Quantitative Analysis
for Management Decisions

Quantitative Analysis
for Management Decisions

MARVIN H. AGEE

Virginia Polytechnic Institute
and State University

ROBERT E. TAYLOR

University of Missouri

PAUL E. TORGERSEN

Virginia Polytechnic Institute
and State University

PRENTICE-HALL, INC., *Englewood Cliffs, New Jersey*

Library of Congress Cataloging in Publication Data

AGEE, MARVIN H (date)
  Quantitative analysis for management decisions.

  Includes bibliographies and index.
  1. Industrial management—Mathematical models.
I. Taylor, Robert Edward, joint author. II. Torgersen,
Paul E., joint author. III. Title.
HD20.4.A5   658.4′033   75-38585
ISBN 0-13-746511-4

Printed in the United States of America

10 9 8 7 6 5 4 3 2 1

PRENTICE-HALL INTERNATIONAL, INC., *London*
PRENTICE-HALL OF AUSTRALIA PTY. LIMITED, *Sydney*
PRENTICE-HALL OF CANADA, LTD., *Toronto*
PRENTICE-HALL OF INDIA PRIVATE LIMITED, *New Delhi*
PRENTICE-HALL OF JAPAN, INC., *Tokyo*
PRENTICE-HALL OF SOUTHEAST ASIA PTE. LTD., *Singapore*

Contents

Preface

The increased use of quantitative methods in structuring and resolving problems confronting the production and the operations manager has resulted in the collection of a large body of systematic knowledge, often described as management science. Continued progress in the application of the scientific method to managerial problems may be expected to extend and refine this analytical approach to decision making. Further, in the years to come, an individual aspiring to a managerial position, or who will be a part of the management process as a member of a staff group, will find an understanding of these exciting developments to be helpful if not essential.

It is not surprising that the teaching of quantitative methods at colleges and universities has kept pace with the requirement. Only eight or ten years ago, many colleges and universities did not have a single course in the discipline; today, courses in quantitative methods are included in many catalogs and found in a number of curricula within the same institution. In a number of cases, entire programs in quantitative methods have been developed. Further, many larger companies have established departments of management science, operations research, operations analysis, or some similar term describing the discipline and its focus.

This text is an attempt to meet the needs of the nonmathematician in acquiring a basic understanding of the fundamentals of management science. We have attempted to develop the topics without requiring mathematical sophistication, but at the same time without an undue sacrifice in pedagogical foundation. In each chapter, where appropriate, examples have been inserted that will permit the student to see the use of the quantitative method under consideration. The only caution offered is that the reader recognize the simplicity of the illustrations. Examples have been developed to illustrate an approach and have often been simplified for purposes of clarity and making a point. Unfortunately, most real-world problems are not simple and will not permit simplification for ease of analysis. Nevertheless, these examples should assist in giving the reader confidence and understanding. At the end of each chapter, questions and additional problems are available for homework assignment. Some statistical tables and random numbers are included in the appendix in support of chapter material.

The text has been designed as an introduction to management science. After two introductory, descriptive chapters, we present a chapter that portrays the firm as an input-output deterministic system, including the relationship between the levels of firm activity and attending consequences. We then introduce probability and some probability distributions. With the exception of the material dealing with linear programming, the remaining chapters build on this foundation in probability. However, the chapters are relatively autonomous and one or more may be omitted without restricting the coverage of other chapters that follow. For those students who have completed a course in probability, these two chapters may be omitted; and following the introductory material, it is possible to move directly into the quantitative methods.

Dr. Fred Silverman of Bernard M. Baruch College and Professors Jay E. Sturm and Myron Uretsky, both of New York University, have helped in reviewing this material. A number of other individuals have assisted in the very important work of editing and typing. We are grateful to these individuals and to the students who have assisted us through the use of the manuscript in the classroom.

MARVIN H. AGEE
ROBERT E. TAYLOR
PAUL E. TORGERSEN

Management and decision making

The manager is a decision maker. Just as a study of management must include an examination of the decision process, so also assistance provided the manager will likely include aids to resolving decision situations. But in a broader frame of reference, we all make decisions. Further, the student of management does not have a monopoly on the study of the decision process. Philosophers, economists, and psychologists are concerned with how decisions are made and why a particular alternative may have been selected. So also are politicians, criminologists, and market research analysts concerned with the means by which individuals evaluate alternatives.

As students of management, we may choose to focus upon the decision-making process and aids to increase the decision-making capacity of the manager. At the same time, we will quickly perceive that decisions—even

1

the most profound decisions—are often made without an individual awareness of the process involved. To some extent, asking the executive how he makes decisions is like asking the halfback how he runs with the football. Perhaps the difficulties involved in capturing the instinctiveness element in decision making may have been best summarized in a statement allegedly made by a former catcher of the New York Yankees, who was asked to describe his thoughts when he was at bat: how did he decide which pitch to hit and where to attempt to hit the ball? His reply was: "I can't think and hit the ball at the same time!" The executive may be similarly hard-pressed to provide an explanation of how or why he made a particular decision. Nevertheless, some situations do lend themselves to analysis—to quantification and explicit review. We will attempt to provide the manager with a few quantitative tools that may be of assistance in describing some decision situations and in contrasting alternatives.

THE DECISION PROCESS

Because the manager is called upon to make decisions, a number of the elements and activities of the organization are designed to facilitate the decision-making process. A cost control system may enable the manager to detect the out-of-control financial condition. A computer-based information system may be installed to provide the manager with reliable and current data. Statistical control charts and inventory models can be introduced to minimize reliance on intuition and the analogous—but never identical—earlier experience as the basis for selecting alternatives.

**A Concep-
tualization**
The activity of the manager, functioning as a decision maker, can be seen in the schematic of Figure 1.1.[1] While not every possible decision situation is captured, a more or less idealized sequence of the steps leading up to and following the decision is presented. The cycle begins with the requirement for a decision—a stimulus. Perhaps a machine has broken down, a district sales report has come in and it is far short of expectations, or a group of employees have indicated that they would like to be represented by a labor union and wish company recognition of that union as the collective bargaining agent. Each (or all) of these inputs may trigger the need for a response—a decision.

Drawing upon his own experiences and possibly employing the information resources of the firm—for example, some accounting records—the manager evolves a conceptualization of the decision situation. At this point, the objectives may be clear, the alternatives may be well-defined, the uncertainty associated with each choice may be at a minimum, and it is possible to make a decision. The manager is prepared to respond to the stimulus, he does so, he observes the consequences of his choice, and the circle is completed when the results become a part of the inventory of the manager's experiences.

In some instances the initial conceptualization may be hazy. The manager

[1] Adapted from William T. Morris, *Management Science* (Englewood Cliffs, N.J.: Prentice-Hall, Inc., 1968), pp. 5–8.

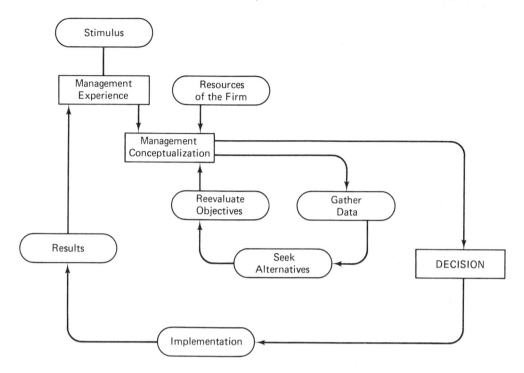

may not be prepared to make a decision and he may seek out additional information. Before deciding whether to repair or replace the machine, he may wish more data on its history. Has it broken down often in the past and was it expensive to repair? How much does it cost to operate? How much might a replacement cost to operate? The answers to these questions will provide additional information.

As a second response, the manager may seek out additional alternatives. Neither replacement nor repair may be altogether satisfactory. Perhaps a third alternative can be identified—that of subcontracting out the work that had been done with the machine. This third alternative may prove to be the most economical choice.

A third response to an inadequate conceptualization may be one of goal clarification: a reevaluation of objectives. What is to be accomplished? Perhaps the part being manufactured on the machine can be eliminated. The triggering of a stimulus often provides the opportunity for redefining objectives.

The gathering of data, the search for additional alternatives, and the reevaluation of objectives are all undertaken to permit a more complete conceptualization of the decision situation. This then leads to the decision itself, implementation, and the observance of the results of the decision. All then become part of the management experience. Hopefully, the manager learns through this experience; he profits from his mistakes; he is reinforced in his judgment. The decision process is also a learning experience.

Goals and Effectiveness

Decisions are made toward some end. However, goal definition is not always a simple task. Consider an individual—the college senior—reviewing two or three job offers. Which offer will be selected? The choice will depend on the objective(s). Each offer may include a specified starting salary, a geographical location, and a type of work. In addition, the perceived opportunities for advancement may be considered. Even in this individual case it is likely that the decision will incorporate multiple goals or objectives. Regarding the decisions made by the manager, Drucker has suggested that the objectives of an enterprise are also multiple:

> There are eight areas in which objectives of performance and results have to be set: Market standing; innovation; productivity; physical and financial resources; profitability; manager performance and development; worker performance and attitude; and public responsibility.[2]

Not only do individuals have multiple goals, but organizations also face decision situations that include multiple indices of success.

While most decisions do involve a number of objectives, we will still assume that a single goal or measure of effectiveness can be defined—particularly for the type of decision that lends itself to quantification. Minimum cost, maximum productivity, or minimum completion time are typical of the measures of effectiveness against which quantitative comparisons will be made. Of more significance *is the shape of the effectiveness function.* This can be illustrated in the context of an example.

Consider the classical economic order quantity problem included in inventory control (described in more detail in Chapter 10). The manager would like to establish an inventory of some raw material, component part, or finished product. This inventory is maintained as a reservoir between the source of supply and the demand for that item. As an example, a retail store is an inventory system; so also is a gasoline station. In a manufacturing operation it is necessary to purchase and then store a quantity of raw materials as input to the production process. In each case, it is usually necessary to order and receive into the reservoir in bulk quantities with individual units then drawn from the inventory on a per unit, per time basis. How large a quantity should be ordered when it is necessary to secure replacements? This can be a significant question. An inventory that is too large requires excessive storage facilities and represents an investment that might be better spent elsewhere. At the same time, with a smaller inventory we are more likely to be caught short, and we spend an inordinate amount of time reordering and placing units into inventory. How large should be our order quantity? Should we order a day's supply each and every day? Should we order on a weekly or monthly basis?

In the most simplified case, two classes of costs are relevant to the inventory system: the ordering cost and the carrying cost. Ordering costs include the expense of bringing a quantity of items into the inventory bank.

---

[2] Peter F. Drucker, *The Practice of Management* (New York: Harper & Row, 1954), p. 63.

They are usually incurred each time an order is placed and can, therefore, be expressed as a dollar cost per order.

Carrying costs are dependent on order quantity. The value of money tied up in inventory, perhaps expressed as an interest charge, is a major carrying cost. Storage facilities and storage operations may also be significant. Even taxes and insurance charges are costs that will increase with increases in the average inventory level.

In the very simplest of cases, assuming a constant demand upon the reservoir and ignoring the likelihood of shortages, the costs involved in establishing an economic order quantity level can be seen in Figure 1.2. Note that the total cost is the sum of the carrying cost and the ordering cost and that a minimum total cost can be established at some specified order quantity. In this example, the total cost is the effectiveness function. The significance of the illustration is seen in the shape of the effectiveness function. *Most such functions are U-shaped rather than V-shaped.* This is an important observation in that it suggests that in those instances where there are a large number of alternatives available, our search should be directed only toward "getting into the ball park." We should not spend (or waste) time in identifying the absolute best choice. In effect the decision maker (and the organization) becomes "concerned with the discovery and

The Measure of Effectiveness **FIGURE 1.2**

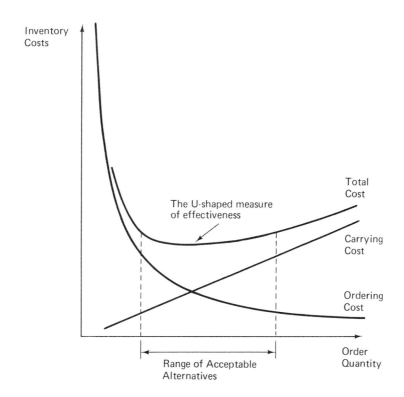

selection of satisfactory alternatives; only in exceptional cases is (he) concerned with the discovery and selection of optimal alternatives."[3] According to this approach, the decision maker seeks a range of outcome that should be adequate. He then selects one alternative that appears to be a good choice. He does this because the superiority of the absolute best over the second or third best choice is rather slight.

TWO QUANTITATIVE DECISION SITUATIONS

Most decision situations do not lend themselves to quantification. From the housewife selecting a flavor of ice cream for the family dessert to the manager assessing two candidates for the position of receptionist, the comparison of alternatives is likely to include qualitative characteristics and to be based upon judgment and intuition. On the other hand, when a decision situation does lend itself to quantification, it is all too easy to assume that the comparisons are more rigorous and the conclusions more certain. This is not always the case. Consider the following two decision situations which are readily quantified.

The Case of the Accident Prone Drivers

The manager of a large metropolitan taxi company is concerned with what he believes to be an excessive number of serious accidents leading to damaged vehicles and passenger accident claims. While all of these claims are covered under a blanket insurance policy, the premiums are based upon the number of accidents. The manager is of the opinion that a few of the drivers are more susceptible to accidents than other drivers and might be classified as "accident prone." For the past year he has been collecting accident data and offers the following information on the 400 taxicab drivers:

Number of Drivers	Number of Accidents
132	0
136	1
90	2
31	3
7	4
4	5

In reviewing driver assignments over the year, it can be established that each driver spent the same number of hours in a taxicab and that each driver spent approximately the same amount of time driving through the different sections of the city during the different hours of the day. In effect, the "exposure and opportunity time" is the same for each of the 400 drivers. (A simplified example, to say the least.) The manager is convinced that the four drivers who had five accidents each and the seven who had four each are accident prone, and that the thirty-one drivers who

[3]James G. March and Herbert A. Simon, *Organizations* (New York: John Wiley and Sons, Inc., 1958), pp. 140–41.

had three accidents each should also be suspect. He is contemplating discharging the forty-two drivers who had three or more accidents and possibly placing the ninety drivers who had two accidents each on probation with their being subject to discharge in the event of two or more accidents in the next year.

 7 Management and decision making

If one plots a *frequency distribution* of these data (described in Chapter 5), one would obtain the sketch of Figure 1.3. We can note that the distribution tails off to the right and perhaps we have the *prima facie* evidence that this *skewness* is indicative of the condition of accident proneness. However, the suggestion that these data demonstrate a condition of accident proneness is in error. In point of fact we have obtained a Poisson distribution describing the number of times an event will occur, given (1) the probability of a specific occurrence is small and (2) the number of such opportunities is relatively large. We are describing the likelihood that any single driver will have an accident during a particular time period and would obtain this distribution *if the probability of having an accident is the same for each driver.* Based upon this information alone, one cannot conclude that the four drivers who have five accidents are more likely than any of the other drivers to have an accident in the next or any succeeding time period. The skewed distribution is the expected distribution for a constant probability of occurrence. If the distribution were skewed more extensively than that shown in Figure 1.3, then we might be led to believe that some drivers are more likely to have accidents than others. However, the identification

Distribution of Drivers and Possible Recommendations **FIGURE 1.3**

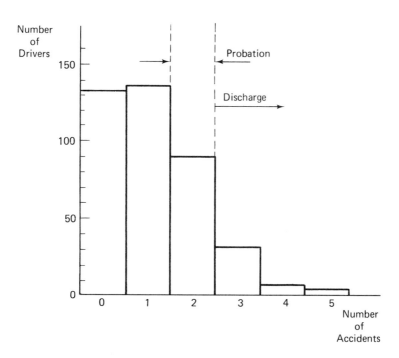

of those "accident prone" drivers is not as easy as the instinctive response of discharging all drivers with a specified number of accidents through a given time period.

A Friendly Game of Chance

Consider the following opportunity to participate in a form of poker. Each participant contributes a sum of money in order to establish a bank against which bets can be made. The dealer addresses the first participant and turns over two cards. The participant may place a wager and he will win the amount wagered in the event the third card falls between the first two. As an example, the dealer might turn over a six of diamonds and a jack of hearts. The player will win if the third card is a seven, an eight, a nine, or a ten of any suit. If any other card results, the individual loses his wager.

The amount to be wagered is a decision that the participant makes after observing the first two cards and before the third card is turned over. Some predetermined minimum bet is mandatory, twenty-five cents, for example. The wager may vary in any amount from the minimum to a maximum, which is the total amount contained in the collected pool, $20.00, for example. For purposes of reviewing and contrasting different possible decisions, assume that the range of wagers is as indicated for every participant. Further, in order to keep the situation simple, assume that in each case the individual placing the wager is the first such individual to have an opportunity and the two cards shown are the first two cards taken from the top of the deck. In effect, and by this assumption, the decision maker does not have to keep track of all the cards that have been played up to the point where he has to make a decision. We simply assume in each case that the decision situation results from the first two cards shown, and any one of the remaining fifty cards in the deck then has an equal chance of being the third card shown after the bet is made. The interesting question is, "What wager should be placed for the different possible pairs of cards?" If the first two cards are of the same value, the seven of spades and seven of diamonds, for example, it is likely that the participant will wager only the minimum required amount because it is certain that he will lose. At the other extreme, if a deuce and an ace (the ace is considered a high card) are shown, there are only six of the remaining fifty cards which could appear and would result in a loss: the three other deuces or the three other aces. Perhaps an individual receiving this opportunity would wish to wager the maximum amount possible. Then what wager should be placed between these two extremes in opportunity?

What follows is a fairly typical response from an individual when confronted with a dozen opportunities:

Cards	Wager
2–9	$ 5.00
3–7	.50
5–J	2.00
4–6	.25
8–K	2.00

3–K	16.00
7–10	.50
4–Q	10.00
5–6	.25
6–A	14.00
2–A	20.00
2–K	15.00

A minimum bet is selected where the odds are rather poor, and it is not uncommon for the amount of the wager to increase in some linear relationship as the odds favoring winning apparently increase. In the next-to-last bet for the most favorable odds, a wager of $20.00 is selected.

In point of fact, *this pattern of betting is not logical* if one accepts only two assumptions. First, we assume the participant is interested in maximizing his winnings and second, that he has some reasonable "bank roll" behind him and a short run of losses will not bankrupt him. Then only two wagers should be placed. If the odds are against the individual winning (the probability of a successful draw is less than one-half), only the minimum wager should be placed. If the odds favor the participant, the maximum wager should be placed. In effect, rather than a linear relationship describing odds of success and possible wagers, a step function should be inserted. Up to the point where the odds do not favor the participant, he should bet the minimum amount possible. Beyond that point and where the odds favor his winning, he should bet the maximum amount possible. By selecting one of these two alternatives and only from these two alternatives, he will maximize his winnings in the long run. Unfortunately (or perhaps, fortunately), even mathematicians and statisticians do not always behave in a logical fashion when confronted with decision situations involving the element of chance.

PLAN OF THE BOOK

As the title suggests this book is an introduction to management science. It is an introduction to some quantitative methods that may be employed by a manager in the evaluation of alternatives. Chapter 2 describes management science within the framework of the scientific method. In the same chapter we introduce the concept of a model as a replica of reality and describe the process of experimentation wherein a model is manipulated to observe the consequences of different alternatives.

Chapter 3 portrays the firm as an input-output system and describes the relationship between the levels of production or service activity and the attending consequences. In Chapters 4 and 5 we introduce some concepts of probability. We review the necessity of measuring certainty (or uncertainty) and discuss probability as the likelihood of the occurrence of an event. Some theorems of probability are stated and illustrated. Revised or *a posteriori* probabilities are also interjected as a means by which one can profit from experience in the estimation of the likelihood of an event. Some probability distributions are treated.

With the exception of Chapters 12 and 13, which deal with linear programming, the remaining material builds upon the foundation in probability provided in Chapters 4 and 5. However, subsequent chapters are relatively autonomous and one or more may be omitted without inhibiting an understanding of other chapters which follow. Chapters 6 and 7 review the decision process in the structured framework of decision theory. More specifically, decisions are defined in the framework of a payoff matrix and are then categorized under conditions of certainty, risk, uncertainty, and conflict.

Chapter 8 is concerned with the methods of scheduling and of sequencing units through a series of operations. Chapter 9 deals with the statistical control chart as a means of insuring the stability of the quality of a product, and acceptance sampling methods as a measure of the quality of the final output of a production process. Chapters 10 and 11 deal with the inventory process and the issue of how many units should be maintained in inventory, including how often and how many units should be placed in inventory. Chapters 12 and 13 provide the manager with a means of approaching the problem of resource allocation. Here we seek an optimal solution to allocations problems where there exists a large number of variables that are linearly related and that interact within boundaries or constraints that are also linear.

Chapter 14, dealing with Monte Carlo analysis, proposes a technique of testing alternatives through trial-and-error approaches. In effect, through the technique of selecting random sequences of numbers from a probability distribution, we are able to test or simulate the outcome associated with alternatives which do not lend themselves to direct analysis and comparison. Chapter 15 deals with queueing or waiting line analysis. Here we are concerned with the level of service that should be provided in order to minimize the service facility cost and the waiting cost.

In each chapter we included a number of examples in order to illustrate the quantitative method under consideration. The reader should be careful to recognize the simplicity of these illustrations. We have deliberately introduced examples to illustrate an approach, and we have sometimes simplified the example for clarity of illustration and to make a point. Unfortunately, most real world problems are not simple and will not permit simplification for ease of analysis. Nevertheless, these examples should adequately demonstrate the applications to be cited.

QUESTIONS

1. List two or three of the more important decisions that you have made to date.

2. List two or three decisions that you have already made today.

3. Within the framework of Figure 1.1, describe a decision that you need to make within the next few days.

4. The manager should profit from his mistakes. Discuss this learning experience with an example and in the context of Figure 1.1.

5. In the context of an example, illustrate the lack of independence of the eight enterprise objectives proposed by Drucker.

6. Drucker's objectives are not equally relevant to all organizations. As an example, market standing is not a meaningful measure of the activities of a local telephone company. Cite some other examples of the lack of universality of these objectives.

7. If V-shaped effectiveness functions were more prevalent in describing decision situations, it would be advantageous to spend more time in evaluating alternatives. Discuss.

8. Do you believe that the odds favor the dealer or the other participants in the card-playing example?

BIBLIOGRAPHY

BARNARD, CHESTER I. *The Functions of the Executive.* Cambridge, Mass.: Harvard University Press, 1938.

DRUCKER, PETER F. *The Practice of Management.* New York: Harper & Row, 1974.

KOONTZ, H., AND O'DONNEL, C. *Principles of Management.* New York: McGraw-Hill Book Company, Inc., 1964.

MARCH, JAMES G., AND SIMON, HERBERT A. *Organizations.* New York: John Wiley and Sons, Inc., 1958.

MORRIS, WILLIAM T. *Management Science.* Englewood Cliffs, N.J.: Prentice-Hall, Inc., 1968.

TORGERSEN, PAUL E., AND WEINSTOCK, IRWIN T. *Management: An Integrated Approach.* Englewood Cliffs, N.J.: Prentice-Hall, Inc., 1972.

An introduction to

management science

One of the more exciting developments to come upon the business and industrial scene since the end of World War II is the growth and infusion of science and of quantitative methods into the management process. The manager of today is likely to be attuned to probabilistic concepts, to the techniques of optimization, and to the methods of simulation. If he has not developed a proficiency, he has at least acquired an appreciation for such diverse tools as statistical control theory, linear programming, and the computer as a means of unraveling complex mathematical relationships. The manager may still be practicing the "art of management"; however, through the use of some quantitative methods he is likely to be aided by rigorous and replicable insights into a wide variety of decision situations.

Although management science is often thought of as the employment of a "bag" of mathematical and statistical tools, in fact it is more than this collection of quantitative techniques. Management science is also an approach, a way of looking at a problem situation, conceptualizing it, and then resolving a mathematical formulation of the situation toward some measure of effectiveness.

The seeds of the scientific approach to management may have been planted by Frederick W. Taylor at the turn of the century. Taylor, who was trained as an engineer, wished to reduce the art of work rules and productivity to a science. In developing procedures, he resorted to a series of careful experimental tests as the basis for developing his improved systems. In particular he attempted to reduce the worker's art and trade knowledge to a set of empirically developed work rules which would greatly increase productivity. Taylor believed that management could be reduced to an applied science, and while a few of his specific studies and applications were subsequently criticized by labor and government officials, the systematic approach was noted and emulated by a number of disciples. Perhaps for the first time, the management process was viewed as both an art and a possible science.

SOME EARLY APPLICATIONS

The past three to four decades have seen a significant increase in the use of the scientific method in decision making. The initial application to military decision making was called *operations research* and undertaken during World War II. In 1940 a group of scientists in England joined forces under the direction of P. M. S. Blackett to provide information and analyses regarding the most effective utilization of military resources. Although this group was first concerned with the description of technical situations, it quickly became involved in problems that were essentially of a management orientation. For example, it analyzed and offered recommendations concerning the radar-interceptor/defense system as an integrated man-machine system involving human, technological, and operational management aspects.

Other diverse problems studied by operations research groups during World War II included: search patterns to be employed against submarines; the arrangement of merchant and escortships within convoys; strategic bombings and their effectiveness; the laying of mines in the Sea of Japan; and evasive action to be taken by a ship under kamikaze attack. This interdisciplinary and scientific approach, frequently employing complex mathematical models, facilitated the solution of a number of interesting and unique wartime problem situations.

After the war operations research moved slowly into civil government and business and began to find its way into American industry in the late 1940's and early 1950's. In more recent years a number of progressive colleges and universities have offered major degree programs in operations research within such fields as engineering, business administration, mathematics, statistics, and economics.

The movement that is referred to as *management science* is partly an outgrowth of operations research. But it also involves an extension of research in mathematical economics, the behaviorial sciences and other fields. While management science borrows heavily from statistics, mathematics, and the physical sciences, it goes further in borrowing liberally from the social sciences. More to the point, management science is a method of approaching an executive problem and decision situation.

THE SCIENTIFIC METHOD

For better or worse today *is* an age of science and technology. The results are evident and at least the positive effects are accepted as a matter of course. Man has amplified the means by which one person may speak to another. He has greatly expanded his capabilities for travel. His diet can be balanced and nutritious. His health can be reasonably secure. His life can be made less a drudgery and more an opportunity for enjoying other, more artistic and creative aspects of his existence. All of this is a product of scientific inquiry—be it the study of flight near the speed of sound or the necessity for oxygenating blood during open heart surgery. But what is *science?* When we speak of *science* or *scientific inquiry*, what do we mean?

A first inclination is to think of science as a collection of subject matter fields and people who work in those fields. We would assume that physics is a science and the physicist is a scientist. The chemist and the astronomer are also scientists. The economist, the sociologist, the historian, and the psychologist are described as social scientists. While some disciplines are often considered more scientific than others (for example, chemistry more than sociology), science can be perceived as a field of knowledge and scientists as people who acquire that knowledge. A second perspective of science is seen in a collection of explanations, that is, laws and/or theories. A physicist might express Newton's second law of motion: the time rate of change of momentum of a particle is proportional to the external force and occurs in a direction coincident with that of the force. If momentum (mass × velocity) is differentiated in regard to time and the mass is assumed to be constant, then the force can be shown to be equal to the product of the mass × the rate of acceleration. In effect, $F = ma$, and this relationship is both an explanation and a prediction. It can be used to describe why something happened the way it did. It can also be used to predict an outcome with a measure of precision and certainty. The physicist will be able to express a number of other such relationships. Similarly in chemistry, economics, and engineering we have explanations which are universal or near universal in their ability to describe and to predict phenomena. These explanations may be the result of scientific inquiry, but they are often perceived as science itself. However, in addition to a subject matter field and to a body of explanations, *science* can be seen as the *approach* for obtaining explanations.

The quest for scientific information is assumed to be regulated by certain standards or ideals which should be approximated if never fully attained. These criteria provide us with a means of obtaining systematic knowledge derived through observation, study, and experimentation. If our knowledge is to be systematized, information has to be generated, stored, and classified. The information is likely to be gathered through observation of actual phenomena, through controlled experimentation, or by inferences drawn from empirical data with the purpose of developing an understanding of the topic under investigation. The criteria are:

Criteria of the Scientific Method[1]

1. *Intersubjective testability*—The knowledge claims can be verified by any person with the relevant education and technical equipment. In effect the "truths" of science are free from cultural and personal bias, and those "truths" that are accessible only to a privileged few, (for example, the mystical insight, the religious ecstasy, and the artistic inspiration) are not scientific. Given the same quality control data, similar statistical control limits should be established regardless of the person analyzing the data.

2. *Reliability*—The evidence or degree of support offered represents a sufficient degree of confirmation. This criterion separates the scientific truth from that of opinion or superstition. For example, with adequate sampling sales data, one can make a reliable forecast of market potential.

3. *Precision*—The "truths" of science are precise, and this is in part a function of the measurement tools. There is a definitiveness which is perhaps more evident in the physical than the social sciences, but which is a criterion of the scientific method. One can speak of the exact probability of an inventory level meeting a production demand.

4. *Systematic Structure*—The "truths" of science are related to each other through a web of knowledge. These truths integrate through some well-connected and consistent accounting of the facts, rather than a "telephone directory" of information. Forecasting, scheduling, production, and product distribution models must be interdependent, for instance.

5. *Comprehensiveness*—Science has often led to the use of devices that permit us to extend our senses. The radio telescope permits the astronomer to see far out into the universe, and the electron microscope permits the metallurgist to see into the structure of a material. Similarly, the personality test or intelligence test permits the psychologist to see into the inherent nature or ability of an individual. Perhaps the management game can be used to orient the new manager to some of the significant decision situations he will face.

It is unlikely that the study of human organizations and the analysis of decision situations within organizations can ever be as precise and generally replicable as studies in the physical sciences, nor can a comparable investment in time precede each management decision. Nevertheless, the body of knowledge and theory in the science of management has increased remarkably over the last few years. The steps preceding a decision are similar in each case.

---

[1]The material in this section has been abstracted from Herbert Feigl, "The Scientific Outlook," in *Readings in the Philosophy of Science*, eds. Herbert Feigl and May Broadbeck (New York: Appleton-Century-Crofts, Inc., 1953), pp. 8–18.

The Science of Management Science

Management science can be seen as the application of scientific methods to problems arising within the management process, embracing integrated systems of men, materials, and equipment. Its purpose is to provide the decision maker with a quantitative basis for evaluating the operations under his control. This aim may usually be achieved with greater success if pursued in accordance with a systematic (scientific) plan. In effect, the approach of management science is similar to the scientific method and calls for the following four steps:

1. *Define the problem.* The manager is well on his way toward effecting a solution if the problem situation is properly defined. Inventory costs may be increasing and appear to be excessive. Labor turnover may be greater than comparable facilities within the region. A product mix may need to be defined that will more effectively utilize existing plant facilities. A level of service may have to be specified that will reduce customer waiting time without an excessive investment in service facilities. All of these preceding problem situations may call for a quantitative evaluation eventually leading to the selection of an alternative and a solution. However, each problem is well on its way toward a solution with a proper definition.

2. *Formulate a model.* The method of science calls for the construction of a hypothesis to explain the observed relationships. In a sense, the hypothesis is formulated with the construction of a model that relates the significant variables and constraints to a measure of effectiveness. Management scientists (and operations researchers) have identified and modeled many recurrent processes. These models, in their aggregate, provide a body of quantitative relationships that are able to be applied, often with little modification, to the operational problem at hand.

3. *Manipulate the model.* The testing and revision of the hypothesis is achieved through the manipulation of the model. In effect, we seek to determine for the variables under the control of the decision maker those values which will lead to optimum system effectiveness. This may be accomplished analytically or numerically. In the first case, we may be taking the derivative of some equation. In the second, we may be employing a digital computer toward a trial-and-error solution. The model is never a perfect representation of reality, but if it is properly formulated and correctly manipulated, the model will be useful in predicting the effect of changes in controllable variables on the overall effectiveness of the system. Hopefully, this will lead to the identification of an alternative and a decision.

4. *Making the decision.* At best, the model of an operation or situation will take the decision maker only part way to the point of decision. It will supply him with a quantitative basis for evaluating operations under his control. Invariably, however, it will be impossible to incorporate some qualitative factors into the quantitative evaluation. At this point in the assessment, these qualitative factors will have to be considered.

The making of the decision and the observation of the results of the decision complete the cycle. The decision maker is now able to observe the consequences of his action. In a very real sense the management process must incorporate a learning component and one must profit from successful or from improper decisions. Just as the scientist is able to progress through negative results, the manager and the management process must improve through the selection of alternatives which were less than satisfactory.

In discussing the science of management science, we alluded to the formulation and manipulation of a model. But what exactly is a model? When used as a noun, the word *model* implies a physical representation. A design engineer may construct a clay model as a possible configuration for a new automobile fender. The word may also be used as an adjective. For example, a man may be referred to as a model husband, and this use carries with it an implication of "ideal." Finally the same word may be used as a verb, as in the case where a girl is employed to model clothes. Here the verb *to demonstrate* could have been substituted. In management science, "model" retains each of these meanings. The model is designed to *represent* operations under study through an *idealized* example of reality in order to *demonstrate* the essential relationships that are involved.

Kinds of Models

Models can be classified by type and a distinction made among *iconic*, *analogue*, and *symbolic* models. The difference includes level of abstractness. Iconic models are those which look like what they represent. A globe may be used in the classroom to demonstrate the shape and orientation of continents, water bodies, and other geographical features of the earth. A model of the solar system is used to demonstrate the orientation of the sun and planets in space. A model of an atomic structure would be similar in appearance, but at the other extreme in dimensional reproduction. Each of these models represents reality and is used for demonstration. None are customarily manipulated in an experimental sense. However, an aeronautical engineer may test a specific tail assembly with a model airplane in a wind tunnel, or a pilot plant might be built to test a new process for the purpose of locating operational difficulties before full production. In these two latter cases, the model itself may be manipulated to demonstrate relationships.

The analogue model uses one set of properties to represent another set of properties. A graph of sales by weeks uses the length of lines as analogous to the magnitude of sales over time. Some physical analogues have been constructed in which fluid or electron flows are used as analogies for traffic and economic systems. An analogue computer establishes a relationship between some variables in the real world and an electrical system. The analogue model is often more useful in the study of a dynamic situation. Because changes in the analogue model are likely to be made more easily than in the iconic model, the former can fit a greater variety of situations and has more generality.

The symbolic model substitutes symbols for components or variables in the real world system, and these symbols are generally related to each other in a mathematical sense. Newton's second law of motion, $F = ma$, has already been stated as describing the relationship between three variables: force, mass, and acceleration. Although the symbolic model may be more difficult to relate to the real world, the symbols do provide a much higher degree of abstraction and precision in their application. Because of the logic incorporated within the symbolic model, it can be manipulated in accordance with established mathematical procedures.

Almost all mathematical models are used either to predict or to control. The outcome of an alternative course of action may be predicted in terms of a selected measure of effectiveness. For example, a linear programming model may predict a profit associated with various production quantities of a multiproduct process. Mathematical models may be used to control the level of inventory in a plant. In a quality control illustration, the model may be employed to monitor the proportion of defectives that will be accepted from a supplier.

Because the model is only an approximation of reality, it is never able to completely capture the system under consideration. In general those factors which lend themselves to quantification are the factors incorporated within the model. The danger in then using the model as a predictive device is the possibility of oversimplifying the problem under consideration. It is easy to become enamored with a representation that appears rigorous and complete, when in fact many qualitative factors have been omitted.

Experimentation

The third step in the science of management science calls for the manipulation of the model. By analogy this is the experimentation step required in the testing of the hypothesis.

The decision maker is likely to have a number of alternatives available to him. Each of these may be tested. For example, a plant manager may experiment with different lengths of the work week. The inventory department may test different inventory policies, including ordering quantities and levels of safety stock. This process of direct experimentation is costly and time consuming and may even be destructive. Models and the process of indirect experimentation provide a convenient means whereby the decision maker may be provided with factual information without disturbing the operation itself.

In direct experimentation, the object, state, or event is subject to manipulation and the results are observed. For example, the housewife might rearrange the furniture in her living room by this method. Essentially, she or her husband under her direction moves the furniture and observes the results. This process may be repeated with a second move and perhaps a third, until all logical alternatives have been exhausted. Eventually, one such move is subjectively judged best; the furniture is returned to this position, and the experiment is completed. Direct experimentation such as this may be applied to the rearrangement of machinery in a factory. Such a procedure is time consuming, disruptive, and costly, and therefore, indirect experimentation is more likely to be employed. In these examples, a layout could have been sketched of the space. Templates representing the furniture or machinery could be constructed to scale and placed on the required space. The templates themselves could then be manipulated until a desirable arrangement is achieved.

Through the use of such mathematical models as inventory control, queueing, statistical control, and so forth, alternatives can be tested through indirect experimentation. If the model has been properly constructed and tested, we can have some confidence that the final choice will be similar to that which would have been obtained through the more costly and time consuming direct experimentation.

QUESTIONS

1. How might one define "science"?

2. Distinguish between *reliability* and *precision* as criteria of the scientific method.

3. Against which criteria might astrology be evaluated to determine whether or not it is a science?

4. Cite an illustration where the improper or incomplete definition of the problem situation would likely lead to an incorrect or inappropriate decision.

5. Discuss the various meanings of the word *model*.

6. Briefly describe iconic, analogue, and symbolic models.

7. In the context of an example, illustrate the advantages and disadvantages of direct experimentation in contrast to the development and manipulation of a model of the real world situation.

8. What caution must be exercised in the use of models?

9. What distinctions can be made between the fields of operations research and management science?

BIBLIOGRAPHY

BIERMAN, H., BONINI, C. P., JR., AND HAUSEMAN, WARREN H. *Quantitative Analysis for Business Decisions.* Homewood, Ill.: Richard D. Irwin, Inc., 1969.

CHURCHMAN, C. W., ACKOFF, R. L., AND ARNOFF, E. L. *Introduction to Operations Research.* New York: John Wiley & Sons, Inc., 1957.

FABRYCKY, W. J., GHARE, P. M., AND TORGERSEN, P. E. *Industrial Operations Research.* Englewood Cliffs, N.J.: Prentice-Hall, Inc., 1972.

LEVIN, RICHARD I., AND KIRKPATRICK, CHARLES A. *Quantitative Approaches to Management.* New York: McGraw-Hill Book Company, Inc., 1971.

TAHA, HAMDY A. *Operations Research.* New York: The Macmillan Company, 1971.

WAGNER, HARVEY M. *Principles of Management Science.* Englewood Cliffs, N.J.: Prentice-Hall, Inc., 1970.

Cost and income models

The business firm provides a service or produces a product. It does
so by accepting inputs of varying kinds and amounts and blending these
in an economical fashion to achieve the desired output. The nature of the
conversion process will vary from one firm to another and will be largely
dependent upon the service or product. If we are to provide furniture,
men's clothing, or wristwatches, the conversion process will be a manufacturing system. If we are to mine coal or raise turkeys, we still require inputs
and provide a product, but the conversion process will have different
characteristics. Even a firm committed to providing a service, such as a
taxicab company or a hospital, will require a blend of inputs in order to
offer that service.

The firm's profits (or losses) will be determined by the relationship
between total revenue and total costs. These in turn will be dependent
upon the level of service or quantity of output provided and the costs needed
to achieve this output and resulting income. In this chapter we will be
concerned with the production decision. How much to produce? How much
service to offer? We will examine the inputs to the firm as well as the
different classes of costs that are likely to accrue in the conversion process.
Finally, we will be concerned with the economic implications—the profit
or loss—growing out of different levels of operation of the firm.

THE PRODUCTION SYSTEM

Literally tens of thousands of inputs may be required in the production
of an airplane or an automobile. Even the inputs to a barber shop or restaurant
would require a lengthy listing. It is hardly possible and certainly impractical
to enumerate all the possible inputs to a firm; therefore, the four classes
of inputs, human service, materials, producer goods, and capital, will be
defined as the ingredients required in the production system.

The successful firm is somehow able to convert ingredients into a good
and/or service which is then offered to the public. The output provides
the revenue (income from sales) which in turn pays for the cost of producing
the product or providing the service, the cost of marketing this product
or service, the general costs of administering the firm, and the amount
of profit remaining after these costs are deducted. Whether the output of
the firm is a product or service and whether the firm is a wholesaler or
retailer, the firm can be considered an input-output system. The wholesaler
and retailer may only differ from the manufacturer in that the former two
purchase rather than manufacture the item that is sold.

The firm has been described as a conversion process, as demonstrated **Production**
in Figure 3.1. The firm must have a labor input. In a sense, the organization **Inputs**
is the combined efforts of people coordinated toward the objective or output

FIGURE 3.1   The Firm as an Input-Output System

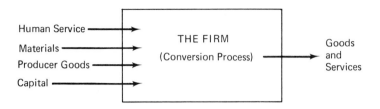

of the firm. An airline requires pilots, stewardesses, baggage handlers, reservation clerks, and mechanics. It also employs accountants, attorneys, and computer programmers. These individuals with their respective talents and skills provide the human service input. In a similar fashion, the automobile company employs engineers, toolmakers and assembly line workers. While some of these employees may be represented by a labor union and others may work outside of the bargaining unit, all contribute their effort to the design, manufacture, and sale of the automobile. Within the various types of organizations, different categories of labor inputs may be established. In the military there are officers and enlisted men; in a university, faculty, staff, and students. It is not uncommon in a manufacturing firm to distinguish between direct and indirect labor, with the former capable of being measured and charged directly to the production units.

Materials are also required to meet the objectives of the firm. Like the labor input, we may wish to distinguish between direct and indirect material. In the first category are those component parts along with raw materials that are physically altered and directly converted into the end product. Tires may be purchased and added to the automobile as it moves down the assembly line. Gray iron may be purchased in ingots, melted down, and poured into engine blocks. Sheet steel may be cut and bent into panel configurations and used to construct the automobile body. These are direct materials. In the second category are those materials that are classified as indirect, those that are consumed in the support of the production process without being directly attributed to production units. The machine shop that is used to support the production facility may consume different quantities of materials, which are not capable of being assigned to specific production units.

Producer goods is the third class of input. These include the land and building, as well as the production facilities that are involved in altering the input materials. Most producer goods are consumed in the production process, and eventually they have to be replaced. This consumption of producer goods is another cost of the product or service that the firm provides. Plants grow old; assembly lines have to be repaired or component machines have to be replaced. All this costs money. The barber must eventually replace his shears and clippers, the taxicab driver must eventually replace his automobile, and the automobile manufacturer must eventually repair or replace the production facility used in the manufacture of the product.

Capital is still another necessary input to the firm. The cost of producer goods, as well as the daily operating expenses, must be met with capital. Insufficient financial support is a frequent reason for business failure. Like the other inputs of producer goods, materials, and human services, capital also costs money. An interest charge must be paid for the use of money, and this interest is a cost of doing business.

A specific firm will likely require inputs from each of these classes but of varying types and in different proportions. For example, the labor input required in an urban mass transit system (a city bus company) may be close to 85 percent of the total cost of operation. A petroleum refinery, on the other hand, may consist of an extensive investment in physical facilities that convert large quantities of a crude oil input into a number of products, and its labor input may be rather minimal. In touring a chemical processing plant, one may actually be hard-pressed to find the human input. In general, an input of extensive physical facilities will also require extensive capital input and will consume or convert large quantities of materials into the end product. This latter facility is likely to operate with a minimal amount of labor input.

Revenue

The firm expects to receive revenue in exchange for the goods or services that are provided. This revenue is likely to be proportional (perhaps linearly proportional) to the quantity of goods provided or the amount of service offered and consumed. If the automobile firm is successful in increasing its level of production and sales by 10 percent, it is ordinarily expected that the revenue received will be increased by 10 percent. Further, the airline firm that is able to raise its passenger loading from 50 percent of capacity to 55 percent is increasing its revenue in direct proportion to this added passenger service. While it is not uncommon for added sales or added service to be offered in a nonlinear price structure, the simplest case is that of a unit sales structure that is constant over the total possible range of sales. If an airline ticket between two points costs the same for the individual purchasing the first ticket as it does for the individual purchasing the last ticket, then this linear revenue relationship will hold true. However, some airlines sell vacant seats to military and young people on a stand-by basis at a reduced fare; under such a program, increasing passenger loading from 50 to 60 percent may not result in proportional increase in revenue, although the revenue may still be the difference between a profit and a loss.

PRODUCTION COSTS

The product or service that the firm provides should result in sales revenue, and this income will likely be proportional to the quantity of the product that is sold or the amount of service provided. Each of the inputs in turn will cost money, and to some extent, the quantity of inputs that will be required will depend on the desired level of output. Thus, the costs of inputs will be at least partially dependent on the level of operation of the firm.

The costs of operation will be classified in this section according to their independence of or dependence on the level of production. In the first class are fixed costs; in the second, variable costs. In addition, costs will be viewed in the framework of cost extensions for added levels of production. This view leads to the concept of incremental (or marginal) cost analysis. Finally, the concept of unrecoverable or sunk costs will also be treated in this section.

Fixed Costs

A cost thought to be fairly constant over a complete range of operational activity is considered to be *fixed*. For example, the expenses incurred in the rental of an insurance office for a month will be the same regardless of the amount of insurance sold that month. Cost items in this class are more or less fixed in amount for a time period, such as a year, regardless of the number of units produced or quantity of service offered. In general, managerial expenses, as well as sales and research inputs, are independent of production levels. The cost of the consumption of producer goods (depreciation), as well as rental expenses and the cost of some indirect materials, are also likely to be fixed. In addition, interest charges on capital will be a constant if the capital requirements do not change with the level of operations.

Fixed costs usually arise because of preparation for the future. For example, research activity is considered an investment in the future; a machine is bought now to reduce labor costs for some time to come; a sales effort is thought to extend beyond any immediate fluctuations in production. We must recognize, however, that not all costs considered to be "fixed" are fixed in an absolute sense, nor are they "fixed" over the complete range of possible operational activity. For example, an expenditure for research may be curtailed somewhat in the event sales and production are less than expected, but on the other hand, a bonus could be granted to management personnel after an exceptionally good year of operation. Either of these actions would modify the so-called "fixed costs of operation."

Costs may also remain relatively fixed within a range of operation and then change markedly when another range is entered. For example, if production in a manufacturing plant that normally operates on a two-shift, five-day-a-week basis were to increase so that three shifts were necessary, the additional supervisory personnel necessary to direct this third shift would lead to a step-function increase in fixed costs.

Variable Costs

Other costs incurred by the firm are assumed to vary directly with output; these are called *variable costs*. Direct labor and direct material are considered in this class. For example, each unit of production might require $1.80 in component parts and $1.70 in other materials. Under a piecework system, the labor cost per piece may be $2.50. This totals $6 per unit of variable costs. If 10,000 units are produced one month, the variable cost that month would be $60,000. Should production the second month be increased to 11,000 units, the variable cost the second month would be $66,000. The relationship between fixed cost, variable cost, total cost, and the level of production can be seen in Figure 3.2.

Variable costs like fixed costs are not as easily defined in practice

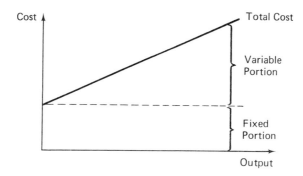

as they are in theory. Increasing production from 10,000 to 11,000 units per month may result in more waste and defective units, thus increasing the material cost per unit. Also, overtime work at time-and-a-half pay may even increase the unit labor cost.

In actual practice, most costs should properly be considered neither fixed nor variable in an absolute sense. Nevertheless, they may be placed in one class or the other over a given range if the approximation does not result in a great sacrifice in accuracy. Alternatively, some costs may be prorated with a portion assigned to one class and the remainder to the other. The advantage to be gained in cost-output analyses may warrant this classification system.

Incremental Costs

The consideration of *incremental (or marginal) costs* in the analysis of alternatives includes more than the simple definition of another type of cost; it represents a way of looking at an opportunity. The outcome of a course of action is estimated in terms of changes in revenue in comparison to changes in cost. With this reasoning a decision is considered to be profitable if it increases revenue more than it increases costs. The measurement of an incremental cost is illustrated in Figure 3.3.

The Incremental Cost, ΔC, Resulting from the Incremental Output, ΔQ **FIGURE 3.3**

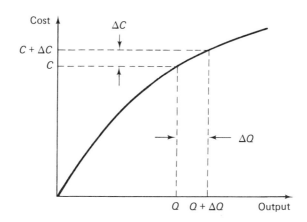

The added cost could be the cost to produce one more unit of output. In the event that the total cost function consists of a fixed and a variable cost, as seen in Figure 3.2, the incremental cost would be the same from any one unit to another. On the other hand, there would be almost no incremental cost in carrying an additional passenger in an airplane that is only half full.

Incremental cost analysis can be useful provided some care is exercised in its application. Consider the following example: the total cost of producing 40 units per year is $72,000. This results in an average cost of $1,800 per unit. The opportunity now presents itself for selling an additional five units for a total price of $7,500. At $1,500 per unit, this appears to result in a loss of $300 per unit or a total loss of $1,500. The total cost of producing 45 units has, however, been estimated at $78,500. Then, the incremental cost per unit of the extra units would be: $C = \$78,500 - \$72,000 = \$6,500$, $Q = 45 - 40 = 5$ units, and $C/Q = \$6,500/5 = \$1,300$. Thus, the sale of the extra five units would result in a profit of $1,000 ($200 per unit) rather than a loss of $1,500 ($300 per unit).

Some caution must be exercised in the use of incremental analysis. Although a decision is sound if it increases revenue more than it increases costs, the total effect of the decision cannot be ignored. In the preceding example, the original customers may learn of the dual price structure and resent paying the higher price for subsequent orders. Then the profit of $1,000 may turn out to be a rather expensive profit. Incremental or marginal analysis is actually a method of reasoning wherein receipts and expenditures that have already occurred are considered beyond our control. Subsequent receipts and expenditures are then evaluated in terms of the added amounts in each case. The decision is made on the basis of these added amounts, provided there is no effect upon the initial or base decision.

Sunk Costs

Sunk costs are similar to incremental costs in that their acceptance and use represent an outlook rather than a simple definition. A *sunk cost* is an expenditure that has been incurred in the past and is now unrecoverable. The significance of a sunk cost is that it should be completely ignored in evaluating alternatives and making future decisions. This is easy to say; it may be more difficult to do.

Consider an example: a machine was purchased one year ago for $60,000. According to our initial estimates of the machine's life, it should now be worth $50,000. (We might assume that $10,000 has been recovered over the past year.) However, a new machine now on the market will do the same job much more efficiently. Should we decide to purchase the new machine, we will be given a $5,000 trade-in on our existing machine. The difference between our projected worth of the machine ($50,000) and the trade-in allowance ($5,000) is a sunk cost, if we go ahead with the purchase of the new machine. Should this $45,000 "loss" influence our decision? The answer is an emphatic "No!" We might consider the initial purchase a mistake, but the failure to purchase the second machine, if in fact it is more economical, would be a second mistake. A sunk cost should be recognized as such and accepted if necessary; it should not influence a future decision.

LINEAR BREAKEVEN ANALYSIS

The breakeven chart is a deterministic model that permits an analysis of the profitability of a firm at different levels of output. As the name suggests, the chart identifies that level of output where revenue equals cost, either for the firm as a whole or for an individual product or service. In addition, the amount of profit (or loss) can also be assessed at other levels of output.

The Simple Linear Case

In this first case, we will assume that a linear relationship exists for costs and income over the range of possible output. We will illustrate the breakeven chart schematically, but first we will define it in algebraic terms, thus facilitating mathematical manipulation of the model. Let:

Q = number of units made and sold each period
p = price per unit
I = Qp, the income per period
F = fixed cost per period
v = variable cost per unit
C = $F + vQ$, the sum of fixed and variable costs for Q units of product
P = $I - C$, the profit per period for Q units of product. A negative value of P represents a loss.

These algebraic relationships are illustrated in Figure 3.4. Assume the fixed cost, $F = \$20$; the variable cost, $v = \$1.50$ per unit; the price, $p = \$4$ per unit; and the production capacity as twelve units per period.

A number of situations may now be defined. The breakeven point occurs at that level of Q where income equals cost, or $Qp = F + Qv$; solving for Q:

$$Q = \frac{F}{p - v}$$

$$= \frac{\$20}{\$4.00 - \$1.50} = 8 \text{ units}$$

The income (and costs) at the breakeven point may be found by substituting $F/(p - v)$ for Q in either $I = Qp$ or $C = F + Qv$. Using income:

$$I = \left(\frac{F}{p - v}\right) p$$

$$= \left(\frac{\$20}{\$4.00 - \$1.50}\right) \$4 = \$32$$

FIGURE 3.4   A Breakeven Chart

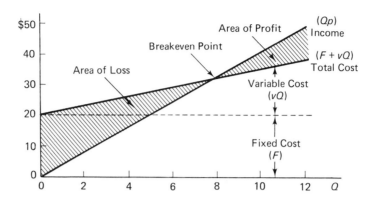

Since profit per period, P, is a function of Q, it may be useful to express this relationship as follows:

$$P = I - C$$
$$= Qp - (F + vQ)$$
$$= Q(p - v) - F$$

In the example, the profit at a capacity of twelve units would be $P = 12$ ($4.00 − $1.50) − $20 = $30 − $20 = $10. The profit at ten units would be $P = 10$ ($4.00 − $1.50) − $20 = $5 and the loss (negative profit) at five units would be $P = 5$ ($4.00 − $1.50) − $20 = −$7.50.

Production Above Normal Capacity   Assume, in an extension of the previous example, that an output of sixteen units is possible, but at a variable cost of $2.50 per unit for the extra four units of output. The price is still $4.00 per unit. Should the sixteen units be produced? On an incremental basis, the added income per unit would be $\Delta I = \$4.00$ and the added cost would be $\Delta C = \$2.50$. Then the incremental profit would be $\Delta I - \Delta C = \Delta P = \$1.50$ per unit or a total of $6.00 in profit for the added four units.

The schematic model of this situation can be seen in Figure 3.5. Letting Q and v represent the units of production and variable cost per unit up to the normal capacity, we can designate the added units and the variable cost of output exceeding normal capacity as Q' and v' respectively. Then the total cost of production, including that in excess of normal capacity, becomes:

$$C = F + Qv + Q'v'$$

28   The total income is simply:

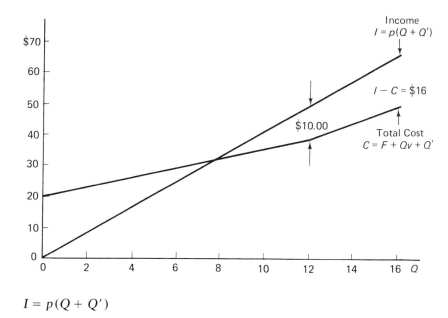

$$I = p(Q + Q')$$

And the total profit will be:

$$P = p(Q + Q') - F - Qv - Q'v'$$
$$= \$64 - \$20 - \$18 - \$10 = \$16$$

As long as the slope of the income function exceeds that of the cost function, production at extended capacity can be pursued with profit. This example could be one where overtime has to be scheduled for the added production. Although the extra units are more expensive, they can still be sold at a profit.

The Effect of Dumping

In some instances, a constant unit price cannot be maintained over the total possible range of output. Perhaps the initial price can be realized for some of the output, but the remainder must be "dumped" at a lower price.

In our initial example, assume that eight of the twelve units are sold for $4 each. The remainder can only be sold for $3 each. The cost of producing twelve units has not changed. Although the income for the first eight units can be defined as $I = Qp$, the income for the remainder should be $Q''p''$ where Q'' is the last four units and the reduced price is $p'' = \$3$.

The income realized under dumping is:

$$I = Qp + Q''p''$$

The total profit will be:

$$P = Qp + Q''p'' - F - Qv - Q''v$$

$$= \$32 + \$12 - \$20 - \$12 - \$6 = \$6$$

Like production above capacity, "dumping" will be profitable if the "dumped" units are sold at a price that is greater than the variable unit cost. A danger exists only if the market price of the initial units is placed in jeopardy. For example, an airline can afford to fill a partially loaded plane with passengers paying reduced fares, but this is profitable only if the subsequent ticket sales of the initial or original passengers are not hurt by the practice.

Some Examples

Problem 1. Solve for the breakeven point described by $F = \$1000$, $v = \$15$ per unit, and $p = \$20$ per unit over the range of 0 to 250 units. Calculate the profit at an output of 225 units.

$$Q_{(breakeven)} = \frac{F}{p - v}$$

$$= \frac{\$1000}{\$20 - \$15} = 200 \text{ units}$$

$$P_{(at\ Q=225)} = Q(p - v) - F$$

$$= 225 \ (\$5) - \$1000 = \$125$$

Problem 2. In the previous problem, an additional fifty units could be produced at a variable cost of $18 per unit. These fifty were to be sold at $20 per unit but unfortunately only forty were sold at that price and the last ten had to be dumped at $15 per unit. Was this a profitable venture?

On an incremental basis, the cost of the additional fifty units was (50) ($18) = $900. The return was (40) ($20) + (10) ($15) = $950, and a profit of $50 was realized.

Problem 3. A firm has the capacity to produce 650,000 units per year. At present it is operating at 60 percent of capacity. Annual fixed costs are $100,000. The variable cost is $0.08 per unit. The selling price is $0.28 per unit.

a) What is the profit at the present level of operation?
b) At what level of operation would breakeven be achieved?
c) What would be the profit at 100 percent of capacity?

Present operations are 650,000 (0.60) = 39,000 units per year. Profit at this level of operation would be:

$$P = Q(p - v) - F$$
$$= 390,000 (\$0.28 - \$0.08) - \$100,000$$
$$= -\$22,000 \text{ per year}$$

Breakeven would be achieved at:

$$Q = \frac{F}{p - v}$$
$$= \frac{\$100,000}{\$0.28 - \$0.08} = 500,000 \text{ units per year}$$

Profit at 100 percent of capacity would be:

$$P = 650,000 (\$0.28 - \$0.08) - \$100,000$$
$$= \$30,000 \text{ per year}$$

NONLINEAR ANALYSIS

The breakeven chart is applicable even when the firm's costs or revenues are not linearly related to output and not easily described in algebraic terms. Sometimes the unit price changes and continues to change with the sale of additional units. At other times the variable cost may change, perhaps increasing as more and more units are produced. It is even possible that additional fixed costs have to be incurred beyond some levels of output. Income and costs can be compared both on a direct and iterative basis and on a change and rate of change basis. Both such comparisons will be illustrated in this section.

Income and Cost Comparisons

Consider the costs and income given in Table 3.1 for the varying production and sale of zero to twelve units of output. In this example, the fixed costs (column B) are a constant. The variable costs (column C) increase, first at a decreasing rate and then, beyond unit 4, at an increasing rate. The unit sale is a constant through the first eight units of output. Beyond this, the unit sale price decreases and income (column E) increases at a decreasing rate. Two breakeven points can be identified—at units 6 and 11—and the profit (column F) is apparently a maximum at unit 9 with income less total cost equal to $55. The data of Table 3.1 are illustrated schematically in Figure 3.6, in which we have a "picture" of the relationship between fixed cost, variable cost, income, profit, and the level of operation. It can also be observed that a range of profitable operation exists and this range is magnified to be able to ascertain the maximum possible profit.

TABLE 3.1   Income and Cost Data for Varying Levels of Output

Output, Q (A)	Fixed Cost (B)	Variable Cost (C)	Total Cost (B + C) (D)	Income (E)	Profit (E − D) (F)
1	$300	$ 100	$ 400	$ 140	−$260
2	300	190	490	280	− 210
3	300	270	570	420	− 150
4	300	350	650	560	− 90
5	300	440	740	700	− 40
6	300	540	840	840	0
7	300	650	950	980	+ 30
8	300	770	1,070	1,120	+ 50
9	300	900	1,200	1,255	+ 55
10	300	1,040	1,340	1,380	+ 40
11	300	1,190	1,490	1,490	0
12	300	1,350	1,650	1,580	− 70

Incremental Comparisons   The data of Table 3.1 can also be analyzed on an incremental basis. This is calculated in Table 3.2 and sketched in Figure 3.7. Note that the average income is a constant through eight units and drops only slightly thereafter. The average cost drops quickly at first as the fixed cost is able to be prorated over more and more units. It is at a minimum at unit 9 and increases thereafter as the effect of the increasing variable cost begins to outweigh the reduction achieved through the prorating of the fixed cost. The average cost and average income are the same at unit 6 ($140) and at unit 11 ($135), the two levels of output at which breakeven is achieved. Although the difference between average income and average cost is the same at unit 8 ($140 −

TABLE 3.2   Average and Incremental Values for the Data of Table 3.1

Output, Q (A)	Average Cost (D ÷ A) (G)	Average Income (E ÷ A) (H)	Incremental Cost $(D_Q - D_{Q-1})$ (I)	Incremental Income $(E_Q - E_{Q-1})$ (J)
1	$400	$140	—	—
2	245	140	$ 90	$140
3	190	140	80	140
4	163	140	80	140
5	148	140	90	140
6	140	140	100	140
7	136	140	110	140
8	134	140	120	140
9	133	139	130	135
10	134	138	140	125
11	135	135	150	110
12	137	132	160	90

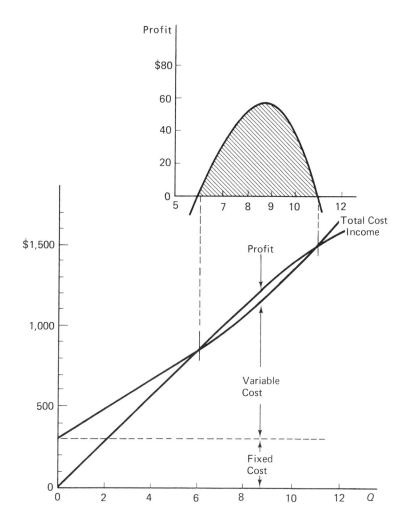

134 = $6) as it is at unit 9 ($139 − 133 = $6), a larger profit is realized at an output of nine units. In effect, the profit at eight units of output is 8 units × $6 average profit per unit = $48 total profit. The profit at nine units of output is 9 units × $6 average profit per unit = $54 total profit. Note that at ten units the profit is reduced: 10 units × $4 average profit per unit = $40 total profit.

The incremental costs and income are also given in Table 3.2 and sketched in Figure 3.7. The incremental income is a constant through eight units and then drops $5, $10, $15, and $20 respectively with the sale of the succeeding four units. The incremental cost increases from unit 4 through unit 12. In each case through the first 9 units the incremental income exceeds the incremental cost. Unit 10, however, will result in an added cost of $140 and an added income of only $125. Thus, if profit is to be maximized,

33

FIGURE 3.7 The Data of Table 3.2

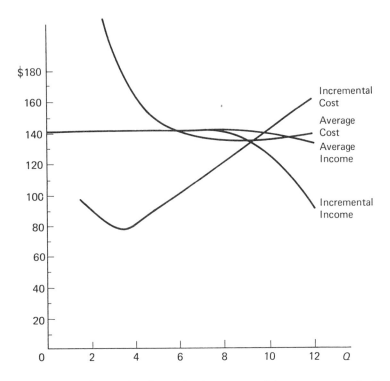

unit 9—the last unit where the incremental income exceeds the incremental cost—should be the last unit of output. Producing more than nine units will result in a reduction in total profit.

Incremental analysis can be an aid in decision making. In some instances it may not be possible to accurately measure the total cost of or the total income from producing a number of units. It might be possible to assess the cost of producing and selling one additional unit with more confidence. If that unit can be sold at a profit, it should be produced. The only reservation in using this approach is that if there is a price break, the most recent sale must not jeopardize initial sales in future periods of time.

An Example *Problem 4.* A plant can operate either through a single-shift, five-day workweek, a two-shift, five-day workweek, three shifts of five days, or three shifts of six days (Monday through Saturday) in the production of small machine tools. While the variable cost of direct labor and materials will run approximately $1,000 per unit and can be assumed to vary directly with output over all levels of production, the fixed costs will increase in steps from one shift condition to the next. Specifically, these fixed costs will run $6,000, $9,000, $14,000, and $19,000 per week through the respective four shift conditions.

Output will not increase proportionally as additional shifts and Saturday are added to the basic single-shift five-day workweek. Four machine tools can be produced each week over the single shift of five days; three more with the second shift; two more with the third shift of five days; and one more (for a total of ten) with the three-shift six-day workweek. If these machine tools are sold for $3,000 each and essentially all that are produced can be sold, at what level of operation will the plant be most profitable?

Because of the step function increases in fixed costs, a tabular or graphic rather than an algebraic formulation is suggested. Cost and income over the different possible levels of output are presented as follows:

Output	Shift	Fixed Cost	Variable Cost	Total Cost	Income	Profit
1	1	$ 6,000	$ 1,000	$ 7,000	$ 3,000	−$4,000
2	1	6,000	2,000	8,000	6,000	− 2,000
3	1	6,000	3,000	9,000	9,000	0
4	1	6,000	4,000	10,000	12,000	+ 2,000
5	2	9,000	5,000	14,000	15,000	+ 1,000
6	2	9,000	6,000	15,000	18,000	+ 3,000
7	2	9,000	7,000	16,000	21,000	+ 5,000
8	3	14,000	8,000	22,000	24,000	+ 2,000
9	3	14,000	9,000	23,000	27,000	+ 4,000
10	3 + S	19,000	10,000	29,000	30,000	+ 1,000

It can be seen that a profit of $5,000 per week is possible under two shifts and an output of seven units per week. Note that the maximum profit is achieved in each case at the highest level of possible output within each shift condition. Under a single shift, two shifts, three shifts, and three shifts plus Saturday, a profit of $2,000, $5,000, $4,000, and $1,000 respectively would be possible.

QUESTIONS AND PROBLEMS

1. Specify a product-oriented firm and list some of the major inputs within each of the four classes of inputs presented in the chapter.

2. Specify a service-oriented firm and do the same.

3. Give some examples of fixed costs and variable costs in a university.

4. Give an example of the concept of incremental analysis in a university.

5. Give an example of a sunk cost. Why do you think it is so difficult for a person to recognize and accept a sunk cost?

6. Solve and graph the breakeven point described by $F = \$10,000$, $v = \$0.50$ per unit, and $p = \$0.75$ per unit over the range of 50,000 units of capacity. Calculate the profit at a level of operation of 60 percent of capacity.

7. In the previous problem, capacity can be increased to 60,000 units. However, the variable cost will increase $0.10 per unit and the fixed cost

will increase another $1,000. If these added units could be sold at the original price, would it be profitable to add to the capacity?

8. A firm has the capacity to produce 850,000 units per year. At present it is operating at 70 percent of capacity. Income is $0.11 per unit for all units, annual fixed costs are $22,500, and the variable cost is $0.068 per unit. What is the annual profit or loss at this capacity?

9. In the previous problem, at what percentage of capacity does the firm break even? What will be the profit or loss at 60 percent and 80 percent of capacity?

10. A market survey of towns X, Y, and Z reveals that it will be possible to sell 10,000, 3,500, and 3,000 loaves of bread per day in each town respectively, six days a week. At the present time two alternatives are under consideration to meet this demand. In the first, one plant with a capacity of 20,000 loaves could be located equidistant between the towns and produce at a fixed cost of $1,000 per day. The variable cost would be $0.08 per loaf. Alternatively, plants with a capacity of 12,000, 4,000, and 4,000 loaves respectively could be located in each town. The fixed costs would be $700, $350, and $350 respectively per day. Because of the reduction in trucking costs, the variable cost per loaf would be $0.06. If the market survey is correct, which alternative would be more desirable? If sales were to increase to production capacity, which alternative would be more desirable?

11. The following cost and income data are projected over the indicated range of output in possible daily levels of production.

Output	Fixed Cost	Variable Cost
60	$ 9,500	$6,000
65	10,000	6,500
70	11,000	6,900
75	12,000	7,400
80	13,000	8,000
85	14,500	8,600

Each unit can be sold for $270. At what level of output is profit maximized?

12. In the previous problem, if the sale price could be raised to $300, what would be the optimal level of production?

BIBLIOGRAPHY

BIERMAN, H. J., AND SMIDT, S. *The Capital Budgeting Decision.* New York: The Macmillan Company, 1966.

OXENFELDT, A. R., AND WATKINS, M. W. *Make or Buy: Factors Affecting Executive Decisions.* New York: McGraw-Hill Book Company, Inc., 1956.

RIGGS, J. L. *Economic Decision Models.* New York: McGraw-Hill Book Company, Inc., 1968.

TERBORGH, G. *Business Investment Policy.* Washington, D.C.: Machinery and Allied Products Institute, 1958.

THUESEN, H. G., FABRYCKY, W. J., AND THUESEN, G. J. *Engineering Economy.* Englewood Cliffs, N.J.: Prentice-Hall, Inc., 1971.

Probability

While man lives in the present, he is oriented toward the future, and he tends to think in terms of tomorrow, next week, or the following month. Sometimes he may reminisce in an attempt to recapture earlier times, and a few people even seem to live in the past. Nevertheless, the inevitable and unknown future faces all of us.

The future can bring pleasant and unexpected surprises; it can also lead to disappointment. Students drop out of school for academic or other unplanned reasons, some marriages end in divorce, people enter trades or professions for which they are not suited, and they carry insurance which they hope they do not have to use in an attempt to protect themselves against the possibilities of sickness and accidents. The nature of the business world would also be quite different if it were possible to predict the future with complete certainty. If the element of chance were eliminated, errors in decisions could only be attributed to the failure to consider a meaningful alternative or the omission of relevant information. Unfortunately (or perhaps fortunately), we do not live in a world where it is possible to forecast the future with certainty. As a result, we have employee turnover, unexpected equipment breakdowns, and material shortages; we produce defective products, overproduce, or ship to the wrong market regions and have special clearance sales; we also have business failures.

MEASURING UNCERTAINTY

Our desire to handle the element of uncertainty in decision making leads us to the concept of probability. Here we have a measure of relative certainty or of relative uncertainty. We have a means of mathematically expressing the possibility of an event or for quantifying the degree of assurance in an outcome. An event that is certain to occur will have a probability of one, while an event that is certain not to occur will have a probability of zero. These extremes rarely exist in reality, but they do serve to establish limits between which measures of relative certainty will have to fall.

Some Definitions of Probability

Over the past few years, there has developed a growing awareness that the occurrence of future events can be described quantitatively in terms of probability. Odds are regularly quoted on football games and at the race track; it is even employed in reporting the weather, as, for example, "The probability of rain tomorrow is 30 percent." The development and use of probability statements, first undertaken in the eighteenth century to analyze gambling games, will be shown to be essential to an understanding of many contemporary management decision situations. However, we sometimes overlook the basis upon which a probability is specified.

A measure of relative certainty can rest upon an objective and/or subjective foundation. An objective probability is one that is established either on the basis of logic and the geometry of the situation—the classical or *a priori* approach—or it is established on the basis of tabulated past experience—the relative frequency approach. A subjective probability is likely to incorporate an objective component, but it is based upon opinion and is a qualitative expression of a degree of belief, stated in quantitative terms. Each will be described.

The *classical* definition of probability suggests that if an experiment can result in a number of equally likely outcomes—the exact number being N, and n of these possessing a specific attribute A—then the probability of the occurrence of A, $P(A)$, is:

$$P(A) = \frac{n}{N}$$

For an example, if we roll a six-sided die that is numbered consecutively from one to six and assume the die is fair and each side is equally likely to land face up, and if we consider a success (the occurrence of A) to be the roll of either a four, three, two, or one, then the probability of success on a given roll would be:

$$P(4 \text{ or less}) = \frac{4}{6} = \frac{2}{3}$$

The key to this definition is the assumption of *equally likely outcomes*. Had this die not been fair, or in another situation if playing cards are not shuffled properly, the probabilities developed through the classical definition will be in error.

The *relative frequency* definition of probability is also an objective approach which suggests that if we repeat an experiment a large number of times, i.e., N, and we denote the number of occurrences of our success by n, then again we find the probability of success, $P(A)$, is:

$$P(A) = \frac{n}{N}$$

For example, if we roll the six-sided die a large number of times, say 10,000 rolls, and we note that 6,650 times we have a four or less, then the probability of a four or less on the next roll would be:

$$P(4 \text{ or less}) = \frac{6,650}{10,000} = 0.665$$

The key to this second objective definition is twofold: we need a reasonable amount of historical data before we can make any predictions about the next event (the probability is theoretically correct only in the case where N approaches infinity), and the collection of this data—the repetitions—must be done under similar conditions. We should not use data that have been amassed over a period of time during which the circumstances affecting the likelihood of an event have been changing. This latter requirement is difficult to meet and is too often compromised with misleading results.

The *subjective* approach to probability is individualistic and personal.

The assessment of the likelihood of an event is a measure of belief and depends not only on the specific experiences of the individual who is involved, but also on his nature—his prejudices, his degree of optimism in the future, and so forth. The individual will weigh the evidence as he sees it and then express a probability as a degree of belief.

Most human decision making will incorporate a degree of uncertainty. Most probability will contain a subjective element. Personal experience, judgment, and intuition will influence the assessment of the degree of uncertainty, but this is not undesirable in the absence of objective, quantifiable data. However, the decision maker should lean on the classical and relative frequency definitions as far as possible in formulating his subjective probability, as demonstrated in Figure 4.1.

Consider the bridge player who must decide whether or not to attempt a finesse. Relying on the classical definition of probability, he can assume that the cards have been shuffled and dealt properly and that the "equally likely" requirement has been met in dealing each card. He can then calculate the probability of certain distributions or splits, which will give him an objective probability. However, he can also review the bidding, and based on his knowledge of his opponents and their actual bidding patterns, he can modify the initial objective probability.

The decision maker is more likely to rely on the relative frequency definition in formulating his subjective probability. He might realize that previous conditions were not the same as existing ones and use this initial information as a reference upon which to add the subjective element. The quality control manager might tabulate the percentage of defective units received over a particular time period from a certain supplier, then modify

Determining the Likelihood of an Event   **FIGURE 4.1**

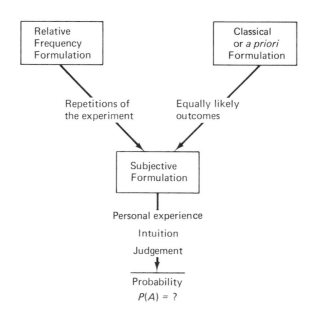

this information to incorporate an apparent trend in quality improvement. A market forecast might be modified to reflect an unusual change in the activity of a competitor. The probability of success attached to a research proposal might be changed from the average figure to reflect the influence of the individual who will be directing the specific project. In each case, judgment will be used to modify the results of the more objective approach.

Probability and Intuition

The establishment of a probability is likely to be based on either the geometry of a situation or the outcomes of similar experiences. In either case and as has been suggested, judgment and intuition may be required either because the logic is incomplete or the experience was similar but not identical to the situation at hand. Intuition can then provide one with a more accurate assessment of the probability involved. At the same time, just as a person can be fooled by an optical illusion, so also can he be deceived by a mathematical illusion.

A rather familiar example of such an illusion occurs with the repeated tossing of a fair coin and the occurrence of a sequence of either heads or tails. Assume an honest coin is tossed and four tails in a row occur. The tosser than pauses while bets are placed on the single next flip. Undoubtedly, people will prefer to bet on a head, and a few people may even provide odds that favor the occurrence of a head, because this event is "due" to come up next. But in fact, the probability of a head or tail on the next toss is exactly 0.5, because preceding flips of the coin are irrelevant past history.

Regarding the apparent geometry of the situation, assume two coins are to be tossed simultaneously. Obviously three outcomes are likely: two heads may occur, two tails may result, or one coin may have a head and the second a tail. Because these outcomes are simple and clearly distinguishable, it is easy to assume that they are equally likely to occur and the respective probabilities are $1/3$, $1/3$, and $1/3$. In point of fact, the outcomes are not equally likely and the respective probabilities are $1/4$, $1/4$, and $1/2$.

It is also not uncommon for an individual in betting on a horse race or similar gambling situation, to wager one or more bets on specific and certain numbers or combinations of numbers because they are considered to be lucky; that is, they have a better chance of occurring. As with the example of the sequential tossing of a coin, preceding events are irrelevant. The fact that an individual has noted or thought he has noted the more frequent occurrence of winning wagers on specific numbered horses does not imply that subsequent winners will follow this same pattern. Horse races and flips of a coin can be considered independent, unless a decided element of bias enters the situation as would be the case if the coin is not fair or favored horses tend to be assigned specific positions in the race.

As another more complex example, consider the situation in which a number of individuals park their cars in a parking lot for the evening. Unfortunately, the lot attendant suffers a mental breakdown and at the

end of the evening simply provides each individual requesting a car with
a car selected at random from those parked in the lot. What is the probability
that no one individual will receive his own car? In other words, in this
situation how often would it occur that every individual will receive the
wrong automobile?

The solution of the problem is a little more involved than we would
wish to undertake at this time. However, as one would suspect, the answers
depend on the number of individuals who brought their cars to the parking
lot, although the intuitive assessment of actual probabilities might well be
in error. If only one person has parked his car, there is no chance that
he will receive the wrong one. With two such cars parked, there is a 50-50
chance that both will receive the wrong car; with three individuals, there
is one chance in three that all three will receive wrong cars; and we can
continue to enumerate the possibilities.

The interesting and not at all intuitive resolution of this problem is
not in the particular answers already provided but in two elements of the
answers:

1. With the exception of the single car, the probability is always higher for an
even number than for either adjacent odd number. In other words, the event is
more likely to occur with six than with either five or seven, more likely with four
than with either three or five.
2. The probability of no single individual receiving his own automobile is essentially
the same if there are 8, 50, 400 or 8,000 people and automobiles. Once the number
exceeds eight, the actual number is largely irrelevant (37 percent of the time this
experiment is tried, no one individual receives his own automobile).

Both of these results are rather surprising and are probably counter
to the intuition of most people. This is not to say that judgment and intuition
based upon logic and/or experience is not valid in many instances. One
must simply be aware of the fact that there are such things as statistical
illusions where one can be deceived in an assessment of the probabilities
involved.

Probability has been defined as a "measure of the likelihood of occurrence
of an event." However, the implications of this measure will depend on
the event in question and the individual or individuals who might be involved
with the event. For example, an individual may be about to enter a hospital
for a rather serious operation, and he may be told that available data indicates
that the probability of full recovery is some value such as 0.7, 0.9, or
0.999. While each of the preceding percentages still report "odds" that
favor the individual in question, nevertheless, the third is almost infinitely
more reassuring than the first; still the individual is likely to worry about
the operation even with the most favorable probability of 0.999. There may
actually be some probability above which the individual would be safer
in the hospital having an operation than going to work or staying at home.
Yet most of us would worry even if the probability of full recovery were
so close to one as to make this a safer situation than the drive to the

**Some
Meanings of
Probability**

hospital. The significance of a probability cannot be divorced from the individual's involvement in the outcome.

A distinction can further be made between a probability that is applied to a group and a probability that is applied in the individual case. From the viewpoint of the company that is selling insurance on individuals who may be afflicted with some disease necessary to require a serious operation, the company can calculate odds with some detachment and express the cost of premiums needed to pay for that proportion of the individuals who do not recover from the operation. On the other hand, the individual involved with the operation derives little comfort from these odds even though they may be favorable. He realizes that the probability only has meaning before the operation. His chances of recovery may be 0.9 prior to the operation, but after the operation has been completed, he will either recover or he will not. In his specific case, the odds will ultimately be reduced to "yes" or "no"; he will make it or he will not.

While there is likely to be a subjective element incorporated in the assessment of a probability, there is also likely to be a subjective assignment of meaning to that probability. If a couple about to enter matrimony is informed that one marriage in three ends in divorce, they will still be convinced that this probability is not applicable to their marriage. On the other hand, if an individual learns that the probability of rain is 20 percent, he will not look upon this as an optimistic forecast for good weather if the consequences of rain are serious. For example, if that individual is responsible for being with a group of Cub Scouts on a picnic and the alternate plan requires that the group spend the day in his basement, the probability of 20 percent may not be small enough to dispel the suspicion that this mob of children will be certain to spend the day in his basement.

THE EVENT

The definition of probability includes mention of the occurrence of an event. But what is an event? It can be the toss of a coin resulting in a head, the selection of a specific playing card, or the birth of a blue-eyed baby. It can also be the occurrence of a defective product or an accident to an employee.

Consider the act of tossing a fair coin. The toss will result in the equally likely occurrence of one of two possible events, a head or a tail. These can be described in probabilistic terms as:

$$P(H) = P(T) = 0.5$$

Consider a deck of fifty-two playing cards. What is the probability that in the selection of a single card, the result will be the ace of spades? The probability can be stated as P(ace of spades), or simply $P(A_S)$, and the likelihood is:

$$P(A_S) = 1/52$$

Using the relative frequency formulation, we might have observed that of the 1,000 children born in the local hospital over the last few years, 250 had blue eyes. Then the probability that the next baby born in the hospital will have blue eyes can be expressed as:

$$P(\text{blue eyes}) = \frac{250}{1,000} = 0.25$$

Similarly using historical evidence, the probability of the occurrence of a defective might be established in a quality control program and accident records may be used in assessing rates for a workmen's compensation plan.

Mutually Exclusive Events

Events or outcomes are said to be *mutually exclusive* if one and only one possible event can take place at a time. Consider again the example of the tossing of the fair coin. There are two possible outcomes—heads or tails. On any one toss of the coin, either the head or the tail may turn up, *but not both.* The events, heads *and* tails, are then said to be mutually exclusive. In the roll of the six-sided die, the outcomes of sides one through six landing face up are mutually exclusive. If the side two lands up, then neither of sides one, three, four, five, nor six may land face up. Only one of the six sides may land face up. As another example, consider an urn containing four balls, identical except that one is red and no two are the same color. We draw out one ball and see if it is the red one. By drawing the red ball, we preclude the possibility of drawing any other color at that time. Consequently, since only one ball can be drawn at a time, the events (or draws) are mutually exclusive.

The critical question in determining whether or not events are mutually exclusive is "Can two or more outcomes or events occur at the same time?" If the answer is affirmative, the events are not mutually exclusive. If the answer is negative, then the events are mutually exclusive.

Collectively Exhaustive Events

When the list of outcomes of every given action includes all possible outcomes of that action, then the list may be said to be *collectively exhaustive.* With the tossing of the fair coin, there are two possible outcomes—heads and tails. Since the result of any toss must be either a head or a tail, the list of these two events is collectively exhaustive. In the case of the roll of the six-sided die, an enumeration of the probabilities of the occurrences of each of the six sides is also collectively exhaustive. The sum of the probabilities of every listing of events or outcomes which are both mutually exclusive and collectively exhaustive must be equal to one.

Independent Events

Events are *independent* if the occurrence of one event has no effect upon the occurrence of a second event. Consider the tossing of two coins. The outcome of the second toss may be considered independent of the outcome of the first. As a further example, consider the sequential tossing of the same coin. The result of the first toss is a head; the second toss also results in a head; so does the third. Is the fourth toss independent of the first three? The answer must be a resounding "yes," and the probability of another head is still $P(H) = 1/2$. These events are independent.

The Probability Tree

It has already been suggested that in a sequence of independent events, the occurrence of the first event has no effect upon the probable occurrence of the second and of succeeding events. A sequence of events and the probabilities associated with this sequence can be pictorially defined with a probability tree. Consider the very simple illustration of the flip of a coin through three sequential tosses. For the first toss, we have two possible outcomes—a head or a tail—each with the probability of 0.5. This can be seen in Figure 4.2.

FIGURE 4.2   One Toss

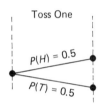

If we now assume that the first toss resulted in a head, the second toss can also result in either a head or a tail, again with the respective probability of 0.5 for each outcome. Likewise, if we assume that the first toss had resulted in a tail, the second toss can be followed with a head or a tail, each with the same probability of 0.5. The outcomes are now expanded through two tosses and can be seen in Figure 4.3.

FIGURE 4.3   Two Tosses

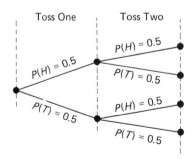

The third toss can also result in either a head or a tail following each of the now four possible outcomes. The third level of branching can be seen in Figure 4.4. Note that we now have a series of eight possible outcomes. The first consists of three heads in a row, the second consists of two heads followed by a tail, the third consists of a head-a tail-a head, and so forth. As we will shortly see, the probabilities associated with each of these outcomes, for example, a head followed by a second head followed by a third head, will be the product of the probabilities of the respective independent events. While this type of analysis will become rather awkward for large numbers of tosses and for events that may result in large numbers of possible outcomes, this picture of sequences of independent events will serve as an introduction in the presentation of some theorems of probability.

Three Tosses   **FIGURE 4.4**

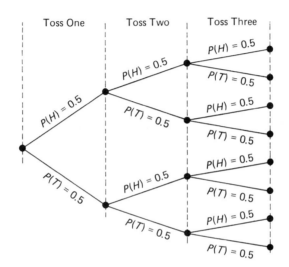

SOME THEOREMS OF PROBABILITY

In working with probabilities, we must follow the rules. To violate these will lead to some erroneous and often bizarre results. As we will see, the question of whether or not one event is *independent* of another and multiple events are *mutually exclusive* will affect what we can and cannot do with probabilities.

The probability of the occurrence of either one or another of a series of mutually exclusive events is the sum of the probabilities of their separate occurrences. Thus in tossing a coin, the probability of either a head or a tail would be:

The Addition Theorem

$$P(H \text{ or } T) = P(H) + P(T)$$
$$= 1/2 + 1/2 = 1.$$

Note these probabilities are also collectively exhaustive in that their sum is unity.

In drawing a card from a thoroughly shuffled deck of playing cards, the probability of drawing an ace would be the sum of the probabilities of drawing each of the separate aces, or:

$$P(\text{ace}) = P(A_S) + P(A_C) + P(A_H) + P(A_D)$$
$$= 1/52 + 1/52 + 1/52 + 1/52 = 4/52 = 1/13.$$

Note that in this latter case the drawing of an ace will not result in an outcome that is collectively exhaustive. There are a total of fifty-two equally likely outcomes, and the drawing of an ace requires the enumeration of only four of these fifty-two outcomes.

If the addition theorem is violated, some rather unusual probabilities may be calculated. For example, assume that a college student is beginning a cross-country trip on four rather bald tires. He is told by a garage mechanic that there is a chance that one or more tires may go flat on the trip, and because of the condition of the tires, they cannot be repaired and will have to be replaced. The probability of each or of any one tire having a flat before reaching the destination is 0.3 or $P(F_1) = P(F_2) = P(F_3) = P(F_4) = 0.3$. Because the student has only the four tires (no spare) and little money to purchase replacements, he is anxious to calculate the probability of having a flat tire and having to spend some of his meager financial resources. By using the addition theorem incorrectly, he could conclude that the likelihood of failure is:

$$P(F_1 + F_2 + F_3 + F_4) = P(F_1) + P(F_2) + P(F_3) + P(F_4)$$
$$= 0.3 + 0.3 + 0.3 + 0.3 = 1.2$$

This is not true, because the failure of tires (even bald tires) is not mutually exclusive. Events may be said to be mutually exclusive if one and only one outcome can take place at a time. Over the period of the cross-country trip in question, it would obviously be possible for more than one tire to go flat. The preceding example yielded a probability of 1.2 which would certainly lead to some suspicion of our analysis. However, had the probability of failure been only 0.2 and the sum of these four probabilities then be 0.8, we might not have been immediately suspicious and detected the error in our reasoning.

The Multi-plication Theorem

The probability of the occurrence of independent events is the product of the probabilities of their separate events. Thus, in tossing two coins, the probability of the occurrence of two heads would be:

$$P(H \cdot H) = P(H)\,P(H)$$
$$= (1/2)(1/2) = 1/4$$

The probability of flipping a coin three times and in the three successive tosses observing a head, a tail, and another head would be:

$$P(H \cdot T \cdot H) = P(H)P(T)P(H)$$
$$= (1/2)(1/2)(1/2) = 1/8$$

Note that this is not the probability of obtaining two heads and a tail in three successive tosses of a coin. This is the probability of obtaining a head, a tail, and a head in that order. One could also obtain two heads and a tail in a number of other different orders. For example, one could obtain a head, a head, and a tail, or one could obtain a tail, a head, and another head. Each of these would yield the final outcome of two heads and a tail, and because these three alternative means of obtaining two heads and a tail are mutually exclusive, the resulting probability is additive. Therefore, we can conclude that the probability of obtaining two heads and a tail on three tosses of a coin would be $1/8 + 1/8 + 1/8 = 3/8$.

The tire failure problem can now also be resolved because these events are independent. The probability of the failure of any tire is independent of the failure of any other tire. Similarly, if $P(F_1)$ is independent of $P(F_2)$, the probability of tire one not failing, $P(\bar{F}_1)$, is independent of $P(\bar{F}_2)$. Then,

$$P(\bar{F}_1) = 1 - P(F_1)$$
$$= 1 - 0.3 = 0.7$$

The probability of no tire failing would be:

$$P(\bar{F}_1 \cdot \bar{F}_2 \cdot \bar{F}_3 \cdot \bar{F}_4) = P(\bar{F}_1)P(\bar{F}_2)P(\bar{F}_3)P(\bar{F}_4)$$
$$= (0.7)(0.7)(0.7)(0.7) = 0.2401$$

And the probability of any tire or of one or more tires failing would be:

$$1 - P(\bar{F}_1 \cdot \bar{F}_2 \cdot \bar{F}_3 \cdot \bar{F}_4) = 1 - 0.2401 = 0.7599$$

So it would appear as though the odds were approximately 3 to 1 against the student's completing his trip without at least one flat tire.

The cross-country trip on four bald tires can also be described in terms of a probability tree. We can enumerate in sequential steps the outcomes and combinations of outcomes that might result through the four tires. The first tire can be described as follows in Figure 4.5, again with $P(F)$ representing the probability of failure and $P(\bar{F})$ representing the probability of the tire not failing. The outcomes associated with tires one and two can be seen in Figure 4.6, with the products noted. Note that the probability of these two tires failing is $P(F_1 \cdot F_2) = 0.09$ and the probability of these two tires not failing is $P(\bar{F}_1 \cdot \bar{F}_2) = 0.49$. The probability of the first tire not failing

FIGURE 4.5   One Tire

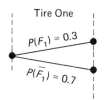

FIGURE 4.6   Two Tires

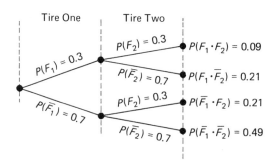

but the second tire failing and the probability of the first tire failing but the second tire not failing are each 0.21. Because these four outcomes are mutually exclusive and collectively exhaustive, the sum of the probabilities add to unity. The event—one tire failing—can occur if either event $(F_1 \cdot \bar{F}_2)$ or event $(\bar{F}_1 \cdot F_2)$ occurs. These are mutually exclusive events and hence, $P(\text{one tire failing}) = P(F_1 \cdot \bar{F}_2) + P(\bar{F}_1 \cdot F_2) = 0.42$.

A probability tree could be constructed for three tires and then for all four. The results of the three-tire sketch would yield the following mutually exclusive and collectively exhaustive outcomes:

$$P(F_1 \cdot F_2 \cdot F_3) = 0.027$$

$$P(F_1 \cdot F_2 \cdot \bar{F}_3) = 0.063$$

$$P(F_1 \cdot \bar{F}_2 \cdot F_3) = 0.063$$

$$P(F_1 \cdot \bar{F}_2 \cdot \bar{F}_3) = 0.147$$

$$P(\bar{F}_1 \cdot F_2 \cdot F_3) = 0.063$$

$$P(\bar{F}_1 \cdot F_2 \cdot \bar{F}_3) = 0.147$$

$$P(\bar{F}_1 \cdot \bar{F}_2 \cdot F_3) = 0.147$$

$$P(\bar{F}_1 \cdot \bar{F}_2 \cdot \bar{F}_3) = 0.343$$

Note that these add to unity. The probability of all three tires failing is 0.027 and of two tires failing is $0.063 + 0.063 + 0.063 = 0.189$. The probability of one tire failing is $0.147 + 0.147 + 0.147 = 0.441$ and of no tires failing is 0.343. The four-tire sketch would yield sixteen outcomes with the probability of no tire failing, $P(\bar{F}_1 \cdot \bar{F}_2 \cdot \bar{F}_3 \cdot \bar{F}_4) = 0.2401$.

The probability of the occurrence of two dependent events (nonindependent events) is the probability of the first event times the probability of the second event, given that the first has occurred. This may be expressed as:

$$P(W_1 \cdot W_2) = P(W_1)P(W_2|W_1)$$

The conditional theorem is similar to the multiplication theorem, except that consideration is given to the lack of independence between events.

As an example, consider the likelihood of selecting two successive white balls from an urn containing three white and two black balls. For the first selection of a white ball, W_1, the probability of W_1 is:

$$P(W_1) = 3/5$$

Assuming success with the first draw, there now remain two white and two black balls in the urn. Then,

$$P(W_2|W_1) = 2/4$$

and

$$P(W_1 \cdot W_2) = (3/5)(2/4) = 6/20 = 3/10$$

A more interesting question is the likelihood of selecting a white and a black ball from the same urn. Two mutually exclusive (but not collectively exhaustive) outcomes would satisfy the requirements a white ball followed by a black ball, and a black ball followed by a white ball. Each of these outcomes can be expressed in probabilistic terms. The first is:

$$P(W_1 \cdot B_2) = P(W_1)P(B_2|W_1)$$
$$= (3/5)(2/4) = 6/20 = 3/10$$

And the second is:

$$P(B_1 \cdot W_2) = P(B_1)P(W_2|B_1)$$
$$= (2/5)(3/4) = 6/20 = 3/10$$

The sum of these yields the probability of selecting a white and a black ball in either order.

$$P(W_1 \cdot B_2) + P(B_1 \cdot W_2) = 3/10 + 3/10 = 3/5$$

By way of verification, the probability of selecting two black balls is:

$$P(B_1 \cdot B_2) = P(B_1)\, P(B_2 | B_1)$$
$$= (2/5)(1/4) = 2/20 = 1/10$$

and the sum of all the possible outcomes: two white, a white and a black (in either order), and two black balls is $3/10 + 6/10 + 1/10 = 1$.

Some Examples

Problem 1. In selecting a card from a deck of fifty-two cards, what is the probability of obtaining a king? A king or a queen? A heart? The king of hearts?

With the *a priori* formulation and assuming a thorough shuffle of the cards, the probability of selecting any one specific card would be $1/52$. Then with the addition theorem, the probability of selecting a king would be the sum of the probabilities of selecting each of the specific kings, or:

$$P(K) = P(K_H) + P(K_S) + P(K_D) + P(K_C)$$
$$= 1/52 + 1/52 + 1/52 + 1/52 = 1/13$$

Again with the addition theorem, the probability of selecting a king or a queen would be:

$$P(K \text{ or } Q) = P(K) + P(Q)$$
$$= 1/13 + 1/13 = 2/13$$

The probability of selecting a heart would be the sum of the probabilities of selecting each of the thirteen cards identified as a heart; that is, the ace of hearts, the king of hearts, and so forth, through the two of hearts, or:

$$P(H) = P(A_H) + P(K_H) + \ldots + P(2_H)$$
$$= 1/52 + 1/52 + \ldots + 1/52$$
$$= 13/52 = 1/4$$

And the probability of selecting the king of hearts would be:

$$P(K_H) = 1/52$$

Problem 2. If the probability of a strike next week at the plant of one of our two suppliers is 0.2 and the probability of a strike at the second supplier is 0.4, what is the probability both plants will be shut down and we will be unable to obtain the needed materials?

In this instance we are working with probabilities that have likely been founded on the *relative frequency* formulation to which may have been added a *subjective* component. Assuming the two events are independent (and this may be a precarious assumption), we can use the multiplication theorem of probability. The probability of both plants being shut down is the product of the probabilities of each of the plants being shut down. Using $P(S_1)$ to indicate the probability of a strike at the first plant and $P(S_2)$, a strike at the second:

$$P(S_1 \cdot S_2) = P(S_1) P(S_2)$$
$$= (0.2)(0.4) = (0.08)$$

Problem 3. In selecting a card from a deck of fifty-two cards and then selecting a second card from a second and separate deck, what is the probability of selecting a king and a queen (in any order)? At least one heart?

With the use of the addition theorem and the results of the first problem, the probability of obtaining a king or a queen on one draw would be:

$$P(K \text{ or } Q) = 2/13$$

Given the occurrence of a king (or a queen), the probability of then drawing the necessary complementary card would be:

$$P(\text{complementary } K \text{ or } Q) = 1/13.$$

The product of these two latter probabilities would be:

$$P[(K \text{ or } Q) \cdot (C)] = P(K \text{ or } Q)P(C)$$
$$= (2/13)(1/13) = 2/169$$

Note that the odds of obtaining a king and a queen are double that of obtaining two kings.

At least one heart can be obtained from the two independent draws through one of three mutually exclusive events: drawing a heart and then drawing a card that is not a heart; drawing a card that is not a heart followed by the selection of a card that is a heart; drawing a heart and then drawing a second heart (which also satisfies the condition of "at least one heart"). Considering each option in turn,

$$P(H \cdot \bar{H}) = P(H)P(\bar{H})$$
$$= (1/4)(3/4) = 3/16$$
$$P(\bar{H} \cdot H) = P(\bar{H}) P(H)$$
$$= (3/4)(1/4) = 3/16$$

$$P(H \cdot H) = P(H)\,P(H)$$
$$= (1/4)(1/4) = 1/16$$

Because these are mutually exclusive outcomes, they can be added and the probability of selecting at least one heart would be:

$$P(\text{at least one heart}) = P(H \cdot \bar{H}) + P(\bar{H} \cdot H) + P(H \cdot H)$$
$$= 3/16 + 3/16 + 1/16 = 7/16$$

Note that the probability of exactly one heart is a slightly different request.

$$P(\text{exactly one heart}) = P(H \cdot \bar{H}) + P(\bar{H} \cdot H)$$
$$= 3/16 + 3/16 = 6/16 = 3/8$$

The determination of the probability of selecting at least one heart might have been approached from a negative direction and with less required calculations. If we assume that the following two outcomes— drawing no hearts and drawing at least one heart—are mutually exclusive and collectively exhaustive, then we might focus on the first outcome. The probability of drawing no hearts on the two draws would be:

$$P(\bar{H} \cdot \bar{H}) = P(\bar{H})\,P(\bar{H})$$
$$= (3/4)(3/4) = 9/16$$

Then the probability of drawing at least one heart could be expressed as:

$$P(\text{at least one heart}) = 1 - P(\bar{H} \cdot \bar{H})$$
$$= 1 - 9/16 = 7/16.$$

This same problem could have also been pictured through a probability tree and the outcomes and associated probabilities might have been presented in schematic form.

Problem 4. In selecting a card from a deck of fifty-two cards and then selecting a second card from that same deck, what is the probability of selecting two kings? A king and a queen? At least one heart?

As the problem is stated, these events are not independent and the conditional theorem will have to be used. We could assume independence of events had the first card been selected, noted, and then returned to the deck; the deck shuffled; and the second card selected. The fact that the first card was not returned prior to the selection of the second will affect the possible outcome of the second draw.

The probability of the occurrence of two dependent events is the probability of the first event times the probability of the second event,

given that the first has occurred. The probability of selecting a king
on the first draw is simply:

55
Probability

$$P(K_1) = 1/13.$$

Now if we assume success on the first draw, there are only three
kings left in the remaining fifty-one cards. Thus, the probability of
success on the second draw, given success on the first would be:

$$P(K_2|K_1) = 3/51.$$

The product of these events would be:

$$P(K_1 \cdot K_2) = P(K_1)P(K_2|K_1)$$
$$= (1/13)(3/51) = 3/663 = 1/221.$$

Note that in selecting two cards, it is more difficult to obtain two
kings from the same deck, or $P(K_1 \cdot K_2) = 1/221$, than it is to obtain
a king from each of two separate decks, or $P(K \cdot K) = 1/169$.

There will be less of a disparity between the conditional and the
independent case in the selection of a king and a queen. For the first
draw, the probability of selecting a king or a queen will be:

$$P(K_1 \text{ or } Q_1) = 2/13$$

Then, the probability of selecting the needed complementary card will
be:

$$P(C_2|K_1 \text{ or } Q_1) = 4/51$$

where C_2 is the king or queen needed to complement the first draw.
Note that there are still four of the complementary cards remaining
in the deck of fifty-one cards. Then,

$$P[(K_1 \text{ or } Q_1) \cdot (C_2)] = P(K_1 \text{ or } Q_1)P(C_2|K_1 \text{ or } Q_1)$$
$$= (2/13)(4/51) = 8/663$$

These latter odds are actually slightly more favorable than the case
of independence in draws.

The probability of selecting at least one heart can be more readily
resolved by the negative approach. The probability of not obtaining
a heart on the first draw would be:

$$P(\bar{H}_1) = 3/4$$

Then assuming success in the first draw, the probability of not selecting a heart on the second draw from the now remaining thirty-eight nonhearts left in the deck of fifty-one cards would be:

$$P(\bar{H}_2|\bar{H}_1) = 38/51$$

and

$$P(\bar{H}_1 \cdot \bar{H}_2) = P(\bar{H}_1)P(\bar{H}_2|\bar{H}_1)$$
$$= (3/4)(38/51) = 57/102$$

The probability of selecting at least one heart would be:

$$P(\text{at least one heart}) = 1 - P(\bar{H}_1\bar{H}_2)$$
$$= 1 - 57/102 = 45/102$$

odds again slightly more favorable than in the independent case.

REVISED PROBABILITIES

The manager should be able to profit from experience. He should be able to revise an estimate or modify a probability when he receives additional information. One means of doing this—of calculating *a posteriori* probabilities—is with Bayesian statistics.

Bayes'
Theorem
We begin with the assumption that an alternative has to be selected. The probability of selecting the correct one is determined on an *a priori* basis. Then additional information is obtained. The revised probability may now be expressed as:

$$P(A|b) = \frac{P(b|A)P(A)}{P(b)}$$

where $P(A|b)$ is the revised or *a posteriori* probability of State A, given the occurrence of b; $P(b|A)$ is the probability of occurrence b, given State A; $P(A)$ is the *a priori* probability of State A; and $P(b)$ is the probability of the occurrence of b.

For example, assume that we have three urns—one containing four white balls and one black ball, a second containing three white and two black balls, and a third containing two white and three black balls—and that we do not know which urn contains which mixture:

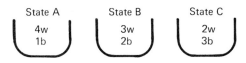

State A   State B   State C

4w   3w   2w
1b   2b   3b

We now select one of the three urns. What is the probability that it is the one designated as State A and containing the four white balls and one black ball? Working with *a priori* probabilities:

$$P(A) = 1/3$$

Now assume that we have the opportunity of reaching into the urn and selecting one ball. We do so and observe that the ball that was selected is black. Now with this added information, what is the probability that we have selected State A?

$P(b|A)$ = 1/5, or the probability of selecting a black ball from the urn designated State A.

$P(A)$ = 1/3, or the *a priori* probability of selecting State A.

$P(b)$ = $P(b$ and State A or b and State B or b and State $C)$

= $P(b$ and A or b and B or b and $C)$

= $(1/3)(1/5) + (1/3)(2/5) + (1/3)(3/5) = 2/5$, or the probability of selecting a black ball.

And the probability we have selected State A is:

$$P(A|b) = \frac{(1/5)(1/3)}{2/5} = 1/6$$

The probability that State B or State C has been selected, given the occurrence of a black ball, would be:

$$P(B|b) = \frac{(2/5)(1/3)}{2/5} = 1/3$$

and

$$P(C|b) = \frac{(3/5)(1/3)}{2/5} = 1/2$$

Note how the odds have changed from an *a priori* probability of $1/3$, $1/3$, $1/3$, for States A, B, and C respectively, to an *a posteriori* probability of $1/6$, $1/3$, and $1/2$. In similar fashion, odds may change any time additional information is acquired. The manager may not be able to define precisely *a priori* probabilities, quantify the influence of incremental information, and finally develop the revised and objective *a posteriori* probabilities. However, he does something similar to this continuously and extensively on an intuitive basis. We have seen that the management experience is a learning experience. Bayesian statistics describes how learning can contribute to the accuracy of probabilities and may assist in conceptualizing the decision-making aspect of the management function.

Problem 5. A die casting machine has just been set up to produce a number of identical aluminum castings. Based upon earlier experiences with this type of machine and the complexity of the die that is to be used, the probability that the machine has been set up correctly is estimated at 0.8. If the machine has been set up correctly, the probability of producing a good unit is 0.9. If, however, the machine has not been set up correctly, only three castings in ten are likely to be acceptable.

The first casting was then made, inspected, and found to be a defective. With this added information, what is now the probability that the machine has been set up correctly?

The *a priori* probability that the machine was set up correctly was given as:

$$P(A) = 0.8$$

The probability of producing a defective, given that the machine was set up correctly, was said to be:

$$P(d|A) = 0.1$$

The probability of producing a defective would be:

$$P(d) = (0.8)(0.1) + (0.2)(0.7)$$
$$= 0.08 + 0.14 = 0.22$$

This latter probability was obtained by first determining the probability of producing a defective, given the machine was set up properly, or $(0.8)(0.1)$; then determining the probability of producing a defective, given the machine was not set up properly, or $(0.2)(0.7)$. Because these two events of the machine either being set up properly or not being set up properly are mutually exclusive, by the addition theorem they may be added to determine the probability of producing a defective.

The *a posteriori* probability that the machine was set up correctly can now be established as:

$$P(A|d) = \frac{P(d|A)P(A)}{P(d)}$$
$$= \frac{(0.1)(0.8)}{0.22} = 0.36$$

Note that the occurrence of a defective should raise some very quick reservations about the work done in setting up the machine. With only one defective, the odds favoring a good job have dropped from $P(A) = 0.8$ to $P(A|d) = 0.36$.

Problem 6. In the previous problem, had the first unit been acceptable, what would have been the probability that the machine was set up correctly?

59
Probability

The *a priori* probability is still:

$$P(A) = 0.8$$

The probability of producing an acceptable item, given that the machine was set up correctly, was said to be:

$$P(a|A) = 0.9$$

The probability of producing an acceptable item would be

$$P(a) = (0.8)(0.9) + (0.2)(0.3)$$
$$= 0.72 + 0.06 = 0.78$$

Note that $P(a)$ from this example and $P(d)$ from the previous example are mutually exclusive and collectively exhaustive and that

$$P(a) + P(d) = 1$$

Now, the *a posteriori* probability that the machine was set up correctly can be reestablished as

$$P(A|a) = \frac{P(a|A)P(A)}{P(a)}$$
$$= \frac{(0.9)(0.8)}{0.78} = 0.92$$

QUESTIONS AND PROBLEMS

1. Give an example of the likelihood of the occurrence of a future event where that likelihood is based upon (a) an *a priori* probability and (b) a relative frequency probability.

2. List some events that are mutually exclusive and some events that are independent.

3. Could one consider the phrase, "Guilty beyond a shadow of a doubt" in probabilistic terms? If so, what subjective probability should be accepted to decide guilt?

4. In taking a twenty question, true-false test you select "false" as the answer to the first three questions. If the correct answers were truly randomly distributed throughout the test, what is the probability that the correct response to the fourth question is "false"?

5. One card is drawn at random from a deck of cards. What is the probability that the card is (a) an ace, (b) a king, queen, or jack, (c) not a heart, (d) not the king or queen of clubs?

6. Two cards are drawn at random from two separate decks. What is the probability that (a) both cards are face cards (that is, jack, queen, or king), (b) both cards are hearts, (c) both cards are of the same suit, (d) neither card is a heart?

7. Two cards are drawn at random from the same deck. What is the probability that (a) both cards are face cards, (b) both cards are hearts, (c) both cards are of the same suit, (d) neither card is a heart?

8. The island of LuMoc has a population of twenty-five Polynesians and five Micronesians. MuLoc, a nearby island, has a population of six Polynesians and eighteen Micronesians. If a shipwrecked sailor arrives on one of the islands but does not know which one, what is the probability that the first person he meets is a Polynesian?

9. If the sailor in Problem 8 landed on an island and the first person he met was a Polynesian, what is the probability he landed on LuMoc?

10. In a newly built manufacturing plant, only 80 percent of the machine tools are connected to the power supply, and 40 percent of the machine tools are not new. Assuming a random ordering of tools and connections, what is the probability that a machine tool is new and connected to the power supply?

11. Four bridge hands of thirteen cards are dealt to four people. Each person is given the opportunity of looking at his cards for only a short period of time and then must place them face down in a pile. The four piles are kept separate but then moved about on the table so that each player can no longer tell which pile is his. One player remembers only that his hand contained three kings. He then specifies a pile as the hand that might have been his hand and is able to look at one card. If the card is a king, what is the probability that the hand was his original hand? If the card is not a king, what is the probability that the hand was his original hand?

12. A transistorized amplifier consists of three transistors, five capacitors, and seven resistors selected from stock of which six, three, and two percent respectively are thought to be defective. What is the probability that the amplifier contains no defective parts?

BIBLIOGRAPHY

The bibliography appearing at the end of Chapter 5 is also applicable to this chapter.

Probability distributions

It is said that we live in an age of standardization. A box of breakfast cereal is expected to contain the same total and proportional amount of ingredients as any other box with the same label. This is assumed to be so whether the box was purchased in one store or a second on the other side of town and whether it was purchased yesterday or last month. In fact the assumption is not true. The differences from one box to another may be slight but there will be differences. Even in an age of conformity and mass production, we can detect differences and we have come to recognize that variability is inevitable. Just as no two snowflakes or fingerprints are the same, so also two successive batches of breakfast cereal or two charges of steel will not contain exactly the same proportion of ingredients, and the resulting products will not have identical characteristics. With the possible exception of those properties that may be reduced to counting, variation is inherent in all objects, states, or events. Variation will occur in the quality of incoming materials, the time required to complete a work cycle, the dimensions of the finished product, the time-to-failure of like pieces of equipment, the number of workers absent from one day to the next, the number of defectives produced over three shifts, and the number of arrivals per hour at a toll booth.

Variation may be a matter of degree but it will occur. As a result, just as probability is useful in describing the likelihood of an event, descriptive statistics are useful in describing the variability associated with the occurrence of different events that have occurred in the past. Also, the probability distribution is a useful method of projecting the likelihood of future possible outcomes. Following an introduction to descriptive statistics, three such simple probability distributions will be introduced in this chapter. Two additional distributions will be helpful in an understanding of waiting lines and will be introduced in the last chapter describing queueing theory.

DESCRIPTIVE STATISTICS

The body of analysis techniques concerned with the description of collected data is called *descriptive statistics.* Such data may be either discrete or continuous and are usually the result of a series of observations taken over time. In its raw form, a mass of data communicates very little information, and as a result, it is often desirable to develop a frequency distribution which describes the data in compact pictorial form. In addition, it is common practice to calculate a measure of central tendency and a measure of dispersion for a mass of data. Each of these descriptive techniques will be developed in this section.

Discrete and Continuous Data

Discrete data consist of separate, individually distinct elements that usually come from a counting process. For example, the data listed in Table 5.1 are the number of people entering a bank each minute for a twenty-minute time span during a portion of the day. Each arrival is a distinct unit. A fraction of a person cannot arrive. For any minute, the number of arrivals is a whole number which may differ from the number of arrivals in any other minute by multiples of one. As can be seen, the data are discrete and they result from a counting process.

The Number of Arrivals per Minute for a Twenty-Minute Period   **TABLE 5.1**

Minute	Arrivals	Minute	Arrivals	Minute	Arrivals	Minute	Arrivals
1	3	6	0	11	2	16	0
2	0	7	3	12	1	17	2
3	1	8	1	13	0	18	1
4	1	9	0	14	2	19	4
5	2	10	3	15	1	20	1

Continuous data can take on any value within some range. The actual recorded observation may appear to be discrete, but this occurs either because of convenience or the physical limitation of the measurement process. As a result, two or more observations may have the same value, although the characteristic under study is unique in each case. For example, consider the data of Table 5.2 pertaining to the distance between two machined surfaces on thirty similarly produced items. The smallest distance is 0.97 inches and the largest is 1.03 inches. Other measurements may fall anywhere within these limits and possibly even outside this range; some measurements are reported as the same. If the distances had been measured to the nearest one-tenth of an inch, it is likely that all would have been recorded as exactly 1.0 inch. These data would still be continuous in nature and each thickness would be different, even though every measurement would have been recorded in identical fashion. If the measurements were made to the nearest one-millionth of an inch, it is likely that no distances would have been recorded as identical. Even then, however, the data would still appear to be discrete; it would appear to vary in increments of one-millionth of an inch. Data that result from a characteristic which varies through a continuum are continuous in nature.

The Distance between Two Machined Surfaces (in inches)   **TABLE 5.2**

0.99	1.00	0.98	1.03	1.00
1.00	1.01	1.01	0.99	1.01
1.01	1.02	0.98	1.02	1.00
1.02	1.00	1.00	1.00	1.02
0.99	0.99	0.98	1.00	0.99
1.00	0.97	1.01	1.01	1.00

The data exhibited in Tables 5.1 and 5.2 can be expressed in a more systematic and compact form by grouping them into frequency distributions. Table 5.3 shows the frequency distribution of the number of arrivals per minute. Table 5.4 shows the frequency distribution of the distance between two machined services. In this latter table, it was necessary to define class intervals into which the continuous data could be grouped. These frequency distributions indicate that the data tend to cluster near the middle and that the frequency of occurrence of higher and lower values decreases. Tabular presentations such as these convey more meaning than the data in its raw form. The tabulated frequencies may also be plotted to facilitate their description, as is shown in Figure 5.1 for the arrival data and in Figure 5.2 for the measurement data. If the ordinate were to be changed from absolute to relative frequency, the area under the distribution will be equal to unity. This transformation is shown in the last column of both Tables 5.3 and 5.4.

Should the ordinate be changed from frequency to relative frequency, then the distributions can be described as relative frequency distributions. In each case they are a picture of what has occurred in the past. Using the relative frequency formulation of probability, these same distributions can be used as probability distributions and used to predict what might

TABLE 5.3   Distribution of the Number of Arrivals

Arrivals	Number of Minutes	Fraction	Relative Frequency
0	5	5/20	0.25
1	7	7/20	0.35
2	4	4/20	0.20
3	3	3/20	0.15
4	1	1/20	0.05
Total	20	20/20	1.00

TABLE 5.4   Distribution of the Distance between Machined Surfaces

Class Interval	Number of Measurements	Fraction	Relative Frequency
0.965–0.974	1	1/30	0.033
0.975–0.984	3	3/30	0.100
0.985–0.994	5	5/30	0.167
0.995–1.004	10	10/30	0.333
1.005–1.014	6	6/30	0.200
1.015–1.024	4	4/30	0.133
1.025–1.034	1	1/30	0.033
Total	30	30/30	1.000

Frequency Distribution of the Number of Arrivals per Minute **FIGURE 5.1**

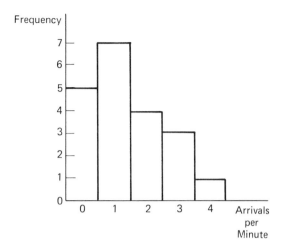

Frequency Distribution of the Distance between Two Machined Surfaces **FIGURE 5.2**

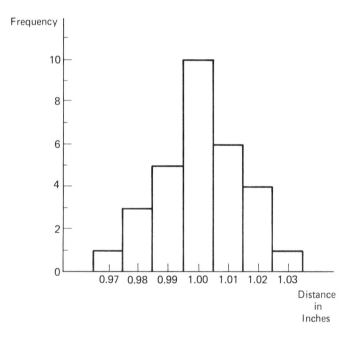

occur in the future. In this context the frequency distribution is a picture of what has occurred; the probability distribution is a prediction of what is likely to occur in the future.

A number of measures may be used to describe the central tendency of a mass of data. Of these, the mean is the most commonly used and may be expressed as:

Measures of Central Tendency

$$\bar{x} = \frac{\Sigma x}{n} = \frac{x_1 + x_2 + x_3 + \ldots + x_n}{n}.$$

This formula suggests that we add each of the values and divide the total by the number of such values. The result is the mean or average.

The mean of the data given in Table 5.1 can be calculated as:

$$\bar{x} = \frac{0.99 + 1.00 + 1.01 + \ldots + 1.00}{30}$$

$$= \frac{30.03}{30} = 1.001.$$

The median is a measure of central tendency defined as that value lying in the middle of an ordered set of data. Its computation requires that data be ranked from the smallest value to the largest and the median is that value lying in the middle if the data consist of an odd number of values. Should the data consist of an even number of values, there is no middle value, and the median is the mean of the two central values. In the data from Table 5.2, the fifteenth value in ascending order is 1.00. The sixteenth is also 1.00; hence, the median would be (1.00 + 1.00) divided by 2 or 1.00.

The mode is another measure of central tendency. It is defined as that value which occurs most frequently. The modal number of arrivals per minute (from Table 5.3 or Figure 5.1) is one. In continuous data there may be no value occurring more than once. The mode is then specified as the midpoint of the class interval of greatest frequency. Referring to Figure 5.2, the modal value would be 1.00. In summary, regarding the data described in Table 5.2, the mean value is 1.001, the median is 1.00, and the mode is 1.00. The mean, median, and mode are likely to be quite similar (if not identical) where the frequency distribution is fairly symmetrical. This is not likely to be the case if the distribution tends to stretch out further in one direction than the other. A distribution is skewed to the right if that distribution tapers off over a more extended range to the right than to the left. In that case the mean is likely to assume a larger value than the median, which in turn is likely to assume a larger value than the mode.

Measures of Dispersion

In addition to information concerning the central tendency of data, it is often desirable to describe the extent to which data cluster about their central value. For this purpose, two measures of variation or dispersion are customarily employed. Of these, the range is the less complex and is obtained by calculating the arithmetic difference between the largest and the smallest value. The range is not a very stable measure of variation, because it depends on only two values, but its advantage lies in the ease with which it may be calculated. For the data of Table 5.2, the range is equal to $1.03 - 0.97 = 0.06$.

The sample variance is a more stable measure of dispersion. It may be calculated as:

$$s^2 = \frac{\Sigma(x - \bar{x})^2}{n - 1} = \frac{(x_1 - \bar{x})^2 + (x_2 - \bar{x})^2 + (x_3 - \bar{x})^2 + \ldots + (x_n - \bar{x})^2}{n - 1}$$

Computing the variance calls for an evaluation of the difference between each value and the mean. These differences are then individually squared and added, and the sum of these squared differences is divided by a number equal to one less than the number of observations. Using the data of Table 5.2, the variance would be calculated as:

$$s^2 = \frac{(0.99 - 1.001)^2 + (1.00 - 1.001)^2 + \ldots + (1.00 - 1.001)^2}{29}$$

$$= \frac{0.00567}{29} = 0.000196$$

It can be seen that this definitional formula for the variance requires the lengthy series of calculations just described. Fortunately, the numerator can be modified by algebraic manipulation and the variance expressed as:

$$s^2 = \frac{\Sigma x^2 - \left[\dfrac{(\Sigma x)^2}{n}\right]}{n - 1}$$

Although this latter equation looks more complex than the previous one, it permits more rapid computation, because the necessity for successive subtraction is eliminated. The variance of the same data would be found by this latter equation as:

$$s^2 = \frac{[(0.99)^2 + \ldots + (1.00)^2] - [(0.99 + \ldots + 1.00)^2/30]}{29}$$

and the calculations are shown in Table 5.5

Table for Calculating the Variance   **TABLE 5.5**

x	x^2	x	x^2
0.99	0.9801	1.00	1.0000
1.00	1.0000	0.98	0.9604
1.01	1.0201	1.01	1.0201
1.02	1.0404	1.03	1.0609
0.99	0.9801	0.99	0.9801
1.00	1.0000	1.02	1.0404
1.00	1.0000	1.00	1.0000
1.01	1.0201	1.00	1.0000
1.02	1.0404	1.01	1.0201
1.00	1.0000	1.00	1.0000
0.99	0.9801	1.01	1.0201
0.97	0.9409	1.00	1.0000
0.98	0.9604	1.02	1.0404
1.01	1.0201	0.99	0.9801
0.98	0.9604	1.00	1.0000

TABLE 5.5 (cont.)

$$\Sigma x = 30.03$$

$$\Sigma x^2 = 30.0657$$

$$s^2 = \frac{30.06570 - \left[\dfrac{(30.03)^2}{30}\right]}{29}$$

$$= \frac{30.06570 - 30.06003}{29} = 0.000196$$

The variance is a useful and descriptive measure of the dispersion of data. It is sometimes converted to a closely related measure of dispersion referred to as the standard deviation. The relationship between these two measures is quite simple; the standard deviation is the positive square root of the variance. In this example calculation, $s = \sqrt{s^2} = \sqrt{0.000196} = 0.014$.

THE PROBABILITY DISTRIBUTION

A frequency distribution describes what has occurred in the past; a probability distribution predicts what might occur in the future. The number of lost-time accidents per month in a plant could be plotted as a frequency distribution as could the won-lost record of a football team. In both cases the distribution is a historical record. A probability distribution for coin tossing could also be established and while this would express the likelihood of a head or a tail, it would ordinarily be established by theoretical rather than historical considerations. On the other hand, the probability of zero, one, two, three, or more accidents occurring per month could be used as a predictive device and this distribution would likely be established from historical evidence.

Probability distributions may be discrete or continuous, depending on the nature of the event they are used to predict. They provide a means for assigning the likelihood of occurrence of all possible outcomes. Variables described in terms of a probability distribution are conveniently called *random variables*. The specific value of a random variable is determined by the distribution with the occurrence of that value then governed by the associated probability. In this section we will examine probability distributions based on the relative frequency formulation of probability, distributions founded on the classical definition or formulation, and distributions based on a subjective assessment. Finally, we will introduce combinations as a stepping stone to developing the hypergeometric probability distribution.

The Relative Frequency Formulation

The relative frequency definition of probability rests upon a simple projection of historical evidence. For example, consider the data of Table 5.1 reporting the number of arrivals per minute at a bank over a twenty-minute period. The same data are summarized in Table 5.3 and finally pictured as a frequency distribution in Figure 5.1. Had the ordinate of this figure been established as relative frequency rather than a number (or frequency), we would have constructed a relative frequency distribution. This latter distribution could have just as easily been labeled a probability distribution and such a distribution is sketched in Figure 5.3. Now we have a projection of what might occur in the future. If someone were concerned with the likelihood of zero arrivals per minute during any given minute, we could examine this probability distribution and conclude that the probability is 0.25, or the odds are one chance in four that there will be no arrivals during the one-minute time period.

A number of comments are now in order. First, this probability distribution rests on the same assumption that underlies the relative frequency definition of probability. We need a reasonable amount of historical evidence before we can make any predictions, and in this case the sample of twenty minutes is a rather limited amount of data. In addition the data that has been collected should be representative of the time period over which the predictions will be made. We collected data over a twenty-minute time period, but are these twenty minutes representative of the time period for which the probabilities will be projected? If the answer is positive, we will have more confidence in our prediction.

Note that the area under the probability distribution is equal to one. We are assuming that the events are mutually exclusive and that they are collectively exhaustive. These assumptions are implicit in any probability distribution. As a result, as we discussed in the previous chapter, the sum of the probabilities of every listing of events or outcomes which are both mutually exclusive and collectively exhaustive must be equal to one.

Probability of the Number of Arrivals per Minute   **FIGURE 5.3**

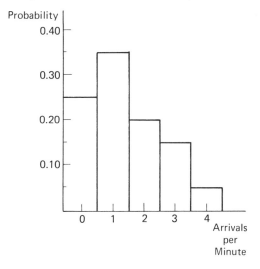

Probability distributions can also be constructed from the logic or geometry of a situation. For example, if one were asked to construct a probability distribution describing the possible outcomes resulting from the

**The
Classical
Formulation**

roll of a six-sided die, one would expect that Figure 5.4 would be the result. Note that this forecast could have been developed without our ever having seen any historical evidence. However, our prediction would be based upon a very critical assumption—namely, that each side of the die is equally likely to land face up. If this assumption of "equally likely outcomes" is not satisfied, the probability distribution will provide us with some very misleading forecasts.

Note that the area under the probability distribution is again equal to unity and that the outcomes are mutually exclusive and collectively exhaustive.

FIGURE 5.4   Probability of the Outcome of the Toss of a Die

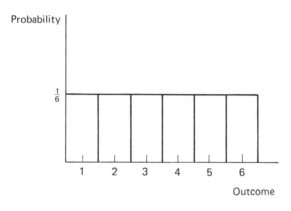

The Subjective Formulation

Some probability distributions have to be established on the basis of either the classical or the relative frequency foundation to which is added a measure of judgment and/or intuition. Consider the production-collection system described in Figure 5.5. We are producing ball bearings and have a large number of machines individually engaged in the production of these bearings. The mean (and possibly the dispersion) of the diameters of the respective outputs are not the same in each case. We desire to collect and ship some quantity of bearings, all of which should fall between the tolerance of 1.045 inches to 1.055 inches. To obtain this desired output, we collect a mix from the machine outputs and pass these bearings over a wire mesh calibrated to allow through all bearings of the diameter of 1.055 or smaller. We then take all those bearings that have passed through the mesh and subject them to a second screen designed to allow through all bearings of a diameter of 1.045 inches or smaller. We retain the larger bearings from this second screening process. Assuming that both meshes are 100 percent effective, we now have a collection of bearings that meet the desired requirement of being within the tolerance of 1.045 to 1.055 inches. But what of the distribution of bearings within this range? What is the probability distribution describing the likelihood of the diameter of a single bearing collected at random from those bearings that have been collected in the barrel to be shipped as the desired output? To obtain the

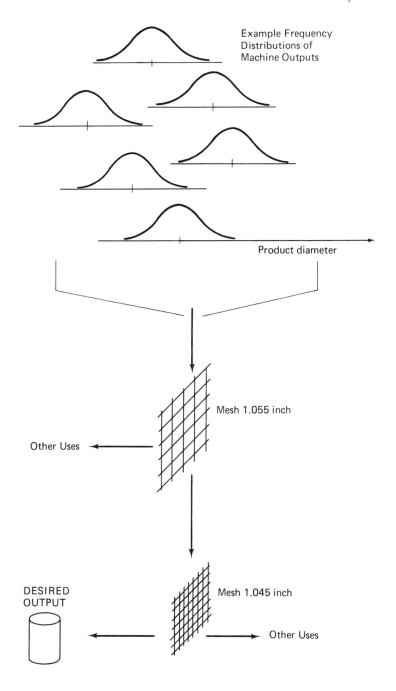

Example Frequency Distributions of Machine Outputs

Product diameter

Mesh 1.055 inch

Other Uses

DESIRED OUTPUT

Mesh 1.045 inch

Other Uses

FIGURE 5.6   Subjective Probability Distribution of the Output of
the Production-Collection System

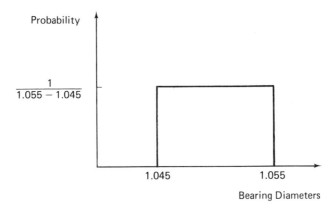

Bearing Diameters

correct answer, one would have to return to the initial distribution of machine outputs and add these over the range of 1.045 to 1.055 inches. Because we are not aware of the form of these initial distributions and we are not likely to have accurate data regarding the exact mean and standard deviation of the output of each of these machines, it would not be unreasonable to assume the continuous uniform probability distribution presented in Figure 5.6 as describing our output. Note that this distribution is a continuous rather than a discrete distribution. The area under this probability distribution is equal to unity. Note also that we are relying on some judgment rather than only historical evidence or the geometry of the situation in the assumption that this probability distribution is uniform. However, with the information that is available, this is not an unreasonable assumption to make.

Cumulative Frequency and Probability Distributions   Sometimes it is advantageous to sum or integrate a frequency or a probability distribution and then express this summation either mathematically or graphically. In subsequent discussions regarding Monte Carlo analysis, we will make particular use of the cumulative probability distribution. As its name suggests, cumulative probability distribution tabulates cumulative frequencies, that is, the total number of occurrences up to and including the interval or event in question. For example and referring again to Table 5.4, we might wish to express as a frequency distribution the number of times we encountered units of a specific thickness (distance between machined surfaces) *or less*. First, we would develop this in tabular form as follows in Table 5.6.

The ogive (pronounced *oh-jive*) is the pictorial representation of a cumulative frequency distribution. Using the data of Table 5.6, we can construct Figure 5.7. Note that in this example, because of the way the ogive will be read, we use the upper boundary of the cell (or even more precisely, the lower boundary of the next cell) along the abscissa. From the ogive a number of interesting observations can be made. For example, the point on the abscissa which lies directly below the intersection of the

curve and the cumulative frequency of fifty is the value above and below
which half of the units are likely to be found. This point is called the
median.

In the same fashion that a frequency distribution can be projected
into a probability distribution, so also can a cumulative frequency distribution
be projected as a cumulative probability distribution. More will be seen
of this in Chapter 14.

Distribution of the Distance between Machined Surfaces   **TABLE 5.6**

Class Interval	Relative Frequency	Cumulative Frequency
0.965–0.974	0.033	0.033
0.975–0.984	0.100	0.133
0.985–0.994	0.167	0.300
0.995–1.004	0.333	0.633
1.005–1.014	0.200	0.833
1.015–1.024	0.133	0.966
1.025–1.034	0.033	0.999 or 1.000
Total	1.000	

Cumulative Frequency Distribution of the Distance between Machined Surfaces   **FIGURE 5.7**

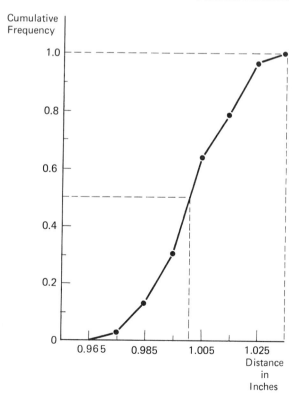

Some probability distributions will have to be developed through the enumeration of all possible outcomes. This can be facilitated by the theory of combinations. Assume we have four items labeled A, B, C, and D. The number of possible pairs which can be made up from these four items are A-B, A-C, A-D, B-C, B-D, and C-D for a total of six such pairs; these are called *combinations*. Alternatively, the number of combinations of n things taken x at a time is given by the expression:

$$C_x^n = \frac{n!}{x!(n-x)!}$$

Note that $n!$ is $n(n-1)(n-2) \ldots (2)(1)$. In our example we are interested in the number of combinations of four things taken two at a time, or:

$$C_2^4 = \frac{4!}{2!(4-2)!}$$

$$= \frac{(4)(3)(2)(1)}{(2)(1)(2)(1)} = 6$$

Likewise the number of combinations of these same four items taken three at a time could be actually specified as A-B-C, A-B-D, A-C-D, and B-C-D. Similarly, we can solve as:

$$C_3^4 = \frac{4!}{3!\,1!}$$

$$= \frac{(4)(3)(2)(1)}{(3)(2)(1)(1)} = 4$$

The number of combinations of four items taken four at a time is obviously:

$$C_4^4 = \frac{4!}{4!\,0!}$$

$$= \frac{(4)(3)(2)(1)}{(4)(3)(2)(1)(1)} = 1$$

Note that $0! = 1$. At the other extreme where very large factorials are encountered, it may be convenient to work with logarithms of factorials.

Consider one more illustration. How many combinations can be made of eight items taken four at a time? We could enumerate these, but using our formula:

$$C_4^8 = \frac{8!}{4!(8-4)!}$$

$$= \frac{(8)(7)(6)(5)(4)(3)(2)(1)}{(4)(3)(2)(1)(4)(3)(2)(1)} = 70$$

This calculation is less time consuming than an actual specification of each combination.

THE HYPERGEOMETRIC DISTRIBUTION

The hypergeometric is the most fundamental of the discrete probability distributions. It is a sampling distribution and describes the case where we wish to establish the likelihood of obtaining two (or more) designated units from a finite or limited population and we chose not to replace units as they are selected. The probabilities associated with various sampling plans used in statistical quality control could be ascertained with the hypergeometric distribution, and the odds of obtaining different poker and bridge hands rest on this distribution. As we will shortly see, the probability distribution is a simple extension of the conditional probability theorem.

The Distribution

The probability distribution can be developed through the theory of combinations, and we do so by defining the probability of each outcome or occurrence as a fraction consisting of all favorable combinations divided by the total number of possible combinations. For example, consider a bowl containing two black balls and one white ball. Two balls are selected at random from this bowl. The probability that one is white and one is black is sought. The denominator of the fraction is the total number of combinations of three balls taken two at a time. In effect we are asking the question: In how many ways can we select two balls from the three contained within the bowl? This will be seen to be three. We implicitly assume that the likelihood of each combination is the same.

The numerator is the number of combinations which will satisfy our requirement of selecting exactly one white and one black ball. This will be seen to be two and is the product of the number of combinations of one white ball selected from the one which is available, times the number of combinations of one black ball selected from the two black balls which are available. The probability of drawing exactly one white and one black ball is calculated as:

$$P(W+B) = \frac{C_1^1 C_1^2}{C_2^3} = \frac{\dfrac{1!}{1!0!}\dfrac{2!}{1!1!}}{\dfrac{3!}{2!1!}} = \frac{\dfrac{(1)(2)(1)}{(1)(1)(1)(1)}}{\dfrac{(3)(2)(1)}{(2)(1)(1)}} = 2/3.$$

The remaining alternative is that of drawing exactly two black balls. The probability of doing so is given by:

$$P(B + B) = \frac{C_2^2 C_0^1}{C_2^3} = \frac{\dfrac{2!}{2!1!} \dfrac{1!}{0!1!}}{\dfrac{3!}{2!1!}} = \frac{\dfrac{(2)(1)(1)}{(2)(1)(1)(1)}}{\dfrac{(3)(2)(1)}{(2)(1)(1)}} = 1/3.$$

Note that in this latter calculation, in the numerator we are suggesting that there really is only one pair of balls which can be selected from the bowl and meets the requirement that both balls be black. On the other hand, there are three possible pairs of balls which can be drawn from the bowl and this three represents the total number of combinations of three balls taken two at a time, or the denominator. The two probabilities of two-thirds and one-third respectively represent the frequencies for this hypergeometric probability distribution. These are mutually exclusive and collectively exhaustive and the area under the resulting probability distribution is equal to unity. As will be further demonstrated through example, hypergeometric distributions have no typical form. They may be symmetrical or skewed to the right or left. They are representative of sampling distributions where the population is limited or finite and replacement between items is not effected during the actual sampling.

Some Examples

Problem 1. Assume that a container of fifty items includes two which are defective. A sample of four is selected from the fifty. We desire to obtain the probability that exactly zero, one, or both defectives will be contained in the sample of four. The first probability, $P[0]$ may be set up as:

$$P(0) = \frac{C_0^2 C_4^{48}}{C_4^{50}} = \frac{\dfrac{2!}{0!2!} \dfrac{48!}{4!44!}}{\dfrac{50!}{4!46!}} = \frac{\dfrac{(2)(1)(48)(47)(46)(45)(44!)}{(1)(2)(1)(4)(3)(2)(1)(44!)}}{\dfrac{(50)(49)(48)(47)(46!)}{(4)(3)(2)(1)(46!)}}$$

Note that in the numerator we are first concerned with the number of ways it is possible to select four units, none of which are defective, from the total of fifty available in the container. This is established by noting the number of combinations of two defectives taken zero at a time and multiplying by the number of ways we can obtain four good units from the remaining forty-eight good units. This numerator is the number of different methods by which four good units may be selected from the fifty available in the container. The denominator is simply the total number of combinations of fifty units taken four at a time. By way of a verification that the probability has been set up correctly, note that in the upper portion of the numerator, the two plus the forty-eight is equal to the upper portion of the denominator.

Likewise in the bottom portion of the numerator, the zero plus the
four is equal to the bottom portion of the denominator. And there
is one further suggestion; when we begin to expand our factorials
in the upper portion of the numerator, the 48! is expanded down to
$48 \times 47 \times 46 \times 45 \times 44!$. The lower half of our numerator also contains
a 44! and these may simply be canceled as they now stand rather
than expanding each of them down to one. Likewise in the denominator,
the two 46!'s will cancel each other. We now may conclude our
calculations as:

$$P(0) = \frac{\dfrac{(2)(1)(48)(47)(46)(45)}{(1)(2)(1)(4)(3)(2)(1)}}{\dfrac{(50)(49)(48)(47)}{(4)(3)(2)(1)}} = 0.8449$$

In similar fashion, the probabilities of selecting one and two defectives
can be calculated as:

$$P(1) = \frac{C_1^2\, C_3^{48}}{C_4^{50}} = \frac{\dfrac{2!}{1!\,1!}\dfrac{48!}{3!\,45!}}{\dfrac{50!}{4!\,46!}} = 0.1502$$

$$P(2) = \frac{C_2^2\, C_2^{48}}{C_4^{50}} = \frac{\dfrac{2!}{2!\,0!}\dfrac{48!}{2!\,46!}}{\dfrac{50!}{4!\,46!}} = 0.0049$$

The probability distribution would assume the form shown in Figure
5.8. Note that the distribution is skewed to the right and that the
area it encompasses totals unity. Because the outcomes of obtaining
zero, one, or two defectives are mutually exclusive and collectively
exhaustive, the sum of these probabilities must be one.

Problem 2. A hungry, near-sighted giant was strolling past the Cotton Bowl
one Saturday afternoon, and hearing a great noise, he peered over
the top of the stands at the field to see if he could find something
to eat. On the field at the time were twelve football players in red
uniforms, eleven players in white uniforms, six officials, one large
dog, and a protesting coach. The giant scooped the thirty people together
(the dog escaped) and randomly selected four for lunch. He knew
that officials were fairly tough to eat and that he could escape indigestion
only if he ate no more than one official. Find the probability that
the giant escaped indigestion.

FIGURE 5.8   The Probability Distribution of the Number of Defectives in a Sample of Four from a Lot of Fifty Containing Two Defectives

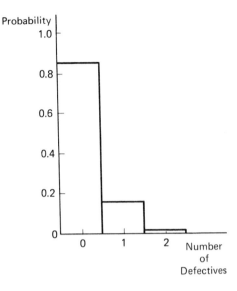

Our solution will require solving for the probability of obtaining zero officials and the probability of obtaining one official in the sample of four. These are:

$$P(0) = \frac{C_0^6 \, C_4^{24}}{C_4^{30}} = \frac{\dfrac{6!}{0!\,6!}\dfrac{24!}{4!\,20!}}{\dfrac{30!}{4!\,26!}} = 0.388$$

$$P(1) = \frac{C_1^6 \, C_3^{24}}{C_4^{30}} = \frac{\dfrac{6!}{1!\,5!}\dfrac{24!}{3!\,21!}}{\dfrac{30!}{4!\,26!}} = 0.443$$

The probability of selecting one or no officials is 0.388 plus 0.443 or 0.831, a high total probability. The other possible outcomes are the likelihood of selecting two, three, or all four officials in the sample of four. The sum of the above two plus these latter three possible outcomes should add to unity.

THE BINOMINAL DISTRIBUTION

The binominal is also a sampling distribution. It is applicable when we are seeking the probability of obtaining two (or more) designated units either from an infinite population *or* from a finite population with the replacement of units as they are selected. In effect, the assumption is made that a constant probability of occurrence exists through the sampling process and from the selection of one unit to the next. This distribution can be used as an approximation to the hypergeometric distribution when the population is relatively large in comparison to the sample which is drawn.

The binominal distribution is often said to describe a *Bernoulli process*. It occurs when each trial (or selected unit) has only two possible outcomes, the probability of each outcome remains constant from one trial to the next (the trials are statistically independent), and the number of trials is known. The binominal distribution is an extension of the multiplication theorem and another form of the probability tree.

The Distribution

The probability of exactly x occurrences in n trials of an event that has a constant probability of occurrence p is given as:

$$P(x) = C_x^n p^x q^{n-x} = \frac{n!}{x!(n-x)!} p^x q^{n-x}$$

where $q = 1 - p$.

As an example of the application of this distribution, assume that a coin is to be tossed five times. The probability of obtaining exactly two tails is:

$$P(2) = C_2^5 (p)^2 (1 - p)^3$$

$$= \frac{5!}{3!2!} (0.5)^2 (0.5)^3$$

$$= 10(0.03125) = 0.3125.$$

Each flip has two possible outcomes—a tail or a head. The probability of a tail is the same from one flip to the next and we are to toss the coin five times.

We could also calculate the probability of obtaining zero and one as well as three, four, and five tails in the five tosses. Because the outcomes are mutually exclusive and collectively exhaustive, the sum of these will be one. Because $p = 0.5$, this distribution will be symmetrical. If p is less than 0.5, the distribution will be skewed to the right; if p is greater than 0.5, the distribution will be skewed to the left.

The mean of a binominal distribution is np and the variance is npq. In our coin tossing exercise, the average number of tails that can be expected in five tosses of a coin will be np or $(5)(0.5) = 2.5$. The variance is npq or $(5)(0.5)(0.5) = 1.25$.

Some Examples

Problem 3. The binominal distribution is frequently used as an approximation for the hypergeometric distribution because of the relative ease with which individual probabilities can be found. It will serve as a good approximation to the extent that the population is large relative to the sample size. This may be demonstrated by reworking Problem 1, used to illustrate the hypergeometric distribution. Since the container of fifty items included two which were defective, $p = 0.04$ and $q = 0.96$, and the respective probabilities are:

$$P(0) = \frac{4!}{0!\,4!}(0.04)^0(0.96)^4 = (1)(1)(0.96)^4 = 0.8493$$

$$P(1) = \frac{4!}{1!\,3!}(0.04)^1(0.96)^3 = (4)(0.04)(0.96)^3 = 0.1416$$

$$P(2) = \frac{4!}{2!\,2!}(0.04)^2(0.96)^2 = (6)(0.04)^2(0.96)^2 = 0.0088$$

While the absolute values are close to those obtained earlier, the percentage error in the calculation for $P(2)$ is:

$$\frac{0.0088 - 0.0049}{0.0049} = 80 \text{ percent}$$

a fairly significant deviation. Had the container held 500 rather than fifty units, the error in the approximation would have been far less serious.

Problem 4. A foundry process yields output that averages 40 percent defective. A batch of twenty units is produced. What is the probability that more than half of these are defective? We are essentially asking for the $P(11) + P(12) + P(13) + \ldots + P(20)$, a rather tedious and time consuming request. Fortunately, we can use the tables describing the cumulative binominal distribution found in the appendix.

From the data already given,

$b = 20$, the number of units to be inspected,
$p = 0.40$, the probability that any single unit will be defective, and
$c = 11$, the number of defectives in question, where we are interested in determining the probability of *11 or more* defectives.

At $n = 20$ in Table 1 in the appendix a value of 1275 can be obtained from the column corresponding to $p = 0.40$ and the row $c = 11$. This means:

$$P(11 \text{ or more}) = 0.1275$$

Again, note that these tabular values represent cumulative probabilities. The probability of exactly ten defectives would be the probability of ten or more, less the probability of eleven or more, or:

$$P(10 \text{ or more}) = 0.2447$$
$$\underline{-P(11 \text{ or more}) = -0.1275}$$
$$P(10) = 0.1172$$

With this same foundry process, the probability of five or fewer defectives could also be resolved. Realizing that $P(5 \text{ or less})$ plus $P(6 \text{ or more})$ must equal one, we can establish our answer as:

$$1.0000$$
$$\underline{-P(6 \text{ or more}) = -0.8744}$$
$$P(5 \text{ or less}) = 0.1256$$

THE NORMAL DISTRIBUTION

The normal is a continuous probability distribution and is often used to define the probability of the occurrence of an object, state, or event that takes on values over a continuum. Under some conditions, it may also be advantageous to use this continuous probability distribution to approximate a discrete process. By doing so tedious summations can be replaced by integrals.

The normal distribution is symmetrical about the mean and possesses an interesting and useful property in regard to its shape. Where distances from the mean are expressed in terms of standard deviations, s, the relative areas defined between two such distances will be constant from one distribution to another. In effect and unlike the hypergeometric and binominal distributions, all normal distributions are identical in form and can be defined in terms of a common value of $\bar{x}$ and s. As a result, a single set of probabilities may be tabulated and used.

The Distribution

The normal (or Gaussian or bell-shaped) distribution is one of the more important of all probability distributions. It describes many real world situations that have a few values which are exceedingly small, a few values which are quite large, and then increasing numbers of values as one moves from each of these extremes toward the mean with a final clustering of values around the mean. For example, the heights and weights of a large number of individuals will likely be normally distributed. As a matter of fact, most physical dimensions will be normally distributed although elapsed time, for example, the time interval between arrivals at a service facility, may be skewed in the direction of the longer time intervals and not bell-shaped. While the data from Table 5.2 consist of only thirty values, these can be approximated by a normal distribution as seen in Figure 5.9.

The area under a normal distribution and the associated probability is usually given from $-\infty$ to any value expressed in standard deviation units.

FIGURE 5.9   The Normal Distribution Approximating the Data of Table 5.2

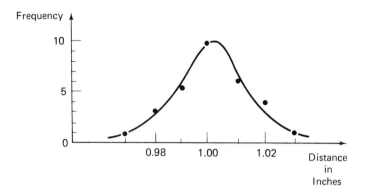

Such probabilities are given in the appendix from $-\infty$ to Z, where Z is the standard normal variate defined as:

$$Z = \frac{x - \bar{x}}{s}$$

This is shown as the shaded area in Figure 5.10.

FIGURE 5.10   The Normal Probability Distribution

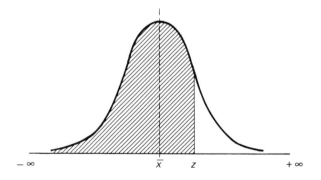

The area from $-\infty$ to $-1s$ is indicated in the shaded area in Figure 5.11. From the appendix the probability of x falling within this range is 0.1587. Likewise, the area from $-\infty$ to $+2s$ is 0.9773. If the probability of a value falling in the interval $-1s$ to $+2s$ is required, the following computations may be made:

$$P(\text{area} -\infty \text{ to } +2s) = 0.9773$$

$$\underline{-P(\text{area} -\infty \text{ to } -1s) = 0.1587}$$

$$P(\text{area} -1s \text{ to } +2s) = 0.8186$$

This can be seen in Figure 5.12. In similar fashion, the probability associated with any event that is normally distributed can be ascertained if the mean and the standard deviation of that distribution is known.

The Area from $-\infty$ to $-1s$ under the Normal Distribution **FIGURE 5.11**

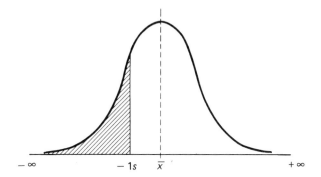

The Area from $-1s$ to $+2s$ under the Normal Distribution **FIGURE 5.12**

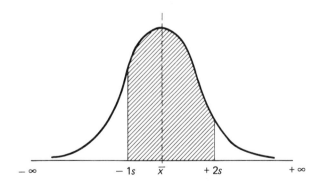

Problem 5. Assume that the data given in Table 5.2 are from a normal distribution and that $\bar{x} = 1.001$ inches and $s = 0.014$ inches are good estimates of the process. What is the probability that the next unit selected is equal to or less than 0.990 inches in thickness? Our standard normal variate is:

Some Examples

$$Z = \frac{0.990 - 1.001}{0.014} = -0.79$$

From the appendix the area from $-\infty$ to $-0.79s$ is 0.2148, and we would conclude that the probability would be:

$$P(x \le 0.990 \text{ inches}) = 0.2148$$

As an extension of this example, what is the likelihood that the next unit will be equal to or less than 1.020 inches *and* equal to or greater than 0.980 inches in thickness? First, the upper standard normal variate is:

$$Z = \frac{1.020 - 1.001}{0.014} = +1.36$$

The lower standard normal variate is:

$$Z = \frac{0.980 - 1.001}{0.014} = -1.50$$

The probability that the next unit will lie between these limits is:

$$P(\text{area } -\infty \text{ to } +1.36s) = 0.9131$$
$$\underline{-P(\text{area } -\infty \text{ to } -1.50s) = 0.0668}$$
$$P(\text{area } -1.50s \text{ to } +1.36s) = 0.8463$$

or more specifically:

$$P(0.980 \le x \le 1.020) = 0.8463$$

Problem 6. Under some conditions the normal distribution can be used as an approximation to the binominal distribution. In general if p is close to 0.5 or if n is large (>50) and $0.20 < p < 0.80$, fairly accurate results may be obtained. From Problem 4, $p = 0.40$, $n = 20$, and we are interested in the probability of eleven or more defectives.

First, our estimate of the mean and the standard deviation would be:

$$\bar{x} = np = (20)(0.4) = 8$$
$$s = \sqrt{npq} = \sqrt{(20)(0.4)(0.6)} = 2.19$$

The probability of eleven or more defectives is the area from 10.5 to $+\infty$. This can be seen in Figure 5.13. Now, expressing the area from a standard normal variate:

$$Z = \frac{10.5 - 8}{2.19} = +1.14.$$

We are interested in the area from $+1.14s$ to $+\infty$. This is:

$$P(\text{area } -\infty \text{ to } +\infty) = 1.0000$$
$$\underline{-P(\text{area } -\infty \text{ to } +1.14s) = 0.8729}$$
$$P(\text{area } +1.14s \text{ to } +\infty) = 0.1271$$

The Binominal Distribution to be Approximated by the Normal Distribution **FIGURE 5.13**

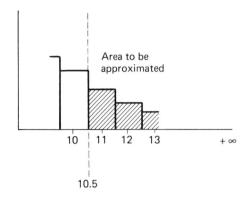

or more specifically:

$P(11 \text{ or more}) = 0.1271$

and this compares to a value of $P = 0.1275$ under the binominal distribution.

QUESTIONS AND PROBLEMS

1. Describe an operational situation that would result in discrete data; in continuous data.

2. Why must continuous data be made discrete in order to construct a frequency distribution?

3. When might the mean be a realistic measure of central tendency? When the median? The mode?

4. When might a measure of dispersion be needed to meaningfully describe some real world situation?

5. What is the difference between the relative frequency distribution and the probability distribution?

6. Cite an example of a probability distribution resting on the relative frequency formulation. The classical formulation. The subjective formulation.

7. Describe a situation that would likely result in a symmetrical frequency distribution. A skewed frequency distribution.

8. Under what circumstances should the hypergeometric rather than the binominal distribution be used to describe a sampling process?

9. What are the requirements for constructing a probability tree (a Bernoulli process)?

10. Under what conditions can the normal distribution be used to approximate the binominal distribution?

11. The data which follow represent the pounds of metal recovered from a casting operation. Plot a frequency distribution of these data.

11.9	12.0	12.2	12.2	11.8	11.9
11.8	11.5	12.6	10.8	12.3	12.6
11.9	11.8	11.7	12.0	12.2	12.1
11.5	11.5	12.7	11.4	11.5	11.4
12.0	11.6	11.8	10.9	11.7	10.9
12.1	12.1	12.3	11.7	11.4	12.2
11.7	11.5	11.6	11.3	11.7	11.2
11.5	11.8	12.3	12.1	11.5	12.0
11.4	11.5	11.3	11.1	11.6	11.9
12.8	11.9	12.4	11.8	12.7	11.5
11.7	11.3	12.9	12.5	12.4	11.6
12.4	12.4	11.9	11.8	12.1	11.5
12.0	11.9	12.0	11.3	11.3	13.0
11.7	11.3	12.5	11.2	11.9	12.0
12.5	11.6	11.1	11.0	11.1	11.0

12. Calculate the mean, the median, and the mode of the data in Problem 11.

13. Calculate the range of the data in Problem 11.

14. If the data of Problem 11 were normally distributed, what would be the probability of the next unit being less than twelve pounds? Between 11.5 and 12.5 pounds?

15. Calculate the probability of obtaining three heads in six tosses of a coin; four heads; five heads; six heads.

16. In a poker hand in which each player is dealt a five-card hand from a standard fifty-two-card deck, what is the probability that any one individual will be dealt two aces? Two or more aces? A flush of all hearts? Any flush?

17. A manufacturing process is 5.0 percent defective. What is the probability of finding no defectives in twenty pieces? Of finding three or less defectives in 100 pieces?

18. What is the probability of a football team playing an eleven game schedule and going through the season undefeated if they can be expected to win each game with $p = 0.8$? (Ignore the possibility of ties.)

19. A baseball team plays a 160-game schedule. Their odds of winning any game are given as $p = 0.6$. What is the probability they will complete the season with 100 or more wins? Solve with the normal as an approximation.

20. Solve Problem 19 using the normal approximation and ascertaining the likelihood the team will end the season with ninety or more wins but less than 100 wins.

BIBLIOGRAPHY

BOWKER, A. H., AND LIEBERMAN, G. J. *Engineering Statistics.* Englewood Cliffs, N.J.: Prentice-Hall, Inc., 1972.

EHRENFELD, SYLVAIN, AND LITTAUER, SEBASTIAN B. *Introduction to Statistical Method.* New York: McGraw-Hill Book Company, Inc. 1964.

KIRKPATRICK, ELWOOD G. *Introductory Statistics and Probability for Engineering, Science, and Technology.* Englewood Cliffs, N.J.: Prentice-Hall, Inc., 1974.

LARSON, H. J. *Introduction to Probability Theory and Statistical Inference.* New York: John Wiley & Sons, Inc., 1969.

LINDGREN, B. W., AND McELRATH, G. W. *Introduction to Probability and Statistics.* New York: The Macmillan Company, 1966.

MARTIN, J. J. *Bayesian Decision Problems and Markov Chains.* New York: John Wiley & Sons, Inc., 1967.

SHUCHMAN, A. *Scientific Decision Making in Business.* New York: Holt, Rinehart and Winston, Inc., 1963.

A structure
for decisions

Decision making has been described as a pervasive and integral part of all human activity, but one often faces a problem in initiating a discussion of the decision-making process. Where does one begin? What can one assume? For our purposes we will begin with the assumption that *a decision is made to achieve some desired state of affairs*. We have also alluded to the fact that an individual or an organization is likely to have multiple goals. Nevertheless, we will assume *a single objective or a single measure of effectiveness*. Finally, we will require that we be able to state exactly which alternatives were considered, how the outcomes associated with each alternative are to be predicted, how these were compared, and so forth. *We will require explicitness.* To the extent that explicitness can be achieved, decisions can be reviewed by others, methods of improving the decision process can be sought, and decision making can be taught.

In this chapter we will introduce some explicit models of the decision process. These will be descriptive and/or predictive, but they will not dictate how decisions ought to be made, because the selection of an alternative as "best" would require a value judgment which we are not prepared to incorporate in an introductory chapter on decision making.

THE PAYOFF MATRIX

One method of describing a decision situation is through the use of a payoff matrix. In order to present this approach, let us consider a situation typically faced by the manager of a retail chain grocery store. If the reader is familiar with grocery store operations, he no doubt will recognize that some realism has been sacrificed for illustration purposes but this sacrifice is minimal.

Let us assume that the grocery store manager places a weekly order for boxes (units) of a perishable fruit each Friday for delivery on the following Monday. Those units not sold during the week are considered worthless, because it is management's policy to promote the high quality of fruit and vegetables sold in the chain stores; hence selling over-ripe fruit at discount prices is against policy.

Boxes of fruit not sold during the week result in a loss of the purchase price plus an "overage" cost per box for disposal. If the weekly demand exceeds the number of boxes ordered, there is a unit "shortage" cost per box. Although the shortage cost is difficult to assess, management realizes a loss due to loss of customer good will, loss of potential profit per box, and other costs. The unit selling price, purchase price, overage cost, and shortage cost are relatively stable throughout the year and average values will be used in the subsequent analysis.

The demand history for this item is not known precisely but managerial experience results in the judgment that weekly demand will be either 9, 10, 11, 12, 13, 14, or 15 boxes. Further, the fruit is a year-round item and management rarely attempts to influence weekly demand by discount or advertising. In this sense, then, demand is outside the control of manage-

An Example—Inventory

ment. The order quantity is of course within the control of management, and we presume it is management's objective to order some constant number of boxes each week to effect some measure of economic advantage. Primary questions therefore concern the measure of economic advantage (a criterion or a principle of choice) and the order quantity (the alternative selected).

The following economic figures are assumed and relevant to our analysis. Let

R	= selling price per unit	=	$10.00
C_0	= purchase price per unit	=	$ 5.00
C_1	= cost of overage (inventory exceeds demand) per unit	=	$ 1.00
C_2	= cost of shortage (demand exceeds inventory) per unit	=	$ 3.00

We further identify elements of the decision as:

Alternatives $\quad = I =$ the number of units to be ordered each week (management's choice).

Possible Futures $\quad = D =$ the number of units demanded per week, a random variable presumed outside management's control.

In general, the outcomes that could occur in a given week can be enumerated as

Outcome 1—The number of units inventoried exceeds the number of units demanded (overage); this number is given by $(I - D)$.

Outcome 2—The number of units inventoried equals the number demanded, that is, $I = D$.

Outcome 3—The number of units inventoried is less than the number of units demanded (shortage); this number is given by $(D - I)$.

Assuming that we are concerned with *profit per week, P,* as a measure of economic advantage, the evaluation of the outcomes are as follows:

For Outcome 1 $(I > D)$,

$$P = RD - C_0 I - C_1 (I - D)$$
$$= (R + C_1)D - (C_0 + C_1)I.$$

For example, if $I = 15$ units and $D = 10$ units, then:

$$P = (\$10 + \$1)10 - (\$5 + \$1)15 = \$20.$$

For Outcome 2 $(I = D)$,

$$P = RD - C_0 D = RI - C_0 I$$
$$= (R - C_0)D.$$

For example, if $I = 10$ units and $D = 10$ units, then:

$$P = (\$10 - \$5)10 = \$50.$$

For Outcome 3 $(D > I)$,

$$P = RI - C_0I - C_2(D - I)$$
$$= (R - C_0 + C_2)I - C_2D.$$

For example, if $I = 10$ units and $D = 15$ units, then:

$$P = (\$10 - \$5 + \$3)10 - \$3(15) = \$35.$$

Thus, for all alternative-future combinations (units inventoried vs. units demanded) over the range of $I = D = 9$, 10, 11, 12, 13, 14, 15 units, the decision can be presented in the matrix format of Table 6.1 where the cell values are values of P, dollars of net profit per week. In these calculations the cost of overages and shortages has been assumed linear in the number of units over or short, respectively.

The choice of the number of boxes to order each week as a matter of policy is not necessarily obvious at this point. For example, if $I = 15$ units were the order policy, the maximum profit of $75 would be possible when $D = 15$, but this policy would also permit the minimum profit of

The Payoff Matrix for the Retail Inventory Example   **TABLE 6.1**

I = Units Inventoried \ D = Units Demanded	9	10	11	12	13	14	15
9	$45	$42	$39	$36	$33	$30	$27
10	$39	$50	$47	$44	$41	$38	$35
11	$33	$44	$55	$52	$49	$46	$43
12	$27	$38	$49	$60	$57	$54	$51
13	$21	$32	$43	$54	$65	$62	$59
14	$15	$26	$37	$48	$59	$70	$67
15	$ 9	$20	$31	$42	$53	$64	$75

$9 to occur when $D = 9$. Indeed, the choice of I as a policy might well vary from manager to manager depending upon his view of "best" or, rather, his *principle of choice.*

We shall not attempt a solution to this inventory decision problem now but have cited the example to serve as an illustration of how the matrix format may be used to display many decision problems. After completing the chapter, the reader may wish to return to Table 6.1 and find his own solution. A generalized version of the matrix representation is presented below and is usually referred to as the payoff matrix.

The Generalized Payoff Matrix

The symbols used in Figure 6.1, can be defined as follows:

a_i = an alternative under the decision maker's control, where $i = 1,2, . . ., n.$

S_j = a state of nature, or possible future, that can occur, given alternative a_i is chosen, where $j = 1, 2, . . ., m.$

θ_{ij} = the outcome of choosing alternative a_i and having possible future S_j occur.

$V(\theta_{ij})$ = the value of outcome θ_{ij}, which may be in terms of dollars, time, distance, utiles, etc.

p_j = the probability that future S_j will occur.

The term, p_j, was not previously introduced in the retail inventory

FIGURE 6.1   The Generalized Payoff Matrix

p_j	p_1	p_2			p_j			p_m
S_j / a_i	S_1	S_2	---	---	S_j	---	---	S_m
a_1	$V(\theta_{11})$	$V(\theta_{12})$	---	---	$V(\theta_{1j})$	---	---	$V(\theta_{1m})$
a_2	$V(\theta_{21})$	$V(\theta_{22})$	---	---	$V(\theta_{2j})$	---	---	$V(\theta_{2m})$
⋮	⋮	⋮			⋮			⋮
a_i	$V(\theta_{i1})$	$V(\theta_{i2})$	---	---	$V(\theta_{ij})$	---	---	$V(\theta_{im})$
⋮	⋮	⋮			⋮			⋮
a_n	$V(\theta_{n1})$	$V(\theta_{n2})$	---	---	$V(\theta_{nj})$	---	---	$V(\theta_{nm})$

decision problem but will subsequently serve as a means by which decisions may be categorized as being under assumed certainty, under risk, or under uncertainty.

Although the payoff matrix is an adequate representation of many practical decision situations, one should not conclude that all decisions can be thus represented. For instance, those situations where a sequence of decisions is involved cannot usually be described by this model. Sequential decisions, introduced in Chapter 9, will be treated separately. Further, when the states of nature (possible futures) are judged under the control of a rational opponent, such as a business competitor, the decision can be represented by a payoff matrix but the solution procedures are quite different. Competitive decisions are considered separately and are treated in Chapter 7.

Even though competitive decisions and/or sequential decisions are not involved in the payoff matrix, other difficulties deserve some discussion. One should not conclude that obtaining the information to create the matrix model is necessarily an easy task. Indeed, there are preliminary decisions that must be made before attempting to select an alternative (or strategy) from the set of alternatives in a payoff matrix. These preliminary decisions concern the alternatives, the possible futures, their probabilities of occurrence, and the values of the outcomes for alternative-future combinations.

What is the feasible set of alternatives? Rarely does the decision maker have the time or even the insight to define all the possible alternatives available to him in a given decision situation. The decision maker may institute a deliberate search for alternatives, rejecting certain alternatives in the process as infeasible, and finally arrive at a "feasible" set of alternatives for further analysis, presumably that set of alternatives in the payoff matrix. How to execute a search procedure and when to terminate the search are interesting and nontrivial questions which are not addressed in this text. Yet another question remains, namely, what constitutes "feasibility?" The answer to this question lies in the original statement of objectives that the decision is to accomplish. Expanding on this statement, if one were considering the replacement of some production machine, an objective might be that the replacement machine must be capable of producing 1,000 units of product A per day. Those machines incapable of reaching this aspiration level of 1,000 units are rejected from further consideration. The machines capable of meeting or exceeding the aspiration level of 1,000 units are "feasible" and the "best" replacement machine is then selected from the feasible set according to a more discriminating rule, such as minimum annual estimated operating cost or maximum estimated profit per year. Finally, the alternatives should be defined as mutually exclusive. This means each alternative is separate and distinct. Alternatives a_1 and a_2, for example, cannot occur together. If such were possible, then the joint alternative would be defined as another alternative, a_3.

Questions of search (extent of and termination of), relevancy, and distinctness apply as well to defining the set of possible futures in a decision problem. Whereas alternatives are often limited by law, social mores, or company policy, the possible futures are usually not so limited. Experience and judgment therefore play an important role in defining the possible futures. It seems, however, that the greater the decision maker's experience, the less judgment is required on his part. Certainly, experience in the form of recorded past history may serve to reduce the amount of judgment required. Using the inventory problem treated earlier in the chapter as an example, records on past demands for the boxes of fruit provide objective values for the futures in terms of units demanded and also provide the range of values (futures) to consider. In any event, once the set of futures has been decided, the futures are treated as mutually exclusive and collectively exhaustive in the subsequent solution of the decision problem.

For each alternative-future combination there is an outcome and an associated value for this outcome. In the previous inventory problem, a given inventory-demand combination during a week yielded either inventory units short, over, or zero. The value of profit per week was then calculated for each specific outcome. However, problems of measurement and value are often more substantial in real world situations. This is particularly true when multiple goals are involved in the problem, which is usually the case. For example, in the production of some product A one might be interested in the unit cost, the unit weight, and repairability. If different production methods are the alternatives in a decision problem about product A, then there are multiple values associated with each production method. What is needed is a common scale to which each different value may be converted; such a scale is that of utility. That is, dollars may be converted to a utility scale, weight may be converted to a utility scale, and so forth, until all different values of multiple outcomes are converted to a common utility scale. Utility values for each outcome (or goal) are then weighted according to relative importance and aggregated by an additive or multiplicative model for each alternative. The decision maker then chooses that alternative which maximizes the weighted utility value. Although we will discuss the concept of utility later in the chapter, it will be in terms of a single goal for each alternative.

Let us now recall the general matrix model presented in Figure 6.1 and classify decisions according to this model and the amount of information available to the decision maker about the probabilities of the possible futures occurring.

DECISIONS UNDER ASSUMED CERTAINTY

The old cliche "Nothing is certain except death and taxes" notwithstanding, it is reasonable to assume in many decision situations that only one future is relevant and then proceed to study the decision as if the future is certain. Such a case is termed a decision under assumed certainty. For example, it may be a matter of company policy to "write off" (or fully depreciate to salvage value) new equipment purchases in five years. If, in an economic analysis of several new equipment candidates, the measure of effectiveness is equivalent annual costs, the determination of these annual costs would be based on a five-year life for each candidate. The outcomes of a five-year life and the associated annual operating costs for each candidate are assumed certain; that is, they will occur with a probability of 1.0. The actual functional life of an equipment candidate might be 4, 5, 6, 7, 8, or more years. However, a judgment is made by the decision maker to suppress uncertainty because of convenience and/or practicality and assume only the single future of a five-year life.

In terms of the general matrix decision model, a decision under assumed certainty would appear as follows:

	S
a_1	$V(\theta_1)$
a_2	$V(\theta_2)$
$\vdots$	$\vdots$
a_i	$V(\theta_i)$
$\vdots$	$\vdots$
a_{n-1}	$V(\theta_{n-1})$
a_n	$V(\theta_n)$

If, in the above model, the values for each alternative were profits (or gains), the principle of choice might be to choose that alternative which maximizes profit. Conversely, if the values were costs (or losses), one might choose that alternative which minimizes costs.

Suppose an investor is considering a $10,000 purchase of U.S. Government securities. Different U.S. Government agencies offer such securities available on the open market. Assuming the various securities have common maturity dates, the investor judges that each agency is financially secure, and payoffs are certain. A logical criterion for choice among the securities would be the effective annual yield, or rate of return, on the $10,000 purchase. (It is assumed there is no reason for allocating the $10,000 to different purchases.) Suppose the investor considers five U.S. Government securities and, for a maturity date of five years hence, has calculated the effective annual yield on each security to be as shown below:

An Example

a_1	8.0%
a_2	7.3
a_3	8.7
a_4	6.0
a_5	6.5

Since the investor would logically desire to maximize the yield on his investment, alternative a_3 would be chosen. Recall that we assumed equal risk and maturity dates for each security.

DECISIONS UNDER RISK

A decision situation wherein the decision maker elects to consider several possible futures and, in his opinion, the probabilities of their occurrence can be stated is called a decision under risk. In some decision problems the probabilities may be objectively known from historical records or objectively determined from analytical calculations. In the inventory problem at the beginning of this chapter, for example, past records may reveal that a demand for nine units has probability of 0.10, a demand for ten units has probability of 0.15, and so forth, such that the sum of the probabilities for all futures (9, 10, 11, 12, 13, 14, 15 units demanded) equals 1.0. This restriction of $\sum_j p_j = 1.0$ agrees with an earlier statement that, once the set of possible futures is decided upon, they are treated as a mutually exclusive and collectively exhaustive set. Further, it is a necessary restriction if we are to use the logic of probability as a guide to decision making.

On the other hand, the decision maker may not have past records available to arrive at objective probabilities. If the decision maker feels his experience and judgment is sufficient to assign subjective probabilities to the possible futures, the decision is still treated as one under risk. The restriction of $\sum_j p_j = 1.0$ also applies to the subjective probabilities assigned by the decision maker. Common principles of choice for selecting an alternative in a decision under risk will now be presented by means of the following example.

An Example— Inventory Size vs. Strike Duration

Consider a small manufacturer whose business consists of purchasing various chemical ingredients, blending these into insecticide mixes (dry and liquid), selling, and distributing. The chemical raw materials are delivered by a trucking firm whose drivers are members of a union. The expiration of the union contract is approaching and a strike is highly probable. The manager of the manufacturing firm is considering purchasing extra inventory and must decide how much extra inventory to purchase. If this decision is structured in the matrix model, the alternatives consist of the supply of inventory for various possible extra weeks, and the possible futures are the various possible weekly durations of the strike. Let us suppose that the values of the outcomes resulting from the extra inventory-strike duration combinations are in terms of incremental costs above regular inventory costs. Further, the manufacturer feels he is able to assign subjective probabilities to the possible futures.

A matrix representation of the decision problem is given by Table 6.2 and the dollar values have been arbitrarily chosen for illustrative purposes. These dollar values were also chosen unrealistically small for convenience of calculation. Four principles for choosing an alternative from the inventory-strike duration decision model will now be presented.

Dominance Principle of Choice

The dominance principle of choice is described as follows: Given two alternatives, if one would always be preferred no matter which future occurs, this preferred alternative is said to dominate the other and the dominated alternative can be deleted from further consideration. Applying this principle will not necessarily solve the decision problem but may serve to reduce the number of alternatives for further consideration. If the values are in terms of costs, a more formal statement of the dominance principle is:

Extra Inventory (Weeks) \\ Strike Duration (Weeks)	$S_1 = 0$ $p_1 = 0.10$	$S_2 = 1$ $p_2 = 0.10$	$S_3 = 2$ $p_3 = 0.50$	$S_4 = 3$ $p_4 = 0.20$	$S_5 = 4$ $p_5 = 0.10$
$a_1 = 0$	$0	$21	$5	$5	$10
$a_2 = 1$	$5	$7	$7	$5	$8
$a_3 = 2$	$9	$9	$9	$9	$9
$a_4 = 3$	$9	$17	$5	$5	$12
$a_5 = 4$	$13	$13	$5	$9	$15

If there is a pair of alternatives a_i and a_k such that $V(\theta_{ij}) \leq V(\theta_{kj})$ for all j, a_i is said to dominate a_k. Alternative a_k may then be discarded from the decision problem.

In the example of Table 6.2 it can be seen that a_2 (one-week's inventory) dominates a_3 (two-weeks' inventory). For any future S_j, the value for a_2 is less than the corresponding value for a_3.

If x is a variable and $p(x)$ denotes the probability of that variable, **Expectation** then the expected value (mean value) of x is defined as $E(x) = \sum\limits_{\text{all } x} x\, p(x)$. **Principle** Interpreting this in terms of the general matrix model of Figure 6.1, the expected value of alternative a_i is given as:

$$E(a_i) = \sum_j V(\theta_{ij})\, p_j$$

In the example of Table 6.2,

$E(a_1) = 0(.10) + \$21(.10) + \$5(.50) + \$5(.20) + \$10(.10) = \$6.6$

$E(a_2) = \$5(.10) + \$7(.10) + \$7(.50) + \$5(.20) + \$8(.10) = \$6.5$

$E(a_3)$ is not applicable since a_3 was dominated by a_2

$E(a_4) = \$9(.10) + \$17(.10) + \$5(.50) + \$5(.20) + \$12(.10) = \$7.3$

$E(a_5) = \$13(.10) + \$13(.10) + \$5(.50) + \$9(.20) + \$15(.10) = \$8.4$

If the principle of choosing that alternative having minimum expected costs is followed, alternative a_2 would be chosen as best. If the values of the outcomes were in terms of profits (or gains), maximum expected profits would serve as the principle of choice.

Most Probable Future Principle

If, in a decision under risk, one future has a probability of occurrence considerably greater than any other, this future is considered certain and all other futures are suppressed. The decision is then treated as one under assumed certainty. In the extra inventory-strike duration matrix of Table 6.2, S_3 has a probability of 0.50 assigned, which is greater than the probability for any other future. Assuming certainty for S_3, the reduced matrix is:

	S_3
a_1	$5
a_2	7
a_3	9
a_4	5
a_5	5

The minimum cost of $5 appears for a_1, a_4, and a_5. Because the decision is now under assumed certainty and intangibles have been excluded from consideration, one would be indifferent among the choices of a_1, a_4, and a_5 because they have the same value under S_3.

Another example of the most probable future principle is the case of a person commuting to work. Each morning that the person leaves for work there is a nonzero probability that an accident will occur and serious injury result. However, the most probable future is that the commuter will reach work safely. The commuter considers this future certain or else he would not go to work.

As a final remark on this principle of choice, it seems appealing only if one future has a significantly higher probability than any other and the values in the total matrix are reasonably close together. One would not wish to suppress the consideration of a future which, albeit with low probability, would inflict a severe loss on the decision maker. An example of this is the matrix below where the positive values are profits.

	$p_1 = .95$	$p_2 = .05$
a_1	$10	$40
a_2	50	−5,000

Following the most probable future principle, a_2 would be chosen. However, the suppression of S_2 does not alter the fact that S_2 could occur by virtue of $p_2 = .05$, and in that event the decision maker would suffer a loss of $5,000.

Aspiration Level Principle

In most real world decisions complexity prevents the discovery of *the* set of optimal actions; most decision makers, therefore, set their goals in terms of outcomes that are good enough, that is, an aspiration level. Interpreting this statement in terms of our original extra inventory-strike duration matrix, a typical aspiration level statement might be to choose that alternative which maximizes the probability of costs being less than or equal to $8. Refer again to the matrix of Table 6.2. Let us now symbolize the aspiration level by P (costs $\leq$ \$8) to mean the probability that costs are less than or equal to \$8. Then, for

a_1, P(costs $\leq$ \$8) $= P(S_1) + P(S_3) + P(S_4)$
$= .10 + .50 + .20 = .80$
a_2, P(costs $\leq$ \$8) $= .10 + .10 + .50 + .20 + .10 = 1.0$
a_3, P(costs $\leq$ \$8) $= 0$
a_4, P(costs $\leq$ \$8) $= .50 + .20 = .70$
a_5, P(costs $\leq$ \$8) $= .50$

Alternative a_2 would therefore be selected to maximize P(costs $\leq$ \$8). In this instance it is certain that the costs will be less than or equal to \$8.

Many varieties of aspiration statements are possible for various decision situations and the reader should not leave the aspiration level principle with the idea that "maximizing probabilities" is the only such statement. Further, the reader should not interpret any of these or any future principles of choice as the way he should select an alternative. Rather, the principles of choice presented result from observing how people seem to decide on alternatives, and thus the principles are offered only as possible guidelines to the decision maker.

DECISIONS UNDER UNCERTAINTY

A decision situation where several futures are possible and sufficient information is not available to assign probability values to their occurrence is termed a decision under uncertainty. It can be argued that any decision maker, if able to define the futures, should have sufficient knowledge to at least make gross subjective probability statements about these futures. On the other hand, sometimes one may feel unable to assign probabilities to futures even if one is experienced. This may be true in such situations as installing new safety devices on machinery where the futures involve the number of injuries per year or the introduction of new products where the futures involve the number of units demanded. The principles of choice subsequently presented are based on the premise that probabilities cannot be assigned. In order to present these principles, let us again recall our extra inventory-strike duration matrix of Table 6.2.

The Laplace Principle

The philosophy of the Laplace principle is simply that if one cannot assign probabilities to the futures, he may as well treat them as equally probable. Using this principle one must consider the decision as one under risk. Applying the principle to our inventory-strike duration example and noting again that a_2 dominates a_3, we calculate:

$E(a_1) = 1/5 \ (0 + \$21 + \$5 + \$5 + \$10) = \$8.2$

$E(a_2) = 1/5 \ (\$5 + \$7 + \$7 + \$5 + \$8) = \$6.2$

$E(a_4) = 1/5 (\$48) = \$9.6$

$E(a_5) = 1/5 (\$55) = \$11.0$

and a_2 would be chosen because of minimum expected costs.

Minimax or Maximin Principle

The minimax or maximin principle holds considerable appeal for the conservative decision maker and suggests that if one is dealing with costs, one should examine the maximum cost associated with each alternative (over all futures) and then select the alternative that minimizes this maximum cost. In other words look for the worst prospect for each alternative and choose the best of the worst. More formally stated, *select the alternative, i, associated with the* $\underset{i}{\text{MIN}} \underset{j}{\text{MAX}} V(\theta_{ij})$. Applying this principle to our example problem, we have:

	$\underset{j}{\text{MAX }} V(\theta_{ij})$
a_1	\$21
a_2	8
a_4	17
a_5	15

Thus, a_2 is selected as the alternative that will minimize the maximum cost one could incur.

An extreme optimist might at this point raise the issue, why not a minimin principle? That is, examine the minimum cost for each alternative and then select the alternative that minimizes the minimum cost, thus possibly obtaining the minimum cost in the matrix. The reader certainly may exercise his prerogative in following such a principle, but it probably would not be the most realistic choice open to him.

In a decision dealing with profits or gains, the parallel for the conservative minimax principle for costs is the maximin principle of choice. That is, *select the alternative, i, associated with* $\underset{i}{\text{MAX}} \underset{j}{\text{MIN}} V(\theta_{ij})$. Again we note that this is choosing the best (MAX) profit from the set of worst (MIN) profits. In the case of profits, the optimist may wish to follow a maximax principle or that of *selecting the alternative, i, associated with the* $\underset{i}{\text{MAX}} \underset{j}{\text{MAX}} V(\theta_{ij})$. He thus desires a chance for the maximum profit in the decision matrix.

Hurwicz Principle

In the case of costs, the Hurwicz principle considers that a decision maker's view may fall between the extreme pessimism of the minimax principle and the extreme optimism of the minimin principle and offers a method by which various levels of pessimism and optimism may be reflected. The Hurwicz principle defines an index of optimism, α, on a scale from 0 to 1. A value of $\alpha = 0$ indicates zero optimism or extreme pessimism. Conversely, $\alpha = 1$ indicates extreme optimism.

Assuming that a decision maker is able to reflect a degree of optimism by assigning a value to α, and again emphasizing that our decision is in terms of costs, we then multiply the minimum cost for each alternative

by α, and the maximum cost for each alternative by $1 - \alpha$. The sum of these products for each alternative is called the Hurwicz Criterion and the alternative which minimizes this criterion is selected. That is, *select an index of optimism α, such that $0 \leq \alpha \leq 1$. For each alternative compute $\alpha \{\underset{j}{MIN}$ $V(\theta_{ij})\} + (1 - \alpha) \{\underset{j}{MAX} V(\theta_{ij})\}$ and select the alternative which minimizes this quantity.* Note that if $\alpha = 0$ (extreme pessimism), we would examine only the maximum costs for each alternative and select the minimum of these costs—the minimax principle. If $\alpha = 1$ (extreme optimism), we would be executing the minimin principle.

Suppose the decision maker concerned with the inventory-strike duration problem was a middle-of-the-road type of person and assigned $\alpha = 0.5$. Then, the Hurwicz Criterion for

$$a_1 = .5(0) + .5(\$21) = \$10.5$$

$$a_2 = .5(\$5) + .5(\$8) = \$6.5$$

$$a_4 = .5(\$5) + .5(\$17) = \$11.0$$

$$a_5 = .5(\$5) + .5(\$15) = \$10.0$$

Choosing the minimum of these quantities selects a_2.

If the decision problem involved profits, a reinterpretation of the Hurwicz principle is necessary, namely, *select an index of optimism α, such that $0 \leq \alpha \leq 1$. For each a_i compute $\alpha \{\underset{j}{MAX} V(\theta_{ij})\} + (1 - \alpha) \{\underset{j}{MIN} V(\theta_{ij})\}$ and select the alternative which maximizes this quantity.* Note that if $\alpha = 0$, only the minimum profits would be examined for each alternative and the maximum of these would be selected—the pessimistic maximin principle. If $\alpha = 1$, the optimistic maximax principle would be executed.

The Savage principle introduces and defines a quantity termed *regret*. **Savage** A matrix consisting of regret values is first developed; then the maximum **Principle** regret value for each alternative a_i is selected. One chooses that alternative **(Minimax** associated with the minimum regret value from the set of maximum regret **Regret)** values.

If the original decision matrix values are costs, the procedure for determining the regret matrix is as follows:

1. For a given future, S_k, search the matrix column values over all alternatives and determine the smallest cost. Assign this cost a zero regret value.

2. For all other cost values under the given future S_k, subtract the smallest cost value from (1) above. The difference is interpreted as units of regret for a particular alternative a_i, given that future S_k occurs.

3. Repeat steps (1) and (2) for each future S_j, $j \neq k$, until the regret matrix is completed.

Again, once the regret matrix is developed, examine each alternative over all futures and select the maximum regret value. Then, choose that alternative which minimizes the maximum regret. This principle of choice is conservative and therefore very similar to the minimax principle applied to the original decision matrix having dollar values. It is emphasized, however, that the Savage principle deals in units of regret rather than dollar values and thus, if both the minimax principle and the minimax regret principle are applied to a common decision problem, different alternatives may be selected.

Some Examples of the Savage Principle

Problem 1. Recalling the extra inventory-strike duration matrix of Table 6.2 after the principle of dominance has been applied, we have:

	S_1	S_2	S_3	S_4	S_5
a_1	$ 0	$21	$5	$5	$10
a_2	5	7	7	5	8
a_4	9	17	5	5	12
a_5	13	13	5	9	15

The regret matrix is determined as:

	S_1	S_2	S_3	S_4	S_5
a_1	0	14	0	0	2
a_2	5	0	2	0	0
a_4	9	10	0	0	4
a_5	13	6	0	4	7

From the regret matrix, the maximum regret value for each alternative and the minimum of these maximum values are determined as:

	Max Regret Value	Min of Max
a_1	14	
a_2	5	5
a_4	10	
a_5	13	

Thus, we choose alternative a_2 in order to minimize the maximum regret.

Perhaps it is beneficial at this point to review the logic of the regret matrix in a somewhat different fashion. Let us choose future S_2 of the original matrix as an illustration:

	S_2
a_1	$21
a_2	7
a_4	17
a_5	13

In creating the regret column for S_2, the decision maker reasons that if S_2 occurs and a_2 had been chosen from the set of alternatives, there will be zero regret because a_2 has the lowest cost of $7 if S_2 occurs. If, on the other hand, a_1 had been chosen and S_2 occurs, there will be fourteen units of regret because a cost of $21 will be incurred and only $7 cost would be incurred if a_2 had been chosen. Similar reasoning applies for a_4 and a_5 to yield ten and six units of regret, respectively.

Problem 2. Assume the following decision under uncertainty where the matrix values are net annual profits.

	S_1	S_2	S_3	S_4	S_5
a_1	$ 0	$21	$5	$5	$10
a_2	5	7	7	5	8
a_3	9	9	9	9	9
a_4	9	17	5	5	12
a_5	13	13	5	9	15

Using the minimax regret principle of choice, which alternative should be chosen? First, applying the principle of dominance, alternative a_3 dominates a_2 and alternative a_2 is therefore dropped from further consideration. We then create the regret matrix. In the case of profits, the logic for creating the regret matrix is the same as in the situation involving costs. Let us use the matrix column under future S_1 as an illustration. The decision maker reasons, if a_5 is chosen and S_1 occurs, there will be zero regret since $13 is the maximum profit under S_1. Relative to the $13 profit of a_5, a_4 has four units of regret ($13 − $9), a_3 has four units of regret ($13 − $9), and a_1 has thirteen units of regret ($13 − 0) if S_1 occurs. Continuing this reasoning for all other futures results in the following regret matrix:

	S_1	S_2	S_3	S_4	S_5
a_1	13	0	4	4	5
a_3	4	12	0	0	6
a_4	4	4	4	4	3
a_5	0	8	4	0	0

Then, choosing to minimize the maximum regret results in:

	Maximum Regret
a_1	13
a_3	12
a_4	4
a_5	8

and the choice of alternative a_4 would achieve the minimum of the maximum regret.

The principles of choice for decisions under uncertainty are mainly attempts to formalize past observations on how persons make decisions. However, the principles were originally developed from more rigorous mathematical premises by decision theorists using utility concepts rather

Summary— Decisions Under Uncertainty

than dollar values. Since many observations of decision makers reveal that they do not always decide to maximize dollar payoffs or expected dollar payoffs (in the case of decisions under risk), a theory of utility has been developed which postulates that a rational decision maker will always decide to maximize utility or expected utility. Decision theory thus holds that a "maximizing utility" principle of choice is a more consistent and defendable principle than a "maximizing (or minimizing) dollars" principle of choice. Utility concepts are discussed in more detail in the next section.

Each of the principles of choice for decisions under uncertainty has received criticism in the literature and whether or not they are useful must remain the judgment of the individual decision maker. It would seem, however, that at the very least it is helpful to the decision maker to create the decision matrix. In doing so alternatives will be conscientiously determined, possible futures seriously considered, and objective values sought for the alternative-future combinations. The very act of such analysis is likely to result in benefits of consistency and thoroughness for the decision maker regardless of the principle of choice used to select an alternative.

Decisions under uncertainty principles of choice do not necessarily select a common alternative when applied to a given decision problem. The different principles of choice reflect different philosophies on the parts of the decision makers. Neither is there any substantiated rationale for choosing an alternative because it was selected by the majority of the several principles of choice.

THE CONCEPT OF UTILITY

The economist normally defines utility as the power to satisfy human wants and has introduced the measurement *utiles* to describe such satisfaction. As a simplified illustration, receiving the grade of A on a final examination might be assigned 95 utiles of satisfaction whereas receiving a C might be assigned 50 utiles. An interesting question is how to determine a person's utility curve (or utility function) for dollars, test scores, time, weight, or whatever objective is relevant; the answer is reasonably complex and somewhat controversial. Further, the problem of scale for the utility measurement is nontrivial, especially if multiple measures of dollars, time, weight, and so forth; are to be converted to a single utility measure. For example, one might wonder why a final examination grade of A should be assigned 95 utiles rather than 1500 utiles or 0.2 utiles. Neither the question of how to determine one's utility function nor what the measurement scale should be will be answered fully in this chapter. However, one method of determining a utility function for a single measure, namely dollars, and defining this on a utility scale from 0 to 1.0 is presented below.

An Example Let us suppose that a manager is presented with the following matrix model of a decision under risk:

	$p_1 = 0.90$	$p_2 = 0.10$
a_1	$15,000	−$20,000
a_2	10,000	10,000

Assume a_1 and a_2 are two mutually exclusive contracts and the manager must choose one or the other. The cell values are estimated net profits that will result from the various alternative-future combinations. If the manager used a maximize expected profit principle of choice, he would calculate:

$$E(a_1) = (0.90)(\$15,000) + (0.10)(-\$20,000) = \$11,500$$

$$E(a_2) = (0.90)(\$10,000) + (0.10)(\$10,000) = \$10,000$$

and choose alternative a_1.

However, let us suppose that the manager chooses a_2 with the explanation that even though the probability of S_2 is only 0.10, he cannot afford the $20,000 loss that will result if S_2 does in fact occur. Choosing a_2 assures a $10,000 profit, a certain amount, whether S_1 or S_2 occurs. The manager exhibits a reasonable aversion to risk in that he chooses $10,000 certain in preference to $11,500 expected. The manager is no doubt aware that the expected profit of $11,500 is but a guide to choice and he would actually receive either the $15,000 profit or the $20,000 loss if a_1 were chosen.

One important point is now emphasized, namely, the maximum expected dollar value principle does not explain the manager's choice of alternative a_2. The utility function in Figure 6.2 is a possible explanation of his preference. The curve through the points c, a_2, b, and d is the manager's utility function for dollars certain over the range of $-\$20,000$ to $+\$20,000$. The utility scale from 0 to 1.0 has been established with the utility of 0 assigned when $-\$20,000$ is certain and of 1.0 when $+\$20,000$ is certain; utility values for other specific dollar values which are certain are determined from the curve ca_2bd. For example, $10,000 certain has a utility value of 0.92. In a more convenient fashion, we can denote:

Utility of $-\$20,000 = U(-\$20,000) = 0$

Utility of $+\$10,000 = U(+\$10,000) = .92$

Utility of $+\$15,000 = U(+\$15,000) = .96$

Utility of $+\$20,000 = U(+\$20,000) = 1.00$

The utility of expected dollar values over the range of $-\$20,000$ to $+\$20,000$ is given by the straight line through the points c, a_1, d. Thus, the utility of the expected dollar value of $11,500 is 0.864.

Let us now revise the original decision matrix by inserting utility values rather than dollar values. That is,

	$p_1 = 0.90$ S_1	$p_2 = 0.10$ S_2
a_1	.96	0
a_2	.92	.92

Then, the expected utility of the contracts are:

FIGURE 6.2   A Risk-Averse Utility Function

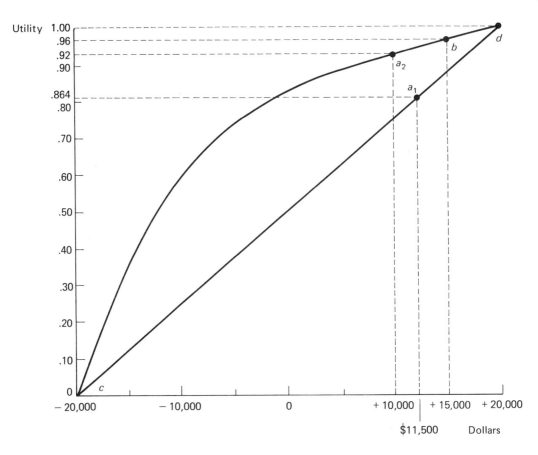

$$U(a_1) = (.90)\ U(\$15,000) + (.10)\ U(-\$20,000)$$
$$= (.90)(.96) + (.10)(0) = .864$$
$$U(a_2) = (.90)\ U(\$10,000) + (.10)\ U(\$10,000)$$
$$= (.90)(.92) + (.10)(.92) = .92$$

If the manager chooses to maximize his expected utility, he would choose alternative a_2. Because a_2 was his preference, the utility model of Figure 6.2 explains this preference and suggests maximizing expected utility as his principle of choice.

Obtaining the Utility Function— A Methodology

One procedure that has been suggested in order to determine a manager's utility function is to pose to him a series of questions concerning two alternatives.

One of the alternatives involves a so-called *basic contract*, which is a gamble. For example, let alternative a_1 be the basic contract consisting of receiving either a $20,000 profit with probability p or a $20,000 loss with probability $1 - p$. Alternative a_2 is to receive a varying amount of money for certain. For a given value of money certain, the task is to find the value of p for which the manager is indifferent between alternative a_1, the basic contract, and alternative a_2, an amount of money for certain. The value of p so determined is interpreted as the utility value for the amount of money certain used in a_2. Hence, one point on the utility function is determined. The questions are repeated for another amount of money certain until the manager assigns a value of p for indifference between alternative a_2 and alternative a_1. A second point on the utility function has thus been determined. This process is repeated for other values of money certain in alternative a_2 until it is judged that a sufficient number of points have been determined to locate the utility curve.

As an illustration, suppose the manager is asked his preference between:

a_1: a \$20,000 profit with $p = 1.0$ and a \$20,000 loss with $(1 - p) = 0$, or
a_2: \$10,000 certain.

He no doubt would choose a_1 because the \$20,000 profit is also certain $(p = 1.0)$ and therefore greater than \$10,000 certain. The manager is then asked to choose between:

a_1: a \$20,000 profit with $p = 0.50$ and a \$20,000 loss with $(1 - p) = 0.50$, or
a_2: \$10,000 certain.

If he chooses a_2 in this case, we then note that he has switched his preference from a_1 to a_2 and conclude that for a value of p between 0.50 and 1.0, he would be indifferent between a_1 and a_2. By continuing to pose the basic choice of a_2 and a_1 to him for given values of p between 0.50 and 1.0, the value of p for indifference is converged upon. Let it be assumed that the value of p for indifference between the above defined alternatives a_1 and a_2 is 0.92. This value of $p = 0.92$ and \$10,000 certain locates one point on the utility curve as shown in Figure 6.2.

This whole series of questions is repeated for another amount of money certain, say \$15,000. That is, we ask the manager to choose between:

a_1: a \$20,000 profit with $p = 1.0$ and a \$20,000 loss with $(1 - p) = 0$, or
a_2: \$15,000 certain.

Given a preference of a_1, we then change the value of p to say 0.50 and ask the question again, and so forth, until a value of p for indifference is found. Let us assume this value of p is 0.96 and it locates another point on the utility curve as shown in Figure 6.2.

Another series of questions might then follow for each of \$5000, \$0, −\$5000, −\$10,000 certain. The respective values of p for indifference between a_1 and a_2 would locate four more points on the utility curve given in Figure 6.2.

The manager whose utility function for dollars has the general concave shape of Figure 6.2 is termed risk-averse. In essence he has a conservative attitude and his utility for dollars increases at a decreasing rate. His utility for $X certain is always greater than the same $X expected (values along the line ca_1d in Figure 6.2).

Other utility functions with different shapes are of course possible. A manager who is attracted to risk may exhibit a utility curve such as Figure 6.3. In this case the manager welcomes opportunities to take risks, desires large profits, and is somewhat unconcerned about large losses. In Figure 6.3 it is noted that his utility for $X certain is less than his utility for $X expected.

Another basic utility curve would be a straight-line or linear utility function. In this case maximizing expected dollar returns would reach the same decision as maximizing expected utility.

FIGURE 6.3   A Risk-Seeking Utility Function

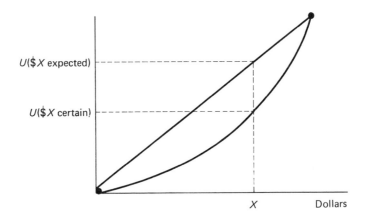

Summary Comments on Utility   Since persons frequently do in fact choose alternatives that do not maximize expected dollar returns in decisions under risk situations, it is logical to assume the existence of nonlinear utility functions for these decision makers. If these utility functions were known with high reliability, they would serve to offer an explanation for alternative choices which do not maximize expected dollar returns. The theory of utility functions has, in fact, a formal axiomatic mathematical base. If a decision maker behaves in a so-called rational and consistent manner in stating his preferences between alternatives (that is, in accordance with the axioms), it can be shown that a utility function does exist for the decision maker. Further, problems of scaling are not severe in the single variable case (for example, utility values for a single variable such as dollars), because a utility scale may be linearly transformed to another utility scale and will not change the decision. That is, assume the two measures $U(a_1)$ and $U(a_2)$, where $U(a_1) > U(a_2)$. Then, for constants a and b, $U'(a_1) = a + b\ U(a_1)$ and $U'(a_2) = a + b\ U(a_2)$ would yield $U'(a_1) > U'(a_2)$ and alternative a_1 would remain the preferred choice.

Whether it is possible to obtain a person's utility function in a realistic sense is, however, highly speculative. Further, it is believed that one's utility function varies in different situations and with time, and in most real world situations the utility for an alternative is dependent on more than any single measure such as dollars. If this is true and if a practical utility measure is a function of, say, dollars, manufacturer's reputation, durability, repairability, and so forth, then a utility surface in n dimensions is applicable. Obtaining a decision maker's n-dimensional utility function with precision seems a practical impossibility, and thus, whether the concepts of utility are useful or not remains a debatable issue. Utility notions are certainly interesting and stimulating in an academic sense and still receive attention in the literature but practical usage, as revealed by published examples, is limited at the present time.

QUESTIONS AND PROBLEMS

1. In the purchase of an automobile for personal use, what are some aspiration level statements one might consider?

2. When is the most probable future principle of choice a reasonable principle to follow for a decision under risk?

3. What distinguishes a decision under risk from a decision under certainty?

4. Sketch a utility curve for a person who is attracted to risk for small dollar payoffs but risk-averse for large dollar payoffs.

5. Which alternative would you select in the decision below if the numbers in the matrix are profits?

	$p_1 = .25$	$p_2 = .25$	$p_3 = .25$	$p_4 = .25$
	S_1	S_2	S_3	S_4
a_1	4	24	0	38
a_2	10	34	22	32
a_3	20	36	24	42
a_4	18	16	18	12
a_5	6	26	8	40

6. An analysis yields a decision under risk given in the matrix below, where the matrix values are annual profits.

p_j	0.1	0.2	0.3	0.2	0.1	0.1
Alternatives \ Futures	S_1	S_2	S_3	S_4	S_5	S_6
a_1	15	8	−5	0	9	12
a_2	10	0	4	8	20	7
a_3	6	6	10	12	−2	8
a_4	3	15	18	5	14	−8
a_5	−10	25	12	3	7	15

a) Which alternative should be chosen in order to maximize the probability of receiving an annual profit of at least 8?

b) If the matrix values are now considered annual costs (negative values will then be annual profits), which alternative should be chosen in order to maximize the probability that annual costs are between six and twelve units, that is, $6.0 \leq$ annual costs ≤ 12.0.

c) Would the most probable future principle of choice be a reasonable one to follow for this decision model?

7. a) If α (an index of optimism) $= 0.4$, apply the various principles of choice to the following matrix model of a decision under uncertainty. The numbers in the matrix are costs.

8	16	8	1
4	5	12	14
15	19	14	13
2	17	8	17
7	15	7	20

b) If the numbers in the above matrix are profits, determine the alternative selected by the various principles of choice.

8. Assume the following decision matrix where the matrix cell values are annual costs:

Alternatives \ Futures	p_1 S_1	p_2 S_2	p_3 S_3
a_1	$ 20	$100	$1200
a_2	180	180	180
a_3	500	120	100

a) If the values of p_j are unknown, which alternative would be chosen by the Laplace, minimax, and Savage principles of choice?

b) If the values of p_j are unknown and α is an index of optimism, for what value of α would one be indifferent between alternatives a_2 and a_3?

c) If $p_1 = 0.20$, $p_2 = 0.70$, $p_3 = 0.10$ and the cell values are considered annual profits, what alternative would be selected by the expectation principle of choice?

9. A manufacturer of seasonal goods must produce in advance of sales. His profit from the production of x units when the demand is D is given by:

$$\text{Profit } (x) \begin{cases} = \$2.00x; & \text{for } 0 \leq x \leq D \\ = \$2.00D - \$1.00(x - D); & \text{for } x > D \end{cases}$$

Suppose that only five values of D are possible: 1,000, 2,000, 3,000, 4,000, 5,000 units, and each of these values have probability of 0.20. The manufacturer wishes to choose among five production quantities also equal to 1,000,

2,000, 3,000, 4,000, and 5,000 units. What would be his choice if:
  a) he chose to produce for the expected demand?
  b) he chose to maximize expected profit?
  c) he chose to minimize the probability of a loss.
  d) he chose to maximize the probability of a profit of $3,000 or more?

10. Let X represent an amount of money in dollars. Suppose a manager's utility for money is given by:

$$U(X) = 1 - e^{-.0003X}, \quad \text{for } 0 \le X \le \$10,000$$

If the manager is presented the following two contracts, predict his choice.

	$p_1 = 0.6$	$p_2 = 0.4$
Contract A	$6,667	$0
Contract B	4,000	4,000

11. Suppose that the acceptance of Contract ABC can result in a $15,000 gain with subjective probability of 0.7 or a $10,000 loss with subjective probability of 0.3. For purposes of illustration, assume the contract can be accepted once or three times. The outcome from each acceptance is independent of the outcome from any other acceptance.
  a) If the contract is accepted three times, what are the possible dollar outcomes and their probabilities of occurrence?
  b) If the following utility table applies, determine the expected utility of accepting the contract once versus the expected utility of accepting the contract three times. (Dollar values are times 10^3).

Utility Table

Dollars	Utility Values
45	1.00
30	.96
20	.91
15	.87
10	.84
5	.80
0	.75
-5	.66
-10	.55
-15	.46
-20	.37
-30	.00

12. Suppose it is reasoned that a manager prefers $100,000 to $10,000 and utility values of $U(\$100,000) = 5.6$ and $U(\$10,000) = 1.0$ are arbitrarily assigned. An attempt is now made to complete and extend the manager's utility function. The approach taken is to pose questions to the manager of the following nature: Choose between (1) $10,000 for certain and (2) a 50-50 chance at either $100,000 or some unknown amount of Y. The amount of Y is varied until the manager is indifferent between (1) and (2) at $Y = \$3,000$.

a) Determine the utility of −$3,000 on the above scale.

b) For the range of dollar values above, namely −$3,000 to $100,000, transform the utility scale to one defined between 0 and 1.0 and determine the utility of $10,000 on the new scale.

BIBLIOGRAPHY

CHERNOFF, H., AND MOSES, L. E. *Elementary Decision Theory*. New York: John Wiley & Sons, Inc., 1959.

HOWELL, J. E., AND TEICHROEW, D. *Mathematical Analysis for Business Decisions*. Homewood, Ill.: Richard D. Irwin, Inc., 1963.

MILLER, D. W., AND STARR, M. K. *Executive Decisions and Operations Research*. Englewood Cliffs, N.J.: Prentice-Hall, Inc., 1960.

MORRIS, W. T. *The Analysis of Management Decisions*. Homewood, Ill.: Richard D. Irwin, Inc., 1964.

SCHLAIFER, R. *Analysis of Decisions Under Uncertainty*. New York: McGraw-Hill Book Company, Inc., 1969.

CHAPTER SEVEN

Decisions under conflict

   In the previous chapter, decisions were viewed in a setting that contained at least a random, if not a benign, future. Certainly, the future which did occur was assumed to be independent of the alternative selected or likely to be selected. However, there are decision situations where one decision maker confronts another and there is a conflict of interest. In this setting the future is influenced by an opponent and one person's gain may be the second person's loss. Some examples of real world situations which result in a conflict of interest between opponents are: (1) manufacturers competing for a share of a market which is essentially fixed, (2) individuals or groups competing for a share of a fixed budget, (3) individuals or political parties competing for elected offices, (4) military battles at a level other than a national or global level, and (5) most recreational games. There are other situations involving conflict of interest which are not strictly competitive in the sense that the loss is equal in value to the gain. Labor-management negotiations, sales campaigns which may increase the size of the market, and individuals competing within an organization are a few examples where one person's gain is not strictly the other's loss.

Decision making under conflict is commonly referred to as *game theory*. While there are not many decision situations that actually lend themselves to the structure required for this type of analysis, some of the insights gained through an understanding of game theory are of more general value in decision situations where one is confronted by an opponent. In addition, while the most common treatment of decisions under conflict is through game theory, there are other competitive decision situations, such as in bidding and purchasing, where the more formal game theoretic construct is not applicable. Nevertheless, most students find game theory interesting in its approach to resolving conflict situations.

GAME THEORY

Decisions under conflict can certainly involve more than two opponents but two-person games play a central role in the whole theory of games. Further, such games have received the most attention in the literature, which is due no doubt to the fact that two-person games are the most readily solved. Only the two-person game will be discussed in this chapter. Indeed, only the special case of strictly competitive games where each person has a finite number of strategies available will be presented.

Terminology

Before considering particular types of strictly competitive two-person games and the logic of solving such games, a general model and terminology should first be established. A general model for the two-person game is given in Table 7.1 where the players have been arbitrarily coded Red and Blue for convenience of reference.

The strictly competitive two-person game is called a *two-person, zero-sum game* because there are two *players* and the gain of one player is exactly the loss of the other player. The sum of these *payoffs* is zero. The individual alternatives available to each player are termed *pure strategies*. Player Red's pure strategies are a_i and player Blue's pure strategies are b_j. Either player's use of a randomized choice of strategies is referred to as a *mixed strategy*. As will be defined subsequently, *optimal strategies* for each player can be determined; the expected outcome when both players use their optimal strategies is called the *value of the game*. A zero value of the game is termed a *fair game*. One *play* of the game consists of a strategy selection

Red's Strategies \ Blue's Strategies	b_1	b_2	----	b_j	---------	b_m
a_1	$V(\theta_{11})$	$V(\theta_{12})$	----	$V(\theta_{1j})$	---------	$V(\theta_{1m})$
a_2	$V(\theta_{21})$	$V(\theta_{22})$	----	$V(\theta_{2j})$	---------	$V(\theta_{2m})$
⋮	⋮	⋮		⋮		⋮
a_i	$V(\theta_{i1})$	$V(\theta_{i2})$	----	$V(\theta_{ij})$	---------	$V(\theta_{im})$
⋮	⋮	⋮		⋮		⋮
a_n	$V(\theta_{n1})$	$V(\theta_{n2})$	----	$V(\theta_{nj})$	---------	$V(\theta_{nm})$

by each player. We shall consider that the strategy selections are made simultaneously by each player. Finding the optimal strategies and the value of the game is called *solving* the game and play is therefore stopped.

For each a_i–b_j combination of strategies there is an outcome with an associated value, $V(\theta_{ij})$. The theory of games has been developed assuming these are utility values and each player has the same utility function. A further simplifying assumption is usually made that each player has a linear utility function for money. *The fundamental basis for solving the game by determining optimal strategies is the minimax theorem which, in part, states that each player seeks to maximize his security level.* Adopting the convention that the payoff values in the decision matrix are gains to Red, then Red seeks to maximize his minimum gain (adopts a maximin strategy) and Blue, in turn, seeks to minimize his maximum loss (adopts a minimax strategy). By so playing, each player will maximize his security level and, in this sense, optimal strategies are found which determine the value of the game and conclude play.

Criterion For Choice of Strategies

In addition to the assumptions above of (1) linear utility functions for each player, (2) player Red using a maximin strategy, and (3) player Blue using a minimax strategy, there are other assumptions that should be stated, namely, each player knows the alternatives available to both him and his opponent and that the outcome depends on these choices (that is, he knows Table 7.1), and if the outcome of the game involves a chance mechanism, then each player is aware of the different possibilities and their respective probabilities.

Other Assumptions

The relevance of these assumptions and the terminology will become more meaningful as we now discuss specific games and their solutions.

TWO-PERSON, ZERO-SUM GAMES

Since all the discussion of games in this chapter is restricted to two-person, zero-sum games, the designations 2×2, $2 \times M$, $M \times 2$, 3×3, and so forth, refer to the number of pure strategies available to the players. The general methodology recommended for solving a game consists of the following steps, each of which will be explained in greater detail later in the chapter.

Step 1. If possible, reduce the size of the game by searching for instances of dominance. For example, if Red strategy a_k is dominated (that is, has a lower payoff for each Blue strategy b_j) by some other Red strategy a_t, then strategy a_k should be deleted from further consideration by Red. Blue strategies should also be examined for instances of dominance. It may turn out in some games that Blue has a dominated strategy only after Red has deleted a dominated strategy or vice versa.

Step 2. After applying the principle of dominance for each player, the remaining game should be searched for an entry in the payoff matrix which is both the maximum value in its column (a Blue strategy b_j) and the minimum value in its row (a Red strategy a_i). Such an entry is called a *saddle point* (or equilibrium pair). If a saddle point is located, the game is solved in the sense that a pure strategy has been found for each player which maximizes his security level. The value of the game is the value of the saddle point entry.

Step 3. If a saddle point for the game does not exist, then additional analysis, depending on the size of the game, is required. The bulk of the remaining discussion on games in this chapter is concerned with this step.

Let us now consider the abstract game given below, where the cell values are gains to player Red.

		Blue's Pure Strategies			
		b_1	b_2	b_3	b_4
	a_1	15	3	0	2
Red's	a_2	0	3	8	16
Pure	a_3	8	4	7	5
Strategies	a_4	12	4	2	25
	a_5	7	3	0	9

Following Step 1 of the above solution methodology, the game is investigated for instances of dominance. First, taking Red's point of view, strategy a_5 is dominated by strategy a_4 (for b_1: 12 is equal to or greater than 7; for b_2: 4 is equal to or greater than 3; for b_3: $2 \geq 0$; and for b_4: $25 \geq 9$). Strategy a_5 can be deleted from further consideration. On the other hand, from Blue's perspective, there are no strategies which are dominated by another. The reduced payoff matrix is then:

		Blue			
		b_1	b_2	b_3	b_4
	a_1	15	3	0	2
Red	a_2	0	3	8	16
	a_3	8	4	7	5
	a_4	12	4	2	25

From Red's point of view, if he knew what Blue's choice of strategy would be, his counterchoice could be determined quite readily, and thus Red reasons:

If Blue uses	b_1	b_2	b_3	b_4	
Red's best counterchoice is	a_1	a_3 or a_4	a_2	a_4	with
a payoff to Red of	15	4	8	25	and
a payoff to Blue of	-15	-4	-8	-25	

Red further considers what Blue's likely response would be for various Red strategies as follows:

If Red uses	a_1	a_2	a_3	a_4	
Blue's best counterchoice is	b_3	b_1	b_2	b_3	with
a payoff to Red of	0	0	4	2	and
a payoff to Blue of	0	0	-4	-2	

Red observes that if he uses a_3 he is assured a payoff of 4 which is greater than the assured payoffs of 0, 0, and 2 from using the a_1, a_2, and a_4 strategies respectively. Thus, strategy a_3 has the property that it maximizes Red's security level, that is, maximizes the minimum payoff.

Assuming that Blue uses a similar line of reasoning, Blue notes from the first argument for Red that strategies b_1, b_2, b_3, and b_4 have security levels of -15, -4, -8, and -25 respectively. If Blue therefore uses strategy b_2, he can be assured of holding Red to a payoff of 4, the smallest assured loss to Blue for his available b_j strategies. In this sense, strategy b_2 maximizes Blue's security level and minimizes his maximum loss to Red.

From this first-order analysis, it seems reasonable to assert that Red would choose a_3 and Blue would choose b_2 as permanent strategies. However, game theory suggests that a second-order analysis be made. Namely, if the fact that when Blue uses his best strategy, b_2 in this case, Red would change from his first-order best strategy, a_3 in this case, then game play is unstable under second-order analysis (as we will see in a later example). On the other hand, if Red does not change from his first-order best strategy, then game play is stable. In this example, Red would not change from a_3 given that Blue uses b_2. Game theory suggests a_3 and b_2 are in *equilibrium* in the sense that neither player could raise his security level unless the other player changes his strategy choice. The strategies a_3 and b_2 are thus termed an equilibrium pair or saddle point. In general, if the minimum of the column maxima equals the maximum of the row minima, then the game has a saddle point. The "optimal" strategy for each player is then the pure strategy associated with the row or column of the saddle point, and the value of the game is the value at the saddle point. If a game has multiple saddle points, they will have the same value.

In all the examples below, it is assumed that Red's strategies are given on the right-hand side of the payoff matrix. Optimal strategies for each player will be coded by binary variables, X_i for Red and X_j for Blue, where the variable will have the value of either 1 or 0. That is, if the optimal strategy for Red is a_1 out of the set of strategies a_1, a_2, a_3, then

**Examples—
Games
With Saddle
Points**

we will note this as (1,0,0), meaning that pure strategy a_1 should be used all the time and strategies a_2 and a_3 none of the time.

Game 1:

	b_1	b_2
a_1	4	9
a_2	2	7

Solution: A saddle point exists at (a_1, b_1). The value 4 is maximum in column b_1 and minimum in row a_1. Thus, Red's optimal strategy is (1,0) and Blue's is (1,0). The value of the game is 4. Red receives 4 and Blue loses 4.

Game 2:

	b_1	b_2	b_3	b_4
a_1	-10	6	2	40
a_2	10	10	8	12
a_3	-8	-4	0	-10

Solution: After some searching, a saddle point can be found to exist at (a_2, b_3). Thus, Red's optimal strategy is (0,1,0) and Blue's is (0,0,1,0). The value of the game is 8. Since the saddle point in this 3 × 4 game may not have been immediately obvious, it may be instructive to first consider dominance. That is, Red strategy a_2 dominates strategy a_3, and a_3 is therefore deleted. Blue strategy b_3 dominates both strategies b_2 and b_4 and these are deleted. This leaves the game as:

	b_1	b_3
a_1	-10	2
a_2	10	8

It can be seen readily that a_2 dominates a_1 and that b_3 dominates b_1; the saddle point of (a_2, b_3) equal to 8 is thereby located.

Game 3:

	b_1	b_2	b_3
a_1	4	1	0
a_2	3	2	3
a_3	0	1	4
a_4	2	1	0

Solution: A saddle point exists at (a_2, b_2). Red's optimal strategy is therefore (0,1,0,0) and Blue's optimal strategy is (0,1,0). The value of the game is 2.

Game 4: We're going camping!

The idea of a "gain" and a "loss" as well as a possible physical representation of the gaming situation can be seen in this example. A husband and wife, Bob and Connie, plan to go camping in the local state park. However, the actual camp site is a matter of some disagreement, because Bob would prefer to camp at a high altitude and Connie would prefer as low an elevation as possible. The campers realize that the park is traversed in the north-south direction by four routes, unimaginatively labeled 101, 102, 103, and 104. The same park has four routes crossing it in an east-west direction, labeled 201, 202, 203, and 204. Bob and Connie have agreed that Bob will select a route that crosses the park in an east-west direction, and Connie will select the north-south route. They will pitch their tent in the vicinity of the junction of two routes so selected. A map of the region is seen in Figure 7.1. The altitudes corresponding to the junctions are listed as follows (in thousands of feet):

		Connie			
		101	*102*	*103*	*104*
	201	6	1	5	1
Bob	*202*	1	2	3	4
	203	4	3	5	5
	204	4	2	1	6

An examination of the game matrix reveals that a saddle point exists at the intersection of routes 102 and 203, and if Connie and Bob choose these respective alternatives, the couple will go camping at an altitude of 3,000 feet. Note that if Bob does select route 203 and Connie selects any route other than 102, Bob will benefit in that they will camp at an altitude greater than that found at the saddle point. From Connie's point of view, if she selects 102 and Bob selects any route other than 203, they will camp

The Camping Alternatives **FIGURE 7.1**

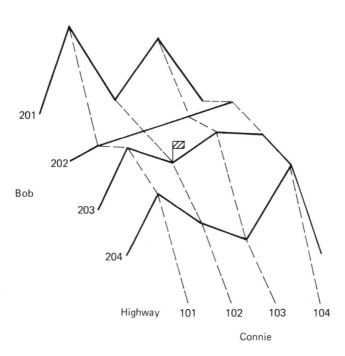

at a site lower in altitude than that found at the saddle point. Interestingly enough, if one examines the region immediately surrounding the intersection of routes 102 and 203 in Figure 7.1, it is possible to visualize the "saddle" configuration of the region.

**2 × 2
Games
Without
Saddle
Points**

The 2 × 2 designation refers to the number of pure strategies available to each player. If a game does not have a saddle point, then the optimal strategy for at least one player will be a *mixed strategy*. A mixed strategy for a player means that he plays the pure strategies a proportionate amount (according to a chance mechanism, with some probability) in order to maximize his security level.

An example of a 2 × 2 game which does not have a saddle point is the following:

	b_1	b_2
a_1	4	2
a_2	3	5

A little reflection on this game reveals that Red will attain his maximum security level of 3 by using a_2 and Blue achieves his maximum security level of 4 by using b_1. However, if Blue uses b_1, then Red no doubt would counter with a_1. This would cause Blue to switch to b_2, which causes Red to switch to a_2, which causes Blue to switch to b_1 and so on in a circular analysis. The game does not have the stability under second-order analysis that a game with a saddle point would have. This situation suggests that a mixed strategy for each player should result. The question then for, say, the Red player is what mixed strategy is appropriate.

Let us denote Red's mixed strategy of choosing a_1 and a_2 with probability p and $(1 - p)$, respectively, as $(p)a_1 ; (1 - p)a_2$. If Blue uses pure strategy b_1, then Red's expected payoff would be:

$$4p + 3(1 - p) = p + 3$$

If Blue uses pure strategy b_2, then Red's expected payoff would be:

$$2p + 5(1 - p) = 5 - 3p$$

The security level of the mixed strategy for Red is the minimum of the two quantities given by these equations. We assume that Red desires to maximize his security level, and it turns out that his security level will be maximized when these two quantities are equal. That is, when $p + 3 = 5 - 3p$. Solving this equation for p yields $p = 1/2$ and $1 - p = 1/2$.

It will be noted from Figure 7.2 that for $p < p^*$ the minimum security level is according to $p + 3$, and for $p > p^*$ the minimum security level is according to $5 - 3p$. The maximum value of these two minimum quantities is when $p = p^*$ or the intersection of the two lines, $p + 3$ and $5 - 3p$. The solution of $p^* + 3 = 5 - 3p^*$ is again $p^* = 1/2$. It is therefore reasoned

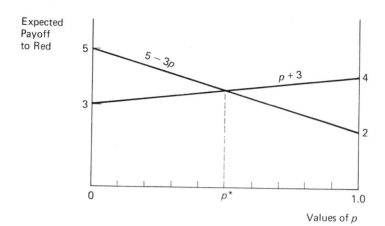

that Red would use the mixed strategy $(1/2a_1, 1/2a_2)$ in order to maximize his security level.

Using the strategy $(1/2a_1, 1/2a_2)$ results in an expected payoff to Red of $4(1/2) + 3(1/2) = 2(1/2) + 5(1/2) = 3.5$, *regardless of the strategy Blue plays* (this will be more readily seen in a later discussion). Whereas our first-order analysis for Red yielded a maximum security level of 3.0 by playing strategy a_2, this level is raised to an expected value of 3.5 by using the mixed strategy $(1/2a_1, 1/2a_2)$.

Player Blue realizes that by playing pure strategy b_1 consistently, Red will win 4 by playing a_1 consistently. Also, if b_2 is played consistently, Red will win 5 by playing a_2 consistently. Blue concludes that he too should play a mixed strategy. Using the same logic as for Red previously, let us denote a mixed strategy for Blue by $(q)b_1, (1 - q)b_2$. If Red uses pure strategy a_1, then Blue's expected payoff would be:

$$-4q + (-2)(1 - q) = -2q - 2$$

If Red uses pure strategy a_2, then Blue's expected payoff would be:

$$-3q + (-5)(1 - q) = 2q - 5$$

By an argument similar to Figure 7.2, the maximum of these two minimum quantities occurs when $-2q - 2 = 2q - 5$. Solving for q yields $q = 3/4$ and $1 - q = 1/4$. Blue's optimal strategy is $(3/4b_1, 1/4b_2)$ and the expected loss to Red is:

$$-4(3/4) - 2(1/4) = -3(3/4) - 5(1/4) = -3.5$$

regardless of the strategy Red plays.

The value of the game was calculated as 3.5. However, in more complete fashion let us state that if Red uses the optimal mixed strategy of $(1/2a_1, 1/2a_2)$ and Blue uses the optimal mixed strategy of $(3/4b_1, 1/4b_2)$, then the value of the game is given by:

$$V = \text{expected payoff to Red}$$

$$= \text{expected payoff given } a_1 + \text{expected payoff given } a_2$$

$$= p[q(4) + (1 - q)(2)] + (1 - p)[q(3) + (1 - q)(5)]$$

$$= 1/2[3/4(4) + 1/4(2)] + 1/2[3/4(3) + 1/4(5)]$$

$$= 1/2(14/4) + 1/2(14/4) = 3.5$$

It is interesting to note that if Red uses the optimal mixed strategy of $(1/2a_1, 1/2a_2)$, then for *any* Blue strategy $(q)b_1, (1 - q) b_2$, Red will expect to gain 3.5. This is shown from the complete value of the game calculation as follows:

$$1/2[4q + 2(1 - q)] + 1/2[3q + 5(1 - q)] = 2q + 1 - q + 3/2q$$

$$+ 5/2 - 5/2q = 3.5$$

Similarly, if Blue uses the optimal mixed strategy of $(3/4b_1, 1/4b_2)$, then for *any* Red strategy of $(p)a_1, (1 - p)a_2$, Blue will expect to lose -3.5. This is also shown by the complete value of the game calculation below, but using negative values for Blue's payoffs:

$$3/4[-4p - 3(1 - p)] + 1/4[-2p - 5(1 - p)] = -3p - 9/4 + 9/4p$$

$$- 1/2p - 5/4 + 5/4p = -3.5$$

From the above analysis of the 2 × 2, two-person, zero-sum game without a saddle point, it can be seen that neither player can unilaterally have any effect on the value of the game if his opponent plays his minimax (implying maximin as well) strategy. The only way either player may expect to gain more than the value of the game is for both players to deviate from these strategies.

Arithmetic Solution Method— 2 × 2 Games Without Saddle Points

For expediency in determining the optimal mixed strategies in 2 × 2 games, an arithmetic solution procedure is given below without proof. However, the algebraic technique discussed previously can be used to verify the results of the arithmetic solution procedure. The procedural steps of the arithmetic technique are presented in terms of the example game used in the previous section, namely:

		Blue	
		b_1	b_2
Red	a_1	4	2
	a_2	3	5

Step 1. For Red strategy a_1, determine the absolute value of the difference in payoff between b_1 and b_2 ($|4 - 2| = 2$ in this example). Call this result x_1.

Step 2. For Red strategy a_2, make a similar calculation as in Step 1 ($|3 - 5| = 2$ in this example). Call this result x_2.

Step 3. Calculate the optimal mixed strategy for Red from:

a. using a_1 with probability $\dfrac{x_2}{x_1 + x_2}$ $\left(\dfrac{2}{2 + 2} = 1/2 \text{ in this example}\right)$ and

b. using a_2 with probability $\dfrac{x_1}{x_1 + x_2}$ $\left(\dfrac{2}{2 + 2} = 1/2 \text{ in this example}\right)$

Step 4. For Blue strategy b_1, determine the absolute value of the difference in payoff between a_1 and a_2 (from the example, $|4 - 3| = 1$). Call this result y_1.

Step 5. For Blue strategy b_2, make a similar calculation as in Step 4 ($|2 - 5| = 3$). Call this result y_2.

Step 6. Calculate the optimal mixed strategy for Blue from:

c. using b_1 with probability $\dfrac{y_2}{y_1 + y_2}$ $\left(\dfrac{3}{1 + 4} = 3/4 \text{ in this example}\right)$

d. using b_2 with probability $\dfrac{y_1}{y_1 + y_2}$ $\left(\dfrac{1}{1 + 4} = 1/4 \text{ in this example}\right)$

Thus, Red's optimal mixed strategy is $(1/2a_1, 1/2a_2)$ and Blue's optimal mixed strategy is $(3/4b_1, 1/4b_2)$ with the value of the game equal to 3.5. These are, of course, the same results determined by the algebraic procedure in the previous section. However, with a minimum amount of practice, the arithmetic procedure can be used to more rapidly solve the 2×2 game.

Assume the following game:

An Example— Arithmetic Solution Procedure

		Blue	
		b_1	b_2
Red	a_1	-1	-6
	a_2	-7	-4

The solution procedure may be summarized in the format below:

		Blue		Red's	
		b_1	b_2	|Difference|	Probability of a_i
Red	a_1	-1	-6	$\|-1-(-6)\| = 5$	$3/(5 + 3) = 3/8$
	a_2	-7	-4	$\|-7-(-4)\| = 3$	$5/(5 + 3) = 5/8$
Blue's |Difference|		$\|-1-(-7)\| = 6$		$\|-6-(-4)\| = 2$	
Probability of b_j		$2/(6 + 2) = 1/4$		$6/(6 + 2) = 3/4$	

Red's optimal mixed strategy is $(3/8a_1, 5/8a_2)$, or $(3/8, 5/8)$, and Blue's optimal mixed strategy is $(1/4b_1, 3/4b_2)$, or $(1/4, 3/4)$, with the value of the game given by:

$$V = 3/8[1/4(-1) + 3/4(-6)] + 5/8[1/4(-7) + 3/4(-4)]$$
$$= 3/8(-19/4) + 5/8(-19/4)$$
$$= -19/4.$$

In the following examples, the algebraic solution procedure has been arbitrarily chosen.

Other Examples —2 × 2 Games Without Saddle Points

Game 1:

	b_1	b_2
a_1	5	8
a_2	10	2

Solution: There are no Red- or Blue-dominated strategies and a saddle point does not exist. Assuming Red uses strategies a_1, a_2 with probabilities of p, $1 - p$ respectively, the optimal mixed strategy is determined from:

$$5p + 10(1 - p) = 8p + 2(1 - p), \text{ or}$$

$$p = 8/11 \text{ and } 1 - p = 3/11$$

Red's optimal mixed strategy is $(8/11, 3/11)$ and the value of the game is:

$$5(8/11) + 10(3/11) = 8(8/11) + 2(3/11) = 70/11$$

Assuming Blue uses strategies b_1, b_2 with probabilities q, $1 - q$ respectively, the optimal mixed strategy is determined from:

$$5q + 8(1 - q) = 10q + 2(1 - q), \text{ or}$$

$$q = 6/11 \text{ and } 1 - q = 5/11$$

Blue's optimal mixed strategy is $(6/11, 5/11)$.

Game 2:

	b_1	b_2	b_3
a_1	8	6	7
a_2	5	9	4

Solution: Blue strategy b_1 is dominated by strategy b_3. No further dominance is applicable, and a saddle point does not exist for the reduced game involving (a_1, a_2) and (b_2, b_3). If Red uses strategies a_1, a_2 with probabilities p, $1 - p$ respectively, the optimal mixed strategy is determined from:

$$6p + 9(1 - p) = 7p + 4(1 - p), \text{ or}$$

$$p = 5/6 \text{ and } 1 - p = 1/16$$

Red's optimal mixed strategy is $(5/6, 1/6)$ and the value of the game is:

$$6(5/6) + 9(1/6) = 7(5/6) + 4(1/6) = 6.5$$

If Blue uses strategies b_2, b_3 with probabilities q, $1 - q$ respectively, the optimal mixed strategy is determined from:

$$6q + 7(1 - q) = 9q + 4(1 - q), \text{ or}$$

$$q = 1/2 \text{ and } 1 - q = 1/2$$

Blue's optimal mixed strategy is $(0, 1/2, 1/2)$.

Game 3:

	b_1	b_2	b_3
a_1	1	8	2
a_2	6	2	8
a_3	5	1	6

Solution: Red strategy a_2 dominates a_3. Then, Blue strategy b_1 dominates b_3. A saddle point does not exist for the reduced game involving (a_1, a_2) and (b_1, b_2). If Red uses strategies a_1, a_2 with probabilities p, $1 - p$ respectively, the optimal mixed strategy is determined from:

$$p + 6(1 - p) = 8p + 2(1 - p), \text{ or}$$

$$p = 4/11 \text{ and } 1 - p = 7/11$$

Red's optimal mixed strategy is $(4/11, 7/11, 0)$ and the value of the game is:

$$4/11(1) + 7/11(6) + 0(5) = 4/11(8) + 7/11(2) + 0(1) = 46/11$$

If Blue uses strategies b_1, b_2 with probabilities q, $1 - q$ respectively, the optimal mixed strategy is determined from:

$$q + 8(1 - q) = 6q + 2(1 - q), \text{ or}$$

$$q = 6/11 \text{ and } 1 - q = 5/11$$

Blue's optimal mixed strategy is $(6/11, 5/11, 0)$.

Game 4: We're going to the Superbowl!

Both the offensive coordinator of the Red team and the defensive coordinator of the Blue team are concerned with establishing a desirable mix of running and passing plays and defenses geared to stop those running and passing plays. After some detailed analysis, both parties independently come to the realization that the following matrix summarizes the likely results of the two classes of offensive and defensive patterns for each team.

		Defensive Team (Blue)	
		Stop Run	Stop Pass
Offensive Team (Red)	Run	+1 yd.	+5 yds.
	Pass	+20 yds.	-10 yds.

The solution for the Blue team is to align their defenses in the "stop run" alignment fifteen times out of every thirty-four (approximately 45 percent of the time) and the "stop pass" alignment approximately nineteen times out of every thirty-four (55 percent of the time). Obviously, these alignments should not be fixed in regard to a specific pattern. However, for a given play the likelihood of the defensive team being in the "stop run" alignment should be 0.45. The Red team would use a running play thirty times out of every thirty-four (approximately 90 percent of the time) and would only resort to a pass four times in thirty-four (approximately 10 percent of the time). Thus, it would appear that the offensive team would stay on the ground almost all the time, but the defensive team would be deliberately attempting to stop the running play only half the time. The other half of the time they would be cautiously guarding against a pass, even though the likelihood of a pass is rather remote.

This illustration points out a number of the implicit assumptions made in game theory. We have to begin with the assumption that a matrix is definable and that both parties would arrive at the same values in the matrix, although they would likely have done so using some independent analyses. We also assume that all possible alternatives are available to both parties. In effect, if the offensive team were to develop a new play for this specific game, the play would not be capable of being evaluated nor included in the matrix. In the third instance, we assume each play is to be run under somewhat similar conditions. That is to say, no difference is made for a play on first down where the offensive team is beginning on its twenty-yard line in contrast to another play, much later in the game, where the offensive team is on its opponent's twenty-yard line and is trailing by two points. Finally, the values in the matrix are assumed to be deterministic. Each time the offensive team chooses to run and the defensive team chooses to stop that run, there will be an exact yardage gain of one yard. In reality, this will obviously vary from one play to another. While the above are typical of the assumptions which restrict the use of game theory, there still are lessons that can be learned from its study. As an example, it is not at all intuitively obvious that a team should be defending against a pass half the time when the likelihood of a pass is very small. Nevertheless, this may well be the best strategy.

TWO-PERSON, ZERO-SUM GAMES CONTINUED

In games where (1) one of the players has more than two pure strategies, (2) a saddle point does not exist, and (3) the game cannot be reduced to a 2 × 2 game by applying dominance, the algebraic and arithmetic solution procedures presented previously do not apply. There is more than one solution procedure for such 2 × M or M × 2 games but only the method of subgames will be presented in this introductory chapter.

For example, let us consider the following M × 2 (or 3 × 2) game:

		Blue	
		b_1	b_2
	a_1	5	2
Red	a_2	3	8
	a_3	1	10

Invoking the principle of dominance does not reduce the game, nor does a saddle point exist. The solution tactic now advocated is to create all possible 2×2 subgames from the $M \times 2$ game and choose that 2×2 subgame for which a mixed strategy for Red will have the highest expected payoff. An intuitive argument for Red choosing a mixture of two pure strategies rather than a mixture of three pure strategies follows.

If Blue uses strategy b_1, then Red would rather choose between a_1 (5) and a_2 (3) than consider the third strategy a_3 (1). Similarly, if Blue uses strategy b_2, then Red would rather choose between a_2 (8) and a_3 (10) than consider the first strategy a_1 (2). Although certainly not a conclusive proof, this rationale at least suggests player Red would prefer a mixture between two pure strategies rather than a mixture among the three pure strategies. Pursuing this line of reasoning, the possible 2×2 subgames are:

Subgame 1:

	b_1	b_2
a_1	5	2
a_2	3	8

Subgame 2:

	b_1	b_2
a_1	5	2
a_3	1	10

Subgame 3:

	b_1	b_2
a_2	3	8
a_3	1	10

Using the arithmetic solution procedure for solving a 2×2 game, we have:

for Subgame 1, Red's optimal mixed strategy is $(5/8a_1, 3/8a_2)$ and Blue's optimal mixed strategy is $(3/4b_1, 1/4b_2)$ with the value of the game equal to:

$$5/8[3/4(5) + 1/4(2)] + 3/8[3/4(3) + 1/4(8)] = 17/4 = 4.25$$

for Subgame 2, Red's optimal mixed strategy is $(3/4a_1, 1/4a_3)$ and Blue's optimal mixed strategy is $(2/3b_1, 1/3b_2)$ with the value of the game equal to:

$$3/4[2/3(5) + 1/3(2)] + 1/4[2/3(1) + 1/3(10)] = 4.0$$

for Subgame 3, the entry (a_2, b_1) is a saddle point. Thus, Red's optimal pure strategy is (1, 0) and Blue's optimal pure strategy is (1, 0) with the value of the game equal to 3.0.

Thus, in this example, Subgame 1 has the highest expected payoff to Red of any of the three subgames and is therefore the solution to the original 3×2 game.

In summary, the solution to the following game is for Red to use the optimal mixed strategy (5/8, 3/8, 0) and for Blue to use (3/4, 1/4) with the value of the game equal to 4.25:

	b_1	b_2
a_1	5	2
a_2	3	8
a_3	1	10

**Example—
2 × M
Game**

Assume the following game:

	b_1	b_2	b_3
a_1	3	4	12
a_2	8	6	3

Solution: There are no dominated strategies for either Red or Blue and a saddle point does not exist for the game. The method of subgames will therefore be used as a solution procedure.

The following subgame:

	b_1	b_2
a_1	3	4
a_2	8	6

yields the saddle point (a_2, b_2). Red's optimal strategy is (0, 1) and Blue's optimal strategy is (0, 1, 0) with the value of the game being 6.0.

The subgame

	b_1	b_3
a_1	3	12
a_2	8	3

yields an optimal mixed strategy of (5/14, 9/14) for Red and an optimal mixed strategy of (9/14, 0, 5/14) for Blue. The value of the game is:

$$5/14 [9/14(3) + 5/14(12)] + 9/14 [9/14(8) + 5/14(3)] = 87/14$$

$$= 6 \ 3/14$$

The subgame

	b_2	b_3
a_1	4	12
a_2	6	3

yields an optimal mixed strategy of (3/11, 8/11) for Red and an optimal mixed strategy of (0, 9/11, 2/11) for Blue. The value of the game is:

$$3/11\,[9/11(4) + 2/11(12)] + 8/11\,[9/11(6) + 2/11(3)] = 60/11$$
$$= 5\ 5/11$$

Because the third subgame above results in the lowest expected payoff of 5 5/11 to Red, the optimal strategies for Red and Blue are (3/11, 8/11) and (0, 9/11, 2/11) respectively. The lowest expected payoff to Red is chosen as the value of the game, rather than the highest expected payoff, because in a $2 \times M$ game, Blue controls the play of the game. In an $M \times 2$ game, as illustrated in the next example, Red will control the play and the subgame having the largest expected payoff to Red will be the value of the game.

Assume the following game:

Example— M × 2 Game

	b_1	b_2
a_1	3	-2
a_2	-4	2
a_3	1	1

Solution: There are no dominated strategies for either Red or Blue, and a saddle point does not exist for the game. The method of subgames will therefore be used as a solution procedure.

The following subgame:

	b_1	b_2
a_1	3	-2
a_2	-4	2

yields an optimal mixed strategy of (6/11, 5/11) for Red and an optimal mixed strategy of (4/11, 7/11) for Blue. The value of the game is:

$$6/11\,[4/11(3) + 7/11(-2)] + 5/11\,[4/11(-4) + 7/11(2)] = -2/11.$$

The subgame

	b_1	b_2
a_1	3	-2
a_3	1	1

yields the saddle point (a_3, b_2). Red's optimal strategy is (0, 0, 1) and Blue's optimal strategy is (0, 1) with the value of the game being 1.0.

The subgame

	b_1	b_2
a_2	-4	2
a_3	1	1

yields the saddle point (a_3, b_1). Red's optimal strategy is $(0, 0, 1)$ and Blue's optimal strategy is $(1, 0)$ with the value of the game being 1.0.

Because the second and third subgames above have the same game value, 1.0, and this value is greater than $-2/11$ from the first subgame, the optimal strategy for Red in either case is $(0, 0, 1)$ and Blue may use either $(1, 0)$ or $(0, 1)$.

$N \times N$ Games and a Summary

Games larger than $2 \times M$ or $M \times 2$ require solution procedures other than those previously presented in this chapter. However, larger $N \times N$ games may contain a saddle point, the existence of which provides the solution to the game. Also, by applying the principle of dominance, the $N \times N$ game may reduce to a smaller game which can be solved by the techniques presented earlier. For $N \times N$ games which do not have a saddle point and cannot be reduced to a 2×2, $2 \times M$, or $M \times 2$ game, the literature advocates linear programming as the most practical solution procedure.

Much of the literature on game theory is reserved for the mathematically sophisticated. This is especially true beyond the two-person, zero-sum games such as nonzero-sum games, n-person games, games with uncertain payoffs, games with an infinite number of pure strategies, and so forth. A considerable amount of literature exists on these advanced games, however.

Authors writing at the introductory level for students of management normally restrict discussion to the two-person, zero-sum games, and this chapter has of course been no exception. Such restriction is primarily due to the fact that useful applications of game theory to real world business situations have been virtually nonexistent up to the present time. Published textbook examples for sales promotion campaigns, labor-management contract negotiations, investment portfolio purchases, political campaigns, and military decisions appear to be hypothesized examples rather than actual real world applications. Such a statement is not intended as a criticism of the examples but rather is made to emphasize the difficulty of applying game theory in practice. A reflection on just a few of the assumptions underlying the solution to a two-person, zero-sum game will suggest reasons for this difficulty. For example, it is rare that both persons would have complete knowledge of all the strategies available to his opponent or the precise value of the outcomes, given a particular strategy pair. Further, the parallel assumption of equal information available to each player concerning opponent strategies and payoffs would seem an unrealistic assumption in most real world situations.

QUESTIONS AND PROBLEMS

1. Distinguish between games which are strictly competitive and those which are not.

2. What is meant by the term *minimax strategies*, as pertains to a two-person, zero-sum game?

3. Develop a 2 × 2 game which has a saddle point and a 2 × 2 game which does not have a saddle point.

4. Distinguish between a pure strategy and a mixed strategy.

5. For the following general 2 × 2 game, give the expression for the value of the game, v.

	b_1	b_2
a_1	x_{11}	x_{12}
a_2	x_{21}	x_{22}

6. For what type of games can the arithmetic solution procedure be used? Determine the optimal strategies and the value for each of the following games.

7. (a)
$$\begin{array}{rr} -10 & 75 \\ 5 & 50 \end{array}$$
(b)
$$\begin{array}{rr} 14 & 8 \\ 10 & 6 \end{array}$$
(c)
$$\begin{array}{rr} -14 & -8 \\ -10 & -6 \end{array}$$

8. (a)
$$\begin{array}{rr} 18 & 6 \\ 14 & 8 \end{array}$$
(b)
$$\begin{array}{rr} -7 & -4 \\ -9 & -3 \end{array}$$
(c)
$$\begin{array}{rrr} 6 & 4 & 2 \\ 10 & -12 & -6 \\ 8 & -2 & -4 \end{array}$$

9. (a)
$$\begin{array}{rr} 2 & -14 \\ -2 & 4 \end{array}$$
(b)
$$\begin{array}{rr} 8 & 14 \\ 10 & 6 \end{array}$$
(c)
$$\begin{array}{rr} -4 & -7 \\ -5 & -3 \end{array}$$

10. (a)
$$\begin{array}{rrr} 18 & 10 & -5 \\ -4 & 20 & 12 \\ 25 & 15 & 7 \end{array}$$
(b)
$$\begin{array}{rrr} -2 & 5 & -1 \\ 3 & -1 & 5 \\ 2 & -2 & 3 \end{array}$$

11. (a)
$$\begin{array}{rrr} 2 & 5 & -3 \\ -1 & -2 & 1 \\ 0 & -1 & 2 \end{array}$$
(b)
$$\begin{array}{rrr} 1 & 3 & 10 \\ 6 & 3 & 1 \end{array}$$
(c)
$$\begin{array}{rrr} 3 & -2 & 1 \\ -4 & 2 & 5 \\ 1 & 1 & 2 \end{array}$$

12. (a)
$$\begin{array}{rrrr} 5 & 3 & 1 & -4 \\ 4 & 2 & -5 & -2 \end{array}$$
(b)
$$\begin{array}{rrrrr} 0 & 12 & -3 & -9 & 18 \\ 6 & 6 & -12 & -3 & 9 \end{array}$$

13. (a)
$$\begin{array}{rrr} 4 & 1 & 0 \\ 3 & 2 & 3 \\ 2 & 1 & 4 \\ 2 & 1 & -1 \end{array}$$
(b)
$$\begin{array}{rrrr} 18 & 18 & 11 & 14 \\ 15 & 15 & 14 & 15 \\ 5 & 26 & 10 & 14 \\ 14 & 22 & 10 & 11 \\ 10 & 12 & 12 & 10 \end{array}$$

14. (a)
$$\begin{array}{rrrr} -5 & 11 & 7 & 45 \\ 15 & 15 & 13 & 17 \\ -3 & 1 & 5 & -5 \end{array}$$
(b)
$$\begin{array}{rrr} 1 & 8 & 2 \\ 6 & 2 & 8 \\ 5 & 4 & 10 \end{array}$$

BIBLIOGRAPHY

HILLIER, F. S., AND LIEBERMAN, G. J. *Introduction to Operations Research.* San Francisco: Holden-Day, Inc., 1967.

LEVIN, RICHARD I., AND KIRKPATRICK, CHARLES A. *Quantitative Approaches to Management.* New York: McGraw-Hill Book Company, Inc., 1971.

LUCE, R. DUNCAN, AND RAIFFA, HOWARD. *Games and Decisions: Introduction and Critical Survey.* New York: John Wiley and Sons, Inc., 1958.

MORRIS, WILLIAM T. *Analysis of Management Decisions.* Homewood, Ill.: Richard D. Irwin, Inc., 1964.

Scheduling

How many times have you heard the saying "Time is money"? In large business and industrial operations, time *does* mean money. Control over the detailed operations of large business and industrial firms has for many years been a subject for very detailed research. An important aspect of industrial control is deciding on the precise use of manufacturing facilities in each instance of time. Several factors must be taken into account in making these decisions, such as the availability of resources, implementation costs, and due dates. It is this kind of decision making that we call *scheduling*.

Industrial scheduling problems differ greatly from one organization to another. Sometimes the operation consists of a series of activities at one work station and only one physical part; sometimes operations require very different labor skills and equipment on each of many thousands of subassemblies. Sometimes finished goods inventories must be maintained to satisfy customer demand. Sometimes such inventories are impossible to keep under all conceivable circumstances. Unique features of the organizational structure of the firm, of the market, or of plant capabilities are always present.

Making certain that a series of activities is completed within a specified period of time is a constraint also applied in situations when the series is to be performed only once. Specifically, when that series of activities constitutes a project which must be completed "in time," the analytical "tools" of this chapter will be of assistance. Construction projects typify these problems in which decisions result in actions that are almost never repeated under similar circumstances. As each activity is completed, it is unlikely to ever be repeated again. This chapter will attempt to present both aspects of scheduling: project and production.

SCHEDULING ENVIRONMENT

In the manufacturing organization, scheduling of production is a problem which draws together such diverse elements of the organization as sales, cost control, purchasing, capital budgeting, and many others. It is worthwhile, therefore, in any discussion of the factory scheduling problem to consider not only the complexities of the problem itself but also the environment within which it exists. In this chapter, we will make a distinction between the *design* of production systems which must operate to accomplish some daily schedule and the *operation* of those systems. Project planning includes the designing and implementation of that design, and it usually requires a great deal of time.

Because of the diversity and complexity of industrial scheduling problems, it is impractical to account for every factor in any single analysis. In this chapter, we are going to investigate two different aspects of the scheduling problem: the production scheduling problem and project scheduling problem.

Production Scheduling

The production scheduling problem generally breaks down into two major facets: job-shop scheduling and finished goods inventory control. Chapters 10 and 11 deal with inventory systems analysis; for this reason it will not be emphasized in this chapter. The *job-shop scheduling* problem revolves around a scenario in which the plant is said to consist of several work centers all with different capabilities. Sometimes duplication of facilities is allowed. There is a list of products to be completed. The routing of each product requires that the first operation must be completed before the second may be started and so on down the list. A specific machine is designed to carry out each of these operations with dates for completion of each of the products possibly having been assigned. How shall the products be scheduled to machines in such a way that: 1) due dates are met whenever possible, 2) the total time to complete all jobs is minimized, or 3) some other criterion function is optimized?

The basic unit of the job-shop process is the *operation.* One can envision an operation as an elementary task to be performed. Three primary attributes of each operation are given as part of the description of the particular job-shop scheduling problem:

1. A symbol identifying the operation with a particular *job.*
2. A symbol identifying the operation with a particular *machine.*
3. A real number representing the *processing time* of the operation.

There is for each job an ordering of the operations which comprise that job. Technological restraints on the order in which the task must be accomplished dictate this order. This ordering between operations is given by a relationship called *precedence.* If A and B are two operations of the same job and if for some reason the processing A must precede the processing of B, then A is said to precede B. The machine in this process is fundamentally a device or a facility which is capable of performing what must be done in the operation. For instance, if the machine in question is a machine lathe, for one job the operation might be a turning operation on the lathe; and for another job the operation might be a thread-cutting operation on the lathe. However, mathematically, the machine is just a time scale with certain intervals available. A *job shop,* therefore, is a set of all the machines that are identified with a particular set of operations. A job-shop process consists of the machines, the jobs, and the constraints of the organization that dictate the order in which operations are assigned during specific points in time. The scheduling of a job-shop process is that of assigning each operation to a specific position on the time scale of a given machine.

Several other assumptions and restrictions are generally placed upon the job-shop process. Among these restrictions are:

1. Each machine is always available for assignment. This implies that there are not significant delays that are caused by machine down time for maintenance, shift changes, or operator unavailability.
2. Each operation can be performed by only one machine in the shop at any time.
3. There is effectively only one machine of each type in the job shop.
4. Preemption by one job of another job is not permitted; that is, once an operation has begun on a given machine, it will run through to completion before another operation can begin on that machine.
5. Processing time of successive operations of a particular job may not be overlapped. This is to say that any given job can only be processed by one operation at a given point in time.
6. Each machine can handle at most one operation at a time.

The production scheduling is generally described by four kinds of information:

1. The jobs to be processed and the arrival process of those jobs to the system.
2. The number of types of machines that comprise the shop.
3. The disciplines that restrict the manner in which job assignments can be made, describing the fundamental flow pattern of the shop.
4. The criteria by which the schedule will be judged, implying the organizational objective function.

Project Scheduling

Project scheduling techniques are generally reserved for large scale one-time projects. Research and design work in the development stage as well as in the installation of systems are certainly unique, one-time projects. Major construction projects of buildings, highways, ships, and airlines also represent one-time projects which lend themselves to description and solution by project scheduling techniques. Generally speaking, project scheduling techniques can be applied economically to any of those projects, provided each is complex or large in scale. Sometimes individual projects are not very complex, but if management considers them only as components of a much larger system, the large system of interest may require some form of project scheduling. For these techniques to operate optimally, the major emphasis must be on completing the project on time. Timing is often primary; cost control is secondary.

Numerous activities must be accomplished in a specific sequence if a major project is to be completed on time. The deadline may have been contracted with the customer or it may be the minimum expected completion date. Often, contracted cost penalties are involved if projects are late, and in rare situations, financial incentives are given to projects to be finished before the deadline. In order to perform activities on schedule, plans must be made to properly allocate resources to the total project. Within timing constraints, efforts are directed toward minimizing total cost. Generally, because of the size of these projects, close attention is given only to the larger and more important activities and to the interactions between them. Project planning is a critical function and serious errors can lead to the destruction of the enterprise. It is not surprising, therefore, that a great deal of effort has been expended to define and develop methods which can deal with the kinds of problems involved in these potential situations.

In the early 1900's, an interesting method for project planning was developed which was known as the Gantt Project Planning Method. The problems which Gantt and the people of his time were faced with had considerably less complexity than the problems which we presently encounter. For his time and situation, however, the Gantt Method was sufficient, and for reasonably small problems today, this method will suffice. For large scale problems, Gantt's trial and error bar chart method provides a means for organizing our thinking but does not satisfy the need for approaching any sort of optimality where serious suboptimization can produce crises. Although the method is inadequate for large scale problems, it has not been forgotten, because the methods employed form the fundamental basis for other more elaborate planning programs.

The weakness of the Gantt technique provided the focus for significant developments in the planning of complex projects. A method was required which would permit optimal or near optimal sequencing and utilization of resources. With the increasing research of the late 1950's in the area of network analysis, an appropriate methodology was found. Beginning around 1957, a number of different approaches to large scale project planning were begun at different locations and for different reasons. Some common examples of project control methods are PERT (Project Evaluation and Review Technique) and CPM (Critical Path Method). PERT initially was developed by the United States Navy to plan and control the Polaris missile program. The DuPont Company developed CPM to control its maintenance and engineering functions. The differences between the approaches arose primarily because of the original job for which each method was developed. Both of them share in common the notion of a critical path, and it is for this reason that we shall study them in this chapter.

The PERT technique was credited with shortening the originally estimated development time on the Polaris submarine system by two years. Similar outstanding contributions have been credited to these techniques since their development. Both PERT and CPM are based on the same concepts, but they differ in some details. Both are based on the network plan that determines the most critical activities to be controlled so as to meet completion dates. Originally PERT methods were based on probabilistic estimates of activity times, whereas CPM methods assumed deterministic activity times. The initial designs of these methods also differed in the way the graphical map part was prepared. Actually, either the probabilistic or the deterministic model as well as either network scheme can be equally applied to PERT or CPM.

Three basic steps are involved in scheduling when using the PERT method: the planning step, the scheduling step, and the final or controlling step. They provide the framework about which a project can be described, scheduled, and then controlled.

The first or planning step is initiated by decomposing the project into distinct activities. The time estimates for these activities are determined (this will be discussed in detail later), and their interdependencies are illustrated by the construction of a network diagram. In this network diagram, each of the arcs represent a distinct activity. The entire diagram gives a network representation of the inter-dependencies of the activities of the project. At this phase, the network diagram is complete and often provides great insight into the project itself. Many planners believe that the basic benefits to be derived from the project planning and scheduling techniques are in the construction of the network diagram itself.

For most project scheduling jobs, the ultimate goal is to be able to determine when each activity must begin in order to assure that the project is completed within the specified time. The scheduling activity must also provide information for the project planner about that series of activities which must be closely watched in order to insure that the project schedule is maintained. This series of activities falls on the *critical path* and represents

tion is delayed. Additionally, for those activities which are not on the critical
path, the *slack time* should be indicated so that the schedule planner will
know how long he might delay certain activities in an attempt to recoup
some resources to place on those activities which are of a critical nature.

The last phase of the scheduling project is that of control. This includes
the use of the diagram and the time charts for making periodic progress
reports. This last step of the scheduling activity is an ongoing one in which
the planner must monitor the progress of the activities on the schedule.
This requires updating the project schedule on a continuing basis in an
attempt to insure that the project schedule is maintained as planned.

PROJECT SCHEDULING USING PERT

Decisions for a given project result in activities and actions that are
generally never repeated under similar circumstances. For instance, the
decision to build a new electric power station in an area is a commitment
by the organization that is best described as a *project*. As each step in
the project is completed, it is unlikely to ever be repeated again. Thus,
developing the first "anything" is generally of sufficient complexity to be
termed a project because it has many activities of a long term nature which
are nonrepetitive. Contrast this with a decision to order some more material
for an ongoing production facility, and we can see how in one case we
have a great deal of prior information to assist our decision making and
in another case we have only estimates to help us.

By their very nature, many of these long term projects are such that
great quantities of financial resources are required for their consummation.
This means very simply that any mistake can cause a great deal of money
to be spent, and the organization can be seriously crippled if anything goes
wrong. As a result there exist limits in a long term planning situation where
a single decision can drive the organization out of business. Obviously,
short term decisions can result in the same end if a poor decision results
in a small penalty over and over again. However, in a situation where
the same decision results in a small loss, corrective action can be taken
in which policy is modified to alleviate the problem. This characteristic
often does not exist in the long term planning project. This is another aspect
of the long term project which differentiates it from the short term project,
and as we develop the PERT technique, we will see how this aspect is
taken into account. In a long term planning operation, experience and judgment
constitute the best sources of information for making decisions. The long
term planning technology of PERT takes into account this aspect of the
problem and uses it to assist in developing project schedules which are
both realistic and effective.

As we discussed in a previous section, the first step of project scheduling   **A Network**
is the *planning step* in which the activities are set down in a network.   **Approach—**
In this section we are going to investigate some of the concepts of activities   **Definitions**

and their interrelationships expressed through a network. The network approach will allow us to illustrate graphically the interdependencies of the activities of a project. Because the project planning function begins with a list of all the activities and their precedent relationships, the network can be constructed through the use of a series of arrows and nodes as will be shown in this section. In a PERT network, the arrows which connect the nodes are called *arcs*. The relationship between the arcs and the nodes are based upon two concepts:

Events denote specific accomplishment which occurs at a recognizable point in time.
Activities are the work required to complete a specific event.

The most general network representation for PERT requires that activities be placed on arcs and the completion events and starting events be placed on the network nodes. Thus, if the two activities were taking a shower and dressing, they would be represented as shown in Figure 8.1.

FIGURE 8.1   Events and Activities

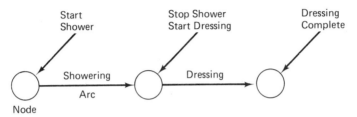

When this method of graphical representation of the project is used, it is easy to relate the length of the arc to the length of time that the activity consumes. Thus, we can draw a reasonably representative project diagram which has graphical significance. It should be emphasized that this particular aspect of the activity-on-arc approach makes it easier to visualize but has no significance in the algorithm for solution.

Let us reiterate: An event is an accomplishment occurring at an instantaneous point in time which requires no time itself or consumes no resources. An activity is a recognizable part of the project requiring time and resources for its completion. Thus, the event "starting the shower" occurred instantaneously in time and required no resources at all. The activity of "taking a shower" required both time and resources.

In constructing a network of activities and events which describes a given project, it is convenient to number each event successively in time such that the high numbered events are those which occur latest in time. Figure 8.2 shows another example where specific activities must be completed before a given activity can start. In Figure 8.2, activities (1–3) and (2–3) must be completed before event 3 or activity (3–4) can be started. Similarly, activity (3–4) must be completed before either activity (4–5) or activity (4–6) can begin. We can now establish some general rules for constructing network diagrams:

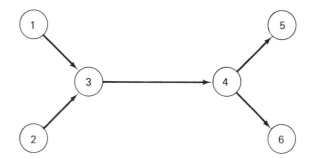

1. Each activity is represented by one and only one arc in the network. Therefore, no single activity can be represented twice in the network. If one activity is broken down into segments, each segment can be represented by a different arc. For instance, if the activity were developing computer programs for a massive information system, then we could draw one arrow to represent an activity "writing computer programs" or we could break that down and draw a series of connecting activities signifying "writing program A," "writing program B," and so forth.

2. No two activities can be identified by the same beginning and end events. In situations where two or more activities can be performed concurrently, the network actually has a given node with several input arcs, and it might be impossible to distinguish the events at that node. In these cases, we introduce a *dummy activity* to resolve this problem. As a result of using the dummy activity, other activities can be identified by unique end events. Dummy activities consume no time or resources. In Figure 8.3a, we have a situation in which both activities A and B have the same end events. In Figure 8.3b, two of four possible representations of the use of a dummy activity (activity D) are shown to alleviate the problem. Dummy activities are also very useful in establishing the proper logical relationship in the arrow diagram which otherwise cannot adequately be represented. When two or more activities have some but not all of their inputs in common, the use of a dummy activity resolves the problem of representation. In Figure 8.4, activity B must precede both activities E and C. Activity A, on the other hand, need only precede activity C. The use of dummy activity D forces the precedence relationship to occur as we desire.

3. Take the following steps to insure that the correct precedence relationship exists in the arrow diagram as it is constructed. Each time an activity is added to the network, it satisfies the following questions:

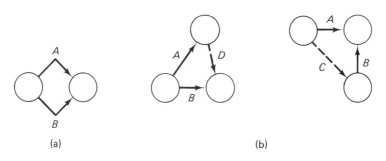

(a)   (b)

FIGURE 8.4 Further Use of the Dummy Activity

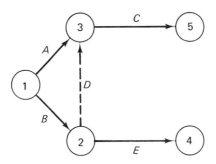

a. What activities must be completed immediately prior to this activity?
b. What activities must succeed this activity?
c. What activities must occur concurrently with this activity?
This rule should be self-explanatory. It insures that the project network is constructed correctly.

An Example   Construct a project network which has activities lettered A through L and in which the following relationships are satisfied:

1. A, B, and C are the first activities of the project and may be begun simultaneously.
2. A and B must precede D.
3. B must precede E and F.
4. C and F must precede G.
5. E must precede H and J.
6. D and H must precede I.
7. G must precede L and K.
8. I must precede L.
9. L, J, and K are the terminal activities of the project.

The resulting network diagram of the project described above is shown in Figure 8.5. Note that two dummy activities were necessary to adequately represent the relationships described. D_1 represents the relationships here in which both activities A and B must precede activity D. D_2 represents a relationship in which both activities G and I must precede activity L. The events of the network are also numbered to represent the increase in time of their occurrence.

Time Estimation   As part of the planning phase of the project scheduling environment for the PERT scheduling method, the planner is required to identify with each activity three time estimates. These time estimates relate to the time that will be required to complete the activity. The planner is asked to develop for each activity:

1. An *optimistic estimate* called *a*.
2. A *pessimistic estimate* called *b*.
3. An estimate of the *most likely* time required called *m*.

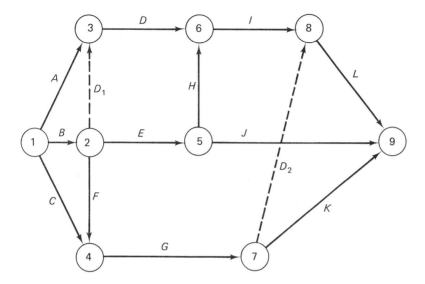

These three estimates are then related mathematically to give an expected elapsed activity time, t_e, where

$$t_e = \frac{1}{6}(a + b) + \frac{2}{3}m$$

This is the formula for the estimate of the mean of a Beta distribution. It uses more information than a single estimate and the range between the shortest and longest time should provide an additional insight into the activity time. However, there is evidence to indicate that this is not always so. The most likely estimate, m, need not coincide with the expected elapsed time, and it may occur to its left or to its right. Because of these properties, it was intuitively justified that the duration for each activity would follow the so-called Beta distribution with its unimodal point occurring at m and its end points occurring at a and b. Figure 8.6 shows the Beta distribution with the intuitively estimated points on it.

A great deal of criticism has been leveled at the use of the Beta distribution assumption. It has been shown on many occasions that expressions developed for the mean and for the variance cannot be satisfied with a Beta distribution unless certain restrictive relationships between a, b, and m exist. It should be noted, however, that the development of expressions for the mean and variance are based on intuitive arguments regardless of the original distribution assumption.

The estimate of the variance associated with the expected value of the elapsed time would also be a helpful piece of information for the project planner. As we discussed in a previous chapter, variance is a measure of the spread of a given distribution. It can be shown that the sum of the

FIGURE 8.6   Beta Distribution Representing Time Estimates

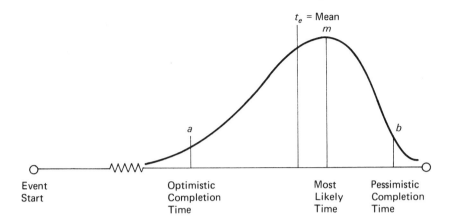

variances of a number of consecutive estimates of independent activities measures the variances of the total sequence. This independence referred to regards the activity times. That is how long it should take to finish each operation. That means that if estimates are given for t_e for each of three activities and these activities have variance measures S_1^2, S_2^2, S_3^2, then the variance of the sum of the activities' time is given by $S_1^2 + S_2^2 + S_3^2$. It should also be noted that the sum of the means for each activity is a measure of the mean of the total sequence. These relationships are depicted in Figure 8.7.

The formulae for the expected activity time t_e and its variance S^2 can be developed intuitively in the following manner. The midpoint of the range, $(a + b)/2$, is assumed to count half as much as the modal point m. Thus t_e is the arithmetic mean of $(a + b)/2$ and $2m$. Thus,

$$t_e = \frac{\dfrac{a + b}{2} + 2m}{3} = \frac{a + b}{6} + \frac{2}{3}m$$

FIGURE 8.7   Summing Means and Variances

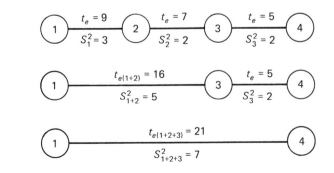

142

In order to develop an expression for the variance, it is often assumed that the range of a given distribution (a,b) encloses roughly six standard deviations of the distribution. This follows since about 90 percent or more of any probability density function lies within three standard deviations of its mean. Thus,

$$S^2 = \left(\frac{b - a}{6}\right)^2$$

Having determined the values of t_e for the activities of the network, it is possible to develop probabilities for the occurrence of any of the events on the network. Using techniques of statistical interval estimation similar to the concepts developed in previous chapters, one can develop relationships using the standard normal distribution so that we may make probability statements that a given event i will occur no later than a specific time. These probabilities represent the chance that succeeding events will occur within certain durations.

Now that we have developed the formulae for determining the expected activity duration time, we can analyze the project network in an attempt to determine the critical path. Remember that in an analysis of this type, the critical path is that series of interconnected activities which, if delayed at all, will cause the entire project to be delayed. Processing at this time should determine those series of activities which are critical and those which are noncritical. A critical activity, then, is one such that a delay in its start will cause a delay in the completion time of the entire project. A noncritical activity is an activity for which the time between its earliest start time and latest completion time as allowed by the project is longer than its actual duration. In this case, the activity is said to have *slack* time.

Making the Critical Path Calculations

Let us begin by using our sample PERT network of Figure 8.8 to determine the critical path. In Figure 8.8, the activities shown contain an estimated time for the duration along with estimates for the variance (contained in parenthesis). The critical path calculations proceed in two phases. The first phase or forward phase begins with the calculations at the start node and moves toward the end node of the project network. At each node in the network, as the calculations proceed, a number is determined which represents the *earliest occurrence of that corresponding event.*

Let E_i represent the earliest start time of all activities emanating from event i, and E_j the completion time. This means that E_i is the earliest occurrence time of that particular event i. Obviously, when $i = 1$, the event is the start event and the convention generally adopted is that $E_1 = 0$. Let d_{ij} be the duration of activity (ij). This means $d_{ij} = t_e$. Now, during the forward calculations, we need to develop the earliest start time for each of the events within the network such that

$$E_j = \max_i [E_i + d_{ij}], \text{ for all arcs where } i \text{ and } j \text{ exist}$$

FIGURE 8.8 PERT Network, with Estimates for t_{ei}, and S_i^2 in Parentheses

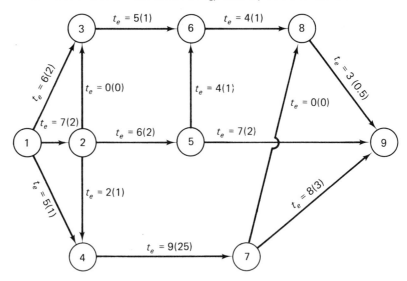

This formula says that the earliest possible start time for a given event is primarily a function of the previous events plus the activity times of all prior activities. Applying this formula to the sample network in Figure 8.8, the following calculations can be developed:

$$E_1 = 0$$

$$E_2 = E_1 + d_{12} = 0 + 7 = 7$$

$$E_3 = \max [E_1 + d_{13}, E_2 + d_{23}] = \max [0 + 6, 7 + 0] = 7$$

$$E_4 = \max [E_1 + d_{14}, E_2 + d_{24}] = \max [0 + 5, 7 + 2] = 9$$

$$E_5 = E_2 + d_{25} = 7 + 6 = 13$$

$$E_6 = \max [E_3 + d_{36}, E_5 + d_{56}] = \max [7 + 5, 13 + 4] = 17$$

$$E_7 = E_4 + d_{47} = 9 + 9 = 18$$

$$E_8 = \max [E_6 + d_{68}, E_7 + d_{78}] = \max [17 + 4, 18 + 0] = 21$$

$$E_9 = \max [E_5 + d_{59}, E_8 + d_{89}, E_7 + d_{79}] = \max [13 + 7, 21 + 3,$$
$$18 + 8] = 26$$

Note that the final calculation, $E_9 = 26$, has been determined by a thorough analysis of the network. This completes the forward phase of the network analysis.

We now begin the backward phase starting from the end event and proceeding backward to the starting event. Our objective in this phase is to compute the L_i or the latest completion time for all activities coming into the given event i for the end event $L_i = E_i$. This initiates the backward pass. Generally, the formula to be used for any given node i to calculate the latest completion time is very similar to that formula used to calculate the earliest start. It is:

$$L_i = \min_j [L_j - d_{ij}], \text{ for all arcs where } i \text{ and } j \text{ exist}$$

Applying this formula to the network shown in Figure 8.8, we can develop the following series of formula values in the network.

$$L_9 = E_9 = 26$$
$$L_8 = L_9 - d_{89} = 26 - 3 = 23$$
$$L_7 = \min [L_9 - d_{79}, L_8 - d_{78}] = \min [26 - 8, 23 - 0] = 18$$
$$L_6 = L_8 - d_{68} = 23 - 4 = 19$$
$$L_5 = \min [L_9 - d_{59}, L_6 - d_{56}] = \min [26 - 7, 19 - 4] = 15$$
$$L_4 = L_7 - d_{97} = 18 - 9 = 9$$
$$L_3 = L_6 - d_{36} = 19 - 5 = 14$$
$$L_2 = \min [L_5 - d_{25}, L_4 - d_{24}] = \min [15 - 6, 9 - 2] = 7$$
$$L_1 = \min [L_4 - d_{14}, L_2 - d_{12}, L_3 - d_{13}] = \min [9 - 5, 7 - 7,$$
$$14 - 6] = 0$$

This completes the backward phase of calculations.

We are now prepared to develop the critical path activity through using the result of the forward and backward analyses. Any given activity (i,j) is said to lie on the critical path if it satisfies the following three conditions:

1. $E_i = L_i$
2. $E_j = L_j$
3. $E_j - E_i = L_j - L_i = d_{ij}$

These conditions simply indicate that there is no slack time between the earliest start and latest start or completion times of the activities. Thus, the activity must be critical. Figure 8.9 has been developed which is another representation of the network shown in Figure 8.8 where the values for L_i and E_i in each of the nodes in the network has been shown. The figures by each node have L_i on top and E_i on the bottom. The critical path is shown by the double hash marks on the arc in the network. This is calculated simply by finding those nodes which have the same L_i and E_i values. Thus, for this network, the critical path is 1-2-4-7-9; and in this case, twenty-six time units is actually the shortest possible time to complete the project. Note that the critical path is in fact a path from start to end in the network.

Now that the forward and backward phases are complete, and the critical path has been determined, it is time to consider other calculations

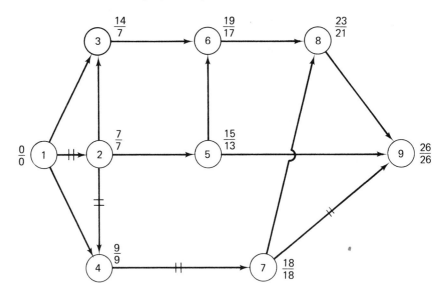

in the network which will provide additional management information. The first development would be in the area of slack time determination. *Slack time* means that a specified activity can slip by a given amount and the total job can still be completed on time. As you would expect, every node on the critical path which dominates the system has no slack time. Any given path besides the critical path through the network can be developed which has slack time. Knowledge of slack time can help us to develop two other time measures associated with each activity: *latest start time* (LS) and *earliest completion time* (EC). These are given for any activity (i,j) by:

$$LS_{ij} = L_j - d_{ij}$$
$$EC_{ij} = E_i + d_{ij}$$

Knowledge of slack time can assist the project planner in resource allocation, and in attempts to shorten the critical path or assure that other activities are not delayed unnecessarily. Using these relationships, we can develop the concept of total slack time. *Total slack time* (TS) for an activity represents the difference between the maximum time available and its duration. That is,

$$TS_{ij} = L_j - E_i - d_{ij}$$

but since $LS_{ij} = L_j - d_{ij}$, we get:

$$TS_{ij} = LS_{ij} - E_i$$

Much of the activity of a PERT project management system revolves around the "trading off" of resources from some activities in order to shorten the time needed for the completion of another activity. The implication is that a better arrangement of resources might be available. Any alternative which reduces the time through the critical path of the project network bears investigation. In order to reduce the time through the critical path of the project, two basic methods or approaches should be used:

1. apply additional resources to the activities on the project critical path in an attempt to reduce activity time, or
2. if possible, shift resources within the other batches of noncritical activities in an attempt to again shorten the time.

Generally, it is unrealistic to expect a great balance of resources to exist in practical situations. However, information of this type is helpful to the project planner in attempts to reduce total project time.

Assume that several planners got together and developed a project. **An Example** The network diagram for that project is shown in Figure 8.10. Each arc has time estimates shown in a-m-b format. As before, the first step is to calculate t_e and S^2. These values are shown in Table 8.1. With those figures in mind, we can proceed to calculate the E_j and L_i values for the network as shown in Tables 8.2 and 8.3 respectively. Then we develop the

Project Network for Example Problem with Time Estimates **FIGURE 8.10**
on Arcs in a-m-b Format

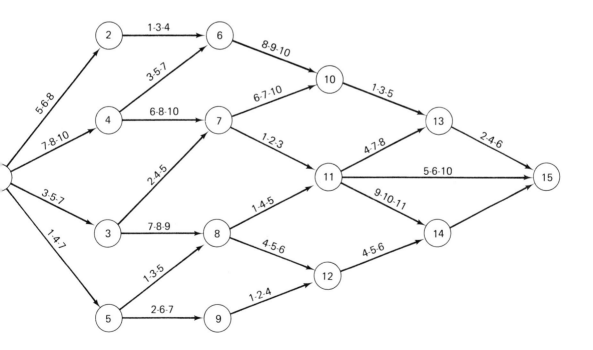

TABLE 8.1   Values for a, b, m, t_e, and S^2 for Example Problem

Activity	a	b	m	t_e	S^2
1–2	5	8	6	6.17	.25
1–3	3	7	5	5.00	.44
1–4	7	10	8	8.17	.25
1–5	1	7	4	3.50	1.00
2–6	1	4	3	2.83	.25
3–7	2	5	4	3.83	.25
3–8	7	9	8	8.00	.11
4–6	3	7	5	5.00	.44
4–7	6	10	8	8.00	.44
5–8	1	5	3	3.00	.44
5–9	2	7	6	5.50	.69
6–10	8	10	9	9.00	.11
7–10	6	10	7	7.33	.44
7–11	1	3	2	2.00	.11
8–11	1	5	4	3.67	.44
8–12	4	6	5	5.00	.11
9–12	1	4	2	2.17	.25
10–13	1	5	3	3.00	.44
11–13	4	8	7	6.67	.44
11–14	9	11	10	10.00	.11
11–15	5	10	6	6.50	.69
12–14	4	6	5	5.00	.11
13–15	2	6	4	4.00	.44
14–15	4	9	7	6.83	.69

TABLE 8.2   Values for E_j, where $E_j = \max_i \left[E_i + d_{ij} \right]$

Node i	E_i
1	0
2	6.17
3	5.00
4	8.17
5	3.50
6	max [6.17 + 2.83, 8.17 + 5.00] = 13.17
7	max [8.17 + 8.00, 5.00 + 3.83] = 16.17
8	max [5.00 + 8.00, 3.50 + 3.00] = 13.00
9	3.50 + 5.50 = 9.00
10	max [13.17 + 9.00, 16.17 + 7.33] = 23.50
11	max [16.17 + 2.00, 13.00 + 3.67] = 18.17
12	max [13.00 + 5.00, 9.00 + 2.17] = 18.00
13	max [23.50 + 3.00, 18.17 + 6.67] = 26.50
14	max [18.17 + 1.00, 18.00 + 5.00] = 28.17
15	max [18.17 + 6.50, 26.50 + 4.00, 28.17 + 6.83] = 35.00

Node i	L_i
15	$L_{15} = E_{15} = 35.00$
14	$35 - 6.83 = 28.17$
13	$35 - 4.00 = 31.00$
12	$28.17 - 5.00 = 23.17$
11	$\min [35.00 - 6.50, 28.17 - 10.00, 31.00 - 6.67] = 18.17$
10	$31.00 - 3.00 = 28.00$
9	$23.17 - 2.17 = 21.00$
8	$\min [23.17 - 5.00, 18.17 - 3.67] = 14.50$
7	$\min [18.17 - 2.00, 28.00 - 7.33] = 16.17$
6	$28.00 - 9.00 = 19.00$
5	$\min [21.00 - 5.50, 14.50 - 3.00] = 11.50$
4	$\min [16.17 - 8.00, 19.00 - 5.00] = 8.17$
3	$\min [14.50 - 8.00, 16.17 - 3.83] = 6.50$
2	$19.00 - 2.83 = 16.17$
1	$\min [11.50 - 3.50, 8.17 - 8.17, 6.50 - 5.00, 16.17 - 6.17] = 0$

Redrawn Network Showing the Critical Path   **FIGURE 8.11**

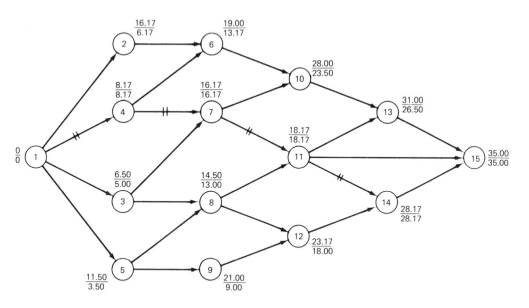

critical path as shown in Figure 8.11. Finally, we calculate total slack. The calculation for LS_{ij}, EC_{ij}, and total slack are summarized in Table 8.4. Note that total slack along the critical path is zero.

TABLE 8.4   Values for Late Start, Early Completion with Total Slack Time

Activity	LS_{ij}	EC_{ij}	TS_{ij}
1-2	$16.17 - 6.17 = 10$	$0 + 6.17 = 6.17$	$10 - 0 = 10$
1-3	$6.50 - 5.00 = 1.50$	$0 + 5.00 = 5.00$	$1.5 - 0 = 1.5$
1-4	$8.17 - 8.17 = 0$	$0 + 8.17 = 8.17$	$0 - 0 = 0$
1-5	$11.50 - 3.50 = 8.00$	$0 + 3.50 = 3.50$	$8 - 0 = 8$
2-6	$19.00 - 2.83 = 16.17$	$6.17 + 2.83 = 9.00$	$16.17 - 6.17 = 10$
3-7	$16.17 - 3.83 = 12.34$	$5.00 + 3.83 = 8.83$	$12.34 - 5.00 = 7.34$
3-8	$14.50 - 8.00 = 6.50$	$5.00 + 8.00 = 13.00$	$6.50 - 5.00 = 1.5$
4-6	$19.00 - 5.00 = 14.00$	$8.17 + 5.00 = 13.17$	$14.00 - 13.17 = 0.83$
4-7	$16.17 - 8.00 = 8.17$	$8.17 + 8.00 = 11.17$	$8.17 - 8.17 = 0$
5-8	$14.50 - 3.00 = 11.50$	$3.50 + 3.00 = 6.50$	$11.5 - 3.5 = 8$
5-9	$21.00 - 5.50 = 15.50$	$3.50 + 5.50 = 9.00$	$15.5 - 3.5 = 12$
6-10	$28.00 - 9.00 = 19.00$	$13.17 + 9.00 = 22.17$	$19.00 - 13.17 = 5.83$
7-10	$28.00 - 7.33 = 20.67$	$16.17 + 7.33 = 23.50$	$20.67 - 16.17 = 4.50$
7-11	$18.17 - 2.00 = 16.17$	$16.17 + 2.00 = 18.17$	$16.17 - 16.17 = 0$
8-11	$18.17 - 3.67 = 14.50$	$13.00 + 3.67 = 16.67$	$14.5 - 13.00 = 1.5$
8-12	$23.17 - 5.00 = 18.17$	$13.00 + 5.00 = 18.00$	$18.17 - 13.00 = 5.17$
9-12	$23.17 - 2.17 = 21.00$	$9.00 + 2.17 = 11.17$	$21.00 - 9.00 = 12$
10-13	$31.00 - 3.00 = 28.00$	$23.50 + 3.00 = 26.50$	$28.00 - 23.5 = 4.5$
11-13	$31.00 - 6.67 = 24.33$	$18.17 + 6.67 = 24.84$	$24.33 - 18.17 = 6.16$
11-14	$28.17 - 10.00 = 18.17$	$18.17 + 10.00 = 28.17$	$18.17 - 18.17 = 0$
11-15	$35.00 - 6.50 = 28.50$	$18.17 + 6.50 = 24.50$	$28.50 - 18.17 = 10.33$
12-14	$28.17 - 5.00 = 23.17$	$18.00 + 5.00 = 23$	$23.17 - 18.00 = 5.17$
13-15	$35.00 - 4.00 = 31.00$	$26.50 + 4.00 = 30.5$	$31.00 - 26.5 = 4.5$
14-15	$35.00 - 6.83 = 28.17$	$28.17 + 6.83 = 35.00$	$28.17 - 28.17 = 0$

PRODUCTION SCHEDULING

Production scheduling problems are very common occurrences whenever any choice is to be made in the order in which a number of operations can be performed. The problem could be jobs in a manufacturing plant, computer programs in a large computer system, the housewife's shopping trip, or even the aircraft waiting for a landing opportunity. It is clear that the very weighty problems in scheduling are somehow solved, because the housewife makes her shopping rounds, aircraft do land, production schedules are implemented. How are they accomplished? Generally speaking, the scheduling process is accomplished by very casual trial-and-error, history-oriented approaches. However, the problem does lend itself to analytical solution. In this section, we will discuss some of the "fringe" solution areas of scheduling problems.

Often one of the basic problems of scheduling is that it becomes confused and intertwined with other problems in the organization. Very often, the order for execution of a series of operations will influence which tasks must be performed or the precise character of the task or method to be used for their performance. Assume that questions concerning what is to be scheduled and how it is to be scheduled have been resolved. Then,

150

the sequence of jobs to be performed can be based on the following assumptions.

1. The tasks or operations to be performed are well-defined and known.
2. The resources available for this activity are completely known and have been specified.
3. The sequence of elemental basic activities of the task is known.

We will discuss two fundamental problems in the production scheduling area: the single-machine, n-job problem and the two-machine, n-job flowshop problem. This is primarily because of the complexity in solving most "practical" problems.

Single Machine, n-Job

This section is concerned with the rather special case of the scheduling problem in which each job consists of a single operation. It is a reasonably realistic problem because in any given job-shop scheduling system, the jobs can be partitioned depending on the machine required to perform the operation. Therefore, each machine in the shop is effectively independent of the others and can be separately scheduled. Under these circumstances, we can direct our attention to that single machine and the set of jobs to be processed on it. Let us assume that the number of jobs is finite and known in advance of the scheduling operation and that each of the n-jobs must be processed. We shall further assume that the machine will not be subject during this processing time to unavoidable delays due to breakdown or other scheduling requirements and that the machine is always available for processing. Further, assume that each of the n-jobs is available for processing simultaneously so that the schedule could begin with any one of the jobs.

There are many theoretical and several practical reasons for examining the rather specialized case of this section. It is obviously the simplest scheduling problem, easily understood, and for those interested in understanding the basic concepts underlying machine shop scheduling, it can serve to illustrate the differences between scheduling procedures. Many of the solutions to this rather simple problem are applicable to problems of a much larger nature. Actually, the applications of this model are more important than may be initially apparent, because there are many shops which contain a single machine as well as many situations in which large complex equipment behaves as if it were a single machine.

The basic objective of the scheduling problem presented here is to arrange these n-jobs in a specific sequence which optimizes some established criterion function. Quite often the criterion function is based on that of flow time. *Flow time* of job i is the total time which that job spends in the shop. Its component times are the waiting time w_i and the processing time of the job p_i.

It can be shown but will be omitted from this section that for the n-job, single-machine problem, the average flow time per job is minimized by sequencing the jobs in order of nondecreasing processing times and is maximized by sequencing the jobs in order of nonincreasing processing times.

One of the areas which has aroused perhaps the most interest in scheduling is that of scheduling to meet preassigned job due dates. The measure of effectiveness is based on satisfaction of these preassigned job due dates. This demonstrates how well we can meet our obligations and fulfill our promised delivery. For this problem it can be shown that the maximum job lateness is minimized by scheduling the jobs in order of nondecreasing due dates.

An Example   For the jobs shown below, produce a processing schedule which minimizes the mean flow time and the schedule which maximizes the mean flow time.

Job	Processing Time
1	8
2	6
3	2
4	7
5	10
6	4

According to the last section, mean flow time is minimized through sequencing the jobs according to nondecreasing processing times. Therefore, the job sequence should be 3-6-2-4-1-5. Figure 8.12 illustrates this sequence in graphical form. Remember that the total processing time is a constant regardless of the sequence. However, the flow time for a specific unit is not independent of the sequence selected. The graph also shows total flow time for each job. As before,

flow time = wait time + processing time.

FIGURE 8.12   Graph of Optimal Schedule

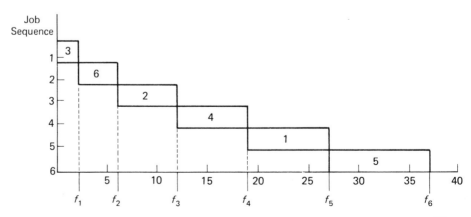

This is shown in Table 8.5. Average flow time is 17.16 time units.

The sequence which produces maximum flow time is 5-1-4-2-6-3. Table 8.6 shows the flow time calculations for this sequence in which average flow time is 26 time units as compared to 17.16 before. It is left to the reader to calculate another schedule in an attempt to exceed the max or min flow time shown.

Flow Time Table for Minimum Flow Time   **TABLE 8.5**

Sequence Number	Job	Wait Time	Processing Time	Flow Time
1	3	0	2	2
2	6	2	4	6
3	2	6	6	12
4	4	12	7	19
5	1	19	8	27
6	5	27	10	37
				103

Flow Time Table for Maximum Flow Time   **TABLE 8.6**

Sequence Number	Job	Wait Time	Processing Time	Flow Time
1	5	0	10	10
2	1	10	8	18
3	4	18	7	25
4	2	25	6	31
5	6	31	4	35
6	3	35	2	37
				156

Two-Machine, n-Job

We now proceed to a situation in which there are two machines which must do processing in sequence on a given number of jobs. We will consider this to be a *flowshop* problem in which the ordering or processing must always proceed from one machine to another in the same order. In other words each job must proceed from machine one to machine two; no jobs will be allowed to begin first on machine two. As before, each job consists of a single operation on that machine. The number of jobs is known and finite and must be processed. All of the jobs are available for processing simultaneously so the scheduling could begin with any one of them. As before, we wish to obtain a sequence of operations which will optimize some criterion function. Generally, in situations where more than one machine exists, a convenient criterion function to use is that of minimizing the makespan. *Makespan* is defined as the elapsed time from the start of the first job to the completion of the last job. It can be shown that the sequences of jobs that minimize the makespan are the same for both machines. The method which we present in this section for computation of the sequencing is given without proof but was developed by S. M. Johnson.

Assume that there are two machines A and B and that the processing time of the n-jobs is A_1, ..., A_n on machine A and B_1, ..., B_n on machine B. The algorithm developed involves the following steps:

1. Pick as the first job of the sequence that which has the smallest processing time occurring in the list A_1, ..., A_n, B_1, ..., B_n. If there is a tie, select either of the smallest processing times.
2. If the minimum processing time observed is A_i, perform the ith job *first*. If it is B_i, perform the ith job last. Note that this decision will apply to both machines A and B.
3. There are now $n - 1$ jobs to be ordered. Apply steps 1 and 2 to the reduced set of processing times obtained by deleting the two machine processing times corresponding to the jobs already assigned.
4. Continue in this manner until all the jobs have been ordered. The resulting ordering will minimize the makespan.

An Example

A local printer has one printing machine and one binding machine. He has several books to process and the printing and binding times are known for each book. Determine the order in which books should be processed in order to minimize the total time required to produce all books.

Book	Printing Time (min)	Binding Time (min)
1	30	70
2	140	120
3	50	60
4	65	90
5	90	40
6	45	10

In this example,

$$A_1 = 30 \qquad B_1 = 70$$
$$A_2 = 140 \qquad B_2 = 120$$
$$A_3 = 50 \qquad B_3 = 60$$
$$A_4 = 65 \qquad B_4 = 90$$
$$A_5 = 90 \qquad B_5 = 40$$
$$A_6 = 45 \qquad B_6 = 10$$

Applying the solution technique of the previous section, we see that the smallest processing time is B_6, so by rule 2 we get a schedule with job 6 last.

					6	

The reduced set of processing times is:

Job	Printing	Binding
1	30	70
2	140	120
3	50	60
4	65	90
5	90	40

The smallest processing time is A_1 so we schedule job 1 first:

1					6

Now we have:

Job	Printing	Binding
2	140	120
3	50	60
4	65	90
5	90	40

leading to:

1				5	6

Similarly,

Job	Printing	Binding
2	140	120
3	50	60
4	65	90

yielding:

1	3			5	6

Finally,

Job	Printing	Binding
2	140	120
4	65	90

which yields the final optimal sequence:

1	3	4	2	5	6

We now can calculate an elapsed time chart for the scheduling of these jobs as shown in Table 8.7. Figure 8.13 shows a time graph of processing activities. Note that the printing machine has no idle time. The binding machine is idle for thirty-five minutes waiting for job number 2. The makespan is 455 minutes.

TABLE 8.7   Schedule Chart for Two-Machine Example

	Printing		Binding	
Job	Time In	Time Out	Time In	Time Out
1	0	30	30	100
3	30	80	100	160
4	80	145	160	250
2	145	285	285	405
5	285	375	405	445
6	375	420	445	455

FIGURE 8.13   Time Graph of Processing

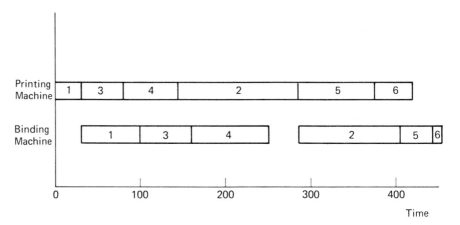

QUESTIONS AND PROBLEMS

1. For the example problem in which the critical path was calculated (see pp. 147–48), determine the variance of the time. What significance has this value?

2. Discuss the conditions in order for an activity to lie on the critical path in terms of sufficiency. That is, what is implied if only two are satisfied?

3. Another concept often employed in PERT calculations is that of *free float*. Free float (*FF*) is defined by assuming that all the activities start as early as possible; it represents the excess of available time over activity duration. That is,

$$FF_{ij} = E_j - E_i - d_{ij}.$$

Discuss free float as it applies to project scheduling and PERT. How do free float and total slack or float relate?

4. Determine the critical path on each of the following networks:

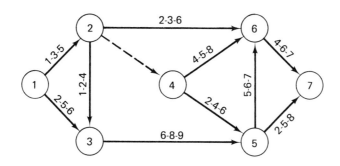

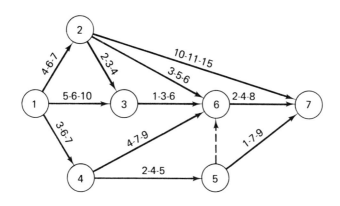

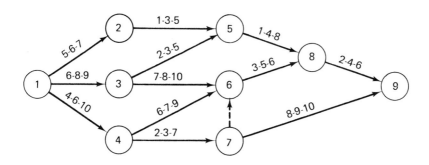

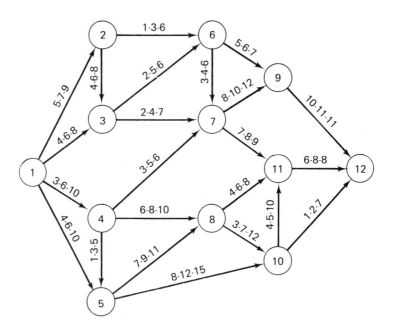

5. For a single machine determine the optimal scheduling sequence for the following jobs according to 1) processing time and 2) due date.

Job	Processing Time (days)	Due Date (day of month)
1	8	July 15
2	12	July 23
3	17	August 4
4	2	August 1
5	4	July 20
6	19	July 25

Assume the scheduling date is July 10.

6. For the two-machine example problem on pp. 154–55, reverse the ordering that was derived by the algorithm and determine the makespan.

7. Determine the makespan for the following two-machine problem.

Job	Machine 1	Machine 2
1	30	60
2	120	60
3	50	40
4	20	80
5	90	120
6	60	120
7	200	150

BIBLIOGRAPHY

LEVIN, RICHARD I., AND KIRKPATRICK, CHARLES A. *Planning and Control with PERT/CPM*. New York: McGraw-Hill Book Company, 1966.

MIZE, JOE H., WHITE, CHARLES R., AND BROOKS, GEORGE H. *Operations Planning and Control.* Englewood Cliffs, N.J.: Prentice-Hall, Inc., 1971.

MUTH, JOHN F., AND THOMPSON, GERALD L. *Industrial Scheduling.* Englewood Cliffs, N.J.: Prentice-Hall, Inc., 1963.

NILAND, POWELL. *Production Planning, Scheduling, and Inventory Control.* New York: The Macmillan Company, 1970.

SASIENI, MAURICE, YASPAN, ARTHUR, AND FRIEDMAN, LAWRENCE. *Operations Research.* New York: John Wiley & Sons, Inc., 1959.

STARR, MARTIN K. *Production Management: Systems and Synthesis.* Englewood Cliffs, N.J.: Prentice-Hall, Inc., 1972.

TAHA, HAMDY A. *Operations Research: An Introduction.* New York: The Macmillan Company, 1971.

TORGERSEN, PAUL E., AND WEINSTOCK, IRWIN T. *Management: An Integrated Approach.* Englewood Cliffs, N.J.: Prentice-Hall, Inc., 1972.

Quality control
and sampling models

Most operations are performed within an environment that includes a number of random elements. In a production operation, the composition or quality of raw materials may vary from one day to the next, machine settings can change through usage and wear, and even temperature and humidity may affect the final product. In any operation that includes a significant human input, variation has to be accepted as inevitable. The control chart is designed to monitor the stability of a process where variability is to be expected, and the issue is not one of attempting to completely eliminate unit-to-unit differences but rather one of assessing whether or not the pattern of variability is stable. As we might expect, these control charts are particularly useful in assessing the quality characteristics of a product.

Statistical control charts are usually applied as a direct monitor on the process through a verification of the output of that process. Acceptance sampling methods tend to be concerned with the output of a process beyond the point of immediate process control. The objective of the latter is to determine whether a discrete quantity of the output of the process is acceptable compared with some criterion of quality. Consequently, a sample from a lot must be assessed and then the lot either accepted or rejected on the basis of the findings of the sample.

THE CONCEPT OF STATISTICAL CONTROL

Statistical control is based on the assumption that there exists *a stable system of chance causes*—a pattern of variation that is consistent and controllable over time. One specific unit may be different from the second, and the second different from the third, and so forth; but if the statistical distribution describing the characteristic in question is stable, then we have a state of statistical control.

As was suggested in Chapter 5, variability is inevitable. Two successive batches of breakfast cereal or two charges of steel will not contain exactly the same proportion of ingredients, and the resulting products will not have identical characteristics. Variation will occur in the quality of incoming materials, in the time required to complete the work cycle, in the dimensions of the finished product, and so forth. However, if we assume in each or any of these illustrations that the pattern of variation is stable, then we can assume a state of statistical control.

Patterns of Variation

Consider the successive rolls of a six-sided die. The first roll yields a three, the second roll is a one, the third is a five, and the fourth roll is another three. It is not unlikely nor unexpected that successive outcomes may be different; however, these outcomes will all be the result of tossing the same die—a die that is assumed not to be changing over time. The die should produce a stable system of chance causes. With enough data and using the relative frequency definition of probability, we could plot the distribution of Figure 5.4—the shape of a rectangle ranging from one to six. This distribution is our stable system of chance causes.

Now assume that someone changes our die (without telling us) by converting the one to a four, the two to a five, and the three to a six so our stable system of chance causes no longer exists in its original form. In effect, we now have a die with two fours, two fives, and two sixes. Assume we are unaware of the change, but we do have the opportunity of continuing to observe the results of successive tosses. First we obtain a four, then a six, another four, and a five. After four tosses, would we know that the die has been modified—that we no longer have the original stable system of chance causes? Not likely! Eventually we might become suspicious, but it might take a few more tosses before we realized we had not seen a one, a two, or a three. On the other hand, had the die been modified by adding two dots to each side, giving us a die reading from three to eight, we would be decidedly suspicious the first time we observed a seven or an eight, and we would then be able to claim that the process has changed!

A probabilistic steady-state or stable pattern of variation exists when the parameters of the statistical distribution describing the system of chance causes remains constant over time. Such a pattern exists, if only for the first day, in Figure 9.1. Assume that we are honing pistons. At twenty-minute intervals through a six-hour day, a unit is selected and the diameter is measured and plotted as in Figure 9.1. The statistical distribution at the end of that day describes the process—the system of chance causes at that point in time. During the first day the process is stable and *in control*. During the second day, however, a trend is evident. The central tendency

FIGURE 9.1   A Stable and Some Unstable Patterns of Variation

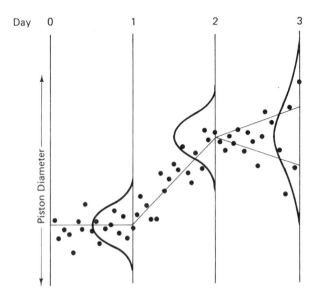

is increasing and the piston diameters are becoming larger. By the end of the day, the average has shifted noticeably upward. The process may be said to be *out of control* during the second day. Another form of instability can be seen during the third day, when the dispersion increases over time. In each of these two cases, the changes were gradual. In another instance the shift to the *out of control* condition might be more severe and erratic. The average piston diameter may suddenly jump upward (or downward) and/or the dispersion may increase radically.

The process under consideration does not have to be limited to a product with a continuous dimension. We could also be concerned with the proportion of defectives in incoming lots of materials, with the duration needed to complete similar types of work, or with the time-to-failure of like pieces of equipment or the number of workers absent from one day to the next. Should the proportion defective increase, and the change represent more than a chance variation, we would like to know that this is occurring. In effect, we would like to know when a stable system of chance causes no longer exists.

Control Limits

In order to detect changes in the basic process, control limits are often placed about the initial stable pattern of variation. This can be seen in Figure 9.2. A sample is taken and the appropriate dimension, for example, the piston diameter, is noted in comparison to the control limits. If the sample falls within the control limits, the process is said to be *in control*. If the sample falls outside the limits, the process is deemed to have changed and is said to be *out of control*. In Figure 9.2 we can assume that Distribution A

Control Limits and Stable and Unstable Patterns of Variation   **FIGURE 9.2**

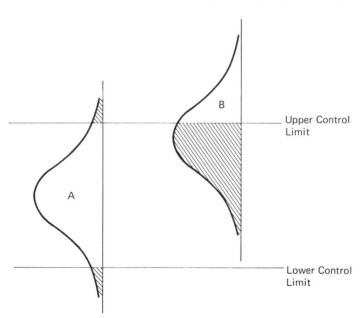

represents the initial stable pattern of variation. Distribution B represents a change—perhaps the condition at noon of the second day in Figure 9.1. At each point in time through the selection and recording of a single value, an error is possible. Perhaps the process has not changed (Distribution A), but a value falls outside the control limits (the shaded area of Distribution A). We would incorrectly assume that the process has changed, and we might take some corrective action when none really was necessary. On the other hand, the process may actually have changed (Distribution B), but out sample value falls within the control limits (the shaded area of Distribution B). Again, we would be in error, this time in not seeking an assignable cause of variation when one actually exists.

The first and most fundamental objective of statistical control is to detect changes from the stable system of chance causes, to detect them as quickly and as economically as possible, and not to be in error too often by inferring that the process has changed when in fact it has not or vice versa. The second objective is that of seeking the cause of variation and taking the appropriate corrective action. However, this latter objective is primarily a function of the technology involved in the process. For example, some mechanical equipment adjustments could be made to bring the average diameter of the pistons back down to the initial condition. If the time to complete a work cycle is becoming excessive, appropriate corrective action would have to be identified. If the time-to-failure of some production equipment is becoming significantly less, again, some assignable reason would have to be noted and corrective action taken. In each case, the detection step must be followed by corrective action.

THE $\bar{X}$ AND R CHARTS

In attempting to control a process where the significant characteristic is measurable as with length or weight, it is customary to employ a pair of control charts—an $\bar{X}$ chart and an R chart. These are used together and might work as follows: a sample, for example, five units, is selected and the mean and the range of this sample are calculated. The mean is then plotted on the $\bar{X}$ chart and is done so in an attempt to ascertain whether or not the process mean is increasing or decreasing. The range of the same sample is also calculated and plotted on the R chart. This latter measure is an attempt to ascertain whether or not the variation is increasing or decreasing over time. By using these together, it is possible to maintain a reliable "picture" of the process output.

The $\bar{X}$ Chart

In constructing an $\bar{X}$ and an R chart, we begin by collecting some samples over a time span when we have reason to believe that the process is in control. Usually each sample will contain four or five observations and we will collect twenty or twenty-five such samples.

The first step in constructing the $\bar{X}$ chart is to estimate the process mean, $\bar{\bar{X}}$, and the mean of the sample ranges, $\bar{R}$. Table 9.1 illustrates a format for obtaining this information.

Sample Number	Sample Values	Mean, $\bar{X}$	Range, R
1	$X_{11}, X_{12}, \ldots X_{1n}$	$\bar{X}_1$	R_1
2	$X_{21}, X_{22}, \ldots X_{2n}$	$\bar{X}_2$	R_2
.	. . .	.	.
.	. . .	.	.
.	. . .	.	.
m	$X_{m1}, X_{m2}, \ldots X_{mn}$	$\bar{X}_m$	R_m

In this format, we are taking m samples of n units each. We are then calculating the mean and range of each sample. Finally,

$$\bar{\bar{X}} = \frac{\Sigma \bar{X}}{m}$$

and

$$\bar{R} = \frac{\Sigma R}{m}$$

The upper and lower control limits for the $\bar{X}$ chart are then usually established as:

$$UCL_{\bar{X}} = \bar{\bar{X}} + A\bar{R}$$
$$LCL_{\bar{X}} = \bar{\bar{X}} - A\bar{R}$$

where A is dependent upon the sample size. Values of A can be obtained from Table 9.2.

Sample Size, n	$\bar{X}$ Chart A	R Chart D_U	D_L
2	1.88	3.27	0
3	1.02	2.58	0
4	0.73	2.28	0
5	0.58	2.12	0
6	0.48	2.00	0
7	0.42	1.92	0.08
8	0.37	1.86	0.14
9	0.34	1.82	0.18
10	0.31	1.78	0.22

It might be noted that these limits are equally spaced about the estimated process mean. As a matter of fact, they are spaced three sigma limits from this mean, but the logic and all the implications of the spread are beyond the scope of this chapter.

The R Chart

If the $\bar{X}$ chart has already been constructed, $\bar{R}$ has been calculated. With $\bar{R}$ and Table 9.2, the upper and lower control limits for the R chart can be specified as:

$$UCL_R = D_U \bar{R}$$

$$LCL_R = D_L \bar{R}.$$

Because $D_L = 0$ for samples of $n = 6$ and less, the $LCL_R = 0$. This means that with samples of six or fewer, it will be impossible for a value on the R chart to fall below the lower control limit. In effect, the R chart will only be capable of detecting increases in the dispersion of the process output unless an unusually large sample, that is, $n \geq 6$, is used.

Some Examples

Problem 1. Assume that control charts are to be established to monitor the weight in ounces of the contents of containers being filled on an assembly line. The containers should hold at least sixty ounces. In order to guarantee the weight, the process must be set to deliver slightly more than this amount. Samples of five containers have been taken every three minutes for the last hour. The sample data, together with the sample means and sample ranges, are given in Table 9.3.

TABLE 9.3 The Weight of the Containers in Ounces

Sample Number	Sample Values					Mean, $\bar{X}$	Range, R
1	61.3	60.5	62.4	62.4	62.0	61.7	1.9
2	59.6	61.7	63.0	61.4	62.8	61.7	3.4
3	61.4	62.4	61.7	61.4	62.4	61.9	1.0
4	62.0	61.9	63.2	61.9	62.2	62.2	1.3
5	62.4	61.9	61.7	61.6	60.5	61.6	1.9
6	63.8	62.5	63.9	61.9	61.4	62.7	2.5
7	63.3	61.6	63.2	60.7	61.4	62.0	2.6
8	61.1	61.3	63.2	62.8	62.0	62.1	2.1
9	62.5	61.9	63.8	61.6	63.0	62.6	2.2
10	62.1	61.7	62.0	61.7	62.9	62.1	1.2
11	61.7	62.6	62.3	61.2	60.8	61.7	1.8
12	63.8	62.3	62.4	64.1	61.3	62.8	2.8
13	60.6	61.8	63.1	62.8	61.7	62.0	2.5
14	62.0	61.2	62.1	61.7	62.1	61.8	0.9
15	61.5	63.1	63.9	61.9	60.7	62.2	3.2
16	63.4	62.6	62.4	61.9	61.8	62.4	1.6
17	62.1	63.1	64.1	61.4	62.3	62.6	2.7
18	61.5	63.2	62.4	62.6	62.2	62.4	1.7
19	61.8	62.2	61.5	61.2	60.8	61.5	1.4
20	61.5	61.4	63.1	61.6	60.8	61.7	2.3

Note that the first sample was made up of five containers whose contents were 61.3, 60.5, 62.4, 62.4, and 62.0 ounces. The mean of this sample $(\bar{X})$ is calculated as $\dfrac{61.3 + 60.5 + 62.4 + 62.4 + 62.0}{5} = \dfrac{308.6}{5}$ = 61.72 or 61.7 ounces. The range (R) is noted as $62.4 - 60.5 = 1.9$ ounces. Similarly, the mean and the range are calculated for each sample, and we are ready to begin constructing our control charts.

It is suggested that the R chart be constructed first. $\bar{R}$ can be calculated as:

$$\bar{R} = \frac{1.9 + 3.4 + 1.0 + \dots + 2.3}{20}$$

$$= 2.05$$

With samples of $n = 5$, the control limits for the R chart can be calculated as:

$$UCL_R = (2.12)(2.05)$$

$$= 4.35$$

$$LCL_R = (0)(2.05)$$

$$= 0$$

These limits are used to construct the R chart of Figure 9.3.

Since all values fell within the control limits, the R chart can be accepted as a method for assessing subsequent process variation. However, had one of these points fallen outside the calculated limit, that point would have had to be discarded and the limits reestablished.

An R Chart from the Data of Table 9.3 **FIGURE 9.3**

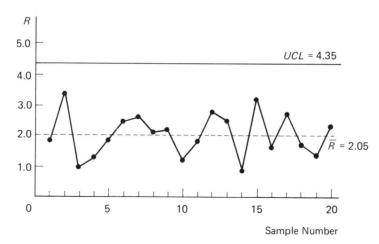

Sample Number

Attention can now be directed to the $\bar{X}$ chart. The mean of the sample means, $\bar{\bar{X}}$, can be calculated as:

$$\bar{\bar{X}} = \frac{61.7 + 61.7 + 61.9 + \ldots + 61.7}{20}$$

$$= 62.09$$

With samples of $n = 5$, the control limits for the $\bar{X}$ chart can be calculated as:

$$UCL_{\bar{x}} = 62.09 + (0.58)(2.05)$$

$$= 62.09 + 1.19 = 63.28$$

$$LCL_{\bar{x}} = 62.09 - (0.58)(2.05)$$

$$= 62.09 - 1.19 = 60.90$$

These limits are used to construct the $\bar{X}$ chart of Figure 9.4.

As with the R chart because all values fell within the control limits, the $\bar{X}$ chart can be accepted in its present form and now be used to detect subsequent changes in the mean of the process. As with the R chart, had an initial value fallen outside the control limits, that point would have had to be discarded and the limits reestablished.

FIGURE 9.4 An $\bar{X}$ Chart from the Data of Table 9.3

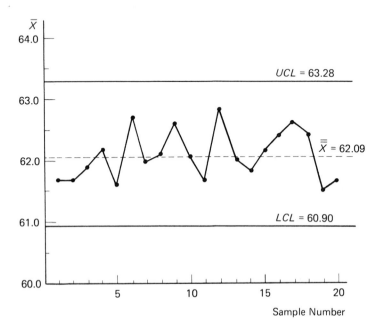

It should be noted that there is an advantage to constructing and testing the R chart first. The value of $\bar{R}$ is used in establishing control limits both on the R chart and on the $\bar{X}$ chart. Had an initial value fallen outside the limits on the R chart, a recalculation of $\bar{R}$ would have been necessary and control limits would have had to be redefined on both the R chart and the $\bar{X}$ chart. The converse is not true. Had an $\bar{X}$ value fallen outside the limits on the $\bar{X}$ chart, only the control limits for that $\bar{X}$ chart would have had to be recalculated.

In our example, both charts are now ready to be used to monitor the process. The control charts would be constructed with the control limits as calculated. Samples of five units would be taken—perhaps every thirty minutes or perhaps only once or twice a day. The mean of this sample of five units would be plotted on the $\bar{X}$ chart, and the range would be plotted on the R chart. As long as both values fell within their respective control limits, we would assume that the process is *in control* and our stable system of chance causes remains in existence. As soon as an $\bar{X}$ value exceeds the control limits, we assume that the mean of the process has shifted. If an R value exceeds the upper control limit on the R chart, we assume that the process dispersion has increased. In either case, we now have to seek the cause of variation and take the appropriate corrective action.

Problem 2. After installing the control charts of Problem 1 (Figures 9.3 and 9.4), samples of five are taken twice a day for the next week with the following results. Was the process ever out of control?

Sample Results for the Next Week **TABLE 9.4**

Sample Number	Sample Values					Mean, $\bar{X}$	Range, R
1	62.4	63.8	60.5	61.4	63.2	62.3	3.3
2	62.1	62.5	63.9	61.9	62.2	62.5	2.0
3	61.5	61.3	63.1	61.9	60.5	61.7	2.6
4	60.6	61.7	62.3	62.8	61.4	61.8	2.2
5	61.7	62.3	63.8	61.7	63.0	62.5	2.1
6	62.5	61.2	63.2	64.1	60.8	62.4	3.3
7	63.3	62.6	61.7	61.7	61.7	62.2	1.7
8	63.5	64.2	63.3	61.8	64.2	63.4	2.4
9	64.6	63.9	62.6	64.1	64.3	63.9	2.0
10	64.2	63.5	62.0	64.5	64.8	63.8	2.8

Yes! It would appear as though the mean shifted upward between the seventh and eighth sample, although no change in dispersion is evident. Plotting the $\bar{X}$ values on Figure 9.4 (or an extension of these control limits) will provide graphic evidence of the occurrence of an assignable cause sometime during the fourth day. The fact that three values in a row exceed the control limit provides fairly conclusive proof of a change. Interestingly enough, and from an examination of

Table 9.4, the change was likely to have been a step-function increase rather than a gradual shifting upward in the process mean.

OTHER FORMS OF CONTROL

Often an observation yields only a two-valued classification: a simple yes or no, correct or incorrect, acceptable or defective. A milling machine may be either in use or idle. The surface finish of a piece of furniture may be acceptable or it may not. The dimension of a part may fall either within or outside a set of specification limits. In other cases an observation may yield a multivalued but still discrete classification system. A clerical operation may have been performed correctly, or it may contain one, two, three, or more errors. An employee may suffer none, one, or more lost-time accidents during a given time period. The number of arrivals to a service facility during a specified hour of the day will be a discrete number. In the first case—that of the two-valued classification—a *p* chart may be employed. In the second case—requiring a counting—a *c* chart can be used. In both cases we are measuring by attributes rather than by variables. We will present the *p* chart and the *c* chart conceptually and without the method for calculating the control limits. In the latter case we would need to develop the Poisson distribution.

The *p* Chart

The *p* chart is designed to control the *percentage* or *proportion* of something, defectives per sample, for example. Each item in the sample is assessed and then placed into one of two defined classes. The proportion of units falling into one of these classes, defectives, for example, may be controlled over time or from one sample to another with this *p* chart. In the simplest case, the sample size remains constant from one sample to another. This will permit the control limits to be constant over the duration of the control chart. On the other hand, when 100 percent inspection is occurring and the production output varies, the sample size will also vary. If this is the case, the control limits will have to be recalculated for each individual sample.

Consider the illustration of Figure 9.5. Assume lots of some component part are delivered to our plant. Over the past few months, these have averaged five percent defective. We select a sample of fifty units from each lot and measure the proportion defective within this sample of fifty. The upper control limit is established as $UCL = 0.143$. The lower control limit is negative and hence cannot be employed. Then, our first sample of fifty units contains one defective. This gives us $p = 0.02$ and this value is plotted on the control chart. Our next sample contains no defectives and we are able to plot $p = 0$ on the control chart. Our third sample contains five defectives and $p = 0.10$ is plotted. Our fourth and fifth samples contain three defectives each and $p = 0.06$ can be plotted. Through our first five samples, all values are within the control limits. It can be noted that it will take eight defectives ($p = 0.16$)

A p Chart Based on Samples of $n = 50$ and $\bar{p} = 0.05$ **FIGURE 9.5**

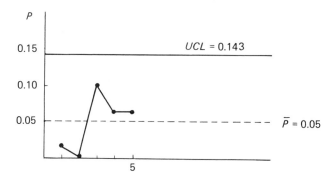

to incur an out-of-control condition. With this occurrence of eight or more defectives, it might be worthwhile to ask the vendor if more than a chance variation is resulting in this increase in the proportion of defectives.

The c Chart

Some processes provide numerical data that are best recorded as a number rather than a proportion. For example, the number of arrivals per hour demanding service at a tollbooth is of interest when deciding upon the level of service capability to provide. If this number of arrivals deviates from a stable pattern of variation, it may be necessary to compensate by either opening or closing additional tollbooths.

As with the p chart, a c chart of constant sample size will permit the construction of control limits that are constant over the life of the control chart. Should the sample size vary, the control limits will have to be varied accordingly.

Consider the c chart of Figure 9.6. We are assuming that in the production of material, a detailed inspection is made at regular intervals of 100 square

A c Chart Based upon Constant Sized Samples and $\bar{c} = 3$ **FIGURE 9.6**

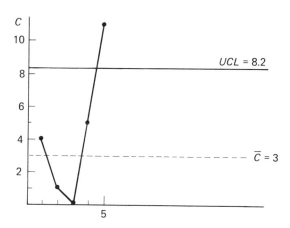

171

yards of material and a count is recorded of the number of defects observed. In the past these have averaged three defects, and the c chart of Figure 9.6 is the result. In now using this to assess the stability of our production process, we observe four defects in the first inspection, one defect in the second, no defects in the third, five defects in the fourth, and a total of eleven defects in the fifth inspection. From our control chart, we would have good reason to assume that the process has gone out of control sometime prior to the recording of the fifth sample.

THE CONCEPT OF ACCEPTANCE SAMPLING

The methods of acceptance sampling also lend themselves to inspection requirements in product quality control. Such inspection can be applied to incoming parts and materials, to components within the manufacturing system moving from one stage of completion to the next, and to the finished product. In addition, through acceptance sampling, inspection may be applied to other tasks such as the verification of accounting records and the determination of the accuracy of clerical work. In each case, the quality of the whole is submitted for judgment, and a decision is made on the basis of a sample taken from the whole.

The Alternatives

Before focusing on the methods of acceptance sampling, it should be noted that essentially three choices are always available to verify (or not to verify) the quality of a group of items. Every item in the lot may be inspected—perhaps even more than once; a sample of items may be taken from the lot and inspected, and an inference made from that sample; or no items may be inspected.

In the first case, the quality characteristic and satisfactory item performance is likely to be deemed rather critical, at least in comparison to the cost of inspection. Perhaps a defective part will result in the malfunction of a much larger system at great expense. For example, each turbine blade to be installed in a jet engine is likely to be meticulously inspected. A sampling plan would be inadequate as a means of insuring the quality of each blade.

Skipping the second case for the moment, in the third case it is at least implicitly assumed that the quality of the units that make up the lot exceeds some minimum acceptable standard. For instance, in purchasing a keg of nails from a lumber yard, a building contractor will not bother to verify the quality of each nail nor probably even select a sample of the nails in the keg for inspection purposes. He may realize that a few will be found to be defective, but the number will be so few that it doesn't warrant his concern at the time of purchase.

The level of verification chosen will ultimately consider the cost of inspection and the cost of accepting and perhaps using defective items. In general, acceptance sampling will be more economical than 100 percent

inspection when the occurrence of a defective in an accepted lot is not
prohibitively expensive, or when the inspection process requires the destruction of the item. Acceptance sampling will also be more economical than no inspection when there is some expense incurred in accepting defectives and the number of defectives is likely to be quite different from one lot to the next.

Returning to the second case—that of sampling inspection—the most elementary acceptance sampling plan calls for the random selection of a sample of size n from a lot containing N items. The entire lot is then accepted if the number of defectives found in the sample is equal to or less than c, the acceptance number. For example, a sampling inspection plan may be defined as $N = 1{,}000$, $n = 50$, and $c = 1$. This means that a random sample of 50 items is to be taken from the lot of 1,000. If zero or one defective is found in the sample, the whole lot is accepted with no further verification. If more than one defective is found, the lot is rejected. In the latter case, the lot can either be returned to the producer or it can be retained and then subjected to a 100 percent screening process and all the defectives removed. The former action is called a *nonrectifying inspection program*; the latter, a *rectifying inspection program*.

Inspection Accuracy

Before proceeding with the development of example acceptance sampling plans, it is well to raise the issue of the detection of defectives. In most discussions regarding inspection choices, it is assumed that 100 percent inspection means the 100 percent screening of all units and the detection of all defectives. Further, if a sample of fifty units is taken and there are three defectives in those fifty units, the three defectives will be noted. This may or may not be a good assumption. The inspection process is often a visual process undertaken by a human being. The person is likely to make some mistakes, particularly if he or she is pressed to verify a number of units within some minimum amount of time, or if the substandard item is difficult to detect, or if the work is boring and monotonous. As a matter of fact, it is not unusual to find improvements in inspection accuracy coming with less inspection rather than more. For example, a 100 percent inspection process may be far less than 100 percent effective in screening substandard units. By reducing the amount of required inspection and establishing an acceptance sampling plan, the inspector may have more time to carefully examine each unit and through the inference of sampling be able to form a more accurate estimate of the quality of a lot.

The fallacy of equating 100 percent accuracy with 100 percent inspection can be seen in the exercise described in Table 9.5. Very few people will come close to reporting the correct count. As a matter of fact, errors of 10 percent or more will not be uncommon. While it is difficult to extrapolate from this textbook illustration to a given "real world" situation, errors in the inspection process also occur in reality and often of this same order of magnitude.

TABLE 9.5

A FAIRY TALE

Assume the letter "G" is a defective product. Read the following story—attempt to comprehend the tale while at the same time counting each "G." You should permit yourself a total of approximately three minutes—time yourself or have someone else provide you with an indication of the passage of time as you are reading to maintain a reasonable pace. Record your total in the box at the bottom. The answer (the number of defectives) is reported in the first question at the end of the chapter.

WHILE STROLLING THROUGH A GLEN, A GIDDY ENGLISH GIRL TRIPPED ON A RATHER LARGE, ALMOST GIGANTIC FROG. THE GIRL STAGGERED BUT REGAINED HER FOOTING AND WAS ABOUT TO GO ON WHEN THE FROG BEGAN TO SPEAK AND GESTICULATE TO GAIN THE GIRL'S ATTENTION. "I HAVE NOT ALWAYS BEEN A FROG," HE CROAKED. THE FROG'S GREEN COLORING SEEMED TO GLOW BRIGHTLY AS HE CONTINUED, "I WAS ONCE A GRACIOUS KNIGHT, A GENTLEMAN CALLED GALLANT GEORGE GRENVILLE, BUT WAS CHANGED INTO THIS GHASTLY FROG YOU NOW SEE BY AN UNGODLY, MAGICAL GENIE. THE SPELL CAN ONLY BE BROKEN IF I GAIN A GIRL'S GOOD GRACES AND SPEND A NIGHT IN HER GARDEN." THE AGOG GIRL WAS SKEPTICAL, OF COURSE. SHE GAZED AT THE FROG'S PLEADING EYES, AND SOON HER GIDDY NATURE GAVE WAY TO HER DOUBTS. GIGGLING, SHE DECIDED TO GRANT THE FROG'S WISH AND TOOK HIM HOME STRAIGHTWAY, PUTTING HIM BY HER GARDEN GATE. THAT NIGHT THE GIRL SLEPT GRANDLY AND SURE ENOUGH, WHEN SHE AWOKE THE FOLLOWING MORNING, THERE ALONGSIDE HER GARDEN GATE WAS THE GRACIOUS KNIGHT, GEORGE GRENVILLE. WELL, STRANGELY ENOUGH, FOR A LONG, LONG TIME THE GIRL'S MOTHER DID NOT BELIEVE THAT STORY.

Total ☐

SINGLE SAMPLING PLANS BY ATTRIBUTES

The type of inspection sampling described by N, n, and c uses inspection by attributes and a single sample of size n. Other attribute inspection plans might use two samples or even three or more samples before requiring the acceptance or rejection of a lot. When it is not feasible to divide a continuous production process into discrete lots, a special class of attribute sampling methods may be used. These continuous sampling models verify

the quality of the process output through inspection of a specified *proportion*
of the items being produced.

Inspection may also be by variables. Here a measurement is obtained and recorded as a continuous dimension, subject only to the limitations of the measuring instrument or the convenience of measurement, rather than as a simple classification of acceptable versus defective units.

In this concluding section, we will concern ourselves only with the most fundamental of acceptance sampling plans—single sampling by attributes.

The Operating Characteristic Curve

Acceptance sampling plans attempt to discriminate between lots of acceptable and lots of unacceptable items. The relative ability of a sampling plan to meet this objective can be demonstrated with an operating characteristic (OC) curve. An OC curve defines the probability of a lot being accepted (of finding c or fewer defectives in a sample) for different levels of proportion defective.

Consider the operating characteristic curve for the sampling plan $N = 1,000$, $n = 50$, $c = 1$, illustrated in Figure 9.7. The abscissa refers to the proportion of defectives which might be found in a lot. The ordinate then refers to the probability of accepting a lot at a specified level of proportion defective. Note that if N contains no defectives ($p = 0$), then the lot is

The Operating Characteristic Curve for the Sampling Plan **FIGURE 9.7**
$N = 1,000$, $n = 50$, $c = 1$

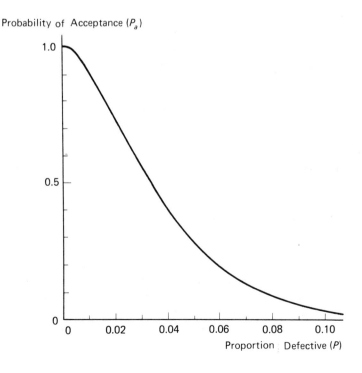

certain to be accepted. If the lot contains ten defectives ($p = 0.01$), then the probability of accepting the lot is approximately 0.91. The probability distribution needed to establish these values is the hypergeometric. For ease of calculation, however, the binomial distribution can be used as an approximation. Then, using the tables describing the cumulative binomial distribution found in the appendix, the OC curve for $N = 1,000$, $n = 50$, and $c = 1$ could have been constructed. We begin by identifying a number of levels of proportion defective and calculating the corresponding probability of acceptance of a lot containing those defectives. In our example, we will work with $p = 0, 0.01, 0.02, 0.03, ..., 0.10$.

At $p = 0$, there are no defectives in the sample; hence, the probability of acceptance is, $P_a = 1.00$.

At $p = 0.01$, there are ten defectives in the lot of $N = 1,000$. Using the appendix for $n = 50$, the probability of obtaining two or more defectives can be read as 0.0894. Then, meeting the acceptance number of $c = 1$, the probability of finding one or less defectives is $1 - 0.0894 = 0.9106$ or $P_a = 0.91$.

We can establish our third point at $p = 0.02$, and again for $n = 50$ and $c = 1$, the probability of obtaining two or more defectives is read as 0.2642; $1 - 0.2642 = 0.7358$ or $P_a = 0.74$.

At $p = 0.03$, the probability of finding two or more defectives is 0.4447; $1 - 0.4447 = 0.5553$ or $P_a = 0.56$.

Similarly, at

$p = 0.04; 1 - 0.5995 = 0.4005$ or $P_a = 0.40$
$p = 0.05; 1 - 0.7206 = 0.2793$ or $P_a = 0.28$
$p = 0.06; 1 - 0.8100 = 0.1900$ or $P_a = 0.19$
$p = 0.07; 1 - 0.8735 = 0.1265$ or $P_a = 0.13$
$p = 0.08; 1 - 0.9173 = 0.0827$ or $P_a = 0.08$
$p = 0.09; 1 - 0.9468 = 0.0532$ or $P_a = 0.05$
$p = 0.10; 1 - 0.9662 = 0.0338$ or $P_a = 0.03$

From these calculations, the OC curve of Figure 9.7 was constructed. Note that this OC curve is unique in that it describes the sampling plan defined as $N = 1,000$, $n = 50$, and $c = 1$. In this sense each acceptance sampling plan can be defined in terms of its own unique operating characteristic curve. However, the lot size will not significantly affect the shape of the curve. The sample size and acceptance number will be quite significant.

A good sampling plan will have a high probability of accepting those lots which contain few defectives and a low probability of accepting lots having an excessive number of defectives. The OC curve illustrates how well a given sampling plan discriminates between good and bad lots. *Good* and *bad* are obviously relative terms, and a lot containing one percent defectives might be considered quite good in one instance and very poor in another.

Problem 3. Through the sketching of operating characteristic curves, contrast the possible effectiveness of the following three sampling plans:

$$N = 500, \ n = 20, \ c = 0$$
$$N = 500, \ n = 20, \ c = 1$$
$$N = 500, \ n = 20, \ c = 2$$

Note that only the acceptance number differs from one plan to the next.

Using the binomial distribution as an approximation, and the tables in the appendix, we can first learn the probabilities of finding one or more, two or more, and three or more defectives in the sample at different levels of proportion defective. These correspond to the three sampling plans and the probabilities are compiled in Table 9.6. Also compiled in this same table are the probabilities of finding zero, one or less, and two or less defectives needed for sketching the three OC curves.

Probabilities Needed for the OC Curves of Figure 9.8 **TABLE 9.6**

Probability of

Proportion Defec- tive, p	One or More Defec- tives	Zero Defec- tives	Two or More Defec- tives	One or Less Defec- tive	Three or More Defec- tives	Two or Less Defec- tives
0	0	1.00	0	1.00	0	1.00
0.02	0.33	0.67	0.06	0.94	0.01	0.99
0.04	0.56	0.44	0.19	0.81	0.04	0.96
0.06	0.71	0.29	0.34	0.66	0.12	0.88
0.08	0.81	0.19	0.48	0.52	0.21	0.79
0.10	0.88	0.12	0.61	0.39	0.32	0.68
0.12	0.92	0.08	0.71	0.29	0.44	0.56
0.14	0.95	0.05	0.79	0.21	0.55	0.45
0.16	0.97	0.03	0.85	0.15	0.64	0.36
0.18	0.98	0.02	0.90	0.10	0.73	0.27
0.20	0.99	0.01	0.93	0.07	0.79	0.21

The relative shapes of the curves in Figure 9.8 are quite similar in that they are nearly parallel through their middle sections. In effect, if one increases the acceptance number, the OC curve slides to the right and is indicative of good lots which contain more defectives.

[1] In this and the next example, as well in as the problems at the end of the chapter, we have restricted our sample sizes to those tabulated in the cumulative binomial tables in the appendix.

FIGURE 9.8 The OC Curves of the Three Sampling Plans from Problem 3

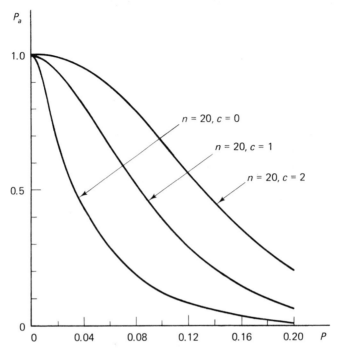

Problem 4. Through the sketching of OC curves, compare the following:

$$N = 500, \; n = 20, \; c = 2$$
$$N = 500, \; n = 10, \; c = 1$$

Note that the ratio of sample size to acceptance number is the same in each case.

Following the format of the previous example, we can develop Table 9.7. Once an acceptable proportion defective has been defined, the relative ability of a sampling plan to discriminate between lots containing more or fewer defectives will, in large measure, depend on the sample size. This is evident in this problem. Note that the OC curves of Figure 9.9 describe sampling plans with the same acceptance number to sample size ratio of one to ten. As the sample size increases, the OC curve becomes steeper. In general, this is desirable in a sampling plan, although the expense involved for this greater ability to discriminate is the cost of a larger sample size. As a matter of fact, the ideal discrimination of a vertical line is indicated in Figure 9.9 with a dashed line. This, however, can only be achieved with 100 percent inspection.

SEQUENTIAL DECISIONS

With some reflection, the reader can no doubt recall decision situations which could appropriately be termed decisions of a sequential nature. For

Proportion Defective, p	At n = 20, c = 2, Probability of		At n = 10, c = 1, Probability of	
	Three or More Defectives	Two or Less Defectives	Two or More Defectives	One or Less Defective
0	0	1.00	0	1.00
0.04	0.04	0.96	0.06	0.94
0.08	0.21	0.79	0.19	0.81
0.12	0.44	0.56	0.34	0.66
0.16	0.64	0.36	0.49	0.51
0.20	0.79	0.21	0.62	0.38
0.24	0.89	0.11	0.73	0.27
0.28	0.95	0.05	0.82	0.18
0.32	0.98	0.02	0.88	0.12

example, one might plan a family outing for the weekend based on mild weather on Monday. As the weekend approaches, one's confidence in the success of the outing fluctuates with the weather forecast from day to day. One might therefore revise one's *subjective evaluation of the chance for success* as more (or more recent) information is available concerning the

The OC Curves of the Two Sampling Plans from Problem 2 **FIGURE 9.9**

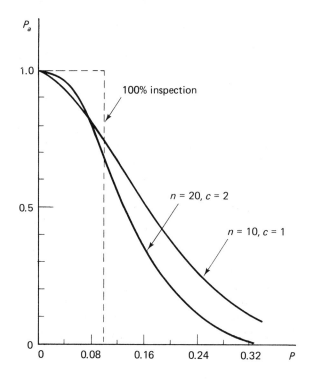

weather. Other examples of sequential decisions can be readily found in retail businesses. The amount of seasonal product A to order for 1976 might depend on the amount of product A sold in 1975, and/or 1974, and/or 1973, and so forth. Another example is what form of advertising to use in the future based on the measured success of various advertising media used in the past. In the field of quality control, the whole area of sampling is concerned with sequential decisions. For example, if a sample of 5 units is taken from some production machine, then subsequent actions taken in regard to the production machine might very well depend on whether 0, 1, 2, 3, 4, or 5 defective units were found in the sample of 5 units taken.

In this section, the technique of *decision tree* representation and the logic of Bayes' Theorem will be applied to sequential decisions under risk.

Decision Trees

The term *decision tree* is given to a particular graphical representation of a decision situation whereby a sequence of decisions is relevant. Before presenting the graphic technique and a solution procedure, it is necessary to define certain symbolism. Let

Δ	= a decision point, which will be labeled D_i for the ith decision point in the tree.
Δ—	= a branch emanating from a decision point, representing an alternative that can be chosen at this point.
$\bigcirc$	= a fork (or node) in the tree where chance events influence the outcomes of an alternative choice.
$\bigcirc$—	= a branch representing a probabilistic outcome for a given alternative. The notation $(\theta;p)$ represents an outcome θ, having an associated value V, which occurs with probability p. It is assumed that branches emanating from a fork in the tree represent mutually exclusive and collectively exhaustive outcomes such that the probabilities sum to 1.0.
$\boxed{V}$	= a value associated with a particular outcome (branch).

In Figure 9.10, a generalized decision tree for a simple sequential decision problem is presented. The sequential decision problem depicted involves two decision points, D_1 and D_2. If alternative a_1 is chosen, it can have two outcomes, θ_1 and θ_2. If θ_1 occurs, then a decision, D_2, is required. If alternative a_{11} is chosen, there can be the two outcomes θ_{111} and θ_{112}. If alternative a_{12} is chosen at D_2, there can be the two outcomes θ_{121} and θ_{122}. For each branch in the tree there is an associated value. For example, if alternative a_1 is chosen *and* outcome θ_1 occurs *and* alternative a_{11} is chosen *and* outcome θ_{111} occurs, then value V_{111} results with the conditional probability p_{111}. The first decision to be made is at D_1, and if alternative a_1 is chosen, then a second decision is required at D_2. The ultimate question to answer is which alternative to chose at D_1.

We shall adopt the criterion of *maximizing expected gain or minimizing expected loss* as a principle of choice at each decision point. The solution procedure advocated is designed to reach the best decision at the decision point (or points) most distant from the base of the tree (the first decision). Then replace the most distant decision point with the best expected value,

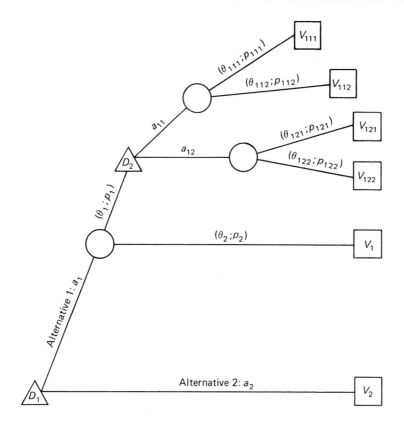

and thus work backwards through decision points until the best decision is made at the first decision point, D_1. In order to illustrate the solution procedure, let us again consider the decision tree of Figure 9.10 and assume all the values are gains. The procedure follows:

1. At decision point D_2, calculate the expected gains for a_{11} and a_{12}. That is,

$$E(a_{11}) = p_{111} V_{111} + p_{112} V_{112}, \text{ and}$$

$$E(a_{12}) = p_{121} V_{121} + p_{122} V_{122}.$$

If $E(a_{11}) > E(a_{12})$, then alternative a_{11} is chosen as best at D_2.

2. Replace D_2 with $E(a_{11})$ and the new reduced decision tree becomes as shown in Figure 9.11.

3. Calculate the expected gains for alternatives a_1 and a_2. That is,

$$E(a_1) = p_1 E(a_{11}) + p_2 V_1, \text{ and}$$

$$E(a_2) = V_2 \text{ (a certain event with } p = 1.0).$$

FIGURE 9.11   The Reduced Decision Tree for Figure 9.10

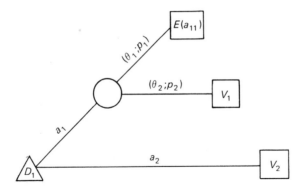

If $E(a_1) > E(a_2)$, alternative a_1 is chosen as best at decision point D_1. If $E(a_2) > E(a_1)$, then a_2 would be chosen. And if $E(a_2) = E(a_1)$, then one would be indifferent between the choice of a_1 and a_2.

Given that $E(a_1) > E(a_2)$ from step (3) above, the optimal sequence of decisions is to choose a_1 at D_1 and then choose a_{11} later on if outcome θ_1 does occur.

An Example: Quality Inspection

Problem Statement.   Assume that lots of solid-fuel rocket engines are received from a manufacturer. They may be tested only by actually firing a sample of a few engines. Suppose that it is known in advance that the engines will come from a process which is either producing an 8 percent defective product or one which is producing a 3 percent defective product. Let us further suppose that we have agreed with the manufacturer to take a sample of two engines from each lot for test firing. For purposes of analysis, the cost of testing an engine is taken to be $1,000, the cost of accepting a defective engine is $15,000, and the cost of rejecting a good engine is $1,000.

Each lot consists of fifty engines, and before any testing of engines is done, we assume that the 8 percent or 3 percent defective product is equally likely. That is,

$p(8\%$ defective lot$) = 0.50$, and

$p(3\%$ defective lot$) = 0.50$.

Problem Analysis.   The first decision which confronts us is whether to accept a lot without sampling or to take a sample of two. It is assumed that there is no reason to reject a lot if sampling is not done. Then if a sample of two is taken, there could be three outcomes. Namely, there could be zero, one, or two defective engines in the sample of two engines. For each of these outcomes, the decision of whether to accept the lot or reject the lot would arise. A decision tree representation of this problem (without probabilities and values assigned) is given in Figure 9.12.

Determination of the Value of the Outcomes.   Let us define:

A Decision Tree for the Quality Inspection Example **FIGURE 9.12**

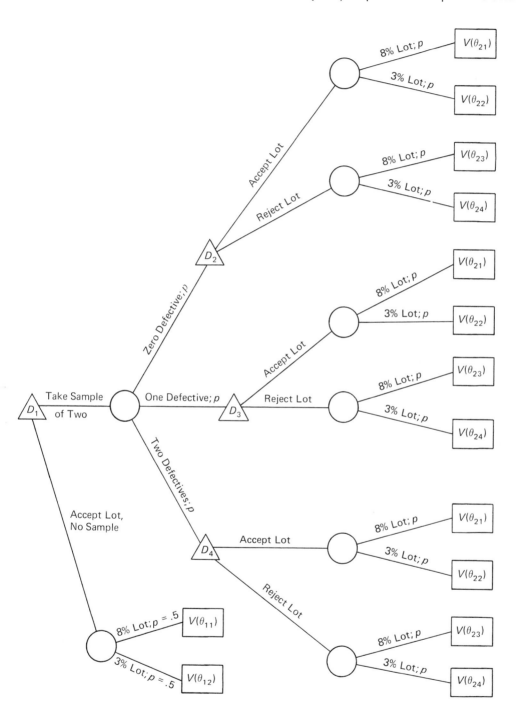

183

a_1 = the alternative "accept a lot without sampling"

$V(\theta_{11})$ = the expected cost of accepting a lot that is 8% defective

= \$15,000/defective unit (.08 × 50 units/lot)

= \$60,000

$V(\theta_{12})$ = the expected cost of accepting a lot that is 3% defective

= \$15,000 (.03 × 50)

= \$22,500

a_2 = the alternative "take a sample of two"

$V(\theta_{21})$ = the expected cost of accepting a lot that is 8% defective, given that a sample of two is taken

= $V(\theta_{11})$ + the cost of sampling

= \$60,000 + 2 (\$1,000) = \$62,000

$V(\theta_{22})$ = the expected cost of accepting a lot that is 3% defective, given that a sample of two is taken

= $V(\theta_{12})$ + the cost of sampling

= \$22,500 + 2 (\$1,000) = \$24,500

$V(\theta_{23})$ = the expected cost of rejecting a lot that is 8% defective, given that a sample of two is taken

= \$1,000/nondefective unit × (expected number of nondefective units) + sampling costs

= \$1,000 (.92 × 50) + \$2,000 = \$48,000

$V(\theta_{24})$ = the expected cost of rejecting a lot that is 3% defective, given that a sample of two is taken

= \$1,000 (.97 × 50) + \$2,000 = \$50,500

Determination of the Probabilities of the Outcomes. Although the prior probabilities of an 8 percent defective lot and a 3 percent defective lot were subjectively assigned to be 0.50 in each case, the probabilities of 0, 1, and 2 defective in a sample of size two may be objectively determined from the binomial probability distribution. For each of the four outcomes following decision points D_2, D_3, and D_4, objective conditional probabilities may be determined by means of Bayes' Theorem presented in Chapter 4.

These probabilities are calculated in the appendix, but let it be sufficient in this example to merely enter the probabilities as shown in the completed decision tree of Figure 9.13.

Solution to the Problem. Using a principle of minimizing expected cost, we arrive at the best decisions at D_2, D_3, and D_4.

For D_2,

$$E(\text{cost of accept}|0\text{ defectives}) = 0.473(\$62,000) + 0.527(\$24,500)$$

$$= \$42,237.50$$

$$E(\text{cost of reject}|0\text{ defectives}) = 0.473(\$48,000) + 0.527(\$50,500)$$

$$= \$49,317.50$$

Thus, the best decision at D_2 is to accept the lot.

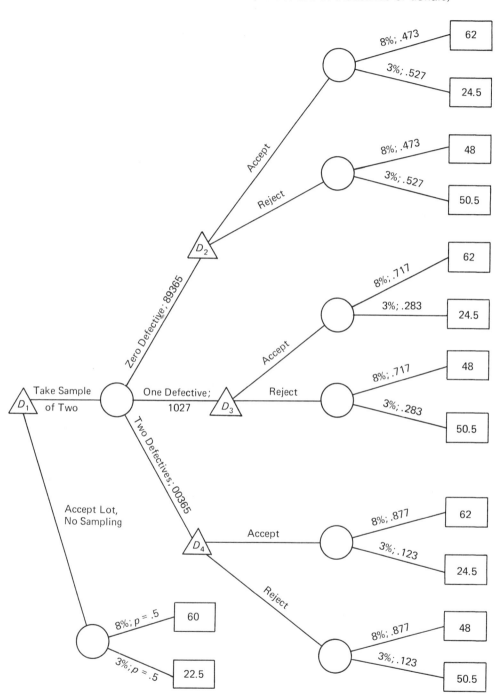

For D_3,

$$E(\text{accept}|\text{one defective}) = 0.717(\$62,000) + 0.283(\$24,500)$$

$$= \$51,387.50$$

$$E(\text{reject}|\text{one defective}) = 0.717(\$48,000) + 0.283(\$50,500)$$

$$= \$48,707.50$$

Thus, the best decision at D_3 is to reject the lot.

For D_4,

$$E(\text{accept}|\text{two defectives}) = 0.877(\$62,000) + 0.123(\$24,500)$$

$$= \$57,387.50$$

$$E(\text{reject}|\text{two defectives}) = 0.877(\$48,000) + 0.123(\$50,500)$$

$$= \$48,307.50$$

Thus, the best decision at D_4 is to reject the lot.

The decision points D_2, D_3, and D_4 are then replaced by their "best" values to yield the reduced decision tree in Figure 9.14 (values are times $1,000).

Finally we calculate the best decision at D_1 by:

$$E(\text{cost of take sample}) = 0.89365(\$42,237.50) + 0.1027(\$48,707.50)$$

$$+ 0.00365(\$48,307.50)$$

$$= \$42,920$$

$$E(\text{cost of not sample}) = 0.5(\$60,000) + 0.5(\$22,500)$$

$$= \$41,250$$

FIGURE 9.14 Reduced Decision Tree

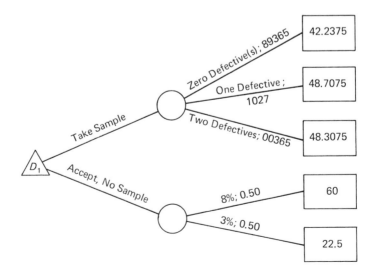

Since $41,250 is less than $42,920, then the best decision is to accept the lot without sampling.

This example has been a rather lengthy one but thus shows the tedium involved in even small decision tree problems. If the example problem were enriched by considering other futures such as 4 percent, 5 percent, 6 percent, and 7 percent defective lots and sample sizes other than two, it should be obvious to the reader that calculations become very burdensome. However, graphically portraying a sequential decision problem in this fashion could prove of considerable benefit to the decision maker even though all the probabilities and values in the decision tree are not readily determined. The simple portrayal of the problem may reveal unimportant branches, suggest the need for obtaining data, and so on. The tedium of calculation may also be reduced in real world problems because it may be necessary to assign subjective probabilities rather than calculate objective probabilities.

Expected Value of Sample Information

In the preceding example problem concerning the decision to accept a lot without sampling or to take a sample of two, the decision was to accept without sampling. The decision was based on an expected cost of $42,920 for sampling and an expected cost of $41,250 for not sampling. Recalling that the cost of sampling was $1,000 per unit sampled, the question naturally arises as to what is the cost of sampling per unit which would make one indifferent between the choices. This question may be answered directly by equating:

$$E(\text{cost of not sample}) = E(\text{cost of take sample}) + \text{cost of sampling, or}$$

$$\$41,250 = (\$42,920 - 2(\$1,000)) + 2C, \text{ where}$$

$$C = \text{the cost per unit sampled}$$

Solving for C yields

$$C = (\$41,250 - \$40,920)/2$$

$$= \$165$$

Thus, if the cost of sampling a unit is greater than $165, one would choose to accept the lot of rocket engines without sampling and if $C < \$165$, then take a sample of two.

The above example leads to the general question of how much to pay for sample information in a decision under risk. In order to answer this question it will be necessary to develop certain definitions and first answer the question of how much to pay for perfect information.

Again using the preceding rocket engine inspection problem, let us recall the following items:

$p(8\% \text{ defective lot})$ = 0.50 = a prior probability
$p(3\% \text{ defective lot})$ = 0.50 = a prior probability

a_1 = the alternative "accept a lot without sampling," where
$V(\theta_{11})$ = the expected cost of accepting a lot that is 8% defective
= \$60,000, and
$V(\theta_{12})$ = the expected cost of accepting a lot that is 3% defective
= \$22,500

Thus, the *prior expected cost, PEC*, of accepting the lot without sampling and any further information is given by

$$PEC = E(a_1) = 0.50(\$60,000) + 0.50(\$22,500)$$

$$= \$41,250$$

Now, if the decision maker could receive perfect information from alternative a_2 (i.e., take a sample of two), how much would this be worth to him? We reason that, if the sample of two provided the certain information of an 8 percent defective lot, the decision maker would choose to reject the lot. This is so because the expected cost of rejecting an 8 percent defective lot is \$46,000 (\$48,000 − \$2,000 cost of sampling) versus the expected cost of accepting an 8 percent defective lot of \$60,000. If the perfect information was a 3 percent defective lot, then the decision maker would choose to accept the lot since the expected cost of acceptance is \$22,500 while the expected cost of rejecting is \$48,500 (\$50,500 − \$2,000 cost of sampling). However, before receiving it, the perfect information could be either the 3 percent or 8 percent defective report with prior probabilities of 0.50 for each report. The *expected cost, given perfect information, EC|PI*, is calculated as:

$$EC|PI = 0.50(\$46,000) + 0.50(\$22,500)$$

$$= \$34,250$$

One can now argue that the *expected value of perfect information, EVPI*, is the *prior expected cost* without any information minus the *expected cost, given perfect information*, or:

$$EVPI = PEC - EC|PI$$

$$= \$41,250 - \$34,250 = \$7,000$$

This figure of \$7,000 represents the maximum amount the decision maker should pay for perfect information.

Information is rarely perfect, however, and in the rocket engine problem the sample of two could merely reveal 0, 1, or 2 defective. Such information serves to revise the decision maker's prior beliefs about the probabilities of either an 8 percent or 3 percent defective lot but does not provide certain information. Thus, before the sample of two is taken, we wish to know the value of the sample information. In order to calculate this, it is only necessary to recall the expected cost of alternative a_2 (take sample of two) minus the cost of sampling. That is, $E(a_2)$ − cost of sampling = \$42,920 − \$2,000 = \$40,920.

Since the *prior expected cost, PEC,* without sampling was \$41,250 and the *expected cost, given sample information, EC|SI,* was \$40,920, then the *expected value of sample information, EVSI,* is \$41,250 − \$40,920 or \$330. For a sample of two, we recognize that this is the indifference cost of \$165 per sample calculated earlier. The summary statement for the *expected value of sample information* is:

$$EVSI = PEC - EC|SI$$

If one were concerned with profits rather than costs in a decision problem, then the above relationships would be modified to

1. expected value of perfect information = expected profit|perfect information − prior expected profit, or

$$EVPI = EP|PI - PEP$$

2. expected value of sample information = expected profit|sample information − prior expected profit, or

$$EVSI = EP|SI - PEP$$

QUESTIONS AND PROBLEMS

1. In Table 9.5 there were 83 G's.

2. What is the difference between a stable and an unstable pattern of variation?

3. What is meant by *measurement by attributes? measurement by variables?*

4. What is the primary function of the $\bar{X}$ chart in relation to detecting unstable patterns of variation? the R chart?

5. What are the two types of control charts for attributes? Give an example of a process that might be controlled by each.

6. What does an operating characteristic curve illustrate?

7. Discuss the general relationship between the sample size and the form of an OC curve.

8. Samples of $n = 5$ were taken from a process for a period of time. The process average was estimated to be $\bar{X} = 0.0200$ inches and the process range was estimated as $\bar{R} = 0.0020$ inches. Specify the control limits for an $\bar{X}$ chart; an R chart.

9. Control charts by variables are to be established on the tensile strength in pounds of a yarn. Samples of five have been taken each hour for the past twenty hours. These were recorded as follows:

Hour

	1	2	3	4	5	6	7	8	9	10	11	12	13	14	15	16	17	18	19	20
	50	44	44	48	45	47	42	52	44	43	47	49	47	43	44	45	45	50	46	45
	50	46	44	52	46	44	46	46	46	44	45	42	51	46	43	47	45	49	47	44
	48	50	44	48	46	43	46	45	46	49	44	41	50	46	40	51	47	45	48	49
	42	47	47	48	48	40	48	42	46	47	42	46	48	48	40	48	47	47	46	43
	43	45	48	46	50	45	46	51	43	45	50	46	42	46	46	46	46	44	45	46

Construct the $\bar{X}$ and R Charts.

10. Sketch the OC curves for the sampling plans $c = 0$, $n = 15$, $N = 200$; $c = 1$, $n = 15$, $N = 200$; and $c = 2$, $n = 15$, $N = 200$.

11. Sketch the OC curves for the sampling plans $c = 1$, $n = 10$, $N = 1,000$; $c = 1$, $n = 20$, $N = 1,000$; and $c = 1$, $n = 50$, $N = 1,000$.

12. Assume you have two special dice. A green die has two surfaces marked head and four surfaces marked tail. A red die has five surfaces marked head and one surface marked tail. Further assume that a person proposes the following game. The person rolls these two dice (hidden from your view) and covers one die. He offers a $5 prize if the color of the uncovered die can be guessed. For purposes of illustration, assume there is no charge to you for playing the game. However, the person offers to provide the additional information of whether a head or tail is exposed on the uppermost surface of the uncovered die but will charge for this information.

A sequenced series of questions now follow about this game to illustrate Bayes' Theorem, the decision tree approach to a sequential decision situation, and the expected value of sample information. Some helpful symbolism and values are first given:

H_0 = the statement "the green die is uncovered"
H_1 = the statement "the red die is uncovered"
h = the report "a head is showing"
t = the report "a tail is showing"

Let:

$PR(H_0)$ = the prior probability (before any additional information) that the green die is uncovered = $1/2$

$PR(H_1)$ = the prior probability that the red die is uncovered = $1/2$

$P(h|H_0)$ = the likelihood (before the report) that the report from the person will be h, given that the green die is uncovered = $2/6 = 1/3$.

$P(t|H_0)$ = the likelihood that the report will be t, given that the red die is uncovered = $1 - P(h|H_0) = 1 - 2/6 = 2/3$.

$P(h|H_1)$ = $5/6$

$P(t|H_1)$ = $1/6$

$p(h)$ = the probability that a report of h will be given = $P(h|H_0) PR(H_0) + P(h|H_1) PR(H_1)$.

$p(t)$ = the probability that a report of t will be given = $P(t|H_0) PR(H_0) + P(t|H_1) PR(H_1)$.

$PO(H_0|h)$, $PO(H_1|h)$, $PO(H_0|t)$, and $PO(H_1|t)$ = the posterior probabilities (after additional information) that the green or red die is uncovered, given the information of h or t.

(a) Using Bayes' Theorem, determine the posterior probabilities. *Answers:*
$PO(H_0|h) = 2/7$, $PO(H_1|h) = 5/7$, $PO(H_0|t) = 4/5$, $PO(H_1|t) = 1/5$.

(b) Create a decision tree for this problem if the person charges $1.00 for the additional information of h or t (three decision nodes should result). Should you (1) buy the additional information, (2) not buy information and guess green die, or (3) not buy information and guess red die, based on a maximize expected profit principle of choice? *Answer:* Buy the additional information with an expected profit of $33/12$ versus an expected profit of $30/12$ otherwise.

(c) Determine the expected profit given sample information ($EP|SI$).

(d) Determine the expected value of sample information ($EVSI$).

13. After receiving somewhat unreliable information concerning enemy troop movement along a supply route, a military commander of an artillery battalion faces the following combat decision (assume the payoff values are loss units, arbitrarily chosen):

Alternatives \ Futures	$p_1 = 0.7$ S_1 = Troop Movement	$p_2 = 0.3$ S_2 = No Troop Movement
A_1 = Bombard Supply Route	0	4
A_2 = Not Bombard Supply Route	12	0

The commander can choose between A_1 and A_2 without additional information or he can send out a reconnaissance plane for additional information. If the plane is sent out, he reasons the mutually exclusive and collectively exhaustive outcomes of the flight are:

Outcome O_1: the plane is shot down, with a loss of 3 units.

Outcome O_2: the plane returns with negative information about troop movement, with a loss of 0.2 units.

Outcome O_3: the plane returns safely with a report of suspicious activity, with a loss of 0.2 units.

The commander assigns the following subjective conditional probabilities to these outcomes:

$P(O_1|S_1) = 0.4$; $P(O_1|S_2) = 0.2$

$P(O_2|S_1) = 0.1$; $P(O_2|S_2) = 0.8$

$P(O_3|S_1) = 0.5$; $P(O_3|S_2) = 0.0$

(a) Determine the posterior probabilities.

(b) Create a decision tree for this problem.

(c) Using the minimizing expected loss principle of choice, what action should the commander take?

(d) What is the expected value of sample information ($EVSI$) in this problem?

BIBLIOGRAPHY

DODGE, H. F., AND ROMIG, H. G. *Sampling Inspection Tables—Single and Double Sampling.* New York: John Wiley & Sons, Inc., 1959.

DUNCAN, ACHESON J. *Quality Control and Industrial Statistics.* Homewood, Ill.: Richard D. Irwin, Inc., 1965.

FEIGENBAUM, A. V. *Total Quality Control.* New York: McGraw-Hill Book Company, Inc., 1961.

GRANT, EUGENE I., AND LEAVENWORTH, RICHARD S. *Statistical Quality Control.* New York: McGraw-Hill Book Company, Inc., 1972.

JURAN, J. M., AND GRYNA, FRANK M., JR. *Quality Planning and Analysis.* New York: McGraw-Hill Book Company, Inc., 1970.

MORRIS, WILLIAM T. *Analysis of Management Decisions,* rev. ed. Homewood, Ill.: Richard D. Irwin, Inc., 1964.

MORRIS, WILLIAM T. *Management Decisions: A Bayesian Introduction.* Englewood Cliffs, N.J.: Prentice-Hall, Inc., 1968.

SHEWHART, W. A. *Economic Control of Quality of Manufactured Product.* Princeton, N.J.: Van Nostrand Reinhold Company, Inc., 1931.

Inventory models I

The inventory process will pose a dilemma and raise some problems for practically every business firm. For example, the highway service station should stock those automotive requirements most likely to be needed by passing motorists, including gasoline, diesel fuel, motor oil and possibly kerosene. In addition it would be advantageous to stock a number of different sizes and types of tires, batteries, seatcovers, tailpipes, and mufflers, as

193

well as numerous other smaller items. At the very least, failure to have a requested item will result in a lost sale, and there is the added possibility that the customer will not return and future sales will also be lost. On the other hand, insuring that all possible customer requirements will be met could require an extensive and even prohibitive investment of space and money in the inventory process. Thus, our service station owner must ask the question: "What and how much should be maintained in inventory?"

The sheer size of the inventory process can be perceived from the fact that in 1972 the total worth of inventories in the United States was estimated to be about $178 billion—nearly $3,000 for each household. Even financing this inventory investment at a prime rate of interest would amount to over $9 billion a year, and these figures do not include inventories which are maintained for the general welfare. As a result, many companies require outside funding to finance their inventories. The point is simple—to maintain items in inventory is an expensive operation and one which must be dealt with analytically.

INVENTORY OPERATIONS

Both wholesale and retail business firms ordinarily establish and maintain inventories to meet the possible demands of the customer. In a sense, these firms *are* inventory systems. In addition, the manufacturing firm must stock raw materials and component parts in order to meet the demands of the production process. Inventory systems exist in many different sizes, shapes, and forms to meet a variety of demands. Even a hospital blood bank functions in a support capacity within the hospital and is another example of an inventory system. Units of the different blood types are maintained as insurance against possible future demand. The accident victim requiring a transfusion in order to stay alive certainly profits from this insurance.

The Inventory System

The answers to such questions as "What should be stocked?" "How many?" "When should replenishments be effected?" "In what amounts?" and others will form the basis for an inventory system. For our purposes, we will begin with the assumption that we have identified those items that will be maintained in inventory. Either the production process is known to require these items or it is likely that a customer will request them; in either case the expected demand is necessary for the success of the firm.

An inventory system functions as a reservoir between a procurement source and a demand. This can be seen in Figure 10.1. It serves as a buffer between a demand, which is likely to be a continuing drain on the system over an extended period of time, and a procurement action, which is likely to be more sporadic or intermittent. For example, a shipment of shoes may be received into a store once or twice a month. These are then sold on a daily and even hourly basis. When the stock level drops to a predetermined point, another order is placed and later received. Occasionally, this buffer system works in reverse—gradually building up, and then being released

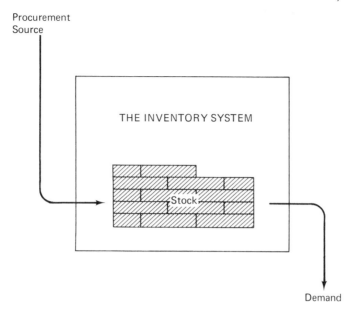

in a surge, as is often the case with the blood bank. Donors who arrive at the hospital on a daily basis provide the blood bank's input, which builds up until there is the demand of an accident victim who requires ten or a dozen pints of blood to stay alive during surgery.

The demand for a given item requires that some procurement action **Fundamental** be initiated to replenish the inventory of that item. As units are withdrawn, **Decisions** a point will be reached at which replenishment action must be initiated. This point is called the *reorder point, R.* When the inventory reaches or falls below the reorder point, replenishment is initiated, usually in the form of an order placed for a supply of units which will raise the inventory level when it arrives. The quantity of units requested on this order is called the *order quantity, Q.* The inventory system is managed by controlling the reorder point and the order quantity. That is, the fundamental decisions in inventory management are:

1. when to replenish the inventory supply (the reorder point—R) and
2. by how much it should be replenished (the order quantity—Q).

The basic system parameter which is the driving force on the inventory **System** system is the *demand, D,* for a product. This is an item-dependent parameter **Parameters** with a rate usually expressed as units per period. The period may be a year, month, or week depending on the inventory situation being studied. As we have already noted, the inventory system may exist to meet demand at many levels—retail, wholesale, or any other level within the production-distribution process. In any case, the characteristics of demand will be dependent on the nature of the demand source.

The most basic demand pattern is classified as *deterministic* and will be used for all cases in this chapter. In this special case, the *future demand* for a particular item *can be predicted with certainty*. At best this is an approximation of reality, although the demand established by a production line might be quite predictable. Generally, future demand is estimated with statistical techniques and is a random variable. Random demand patterns will be considered in Chapter 11.

Deterministic demand situations will allow us to develop an operating policy that will eliminate the possibility of the occurrence of an out-of-stock condition. However, if we can predict demand only in a probabilistic sense, the resulting operating policy will require safety stock to guard against an excessive stockout should a period of high demand occur.

Obviously the demand for a product will influence the size of the inventory of that product which is maintained. In a retail system the demand occurs whenever an attempt to purchase the item occurs. It is wise to recognize the distinction between a demand and a sale which occurs only when the customer successively attempts to purchase the item. If, for example, a customer attempts to purchase an item but none is available, then a demand has occurred, but a sale has not. The customer in this case may take his business elsewhere in which case the sale is lost. On the other hand, the customer may be willing to wait until the stock is replenished to purchase the item in which case the demand is said to be back ordered.

Once the reorder point has been reached and an order has been placed we must wait until items arrive to replenish the stock. The amount of time we wait is called *procurement lead time, T,* or simply lead time. Formally stated this is the elapsed time between the initiation of an order and the receipt of replenishment stock. Its basic dimensions are in periods or fractions of periods. Furthermore it is a parameter that is both item-dependent and supplier-dependent. For example, we can imagine a supplier saying, "If you want 3/4″ galvanized elbows it will take you six weeks." In this case we may wish to investigate the procurement lead time of another vendor in an attempt to receive faster service.

As was the case with demand, lead time is also either deterministic or probabilistic. Although the discussion of inventory systems with probabilistic lead time is far beyond the scope of this text, we must remember that the deterministic lead time case is usually an approximation of reality.

In every inventory system the *replenishment rate, p,* must be considered. This parameter is both item-dependent and supplier-dependent and the rate is expressed in units per period. The parameter describes just how units are added to inventory—for example, item by item over some extended number of periods or in one complete lot. When the replenishment source is an external supplier, it is likely that the entire order will be delivered at once and the replenishment rate is infinite. On the other hand, if the supplier is an internal production operation, then the rate of replenishment is more likely to be finite. This should be attributed to the fact that the item accumulates as it is made. Source- or supplier-dependency for this parameter is reasonably obvious and may in fact play an important factor in the choice of a supplier.

In order to develop the decision rules for managing the inventory system, it is necessary to consider the costs involved. The purpose of this section is to identify the component cost parameters and to discuss their makeup. The ultimate decision rules which are developed will be based on the criteria of operating the inventory system at a minimum cost. Thus, it is necessary to discuss which cost parameters must be evaluated in the process.

The first cost parameter we should consider is the *item cost*, C_I. This is the price of the item in dollars per unit. The parameter is dependent on the item as well as the procurement or production source of the item. Each vendor operates in a unique environment and produces varying quantities of product mixes for different customers. As a result, the quoted unit price may vary from one vendor to another. Further, it is rather unlikely that all vendors will quote an identical price discount schedule. In a manufacturing situation the item cost involves summation of the cost elements of direct labor, direct material, and factory burden elements. Many times in a manufacturing situation, a learning curve effect exists which will result in a significant reduction in the number of direct labor hours per unit as the number of units produced increases. This effect tends to reduce the manufactured item cost in a manner analogous to the price discount schedule for a purchase alternative. For example, if the direct labor hours are twenty per unit in a given situation for the first one hundred units, it is not unlikely to suspect that these direct labor hours will be reduced to say sixteen per unit for the second one hundred items produced, twelve per unit for the next one hundred items produced and so on to some normal lower limit. The learning curve effects in a manufacturing situation are very important to consider.

The next cost parameter to be considered is the *procurement cost*, C_P, which is the combination of those cost elements arriving from the series of activities beginning with the initiation of procurement action and ending with the receipt of replenishment stock. This is a parameter which depends upon both the item as well as the source and has the dimension of dollars per procurement.

When items are purchased, procurement cost involves expenses for paper work preparation, communication, receiving, vendor payment, as well as certain overhead items regarding these activities. Procurement costs for manufacturing activities would be composed of the elements for production planning, production set-up, scheduling, and other costs resulting from those activities required during the initiation of the manufacturing activities. Generally, the major component of this cost parameter arrives from salary.

The most significant cost parameter in the inventory system is known as the *inventory holding cost*, C_H, which is calculated as a function of the number of units on hand and the time duration for which these items are held. This is a cost parameter with dimension of dollars per period.

The holding cost, also known as the carrying cost, is made up of various out-of-pocket expenses such as insurance, obsolescence, taxes, warehouse rental, light, heat, and maintenance. Additionally, the capital invested in inventory is therefore unavailable for other investment opportunities and this foregone interest represents another cost of carrying inventory. Many of these costs are a function of maximum inventory levels while others may depend on average levels. Still others, such as the cost of capital investment, depend on the value of inventory during a given period of time. Many times the inventory carrying charges are expressed as a percentage of the total inventory investment for a year.

The final cost parameter which we will consider in this chapter is the *shortage cost*, C_S, which is the penalty incurred for being unable to meet a demand when it occurs. This cost parameter does not depend on the source of replenishment but on the item. Generally speaking, the specific penalty will depend on the nature of the demand. In cases where the demand is from a customer of the retail establishment, the shortage condition may result in a cost relatively small compared with the item cost. If, on the other hand, the demand arises in a manufacturing activity, the penalty cost for shortage may be extremely high relative to the cost of the item, because the entire manufacturing activity would necessarily have to wait for the item which is short.

A MODEL FOR INVENTORY SYSTEMS

Remember that the basic objective of an inventory system is to meet the demand for the item at a minimum cost. This involves deciding when to procure and how much to procure, in addition to deciding from what source to procure an item. The assignment of values to the decision variables is accomplished by formulating and manipulating a model of the system. Formulation of a mathematical model requires the construction of an *effectiveness function* which contains two types of variables. An effectiveness function is a mathematical statement which links a measure of effectiveness with variables under the control of the decision maker and variables not under control of the decision maker. The function provides the means whereby controllable variables can be evaluated while also considering the effect of the uncontrollable parameters. For the inventory process, the effectiveness function is equivalent to the total system cost. *Optimizing* the effectiveness function means here to find the minimum total system cost.

For clarity in this chapter it will be helpful to define two terms regarding time elements involved in the inventory process:

1. *Period* is the element of time between successive reviews of the stock position. This is generally a day but it may be any other time unit selected for the inventory system.
2. A *cycle* is the number of periods occurring between successive procurement actions.

The inventory system we shall consider here is that of a single item maintained to supply a known and predictable demand. When the number of units on hand is depleted to a specific level, replenishment is initiated which will procure a reorder quantity instantaneously from a single source. Our objective will be to determine the reorder point and the order quantity, taking into account the system and cost parameters so that the sum of all the costs associated with this process will be minimum. As we mentioned earlier, we assume that the demand rate as well as the procurement lead time are deterministic.

In this system it is assumed that the replenishment rate for the inventory is infinite in that the total quantity ordered is delivered at one time. Furthermore, it is to be assumed that the shortage cost per unit short per period is also infinite. In this case then the system must never be out of stock. Figure 10.2 illustrates the inventory activity for the system.

It is well to try to visualize some systems that might exist in inventory management in which an infinite shortage cost is not unrealistic. Certainly in hospital management, infinite shortage costs do exist for all practical purposes. Among these systems would be the life support systems of blood and oxygen. Shortage costs in this situation could be considered infinite due to the potential loss of life resulting from a shortage.

Inventory situations in industry are not difficult to envision when near-infinite shortage costs exist. Among these is the shortage of raw materials fundamental to a production operation. Shortages like these result in the loss of production and plant operation and although obviously not infinite, costs would be far too great to allow shortages to occur.

In our situation when shortage cost is infinite, the total variable cost per year will consist of procurement cost per year and holding cost per year. Trading off these two costs will provide us the means to develop optimal strategies. Item cost per year, while of interest, will not directly affect operating strategy in this case, as will be seen later. Generally, item cost bears consideration when a choice of vendor or supplier exists. Item cost often plays the major role in the determination of a vendor.

The total system cost per year, TC, is represented below as the aggregate of item cost, IC, procurement cost, PC, and holding cost, HC. That is,

$$TC = IC + PC + HC$$

The item cost per year will be the item cost per unit of product multiplied by the demand for that item.

$$IC = C_I D = \text{cost/unit} \times \text{unit/year} = \text{cost/year}$$

The procurement cost for the year will be obtained by recognizing that N is the time needed for Q units of demand for a product. Demand rate per year is uniformly distributed throughout the year. Therefore,

FIGURE 10.2 Simple Inventory System: Instantaneous Replacement—Infinite Shortage Cost

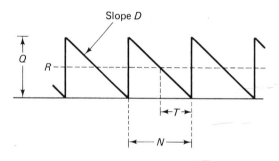

$$N = \frac{Q}{D} = \frac{\text{units}}{\text{units}/\text{year}} = \text{year}$$

Procurement cost per year is equal to procurement cost per procurement divided by the number of years per inventory cycle, or

$$PC = \frac{C_P}{N} = \frac{\text{cost}}{\text{year}}$$

Substituting for N from above, we get

$$PC = \frac{C_P}{Q/D}$$

$$= \frac{C_P D}{Q} = \frac{\text{cost} \times \text{units}/\text{year}}{\text{units}} = \text{cost}/\text{year}$$

In order to assess the holding cost per year we need to recognize that in this case of constant demand average on-hand inventory is $Q/2$. Multiplying this average inventory by the number of years per inventory cycle will give us the total number of unit-years of stock on hand during the cycle, or

$$I = \frac{NQ}{2}$$

Substituting for N, we get

$$I = \left(\frac{Q}{D}\right)\left(\frac{Q}{2}\right) = \frac{Q^2}{2D} = \frac{\text{units} \times \text{units}}{\text{units}/\text{year}} = \text{unit-years}$$

Now holding cost per year will be cost per unit held per year times average inventory during the year, or

$$HC = \frac{C_H I}{N}$$

$$= \frac{C_H Q}{2} = (\text{cost/unit/year})(\text{unit}) = \frac{\text{cost}}{\text{year}}$$

The total annual cost is

$$TC = C_I D + \frac{C_P D}{Q} + \frac{C_H Q}{2}$$

Problem 1. An aircraft manufacturer orders its engines from a supplier at a cost of $10,000 per engine. The anticipated annual demand for these is 1,000. Due to an automated ordering system, procurement or ordering cost has been reduced to $10 per procurement. However, the holding cost is estimated to be $200/unit/year. Graph the two major cost components based on varying order quantities. **Some Examples**

Table 10.1 shows the various cost components for increasing values of Q. Note that when $Q = 10$ the total annual cost is a minimum. Similarly, upon examination of Figure 10.3, which shows graphically the cost components, the minimum total cost point is achieved when holding cost equals procurement cost. Is this to be expected? As a matter of fact it is accidental that the ordering cost equals the holding cost at the minimum total cost, or the point of optimality. What is relevant is that incremental ordering cost and incremental holding cost are equal and balance each other at optimality.

Cost Components (Excluding Item Cost) **TABLE 10.1**

Q	Ordering Cost	Holding Cost	Total Cost
0	$ 0	0	
1	10,000.00	100.00	10,100.00
2	5,000.00	200.00	5,200.00
3	3,333.33	300.00	3,633.33
4	2,500.00	400.00	2,900.00
5	2,000.00	500.00	2,500.00
6	1,666.67	600.00	2,266.67
7	1,428.57	700.00	2,128.57
8	1,250.00	800.00	2,050.00
9	1,111.11	900.00	2,011.11
*10	**1,000.00**	**1,000.00**	**2,000.00**
11	909.09	1,100.00	2,009.09
12	833.33	1,200.00	2,033.33
13	769.23	1,300.00	2,069.23
14	714.29	1,400.00	2,114.29
15	666.67	1,500.00	2,166.67

FIGURE 10.3 The Cost Curves for the Data of Table 10.1

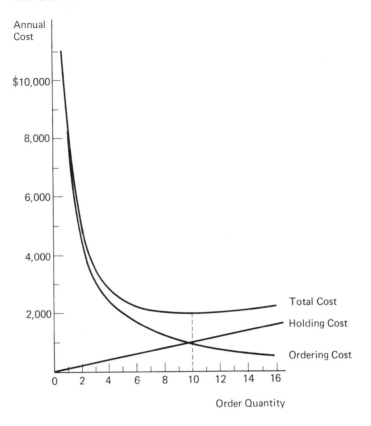

Without developing the accompanying logic, it can be stated that the optimal order quantity can be ascertained through equating component costs:

$$\frac{C_P D}{Q} = \frac{C_H Q}{2}$$

Collecting terms we get

$$Q^2 = \frac{2C_P D}{C_H}$$

$$Q^* = \sqrt{\frac{2C_P D}{C_H}}$$

Here Q^* means the optimal value of Q. This result is derived using differential calculus. From the previous example,

$$Q^* = \sqrt{\frac{2 \times (\$10/\text{procurement}) \times (1{,}000 \text{ units}/\text{year})}{(\$200/\text{unit}/\text{year})}}$$

$$Q^* = 10$$

This agrees with both previous calculations.

Now let us turn our attention to a determination of the optimal reorder point. From Figure 10.2 we see that the lead time, T, is the time needed to receive replenishment stock. Remember that in this basic case we have assumed T to be zero (instantaneous replenishment). Therefore, the reorder point, R, must also be zero. What this says is simply that if you can get items from your supplier instantaneously, then you need to order more *only* when your stock has been depleted to zero. Admittedly, this is not very realistic and we shall soon relax the assumption.

How many times during the year will we need to order? This can be found by dividing the optimal order quantity into the total number of units demanded, or

number of orders placed per year $= D/Q^*$

In our simple example,

orders $= 1,000/10$

$= 100$

Figure 10.4 illustrates the simplified version of the inventory geometry for this case.

Inventory Geometry for the Simplest Case   **FIGURE 10.4**

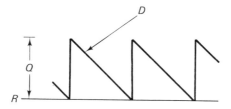

Problem 2. A small company produces high quality electric motors. These motors are used primarily for servo-mechanisms and the company is the sole-source supplier for several other companies. Present figures show that the item costs the company $500 to make. They sell the item for $750. One particular buyer purchases 300 of these motors per year. For that buyer it is assumed that this company can deliver instantaneously. The company which is buying the product says it costs them $1,000 for each order placed and $20/unit/year for each motor kept. What is the optimal number of orders the company should place each year? In this example,

$C_I = \$ \ 750.$
$D = \ \ \ \ 300.$
$C_P = \$1,000.$
$C_H = \$ \ \ \ 20.$

Therefore,

$$Q^* = \sqrt{\frac{2C_P D}{C_H}} = \sqrt{\frac{2(1,000)(300)}{20}} = \sqrt{30,000}$$

$$Q^* = 173.2 \text{ units}$$

Now the optimal number of orders which should be placed each year can be determined by the formula,

$$\text{orders} = D/Q^*$$

$$= \frac{300}{173.2}$$

$$= 1 + \frac{126.8}{173.2} = 2 \text{ orders}$$

Because this is not an integer result, we should round off.

In this example only two orders were placed, because of the very high procurement cost. Had this cost parameter been less, it probably would have been more advantageous to order more frequently. What is the average on-hand inventory level? What would have happened if the company in question had only enough space to store 125 units in the warehouse? Can you speculate about what the best operating policy would have been in this case?

A Modification
Instead of instantaneous replenishment with zero lead time, let us now develop the conditions for a constant but nonzero lead time. In this case we will say it always takes exactly T time units to receive an order once it is placed. All other conditions are exactly as before. Refer to Figure 10.2 again and note that T is that amount of time required to deplete the inventory from a level, R, to zero. At this time another order is received raising the on-hand inventory level to Q units again.

The question we must ask is, "When should I place an order?" This is relatively simple when we remember that demand is known and constant. Therefore, if it takes T time units to receive an order, then the units consumed during that time will be DT. For example, if demand is 1,200 units a year and lead time is one month (1/12 of a year), then *lead time demand* is 1,200 (1/12) or 100 units. Thus, in this case the reorder point is 100 units. So the inventory manager should place his order each time the inventory level reaches 100 units.

A SECOND MODEL

In the previous section, we assumed that the cost of incurring an out-of-stock condition was infinite. This assumption created a system in which the operating policy would never allow an out-of-stock condition to occur. There are many cases in practice which clearly do not operate under this assumption. In this section we will develop the operating policy for systems with a finite stockout cost. We will see that for these systems it may well be economically advisable to allow a stockout condition to occur.

When a stockout condition occurs two possibilities exist: the item can be back ordered and the demand will be satisfied at a later date, or the demand can be lost forever to the system. The first case is the *back order case* and will be treated here. The second case is called the *lost sales case.*

The back order case is very common. How many times have you heard, "I don't have it here now but expect it here with my order on Wednesday," or "I'm sorry we're out of that item now but we have back ordered it." In these cases, if the buyer chooses to return to this source for satisfaction, a time back order condition exists. If the sale is lost—that is, if the demand is not satisfied—then the model is in fact a lost sales case.

For systems in which stockout conditions exist, the total system cost equation must be modified by adding a component for the stockout cost. Thus,

$$TC = IC + PC + HC + SC$$

In this section we will develop the cost parameters for the stockout component. Figure 10.5 shows the inventory geometry for this case.

Once again we will develop the operating policy of when and how much to order in an attempt to minimize the total system cost. In the previous section we based the reorder point decision on units on-hand. This on-hand inventory, often called *inventory level,* is now going to be a deceiving basis for the decision to place an order. Let us analyze what might happen if we were to use this intuitive approach for reorder point. Suppose the operating policy is to order fifty units whenever the inventory level falls to twenty

The Stockout Condition   **FIGURE 10.5**

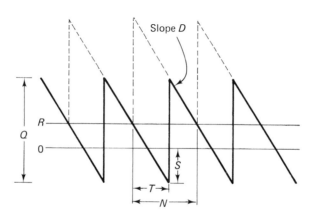

or below. Now assume that when the demand that put the inventory position at twenty occurred, an order for fifty units was placed. Based on the order lead time, say fifteen more demands occurred, and each demand that occurred resulted in replenishment action, thus causing not one but sixteen orders to have been placed. A simple procedure can eliminate the problem. That is, to base reorder point on stock-on-hand plus stock-on-order. This quantity (on-hand plus on-order) is called *inventory position* and is represented by the dotted line in Figure 10.5.

As before we must proceed to develop the cost parameters by analyzing the inventory geometry of Figure 10.5. Remember that demand is known with certainty and does not fluctuate. Therefore Figure 10.5 can be redrawn somewhat to reflect the operating situation; as shown in Figure 10.6. Now, obviously as before

$$N = Q/D$$

The total number of unit-years of inventory on-hand during the cycle can be determined by simple geometry:

$$I = 1/2(N - S/D)(Q - S)$$
$$= 1/2(Q/D - S/D)(Q/S)$$
$$= 1/2 \frac{(Q - S)^2}{D}$$

Now let us look at the back order level, S. It is obvious that

$$-S = R - DT$$

So now by substitution

$$I = 1/2 \frac{(Q + R - DT)^2}{D}$$

The unit-years of shortage can be calculated by

FIGURE 10.6   The Redrawn Shortage Condition

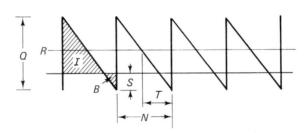

$$B = 1/2(S)(S/D)$$

$$= 1/2(DT - R)\left(\frac{DT - R}{D}\right)$$

$$B = \frac{(DT - R)^2}{2D}$$

So now we can develop the cost components. First, notice that item cost and procurement costs should not change. So

$$HC = \frac{C_H I}{N}$$

$$= \frac{C_H\left[1/2\dfrac{(Q + R - DT)^2}{D}\right]}{Q/D}$$

$$= \frac{C_H(Q + R - DT)^2}{2Q}$$

The shortage cost is

$$SC = \frac{C_S B}{N} = \frac{C_S(DT - R)^2}{2DN} = \frac{C_S(DT - R)^2}{2\left(\dfrac{Q}{N}\right)N} = \frac{C_S(R - DT)^2}{2Q}$$

Now the total system cost is

$$TC = C_I D + \frac{C_P D}{Q} + \frac{C_H(Q + R - DT)^2}{2Q} + \frac{C_S(R - DT)^2}{2Q}$$

Due to the back order nature of the system, the key difference between the expression above and the total cost expression developed in the previous section is the term $R - DT$, which reflects the lead time demand. Previously, this was zero. In this case, however, it is not. Note how the above equation is affected if we let $R = DT$, that is, if we never incur a stockout.

$$TC = C_I D + \frac{C_P D}{Q} + \frac{C_H[Q + (R - DT)]^2}{2Q} + \frac{C_S(R - DT)^2}{2Q}$$

so that

$$TC = C_I D + \frac{C_P D}{Q} + \frac{C_H Q^2}{2Q}$$

which is exactly what we derived in the previous section.

The optimal operating policy may now be calculated. Once again we must determine the respective values of R and Q which minimize the total system cost. In that it is now somewhat more complicated to optimize the total cost equation we must resort to the use of calculus. The complete derivation of the optimal order quantity and reorder point is not presented. However, after application of calculus we can determine that

$$Q^* = \sqrt{\frac{2C_P D}{C_H} + \frac{2C_P D}{C_S}}$$

Note the similarity between this equation and that for the basic inventory model. The difference arises from the back order component. If, as before, the shortage cost goes to infinity, this relation becomes exactly the same as the previous one.

Now let us determine the optimal reorder point, R, using calculus. This is

$$R^* = DT - \sqrt{\frac{2C_H C_P D}{C_S(C_H + C_S)}}$$

Compare this with the previous result and notice once again that if the shortage cost becomes infinite then the formula is exactly as before. That is, if shortage cost is infinite then $R = DT$. Note that as the shortage cost, C_S, becomes smaller, the denominator of the second term becomes smaller and that term becomes larger. The net effect is that when the shortage cost is zero or trivial, then it may be more economical to reorder only after several back orders exist. In other words, never maintain an on-hand inventory. How would this line of reasoning affect the optimal order quantity? Generally speaking, the result is to order less often but order more *when* you order. The minimum total cost expression is given by

$$TC = C_I D + \sqrt{\frac{2C_P C_H C_S D}{C_H + C_S}}$$

Some Examples

Problem 3. A television manufacturer sells over ten thousand 25-inch color televisions per year. The picture tubes for these sets are subcontracted at a unit cost of $250 each. Generally the order lead time is one month and it costs the manufacturer $20 to process an order. An internal analysis reveals that the holding cost for these items is $8 per unit held per year while the expected cost per each item short per year is $5. All items demanded during a shortage condition will be filled upon receipt of the order; that is, this is a full back order case. What is the optimal order quantity and reorder point?

In the example

$$D = 10{,}000 \text{ units/year}$$
$$T = 1/12 \text{ year}$$
$$C_I = \$250/\text{unit}$$
$$C_P = \$20.00/\text{procurement}$$
$$C_H = \$8.00/\text{unit/year}$$
$$C_S = \$5.00/\text{unit/year}$$

The optimal order quantity, Q^*, is given by

$$Q^* = \sqrt{\frac{2C_P D}{C_H} + \frac{2C_P D}{C_S}} = \sqrt{\frac{2(20)(10{,}000)}{8} + \frac{2(20)(10{,}000)}{5}}$$

$$= 360.55 \approx 361$$

Now

$$R^* = DT - \sqrt{\frac{2C_H C_P D}{C_S(C_H + C_S)}}$$

$$= 10{,}000 \times 1/12 - \sqrt{\frac{(2)(8)(20)(10{,}000)}{5(8 + 5)}}$$

$$R^* = 611.45 \approx 611$$

Now what is total minimum cost?

$$TC = C_I D + \sqrt{\frac{2C_P C_H C_S D}{C_H + C_S}}$$

$$= 250(10{,}000) + \sqrt{\frac{2(20)(8)(5)(10{,}000)}{(8 + 5)}}$$

$$= \$2{,}501{,}109.00$$

Note that the vast majority of the total system cost arises from the item cost. Only $1,109 is a variable cost, assuming that the 10,000 items are to be sold. Keep in mind as you apply these tools that many times the variable cost components under the control of the decision maker are relatively small compared with the fixed charge.

Problem 4. For the previous example, investigate the sensitivity of the model to changing shortage costs. Remove item cost from consideration and determine what happens when the shortage costs above varies.

Figure 10.7 illustrates the effect on R^* and Q^* as the shortage cost component varies. Note that as shortage cost decreases so also does the reorder point. For example, when the shortage cost C_S was $0.50/unit/year, the optimal reorder point turned out to be about -34 units, which indicates that it is much cheaper to back order demand

FIGURE 10.7 Sensitivity Analysis of Some Decision Variables

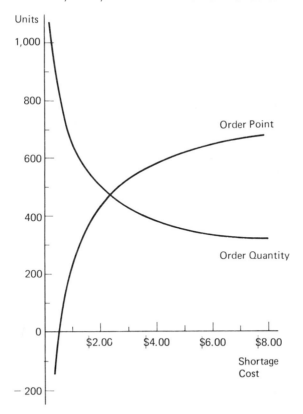

than to worry about filling it. Parenthetically, when $C_S = \$.50$ with a holding cost of $8/unit/year, an order-of-magnitude difference exists between the two costs. Thus, one can easily see why it is much cheaper to back order than to keep an item in stock. In other words, "Why pay holding costs if you can back order everything so cheaply?" Good question!

QUESTIONS AND PROBLEMS

1. How do changes in procurement lead time affect the operating policy of an inventory system?

2. Discuss the changes in inventory operating policy in an inflationary economy assuming that inflation primarily affects item cost.

3. In the models discussed in this chapter the demand for an item was assumed to be known and constant but not under the control of the decision maker. Is this entirely true? How can the decision maker affect demand?

4. In the models discussed in this chapter, how would the operating policy be affected if procurement cost was zero?

5. In this chapter, orders were placed when the inventory fell below a certain point. This implies that the inventory manager is constantly aware

of the status of inventory. In fact this could not be accomplished practically when many items need to be managed. What then are the events which need to be observed regarding inventory management? Under what conditions will the inventory need to be reviewed?

6. What are the components of the stockout cost when the stockout results in a lost sale?

7. Draw the inventory geometry for a lost sales case.

8. Cite three examples of a stockout situation in which all back orders are filled upon receipt of the order.

9. Discuss an inventory system which is a combination of a back order and lost sales situation, that is, when back orders ultimately result in lost sales. Cite at least one example of this.

10. What would the net effect be on the operating policy of an inventory system if a quality control inspection plan were involved on each order quantity received?

11. Calculate the economic order quantity for the following cases:

    (a) $C_P = \$15/\text{order}$
        $C_H = \$150/\text{unit}/\text{year}$
        $D(\text{demand}) = 100 \text{ units}/\text{year}$
    (b) $C_P = \$20/\text{order}$
        $C_H = \$150/\text{unit}/\text{year}$
        $D = 100 \text{ units}/\text{year}$
    (c) $C_P = \$50/\text{order}$
        $C_H = \$150/\text{unit}/\text{year}$
        $D = 100 \text{ units}/\text{year}$
    (d) $C_P = \$50/\text{order}$
        $C_H = \$250/\text{unit}/\text{year}$
        $D = 100 \text{ units}/\text{year}$
    (e) $C_P = \$50/\text{order}$
        $C_H = \$20/\text{unit}/\text{year}$
        $D = 100 \text{ units}/\text{year}$

Assume 360 days in a year and 30 days in a month.

12. Using a lead time of 15 days, calculate the reorder inventory level for all of the above cases.

13. The owner of an ice cream store specializing in a single flavor anticipates the daily demand to be fifty gallons/day during the peak summer months. The ordering cost is $10 per order. His estimate of the holding cost is $.25 per gallon per day. (This is mainly the electricity charges for the cold storage.)

    (a) What is the economic order quantity?

    (b) Assuming that his cold storage has a maximum capacity of fifty gallons, would you advise him to rent additional storage space of similar capacity at $2 a day rental charges?

    (c) What will be the decision if the ordering cost is $15 per order, instead of $10?

    (d) Assuming ordering cost to be $10 per order, what should be the minimum daily demand to justify the rental of an additional storage facility?

14. Compute the optimum order quantity when the total yearly demand is 5,000 units per year, the cost of holding is $20 per unit per year, and the cost of ordering is $25 per order. If the order quantity is restricted to multiples of 100 units, what should be the optimum policy?

15. Calculate the economic order quantity for all the cases in the first problem, assuming shortages (back orders) are permitted and shortage cost is $50 per unit per year.

16. Calculate and plot the curve of the total cost versus shortage cost for the following situation.

$C_I = \$5/\text{unit}$
$C_H = \$20/\text{unit}/\text{year}$
$C_P = \$40/\text{order}$
$D = 100 \text{ units}/\text{year}$
$C_S = \$5, 10, 15, 20, 25, \text{ and } 50.$

17. What do you anticipate the optimum policy to be if the shortage cost is zero in a single item inventory situation with back orders? Justify and illustrate the situation.

18. The ABC Company estimates the cost of ordering a raw material to be $50 per order. The monthly demand is 2,000 units and inventory carrying cost is $5 per unit per month. Obtain the economic order quantity assuming (a) shortages are not permitted, and (b) shortage cost is $100 per unit per month.

19. The XYZ Company, the supplier of the raw material to the ABC Company, offers the following pricing policy:

Order Quantity:

$Q \le 150, C_I = \$25/\text{unit}$

$Q > 150, C_I = \$24/\text{unit}$

Assuming shortages are not permitted, should ABC Company change their ordering policy obtained in problem 18? Graphically illustrate your answers.

20. The XYZ Store has a policy of ordering 2,000 cans of Brown Giant Pork & Beans when the inventory level goes below 200 cans. The lead time is one week. The weekly demand, ordering cost, and holding cost are estimated to be 100 cans, $20 per order, and $0.10 per can per week respectively. How much cost saving can you offer them? Shortages are not permitted.

21. The Brown Giant Company of problem 20 offers the following discounts to XYZ Store.

Order Quantity:

$Q \le 300 \text{ cans}, C_I = \$0.35/\text{can}$

$300 < Q \le 400 \text{ cans}, C_I = \$0.33/\text{can}$

$Q > 400 \text{ cans}, C_I = \$0.30/\text{can}$

Assuming shortages are not permitted, determine the optimum order quantity.

213

Inventory
models I

22. Based on past experience the owner of the General Store in Remote County believes that the optimum order quantity of a certain merchandise is 160 units per order. The weekly demand is 500 units and the cost of procurement is mainly the cost of picking up the merchandise from the nearest retailer 40 miles away. The gas price is $.35 per gallon and his pick-up truck has an average gas mileage of 10 miles/gallon. He also adds $5 to the total gas cost to cover the man-hours lost, depreciation of the truck, and so forth. If the price of gas in Remote County increases to $ .40 per gallon, what would be his new optimum policy?

BIBLIOGRAPHY

The references for this chapter can be found at the end of Chapter 11.

Inventory models II

In this chapter we will continue our discussion of inventory systems by looking at some other aspects of the total inventory spectrum. The simple models of the previous chapter will serve as a basis for this discussion, and we will employ the same symbols as before.

In most manufacturing activities the inventory manager can deal with two types of inventory operations. The first of these is the *purchase option* for inventory replenishment, which was discussed in the previous chapter. In such a situation, an infinite replenishment rate is usually assumed. In effect, the total order quantity is delivered at a point in time. In this chapter we will discuss the other option for inventory replenishment, namely the *manufacture option,* in which a finite rate of replenishment is likely to exist.

We will also investigate the effects of nondeterministic demand patterns on our inventory systems. Generally, we will see that as our ability to accurately predict demand decreases, our cost to operate the system will increase, which results from not having as "tight" a control over the system.

MANUFACTURING ACTIVITIES

We have already discussed the routine basic purchase option for inventory replenishment—the case in which the inventory level is increased by an amount equal to the order quantity at the instant the order is received. Many times, the inventory replenishment activity is a result of some manufacturing activity which can deliver the items to inventory as they are produced and in quantities less than the total order quantity. This situation is particularly characteristic of an internal activity which produces subassemblies for a total system. For example, in support of the manufacture of a finite quantity of automobiles, a similar quantity of engines may be produced. Each engine produced in-house can be delivered as it is completed rather than as a part of a total quantity so that the support activity takes place at a finite rate until the total order quantity is delivered.

Inventory Replenishment

Figure 11.1 illustrates the basic relationship between production rate, P, and demand rate, D, for a given item in terms of inventory replenishment. The case discussed in the previous chapter was that in which P is infinite and therefore $P - D$ is also infinite. The entire order was delivered at one time. It is rather easy to visualize an arrangement with a supplier whereby the order quantity, Q, is broken into n parts with the result being that during each cycle, n shipments, each of size Q/n, are received and placed

Inventory Replenishment and Item Demand   **FIGURE 11.1**

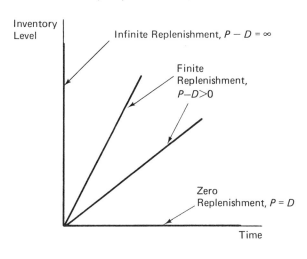

in inventory. Carrying this as far as possible, $Q = n$, or $Q/n = 1$, and each item is delivered to inventory as it is produced. Here, P is the *production rate* in units per period and as long as P is greater than D, the inventory level will continue to grow. This is illustrated by the middle two lines of Figure 11.1.

The opposite of infinite replenishment is when $P = D$ or when the production rate equals the demand rate. In this case the inventory level will never change and each item produced is immediately consumed by demand. In some respects, this is an ideal situation, but it requires a balance of P against D, which may be difficult to accomplish. Generally, we will consider those cases where P exceeds D by some amount sufficient to cause the inventory level to increase. As before, our objective will be to operate the system at minimum cost.

The Basic Production Model

The first case we will study here is similar to the basic model discussed in Chapter 10. In this inventory system we will consider the shortage cost C_S to be infinite. Therefore, we know that the system will never be out of stock. Demand and lead time are known and deterministic. Hence, we can specify an operating policy which will prevent stockout conditions.

An interesting question now arises, namely: What is the interpretation of order lead time in a manufacturing example? The components of this time will include paperwork processing and production scheduling. Production scheduling is yet another topic but plays a large part in the magnitude of lead time. Poor scheduling practices will result in higher costs, because more inventory will have to be maintained to guard against stockouts. Keep in mind, however, that in the total systems view, all decisions such as these must be made in the context of the total system's objective. Therefore, shorter lead times might be achieved only through procurement of additional equipment at a very high cost. As a result, production scheduling and inventory replenishment must go hand-in-hand. This is illustrated in Figure 11.2. Note

FIGURE 11.2 The Production-Inventory System

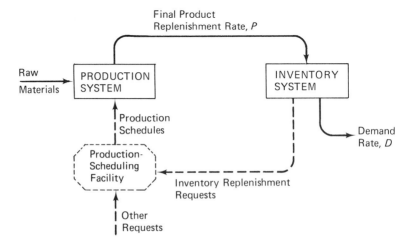

the circular or feedback effect wherein units are provided the inventory system by the production system following the request for such units.

The inventory process under discussion is shown in Figure 11.3. As before, we wish to operate the system at minimum cost, which means that we wish to minimize the sum of the cost components. That is, we wish to minimize TC where TC is represented symbolically as

$$TC = IC + PC + HC$$

As before the item cost is primarily a function of demand, or

$$IC = C_I D$$

And as before the procurement cost remains a function of the number of procurement actions necessary. This was shown to be

$$PC = \frac{C_P D}{Q}$$

Finite Production Rate—Infinite Shortage Cost   **FIGURE 11.3**

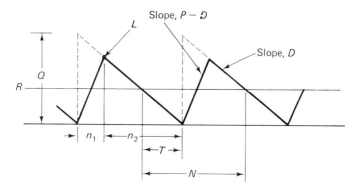

In order to determine holding cost, we must determine the average on-hand inventory per period, which may be accomplished by calculating the area under the inventory curves as follows:

$$N = n_1 + n_2$$

Note also that $N = Q/D$, $n_1 = \dfrac{L}{P - D}$, and $n_2 = \dfrac{L}{D}$.

Therefore,

$$N = \frac{L}{P - D} + \frac{L}{D} = Q/D$$

Collecting terms and factoring we get

$$Q/D = L\left[\frac{1}{P-D} + \frac{1}{D}\right]$$

or

$$Q = L\left[\frac{P}{P-D}\right]$$

Solving for L, we get

$$L = Q(1 - D/P)$$

Referring to Figure 11.3 we see that L is the maximum number of units ever in inventory at any one time. Hence, it is obvious that if the inventory level varies from 0 to L, then the average on-hand inventory level is $L/2$. Therefore, inventory holding cost per period is given as:

$$HC = \frac{C_H L}{2}$$

$$= \frac{C_H Q(1 - D/P)}{2}$$

Now the total system cost TC can be calculated as

$$TC = C_I D + \frac{C_P D}{Q} + \frac{C_H Q(1 - D/P)}{2}$$

And as before we can rationalize that the item cost component is not under control of the inventory manager and therefore it need not affect decision variables. This leads us to realize that total cost is minimized when the procurement cost is equal to the holding cost, or

$$PC = HC$$

$$\frac{C_P D}{Q} = \frac{C_H Q(1 - D/P)}{2}$$

Now, solving for Q, we get

$$Q^2 = \frac{2 C_P D}{C_H(1 - D/P)}$$

or

$$Q^* = \sqrt{\frac{2 C_P D}{C_H(1 - D/P)}}$$

In the above equation, Q^* once again represents the value of Q which minimizes the total system cost. Compare this formula for Q^* with that in Chapter 10. Note what happens to the above equation when the value of P becomes infinite.

The optimal reorder point, R^*, is again given as

$$R^* = DT$$

The minimum total system cost may now be found by substituting the value of Q^* into the total cost equation. This becomes

$$TC^* = C_I D + \sqrt{2C_P(1 - D/P)C_H D}.$$

Problem 1. A manufacturer of shoes has established a production line for certain popular styles of men's shoes. The assembly operations on the production line include the attachment of the soles to the shoes. A small unit in the building which produces the sole blanks used in the production operation is capable of producing 5,000 per month. The production operation requires only 2,500 shoe soles per month. Excessive costs are incurred, however, if a stockout condition occurs and the plant manager has stated that shortages should never occur. Each blank costs about $1.00 and it generally takes one week to get into the production cycle of the blanking unit. The paperwork and set-up costs are about $6 for each replenishment order and inventory holding costs are $0.25 per blank per year. Help this manager determine a minimum cost policy.

Some Examples

In this example,

$$P = 5,000/\text{month} = 60,000/\text{year}$$
$$D = 2,500/\text{month} = 30,000/\text{year}$$
$$T = 1/52 \text{ year}$$
$$C_I = \$1.00$$
$$C_P = \$6.00$$
$$C_H = \$0.25/\text{unit}/\text{year}$$

$$Q^* = \sqrt{\frac{2C_P D}{C_H(1 - D/P)}}$$

$$= \sqrt{\frac{(2)(6)(30,000)}{.25\left(1 - \dfrac{30,000}{60,000}\right)}} = \sqrt{\frac{360,000}{.125}}$$

$$= \sqrt{2,880,000} = 1,696.96$$

The reorder point is

$$R = DT = 2,500/52$$
$$= 48.077$$

Problem 2. What is the total cost of the operation in Problem 1? Using the optimum order quantity, Q^*

$$TC^* = C_I D + \sqrt{2C_P(1 - D/P)C_H D}$$
$$= \$1.00(30,000) + \sqrt{2(\$6.00)(1\text{-}2,500/5,000)(\$0.25)(30,000)}$$
$$= \$30,000 + \sqrt{\$45,000}$$
$$= \$30,000 + \$212 = \$30,212$$

Note that the procurement and holding cost components are only a small part of the total cost in this illustration.

If the item cost could be reduced by one percent ($0.01/unit), what savings in total system cost could be achieved? Because the order quantity, Q^*, is not dependent on C_I, we can use the same order quantity. Then,

$$TC^* = \$0.99(30,000) + \sqrt{\$45,000}$$
$$= \$29,700 + \$212 = \$29,912$$

And the savings would be

$$\$30,212 - \$29,912 = \$300$$

In effect, this savings would pay for the total cost of ordering and holding inventory.

INVENTORY OPERATIONS UNDER UNCERTAINTY

In all of our discussions up to this point, we have assumed that demand was both constant and deterministic. These fundamental assumptions have given us the opportunity of developing models for inventory management with relative ease. But how often can these basic assumptions be validated in the business world? How often can demand be *totally* predictable? How often is demand *totally* constant? Unfortunately, the answers to these questions will require that we proceed with the development of some more sophisticated inventory models.

The next logical questions we need to ask are: what utility do our models have for real life problems? and what impact does the relaxation of these assumptions have on our models? In this section we will address ourselves to these issues and attempt to develop a feel for the nature of inventory systems under uncertain demand.

Consider the service station owner described at the beginning of Chapter 10 who may *assume* that he sells 30,000 gallons of high test gasoline each month. In reality he may sell an *average* of 30,000 gallons each month. Some months' demand may actually reach 37,000 gallons, while other months' demand may dip as low as 25,000 gallons. Likewise, daily demand may be even more unpredictable. **Lead Time Revisited**

The daily differential between average and actual sales is shown in Figure 11.4 for a hypothetical two-week period. Note that on some days the demand rate was in excess of the average while on others it was far less than average. Although it occurred on a daily basis, the basic differences do average out over the two-week period in question. This will not always be the case.

Average and Actual Demand for the Gasoline Illustration **FIGURE 11.4**

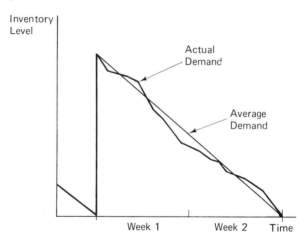

In Chapter 10 we said that lead time was the elapsed time between the initiation of an order and the receipt of that order. We have assumed to date that the time value is constant and known. Although this is a very elementary assumption, we will not violate it in the present chapter. Remember that a key issue in our models was determination of lead time demand, or the reorder point. This was simple to calculate when demand was known and deterministic, but the problem becomes more interesting when random demand patterns are introduced.

As long as demand was constant and lead time was known exactly, then the reorder point, R, could be calculated by multiplying the demand rate times the order lead time. In this ideal situation (under an infinite shortage cost model) the desired parts would arrive on the day the stock was exhausted.

Since reality is not always ideal, such a policy would sometimes result in lost sales or back orders and a possible loss of customer good will. A higher demand rate than expected can result in an out-of-stock period as shown in Figure 11.5. This is highly undesirable if it is unanticipated.

221

FIGURE 11.5   The Effect of Increased Demand During Lead Time

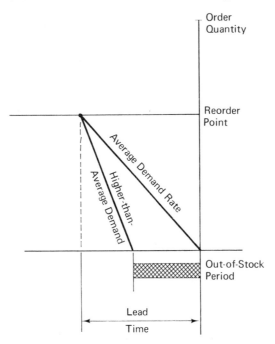

Note also that a delayed delivery would have the same net effect, namely to cause an out-of-stock condition. The latter condition differs from the back order model described earlier in that it is an unwanted condition. The inventory manager does not want an out-of-stock condition to occur.

The key point to note in this section is that when random patterns of demand introduce uncertainty into our model, their effects can be isolated by treating lead time demand. That is, random demand effects can be conveniently treated from a lead time demand standpoint. This in turn can be compensated for by employing a *safety stock* method to address the characteristics of lead time demand. We, as inventory analysts, can focus on lead time demand patterns and their effects on inventory management. Thus, rather than being concerned with the total nature of demand, all we need do is worry about demand averages and lead time demand characteristics.

An Example   *Problem 3.*   The gasoline station owner discussed previously has found that his demand for high test gas averages about 1,000 gallons per working day. Generally, his order lead time is five working days and for this time he finds that demand appears to be normally distributed with a mean of 5,000 gallons and a standard deviation of 600 gallons. What is the probability that lead time demand will exceed 6,000 gallons? From Chapter 5 we calculate our standard normal variate Z as

$$Z = \frac{X - \bar{X}}{S}$$

$$= \frac{6{,}000 - 5{,}000}{600} = \frac{1{,}000}{600} = +1.667.$$

Figure 11.6 illustrates the problem at hand. From Appendix A, the area from $-\infty$ to $+1.667s$ is 0.952. Therefore,

P(lead time demand exceeds 6,000 gallons) $= 1 - .952 = .048$

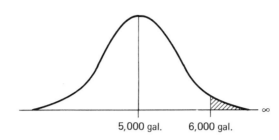

The Normal Curve for Problem 3   **FIGURE 11.6**

5,000 gal.   6,000 gal.

Safety Stock

We often find that in dealing with uncertainty, we add or build up defensive mechanisms to assist us through unexpected situations. A football team will carry some extra players, for example, a second punter, on the bench. A farmer may plant a little more corn than he would ordinarily need to provide food for his livestock over the winter. A production facility may be designed and constructed with some anticipated excess capacity. In inventory management, safety stock is a defense against the unexpected. We build an added reservoir of units to guard against possible stockout conditions. We do this when we are not completely sure of the demand for our product or the lead time prior to the delivery of an order quantity. The use of this buffer can be seen in Figure 11.7. It should be noted that with the use of safety stock, we are assuming that for all practical purposes, a shortage condition will result in a lost sale and that we give up the opportunity of filling a demand once it is lost.

The rationale for safety stock is easy to establish, but what is a sensible level of safety stock? Clearly, the continuous inclusion of safety stock will increase operating expenses because holding costs will increase. Average on-hand inventory will have to increase by the average safety stock level. This cost will then have to be contrasted to the possible cost of lost sales.

A relatively simple method of establishing a level of safety stock calls for the use by the inventory manager of a *customer service* criterion. This approach is easy to visualize and does not require any profound calculations. It is based on a statistical method developed previously. We first need to specify a level of service that we desire to provide. For example, initially we might wish to fill 90 percent of customer orders. However, as soon

FIGURE 11.7 The Value of Safety Stock

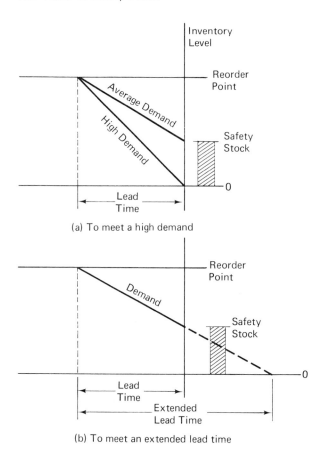

(a) To meet a high demand

(b) To meet an extended lead time

as 90 percent is specified, someone is likely to suggest raising this to 95 percent. The question (and the answer to this suggestion) ultimately reduces to whether these added sales (and profit) will pay for the cost of maintaining the additional inventory. Referring to Figure 11.8, this statistical interpretation of safety stock may answer the previous question.

The inventory manager will have to specify a high demand that will trade-off the cost of safety stock against the probability (or proportion) of out-of-stock conditions. In our examples, he must assume a normal distribution of lead time demand, but this is not unrealistic.

Some Examples

Problem 4. In support of a manufacturing activity in a large machine shop, the organization must maintain a large inventory of tool bits. Each of these bits costs about $10.00 and they are consumed at the rate of 100 bits per week on the average. It generally takes about two weeks for the company to receive a new order of bits once processing has begun. An analysis of the demand activity has shown that the

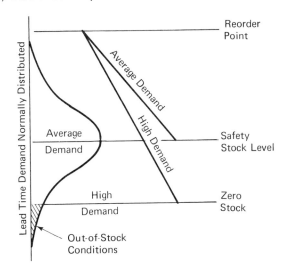

average lead time demand is 200 bits with a standard deviation of 10 bits. Also, analysis has produced the following cost figures

$C_H = \$1.50/\text{unit}/\text{year}$
$C_P = \$50/\text{procurement}$

If the inventory manager wishes to be 90 percent sure of eliminating stockouts, what should the amount of safety stock be?

Assuming no variation, the normal lead time demand is 200 units. The question we are asking is, "What inventory level must we maintain in order to be 90 percent sure it will not be exceeded?" That is, we want to determine a value of R so that

$P(\text{lead time demand} \leq R) = .90$

Assuming a normal demand pattern, we are seeking to determine the point on the curve, as shown in Figure 11.9, at which 90 percent

The Normal Curve for Problem 4 **FIGURE 11.9**

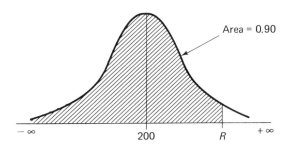

of the area falls to its left. This is a somewhat different approach than that used in Chapter 5, but equally simple. The Z value is now

$$Z = \frac{R - 200}{10}$$

By referring to the table in Appendix A for the area equal to .90 and interpolating if necessary, you can find the Z value with which you need to work. In this example, by referring to the leftmost column for .90 we find that

$$Z = 1.282$$

Therefore we can say

$$1.282 = \frac{R - 200}{10}$$

$$R = 200 + 12.82 = 212.82 = 213$$

This says that if we keep our reorder point at 213 units through any given inventory cycle, we can be 90 percent sure there will be no stockout. That is, we will have only 10 percent stockout conditions and the safety stock for this example is 13 units. How much does this cost us on a yearly basis? We will look at this in the next problem.

Note how safety stock is directly affected by the system variability. We have a standard deviation of 10 which gives us about 13 units safety stock. If the standard deviation had doubled, then the safety stock would also have had to be increased.

Problem 5. For the system in Problem 4, how much does it cost on an annual basis to maintain the safety stock?

This is a simple calculation. By multiplying the holding cost by the safety stock level of 13, we obtain

$$\text{Annual cost of maintaining safety stock} = C_H(13)$$
$$= (1.50)(13)$$
$$= \$19.50$$

QUESTIONS AND PROBLEMS

1. How would a quality control program likely affect the value of P, the production rate, if it is imposed on items entering the inventory system?

2. Discuss what might happen if demand were constant but lead time varied.

3. Is the safety stock model developed in this chapter applicable for the full back order inventory model?

4. Discuss the components of shortage cost in detail.

5. How would continued mismanagement of an inventory system likely affect demand?

6. Cite some examples of inventory systems in which holding cost is greater than item cost.

7. Develop the operating policy for an inventory system with a finite production rate and a finite shortage cost.

8. How would the inventory models developed in this chapter change if demand were in n batches of size D/n?

9. Determine the operating policy for the following inventory system.

$$
\begin{aligned}
D &= 100 \text{ units}/\text{month} \\
P &= 200 \text{ units}/\text{month} \\
T &= 2 \text{ months} \\
C_I &= \$1.50/\text{unit} \\
C_P &= 8.00/\text{order} \\
C_H &= \$2.00/\text{unit}/\text{month}
\end{aligned}
$$

10. The ACE Manufacturing Company produces items which consume four cubic feet of space. The operating parameters of the operation are:

$$
\begin{aligned}
D &= 10{,}000/\text{year} \\
P &= 15{,}000/\text{year} \\
T &= 1 \text{ month} \\
C_I &= \$200 \\
C_P &= 80.00 \\
C_H &= \$25.00/\text{unit}/\text{year}
\end{aligned}
$$

What space requirements will the company need to provide for? What is the maximum inventory space requirement? the average?

11. The average lead time demand of an item is twenty-five units with a standard deviation of ten units. Assuming normality, what safety stock would be necessary to be 90 percent sure that a stockout would not occur?

12. Assuming a $5.00/unit/month holding cost, graph the total holding cost versus the safety factor for the following system:

demand/week = 100 units, standard deviation 20
lead time   = 4 weeks.

Graph this for a safety factor range of .85 to .95.

13. Lead time demand for an item has changed over the year from 100 to 200 units. The standard deviation has changed from ten units to fifteen units. For a 90 percent safety factor, how has the safety stock aspect changed? Discuss the ramifications of this.

BIBLIOGRAPHY

BOWMAN, EDWARD H., AND FETTER, ROBERT B. *Analysis for Production and Operations Management.* Homewood, Ill.: Richard D. Irwin, Inc., 1967.

FABRYCKY, W. J., AND BANKS, JERRY. *Procurement and Inventory Systems: Theory and Analysis.* New York: Reinhold Publishing Corporation, 1967.

HADLEY, G., AND WHITIN, T. M. *Analysis of Inventory Systems.* Englewood Cliffs, N.J.: Prentice-Hall, Inc., 1963.

HILLIER, FREDERICK, AND LIEBERMAN, GERALD. *Introduction to Operations Research.* San Francisco, Calif.: Holden-Day, Inc., 1967.

NILAND, POWELL. *Production Planning, Scheduling, and Inventory Control.* New York: The Macmillan Company, 1970.

TAHA, HAMDY A. *Operations Research: An Introduction.* New York: The Macmillan Company, 1971.

Linear programming I

One of the production managers of a manufacturing plant was recently asked if his department used *linear* programming in any of its activities. He responded that all *computer* programming was handled by another department and that its operation was a complete mystery to everyone in his department. However, he was sure, he said, that all programming was done in either FORTRAN or COBOL. This attitude of grouping linear programming and computer programming together is a common one in many facets of industry. However, on the contrary, linear programming is entirely different from computer programming. In this chapter we shall come to terms with linear programming and learn that it is a very powerful technique for solving a certain class of problems.

The term *linear programming* evolved from a series of earlier names for a technique which selects the best *program* from a series of feasible alternatives. This program has to do with allocation of resources in a manner that maximizes or minimizes some objective of the company. For instance, the company may be concerned with the best production mix of items for a given week knowing both production requirements as well as equipment availability. Using this tool, this problem and many others can be treated. But why call it linear programming? *Linear* describes the relationship between variables in the problem and *programming* refers to mathematical techniques.

RECIPE FOR A LINEAR PROGRAM

We have said that the linear programming method is a mathematical technique for choosing the best alternative from a set of feasible alternatives. In order to employ the linear programming technique, it is important to understand the system of concern. In this case the system could be any activity within the company from a production to a financial to a sales operation in which limited resources must be allocated in an attempt to achieve some basic objective, which has to do with maximization of profits or minimization of costs. In this section we will consider the basic ingredients for the linear programming problem.

There are several requirements inherent in employing the linear programming method, and it is important to understand these before we continue with development of the technique. These requirements are:

1. The organization must have a stated objective which it is attempting to achieve. As mentioned above, the stated objective might be to maximize profits or to minimize costs.

2. The resources of the system which are to be allocated in an attempt to achieve the objective must be in a limited supply. The technique will rely upon the allocation of these limited resources in some manner which trades off the returns on the investment of the resources toward the achievement of the objective.

3. There must be a series of feasible alternative courses of action or strategies which are available to the decision maker. In many practical applications, the number of alternatives becomes almost infinite.

4. All relationships representing the objective as well as the resource limitation considerations must be expressible in the form of mathematical equations or inequalities. These equations or inequalities must be linear in nature.

The Objective Function

The first major requirement of a linear programming problem is that we must be able to establish the goal of the organization in terms of an objective function. This function relates mathematically (and linearly) the important variables with which we are dealing in the problem. For purposes of discussion, let's say we are going to maximize the profit obtained through production of two separate items, namely bolts and screws. Our total profit then is a function of the number of cases of bolts and screws we sell. For each case of bolts sold, we make $1.50 profit and for each case of screws sold, we make $1.00 profit. Therefore, our total profit resulting from the sale of bolts and screws, P, is given by $P =$ $1.50 (number of cases of bolts) + $1.00 (number of cases of screws).

This relationship formulates the objective of our company, namely to earn profit through making and selling cases of bolts and screws. The *objective function* is a linear relationship between the profit and the sales level of each of these items.

Constraints and Inequalities

As we have just suggested, one of the requirements for a linear programming problem is that the resources of the system must be in limited supply. The mathematical relationship which we use to explain this limitation is called an *inequality*. The limitation itself is generally referred to as a *constraint*. Thus, we use mathematical relationships known as inequalities to represent the constraints on the problem.

How does an inequality differ from an equality? An equality basically states the relationship among variables and employs the use of an equal sign. Thus, when we say $A = B$, we state an equality. If A is always less than or equal to B, we state an inequality and notationally write it $A < B$. If we continue the above example of the bolts and screws and say that the total cost to make the bolts and screws on any given day must not exceed $40.00 and it costs $8.00 to make a case of bolts and $10.00 to make a case of screws, the relationship that states the constraint that is imposed upon the system is $8.00 (number cases bolts) + $10.00 (number cases screws) $\leq$ $40.00. This constraint is expressed as a mathematical inequality and such inequalities may be employed to establish upper and/or lower limits on the levels of given variables. In most practical problems there are several constraints, which determine a *region of feasibility* that can be defined as that set of points which produces a feasible solution to the problem.

A GRAPHICAL APPROACH

The basic methodology of the linear programming method can be illustrated quite handily through the use of graphical methods. Actually, graphical methods can be used successfully to solve linear programming problems which contain either two or three variables under manipulation. For those problems with greater than three variables, it is impossible to graphically represent the problem. However, the basic technique of the linear programming method can be illustrated using two variable problems. In this section we will investigate the methodology of the linear programming method through use of the graphical approach. We will show how the problem can be set up graphically and how a solution can be achieved. Although larger problems cannot be handled with this method, we will see that the basic concepts employed in a graphical approach will transfer quite readily to a more systematic mathematical approach presented in a later section of this chapter.

Setting Up the Problem

The classic example for the linear programming method is the allocation of resources to a production problem in which a manufacturer is assumed to produce two products, A and B. Each of the products must be processed by two machines, I and II. To manufacture one unit of product A it is necessary to use two hours of time on machine I and one hour of time on machine II. One unit of product B requires one hour each on machines I and II. Machine I may not operate longer than ten hours a day, while machine II, due to its age and nature, is never available for longer than six hours a day. Each unit of product A contributes $1.50 to profit and each unit of product B contributes $1.00 to profit.

The question we must answer is: how should the manufacturer allocate his facilities for production? That is, what amount of each product should be produced daily in order to maximize profit? The data is summarized as follows:

	Product A (Hours Required)	Product B (Hours Required)	Maximum Machine Hours Available per Day
Machine I	2	1	10
Machine II	1	1	6
Profit Contribution per Unit	$1.5	$1	—

Note that the rows focus attention on the machines while the columns focus attention on the products. For example, the product A column tells us that in order to produce one unit of product A, we must use two hours on machine I and one hour on machine II. The product B column is interpreted in a similar fashion.

Since the profit contribution on product A is larger than that on product B, it might seem that we ought to produce only product A. How many units of product A could we produce daily? How many units of product B could we produce daily? As we develop this problem, it will be seen that a *program* of activity will define a specific production mix for product A and B on machines I and II. Thus, what we are going to seek is the optimal program of operation.

Let us now further define the problem, for purposes of illustration, to include the following restrictions. Let us say that on a daily basis no more than 4.5 units of product A can ever be produced and no more than 4 units of product B can ever be produced due to internal cash flow restrictions. Let us now express the problem for solution via graphical technique. Let us assume that x_1 is the number of units of product A produced daily and x_2 is the number of units of product B produced daily. Daily profit in dollars can then be denoted by

$$P = \$1.5x_1 + \$1.0x_2$$

Using the mathematical notation, our production problem is reduced to finding values of x_1 and x_2 which maximize $P = \$1.5x_1 + \$1.0x_2$, subject to the inequality constraints:

$$
\begin{align}
2x_1 + x_2 &\leq 10 && (1) \\
x_1 + x_2 &\leq 6 && (2) \\
x_1 &\leq 4.5 && (3) \\
x_2 &\leq 4.0 && (4) \\
x_1 &\geq 0 && (5) \\
x_2 &\geq 0 && (6)
\end{align}
$$

Constraints (5) and (6) express the fact that it is impossible to manufacture a negative amount of any product. Constraints (1) through (4) indicate the limitation on specific production activity on machines as well as products.

Note that our problem has two parts: an objective function to be maximized and inequalities (1) through (6) which describe the constraints on our problem. These constraints determine our region of feasibility and determine the totality of points (x_1, x_2), representing the feasible production programs, which jointly satisfy all constraints.

We now exhibit graphically the region of feasibility determined by constraints (1) through (6). Constraints (5) and (6) correspond to all of the points on and to the right of the line $x_2 = 0$ and above the line $x_1 = 0$, as shown in Figure 12.1. In the shaded area, both constraints (5) and (6) hold simultaneously.

The Constraints

Let us now proceed to further define the feasible region by investigating the effect of constraints (3) and (4). Figure 12.2 illustrates the region defined by the intersection of constraint (3) $(x_1 \leq 4.5)$ and constraints (5) and (6) as shown before. Figure 12.3 defines the resulting space when constraint (4) $(x_2 \leq 4)$ is intersected with the other constraints. We have now defined the rectangular region which is, at this point, the feasible region of solutions for the maximization of the objective function P.

In order to graph constraint (1), we first graph the equality $2x_1 + x_2 = 10$ as a linear line and then determine the side of the line which satisfies the inequality. A line segment representing the equation $2x_1 + x_2 = 10$ can be graphed by solving the equation for x_2 when $x_1 = 0$ and for x_1 when $x_2 = 0$. That is, the two points $(x_1 = 0, x_2 = 10)$ and $(x_1 = 5, x_2 = 0)$ define the linear line segment. The feasible solution region defined by the inequality is then determined by arbitrarily choosing values for x_1, x_2 and checking the validity of the inequality. For example, $x_1 = 3$ and $x_2 = 3$, when substituted into constraint (1), yield $2(3) + (3) < 10$, so the point $(3,3)$ satisfies the constraint. This fact determines the feasible solution space to be on

FIGURE 12.1   Region Defined by $x_1, x_2 \geq 0$

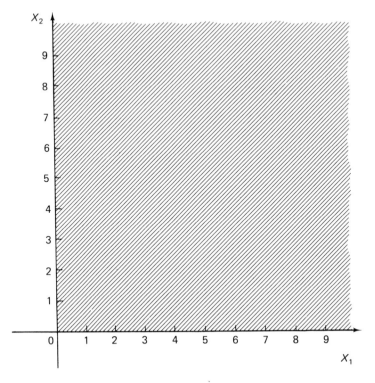

and below the line $2x_1 + x_2 = 10$ in Figure 12.4. The feasible solution space defined by constraints (1) and (3)–(6) is the shaded area of Figure 12.4. *Any* set of points (x_1, x_2) in this space or on the boundary is a feasible solution to our problem (excluding constraint (2)).

Finally, let us investigate the effects of adding constraint (2) to our problem. This is shown in Figure 12.5, which represents the final feasible region of solution for the problem. The region of feasible production programs is now completely represented by all points in the interior or on the boundary of the polygon *OABCDE*. Point *O* has coordinates $(0,0)$; point *A* has coordinates $(0,4)$; point *B*, $(2,4)$; point *C*, $(4,2)$; point *D*, $(4.5,1)$; and point *E*, $(4.5,0)$. For example, in order to determine the coordinates of point *C*, note that this point lies at the intersection of the limiting lines whose equations constitute the system

$$2x_1 + x_2 = 10$$

$$x_1 + x_2 = 6$$

This system has the solution $x_1 = 4$ and $x_2 = 2$ (the reader should verify this).

The points *O, A, B, C, D,* and *E* are termed *vertices* or *extreme points* of a convex polygon. A theorem of linear programming states that both a maximum value (to the objective function) or a minimum value occurs

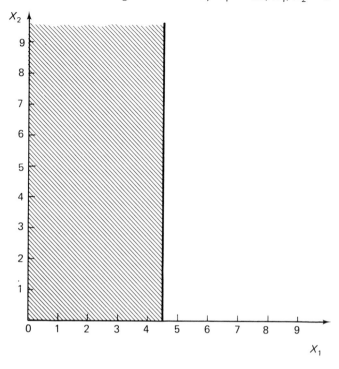

Region Defined by $x_1 \leq 4.5$, $x_1, x_2 \geq 0$ **FIGURE 12.2**

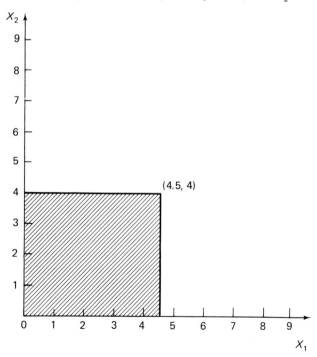

Region Defined by $0 \leq x_1 \leq 4.5$, $0 \leq x_2 \leq 4$ **FIGURE 12.3**

(4.5, 4)

FIGURE 12.4 Region Defined by $2x_1 + x_2 \leq 10$
$$0 \leq x_1 \leq 4.5$$
$$0 \leq x_2 \leq 4$$

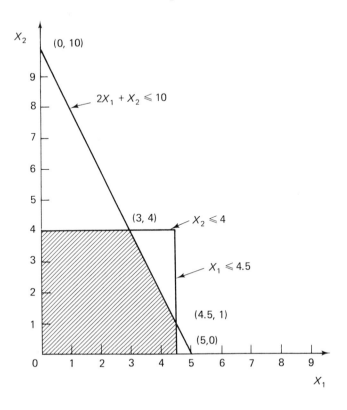

at an extreme point. Since this is true, an exhaustive search of all feasible solution points (x_1, x_2) of the polygon does not have to be made—only the extreme points. A substitution of the (x_1, x_2) extreme points into the objective function yields the following results:

Label	Coordinates	Profit
O	(0,0)	$0.00
A	(0,4)	$4.00
B	(2,4)	$7.00
C	(4,2)	$8.00
D	(4.5,1)	$7.75
E	(4.5,0)	$6.75

The objective function P is maximized for $x_1 = 4$ and $x_2 = 2$, with a value of $8.00. This solution will also be determined in the next section by graphing the objective function.

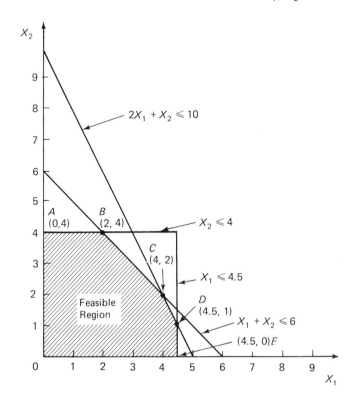

Region Defined by
$$x_1 + x_2 \leq 6$$
$$2x_1 + x_2 \leq 10$$
$$x_1 \leq 4$$
$$x_2 \leq 4.5$$
$$x_1, x_2 \geq 0$$

FIGURE 12.5

In Figure 12.6 the lines representing the profit schedules (objective functions) have been superimposed on the polygon of Figure 12.5. These profit schedules correspond to the values of the profit function at the corners O, A, B, C, D, and E. Recall that, in order to draw any such limiting linear line, we need to find only two of its points. For instance, to draw the line whose equation is $P = 6.75 = 1.5 x_1 + x_2$, note that if $x_1 = 0$ in this equation, then $x_2 = 6.75$ and when $x_2 = 0$, then $x_1 = 4.5$. Hence, the points (4.5,0) and (0,6.75) lie on the line. Plotting these points and drawing the connecting line determines the graph of $1.5x_1 + 1.0x_2 = 6.75$.

Suppose K represents an arbitrary constant. Obviously the function $P = 1.5x_1 + 1.0x_2$ is constant all along the line $1.5x_1 + 1.0x_2 = K$. For this reason any equation of the form $1.5x_1 + 1.0x_2 = K$ is often called an iso-profit line or simply a line of constant profit. By varying K we obtain a family of parallel lines like the six we graphed in Figure 12.6.

If we wish to maximize our objective function and profit P, we must move the line $1.5x_1 + 1.0x_2 = 0$ parallel to itself up and to the right as

237

FIGURE 12.6 Maximizing the Objective Function

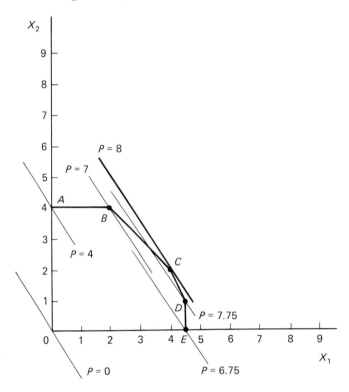

far from the origin as the feasible region permits. This is easy to do graphically by placing a straight edge along the line $1.5x_1 + 1.0x_2 = 0$ and then moving it parallel to itself up and across the region of feasibility in the direction of increasing profit until further movement carries it beyond the region of feasibility. One can see that the largest profit obtainable is at point C, where $P = \$8.00$ for the values $x_1 = 4.0$ and $x_2 = 2.0$. An analytical solution can be determined by noting that the iso-profit line leaves the solution space at the extreme point defined by the intersection of the lines for $2x_1 + x_2 = 10$ and $x_1 + x_2 = 6$. Solving these simultaneously yields $x_1 = 4.0$ and $x_2 = 2.0$.

An Example **Problem 1.** Solve the following problem graphically.

Maximize

$$y = 5x_1 + 6x_2$$

subject to the following restrictions

$$x_1 + 2x_2 \leq 24$$
$$18x_1 + 12x_2 \leq 216$$
$$x_1 \qquad\quad \leq 10$$

238

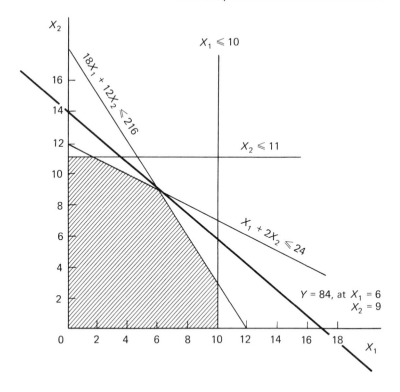

$$x_2 \leq 11$$
$$x_1 \quad \geq \quad 0$$
$$x_2 \geq \quad 0$$

As can be seen in Figure 12.7, the solution is $y = 84$ and occurs at $x_1 = 6$, $x_2 = 9$.

A MATHEMATICAL APPROACH

The method we illustrated in the previous section for solving linear programming problems works very well in certain ideal situations. It is, however, totally unworkable in most practical applications because of our inability to graphically handle problems with more than three variables. Consider the machine center example in the previous section in which there were two products being produced. The graphical solution illustrated was relatively simple. How would we have handled the problem, however, if we had three or more products with which to deal? It would be very difficult in the three dimensional case and certainly impossible in four or more dimensions to handle this problem graphically. We therefore must turn our attention to other methods for handling these types of problems.

In this section we will consider the tabular method for setting up and solving linear programming problems. This method will be shown to be most efficient for the vast majority of problems which are encountered. It is a totally mathematical approach and is iterative in nature in that successive problem solutions are generated by it. The procedure will terminate when a solution is found which meets a certain criterion, called the *optimality criterion;* the corresponding solution is called the *optimal solution.* Our solution procedure is called the simplex method, which was developed several years ago by a mathematician in an attempt to solve problems with linear objective functions having a set of linear constraints. Vast amounts of research have gone into the development and refinement of the simplex method, and indeed many textbooks have been written on this subject alone. In this section we hope to develop an appreciation for this method and demonstrate the steps involved in solving problems with it. As mentioned earlier, the procedure is iterative. The question naturally arises, "How do we know that the iterative procedure stops?" It has been established that the simplex procedure converges to the optimal solution in a finite number of steps. The proof of the assertion is beyond the scope of this text.

Some New Kinds of Variables

In order to deal with the problem from the simplex standpoint, we must introduce some new kinds of variables which allow us to deal more conveniently with the set of inequalities. In fact, the first step in our procedure must be to convert inequalities into equalities by using *slack variables.* The need for slack variables arises when a certain solution to a problem may not cause a given constraint to be satisfied as an inequality. For instance, the problem presented in the previous section had the following constraints:

$$2x_1 + x_2 \leq 10$$
$$x_1 + x_2 \leq 6$$
$$x_1 \leq 4.5$$
$$x_2 \leq 4$$

The first inequality states that the total number of hours available on machine I for daily production must not exceed ten. The second inequality states that the total number of hours available on machine II for daily production must not exceed six. Both of these inequalities recognize the relative differences between products and machines. Accordingly, the optimal solution in terms of a production schedule may well indicate that, all factors considered, one machine need not operate its maximum allotted time. For instance, it may turn out that machine I need operate only 8.5 hours a day to meet optimality conditions. In these cases, slack variables are introduced to take up the slack between the solution and the total amount of resources available, allowing us to convert inequalities to equalities. Thus, our new constraint set with slack variables s_1 through s_4 now becomes:

$$2x_1 + x_2 + s_1 \qquad\qquad = 10$$
$$x_1 + x_2 \quad + s_2 \qquad\quad = 6$$
$$x_1 \qquad\qquad + s_3 \quad = 4.5$$
$$x_2 \qquad\qquad + s_4 = 4$$

The introduction into our solution of four slack variables allows us to construct equality constraints. In this case s_1 is the amount of unused time on machine I, s_2 the amount of unused time on machine II, s_3 the number of units of product A which were not produced, and s_4 the number of units of product B not produced below their respective maxima. In each case, the slack variables are introduced to assume whatever value is required to make the equality relationship hold. However, the slack variables have no profit value associated with them so that the objective function can be written as:

Maximize

$$P = \$1.5x_1 + \$1.0x_2 + 0s_1 + 0s_2 + 0s_3 + 0s_4$$

Our entire problem becomes that of maximizing the profit P (with the slack variables introduced) subject to the set of equality constraints shown above. The problem has more variables, but all the constraints are now equalities instead of inequalities. We have now developed a new problem form, which can be said to consist of n variables and m constraints where n is greater than m in all cases. It can be shown that when n equals m, the problem has only one solution and thus is much simpler. A *basic solution* to this new problem form is achieved when m of the n variables are positive and the $n - m$ remaining variables are equal to zero. A *feasible solution* is a solution which satisfies *all* constraints. This procedure works by generating *basic feasible solutions* to the problem. Geometrically, the basic feasible solution corresponds to an extreme point of the feasible region defined by the constraints. Generally speaking, we begin the solution procedure by creating an *initial basic feasible solution* to the problem. This initial basic feasible solution is one in which only the slack variables are positive and equal to the right-hand portion of the equation. Thus, our initial basic feasible solution to the problem above would be

$$s_1 = 10$$
$$s_2 = 6$$
$$s_3 = 4.5$$
$$s_4 = 4$$

with x_1 and x_2 equal to zero. In this case, $n = 6$ and $m = 4$. So we have four variables with a positive solution and two variables which equal zero as the definition of a basic feasible solution indicates.

This initial basic feasible solution is obviously meaningless because the profit is zero and needs improvement. It is, however, a feasible point at which to begin searching for an optimal solution and that is the basic objective at this point.

In this section we have developed the concept of a slack variable and have shown its employment in the reformulation of the problem developed in the previous section. We will take these concepts and apply them in the next section to the formulation of the solution procedure which will allow us to develop optimal solutions to this type of problem.

The Simplex Method

As mentioned earlier, the simplex method is a tabular method which has been established to provide an iterative solution procedure for the problem type discussed in this chapter. In this section the concept of the simplex method will be developed and its techniques shown in a number of problem settings. Table 12.1 illustrates the basic format of the fundamental simplex tableau. We will discuss the columnar headings in the tableau as we develop the solution methodology, using as an example the problem presented and carried through this entire chapter.

In Table 12.1 the row at the top of the tableau entitled *Cost* will contain the coefficients for each variable, including slack variables, in the objective function. A given feasible solution is termed an iteration of the simplex

TABLE 12.1   The Fundamental Simplex Tableau

procedure and, in tabular form, is termed a simplex tableau as well. In Table 12.2 note that the cost row has those cost components (1.5, 1, 0, 0, 0, 0) entered over the appropriate variables (x_1, x_2, s_1, s_2, s_3, s_4). The *Solution Variables* column contains a listing of the variables in the *current* solution. Remember that the simplex technique is an iterative procedure. This column keeps track of those variables presently in the solution. Remember also that we will be dealing with basic solutions to the problem.

The *Solution Cost* column contains the objective function coefficients of those variables in the solution. In Table 12.2 all initial solution variables are slack variables and the corresponding objective function coefficients are zero. The other major column headings provide column entries for each of the coefficients associated with the variables in the constraint equations as developed in the previous section, including the slack variables. The column headed b contains the value at which the basic variable is in solution. That is, $s_1 = 10$, $s_2 = 6$, $s_3 = 4.5$, and $s_4 = 4$. The value of x_1 and x_2 are zero with the present solution. For the initial basic feasible solution shown in the previous section, this is simply the right-hand-side value of the constraint set. This particular column is sometimes referred to as the *right-hand-side vector* or the *resource vector*. Note that it represents the total amount of

Initial Simplex Tableau for Example Problem   **TABLE 12.2**

Solution Variables	Solution Cost	COST 1.5 X_1	1.0 X_2	0 S_1	0 S_2	0 S_3	0 S_4		b	Ratio
				VARIABLES						
S_1	0	2	1	1	0	0	0		10	$\frac{10}{2} = 5$
S_2	0	1	1	0	1	0	0		6	$\frac{6}{1} = 6$
S_3	0	1	0	0	0	1	0		4.5	$\frac{4.5}{1} = 4.5$
S_4	0	0	1	0	0	0	1		4	$\frac{4}{0} = \infty$
Reduced Cost		1.5	1.0	0	0	0	0		0	

Entering   Pivot   Solution   Departing
Variable   Element   Value   Variable

resources which can be consumed in the solution procedure. The final column entitled *Ratio* will be described later and is used to establish certain decisions that will lead to a new solution. Elements of the bottom row entitled *Reduced Cost* will be calculated as shown in the next few paragraphs. The elements of the reduced cost row reflect a rate of increase in the objective function and will be used to help us decide on the best potential direction (next extreme point solution) in moving toward the optimal solution.

The first step in the simplex method after filling in the tableau as shown in Table 12.2 is to calculate the reduced cost row. Remember that we will be working with basic feasible solutions to the problem; the initial basic feasible solution used for the simplex method is shown in the previous section in which the initial solution variables are the slack variables. So the reduced cost for each variable (column) can be calculated by the following formula:

$$\text{reduced cost} = \text{cost} - \text{solution cost} \times \text{variable column}$$

Calculating the reduced cost elements for x_1

$$\text{reduced cost} = 1.5 - [0(2) + 0(1) + 0(1) + 0(1) + 0(0)]$$
$$= 1.5$$

For x_2

$$\text{reduced cost} = 1.0 - [0(1) + 0(2) + 0(0) + 0(1)]$$
$$= 1.0$$

Following the same formula we will see that the reduced cost elements for all variables in the current solution are zero. This is always true when only slack variables are in the solution. Notice in Table 12.2 that all of the reduced cost elements have been calculated. We now calculate the solution value for this tableau. This is done by multiplying the solution cost column by the b column. In Table 12.2 this value is

$$[0(10) + 0(6) + 0(4.5) + 0(4)] = 0$$

The next step in the procedure is to identify a new variable to bring into the solution, which is accomplished by investigating the reduced cost row and selecting the variable with the *greatest positive* value as the *entering variable*. The reduced cost values reflect potential rates of increase in the objective function and therefore indicate the best potential direction in which to move toward a solution. The iterative nature of the simplex procedure will become clearer now as we select a variable to enter the next solution. In this case it is variable x_1. This indicates that as we move toward an optimal solution, the rate of increase in the objective function will be largest if variable x_1 is introduced.

Now we must decide which variable must leave the current basic solution
in the iterative process to make room for variable x_1 to enter. This involves determining the maximum value which x_1 can assume on entry to the solution without violating any constraints. The ratio column provides the facility for this and elements of this column are calculated using the formula

$$\text{ratio}_i = \text{ratio value for the } i\text{th row}$$

$$= \frac{\text{row element of } b \text{ vector}}{\text{corresponding row element under entering variable column}}$$

That is, $\text{ratio}_1 = 10/2 = 5$, and other ratio values are given in Table 12.2.

We select as the *departing variable* that variable currently in solution with *minimum positive ratio*. In case of ties an arbitrary decision may be made (this will be covered in Chapter 13). In our example, variable s_3 with a ratio value of 4.5 represents the departing variable. This says that x_1 may be entered into solution in place of s_3. The element in the tableau at the intersection of the entering variable column and the departing variable row is called the *pivot element*, and it plays an important role in the development of the next solution tableau.

Now that we have determined the variable which will yield the greatest solution improvement, x_1, and the variable which will be replaced in the solution, s_3, we are ready to develop a new tableau. The steps necessary to accomplish this, outlined below, provide the means to move to the next basic feasible solution. They are as follows.

1. **With the exception of the solution cost element, divide each element in the row of the departing variable by the pivot element.** In this particular example, the pivot element has the value of 1.0 and the new row elements will be the same as the old row elements. The pivot element will, of course, not always have the value of one. The new row elements are entered into a new tableau, replacing the elements of the old departing variable row. The solution variable corresponding to this new row in the next tableau will be the entering variable, x_1, which has replaced the departing variable, s_3.

2. **Enter the new solution variables and their solution cost values into the new tableau.** In obtaining a new solution to the linear programming problem, only one variable is changed with each iteration. Thus, in this example, the new solution consists of the s_1, s_2, x_1, and s_4 variables and these are entered in the next tableau as shown in Table 12.3. The solution cost values for these variables are the coefficients of these variables from the modified objective function. These values are 0, 0, 1.5, and 0 for s_1, s_2, x_1, and s_4, respectively, as shown in Table 12.3.

3. **With the exception of the pivot element, enter the value of zero for every element in the column of the entering variable (x_1, in this instance) in the new tableau.**

4. **Determine the remaining row elements for each solution variable in the new tableau.** The procedure for accomplishing this step is in accordance with elementary operations on rows of a matrix. The operations performed on one element of a row must be performed on all row elements. For instance, the zero element at the intersection of the new s_1 row and new x_1 column is obtained by multiplying the pivot element by two and subtracting the product from the (x_1, s_1) element of the old tableau. Thus, for the complete new s_1 row, the new row elements are obtained by multiplying

TABLE 12.3   The Second Simplex Solution

Solution Variables	Solution Cost	COST 1.5	1	0	0	0	0		b	Ratio
		X_1	X_2	S_1	S_2	S_3	S_4			
S_1	0	0	1	1	0	-2	0		1	
S_2	0	0	1	0	1	-1	0		1.5	
X_1	1.5	1	0	0	0	1	0		4.5	
S_4	0	0	1	0	0	0	1		4	
Reduced Cost		0	1	0	0	-1.5	0		6.75	
									Solution	

each element of the new x_1 row by the value 2.0 and subtracting the product from each corresponding element of the old s_1 row. By similar operations on the new x_1 row, the new s_3 and s_4 rows are obtained. The results of this step are shown in Table 12.3. It is important to emphasize that elementary operations are always performed on the new row of the entering variable in conjunction with the old rows of the variables remaining in solution in order to get the new rows for these remaining variables. This complete step will again be explained in greater detail in Chapter 13.

5. **Calculate a new solution value according to the relationship**
solution value = solution cost × b vector
$$= 0(1) + 0(1.5) + 1.5(4.5) + 0(4)$$
$$= 6.75$$
This value is shown in Table 12.3 and represents the profit achieved with the present solution. From the previous section we know that this is not optimal. Review the section on the graphical approach and attempt to draw some similiarities between our current solution and the graphical equivalent.

6. **Calculate reduced costs again by the relationship**
reduced cost = cost − solution cost × variable column
For x_1 this becomes
reduced cost $= 1.5 − [0(0) + 0(0) + 1.5(1) + 0(0)]$
$$= 0$$
For x_2 this becomes
reduced cost $= 1.0 − [0(1) + 0(1) + 1.5(0) + 0(1)]$
$$= 1$$
We see the remainder of the reduced cost elements in Table 12.3

The optimality criterion or stopping rule for the simplex procedure depends on the values of the elements in the reduced cost row. When all elements in this row become negative or zero, then the procedure terminates because it indicates that there is no suitable direction in which to move to increase the value of the objective function. This condition has not yet been reached since the elemental value under the x_2 column is 1, indicating a new entering variable x_2 would increase the objective function value.

Once again, we calculate ratios according to the previous formula for ratio$_i$. This produces the ratio column as given in Table 12.4. Based on our rule for selecting the departing variable it appears that s_1 is the candidate. The results of these calculations are given in Table 12.4.

Determining the Third Simplex Solution   **TABLE 12.4**

Solution Variable	Solution Cost	COST 1.5 X_1	1.0 X_2	0 S_1	0 S_2	0 S_3	0 S_4		b	Ratio
				VARIABLES						
S_1	0	0	(1)	1	0	-2	0		1	1
S_2	0	0	1	0	1	-1	0		1.5	1.5
X_1	1.5	1	0	0	0	1	0		4.5	$\frac{4.5}{0} = \infty$
S_4	0	0	1	0	0	0	1		4	4
Reduced Cost		0	1	0	0	-1.5	0		6.75	
			↑						Solution	

Entering Variable

Departing Variable

(1) = the pivot element

We are now prepared to generate a new tableau according to our rules. This tableau is shown in Table 12.5. Note that the solution has been improved to \$7.75. The procedure is causing us to move in a manner which improves the solution at each iteration.

Calculating the new reduced cost elements as shown in Table 12.5 indicates that the new entering variable is s_3. The ratio vector now becomes

TABLE 12.5   The Third Simplex Solution

Solution Variable	Solution Cost	COST	1.5 X_1	1.0 X_2	0 S_1	0 S_2	0 S_3	0 S_4		b	Ratio
X_2	1		0	1	1	0	-2	0		1	
S_2	0		0	0	-1	1	1	0		.5	
X_1	1.5		1	0	0	0	1	0		4.5	
S_4	0		0	0	-1	0	2	1		3	
	Reduced Cost		0	0	-1	0	.5	0		7.75	
										Solution	

Entering
Variable

as shown in Table 12.6. Note that variable s_2 is the departing variable from the ratio values below.

Ratio

-0.5
0.5 . . . . Departing Variable
4.5
1.5

By invoking the previous rules still another tableau can be generated. This tableau is shown in Table 12.7. After calculating the reduced cost row it becomes apparent that an optimal solution has been achieved. All reduced cost elements are zero or negative values. As was the case before, the solution value is $8. The solution is

$x_2 = 2$
$s_3 = 0.5$
$x_1 = 4$
$s_4 = 2$
$s_1 = 0$
$s_2 = 0$

Solution Variable	Solution Cost	COST	1.5	1.0	0	0	0	0		b	Ratio
			VARIABLES								
			X_1	X_2	S_1	S_2	S_3	S_4			
X_2	1		0	1	1	0	-2	0		1	$-\frac{1}{2}$
S_2	0		0	0	-1	1	(1)	0		.5	.5
X_1	1.5		1	0	0	0	1	0		4.5	4.5
S_4	0		0	0	-1	0	2	1		3	$\frac{3}{2}$
Reduced Cost			0	0	-1	0	.5	0		7.75	
										Solution	

Entering Variable

Departing Variable

(1) = the pivot element

Substituting $x_1 = 4$ and $x_2 = 2$ into the constraint equations, we see that all are satisfied by this solution. The solution also agrees with that achieved by the graphical approach.

Problem 2. In the first section an example problem was solved using the graphical method. Use the simplex method to solve that same problem. We first rewrite the problem with slack variables included.   **Some Examples**

Maximize

$$P = 5x_1 + 6x_2 + 0s_1 + 0s_2 + 0s_3 + 0s_4$$

This is subject to the following constraints:

$$
\begin{aligned}
x_1 + 2x_2 + s_1 & = 24 \\
18x_1 + 12x_2 + s_2 & = 216 \\
x_1 + s_3 & = 10 \\
x_2 + s_4 & = 11 \\
x_1 & \geq 0 \\
x_2 & \geq 0
\end{aligned}
$$

TABLE 12.7   Final Simplex Solution

Solution Variable	Solution Cost	COST	1.5	1.0	0	0	0	0		b	Ratio
			X_1	X_2	S_1	S_2	S_3	S_4			
X_2	1		0	1	-1	2	0	0		2	
S_3	0		0	1	-1	1	1	0		.5	
X_1	1.5		1	0	1	-1	0	0		4	
S_4	0		0	0	1	-2	0	1		2	
Reduced Cost			0	0	$-.5$	$-.5$	0	0		**8**	
										Solution	

Based on our discussion we know that the initial basic feasible solution may be arrived at by setting all nonslack variables equal to zero. The initial basic feasible solution is then

$$s_1 = 24$$
$$s_2 = 216$$
$$s_3 = 10$$
$$s_4 = 11$$
$$x_1 = x_2 = 0$$

As before, we proceed by developing the best directions for movement. This is accomplished by calculating the reduced cost elements. The initial simplex tableau, along with the reduced cost elements, is shown in Table 12.8. The *entering variable* (x_2), *ratios, leaving variable* (s_4), and *pivot element* are also shown.

We now proceed to develop our second tableau by performing operations about the pivot element to make all other columnar values equal to zero in the entering variable column. This is shown in Table 12.9. The remaining calculations for this are presented in Tables 12.10 and 12.11. Note that the net effect of the operations of Tables 12.10 and 12.11 is to take up the slack and improve the solution.

Solution Variables	Solution Cost	COST	5	6	0	0	0	0			
					VARIABLES						
			X_1	X_2	S_1	S_2	S_3	S_4		b	Ratio
S_1	0		1	2	1	0	0	0		24	$\frac{24}{2} = 12$
S_2	0		18	12	0	1	0	0		216	$\frac{216}{12} = 18$
S_3	0		1	0	0	0	1	0		10	$\frac{10}{0} = \infty$
S_4	0		0	①	0	0	0	1		11	$\frac{11}{1} = 11$
Reduced Cost			5	6	0	0	0	0		0	
										Solution	

Entering Variable

Leaving Variable

① = the pivot element

The final tableau generated in Table 12.11 represents an optimal solution. The termination criterion has been met. The optimal solution is 84 with $x_1 = 6$ and $x_2 = 9$. Place these values back into the constraint equations for proof that this solution meets all constraints.

Problem 3. Consider the following problem:

Maximize

$$P = 8x_1 + 2x_2 + 7x_3$$

subject to the constraints

$$
\begin{aligned}
x_1 + x_2 + x_3 &\leq 30 \\
-2x_1 + x_2 &\leq 15 \\
x_2 - 2x_3 &\leq 24 \\
4x_1 - x_2 + 2x_3 &\leq 80 \\
x_1 &\geq 0 \\
x_2 &\geq 0 \\
x_3 &\geq 0
\end{aligned}
$$

251

TABLE 12.9   Second Solution—Example Problem 2

Solution Variables	Solution Cost	COST	5	6	0	0	0	0		b	Ratio
			X_1	X_2	S_1	S_2	S_3	S_4			
S_1	0		1	0	1	0	0	-2		2	$\frac{2}{1} = 2$
S_2	0		18	0	0	1	0	-12		84	$\frac{84}{18} = 4\frac{2}{3}$
S_3	0		1	0	0	0	1	0		10	$\frac{10}{1} = 10$
X_2	6		0	1	0	0	0	1		11	$\frac{11}{0} = \infty$
	Reduced Cost		5	0	0	0	0	-6		66	
										Solution	

Entering Variable

Leaving Variable

As before, we need to introduce slack variables for each constraint. Upon rewriting, the problem now becomes:

Maximize

$$P = 8x_1 + 2x_2 + 7x_3 + 0s_1 + 0s_2 + 0s_3 + 0s_4$$

subject to

$$
\begin{aligned}
x_1 + x_2 + x_3 + s_1 &= 30 \\
-2x_1 + x_2 + s_2 &= 15 \\
x_2 - 2x_3 + s_3 &= 24 \\
4x_1 - x_2 + 2x_3 + s_4 &= 80
\end{aligned}
$$

Tables 12.12 through 12.15 illustrate the successive simplex tableaus generated in the solution of this problem. It is interesting to note the following optimal solution from the standpoint that x_2 becomes zero after entering a solution and then being replaced.

Third Solution—Example Problem 2 **TABLE 12.10**

Solution Variables	Solution Cost	COST 5	6	0	0	0	0		b	Ratio
		VARIABLES								
		X_1	X_2	S_1	S_2	S_3	S_4			
X_1	5	1	0	1	0	0	-2		2	$\frac{2}{-2} = -1$
S_2	0	0	0	-18	1	0	$\boxed{24}$		48	$\frac{48}{24} = 2$
S_3	0	0	0	-1	0	1	2		8	$\frac{8}{2} = 4$
X_2	6	0	1	0	0	0	1		11	$\frac{11}{1} = 11$
Reduced Cost		0	0	-5	0	0	4		76	

Entering Variable (column S_4)

Solution (76)

Leaving Variable

Final Solution—Example Problem 2 **TABLE 12.11**

Solution Variables	Solution Cost	COST 5	6	0	0	0	0		b	Ratio
		VARIABLES								
		X_1	X_2	S_1	S_2	S_3	S_4			
X_1	5	1	0	$-\frac{1}{2}$	.08	0	0		6	
S_4	0	0	0	$-\frac{3}{4}$	.04	0	1		2	
S_3	0	0	0	$\frac{1}{2}$	$-.08$	1	0		4	
X_2	6	0	1	$\frac{3}{4}$	$-.04$	0	0		9	
Reduced Cost		0	0	-2	$-.167$	0	0		84	

Solution

TABLE 12.12 Initial Solution—Example Problem 3

Solution Variables	Solution Cost	COST	8	2	7	0	0	0	0		
			VARIABLES								
			X_1	X_2	X_3	S_1	S_2	S_3	S_4	b	Ratio
S_1	0		1	1	1	1	0	0	0	30	$\frac{30}{1} = 30$
S_2	0		-2	1	0	0	1	0	0	15	$\frac{15}{-2} = -7\frac{1}{2}$
S_3	0		0	1	-2	0	0	1	0	24	$\frac{24}{0} = \infty$
S_4	0		(4)	1	2	0	0	0	1	80	$\frac{80}{4} = 20$ ←
	Reduced Cost		8	2	7	0	0	0	0	0	
										Solution	

Entering Variable

Leaving Variable

$$P = 220$$
$$x_1 = 10$$
$$x_2 = 0$$
$$x_3 = 20$$

It is also interesting to note that when the solution values are entered into the constraint equations, only the first and fourth are satisfied fully. In fact, constraints two and three are far from satisfied as equalities. This is reflected in the nonzero values for s_2 and s_3. This says that constraints one and four are *binding* or *active*, which means that the maximum value of the objective function is restricted by only those two constraints. The other two constraints are not binding.

PROBLEMS

1. Consider the following linear programming problem.

Maximize

$$z_0 = 5z_1 + 4z_2$$

Solution Variables	Solution Cost	COST	8	2	7	0	0	0	0		
			X_1	X_2	X_3	S_1	S_2	S_3	S_4	b	Ratio
S_1	0		0	1.25	.50	1	0	0	−.25	10	$\frac{10}{5/4} = 8$
S_2	0		0	.50	1	0	1	0	.50	55	$\frac{55}{.5} = 110$
S_3	0		0	1	−2	0	0	1	0	24	$\frac{24}{1} = 24$
X_1	8		1	−.25	.50	0	0	0	.25	20	$\frac{20}{-.25} = -80$
Reduced Cost			0	4	3	0	0	0	2	**160**	
										Solution	

Entering Variable

Leaving Variable

subject to

$$z_1 + z_2 \leq 15$$
$$3z_1 + 2z_2 \leq 40$$
$$z_1 \geq 0, z_2 \geq 0$$

Solve this problem graphically.

2. Solve the following linear programming problem by the graphical approach.

Maximize

$$x_0 = 2x_1 + 3x_2$$

subject to

$$x_1 + 2x_2 \leq 50$$
$$x_1 - x_2 \geq 10$$
$$x_1 \geq 0, x_2 \geq 0$$

3. Solve the following linear programming problem using the simplex method.

TABLE 12.14   Third Solution—Example Problem 3

Solution Variables	Solution Cost	COST	8	2	7	0	0	0	0		
			VARIABLES								
			X_1	X_2	X_3	S_1	S_2	S_3	S_4	b	Ratio
X_2	2		0	1	(.4)	.8	0	0	−.2	8	$\frac{8}{.4}=20$
S_2	0		0	0	.8	−.4	1	0	.6	51	$\frac{51}{.8}=63\frac{3}{4}$
S_3	0		0	0	−2.4	−.8	0	1	.2	16	$\frac{16}{-2.4}=-6.67$
X_1	8		1	0	.6	.2	0	0	.2	22	$\frac{22}{.6}=36\frac{2}{3}$
Reduced Cost			0	0	1.4	−3.2	0	0	−1.2	192	
										Solution	

Entering Variable (↑ under X_3)

Leaving Variable

Maximize

$$z = 2x_1 - 2x_2 + x_3$$

subject to

$$x_1 - x_2 \leq 2$$
$$2x_1 + 3x_2 + 4x_3 \leq 10$$
$$x_1 \geq 0, x_2 \geq 0, x_3 \geq 0$$

4. Solve the following linear programming problem by the simplex method. Check your solution by use of the graphical method.
Maximize

$$z = 7x_1 + 6x_2$$

subject to

$$3x_1 + 2x_2 \leq 24$$
$$x_2 \leq 10$$
$$x_1 \geq 0, x_2 \geq 0$$

Solution Variables	Solution Cost	COST 8	2	7	0	0	0	0		
		VARIABLES								
		X_1	X_2	X_3	S_1	S_2	S_3	S_4	b	Ratio
X_3	7	0	2.5	1	2	0	0	− .5	20	
S_2	0	0	− 2	0	− 2	1	0	1	35	
S_3	0	0	6	0	4	0	1	− 1	64	
X_1	8	1	− 1.5	0	− 1	0	0	.5	10	
Reduced Cost		0	− 3.5	0	− 6	0	0	− .5	220	
									Solution	

5. A manufacturing company is considering buying any of three types of new machines. Machine A costs $6,700; machine B, $5,000; and machine C, $3,500. The maximum amount of money which can be spent is $150,000. The expected net profit for these machines is $420 annually for A, $300 annually for B, and $230 annually for C.

There are several other constraints: There is floor space available for only thirty machines. If only type C machines were purchased, the maintenance department could handle forty, but the maintenance on a type B machine is 1-1/3 times that of C and on a type A it is 1-2/3 more than C.

From the above information, formulate the linear programming model and solve. Disregard the fact that the number of machines bought must be integer.

6. The profits for production of two types of products are $2 and $5 respectively. The requirements for production are three machine hours and ten units of raw materials for product 1 and five machine hours and seven units of raw materials for machine 2. The maximum available machine-hours are 200, and the maximum number of raw material units available is 300. At least 15 units of product 1 must be produced. Determine the optimal amount of each product to produce.

7. Solve the following linear programming problem by the simplex method.

Maximize

$$x_0 = 3x_1 + 9x_2 + 5x_3$$

subject to

$$x_1 + 4x_2 + 5x_3 \leq 8$$
$$x_1 + 3x_2 + 6x_3 \leq 4$$
$$x_1 \geq 0, \, x_2 \geq 0, \, x_3 \geq 0$$

8. Solve the following problem by (a) the graphical approach; and (b) the simplex method.

Maximize

$$x_0 = 2x_1 + x_2$$

subject to

$$x_1 + 4x_2 \leq 24$$
$$x_1 + 2x_2 \leq 14$$
$$2x_1 - x_2 \leq 8$$
$$x_1 - x_2 \leq 3$$
$$x_1 \geq 0, \, x_2 \geq 0$$

9. Consider the following linear programming problem.

Maximize

$$z = 20x_1 + 6x_2 + 8x_3$$

subject to

$$8x_1 + 2x_2 + 3x_3 \leq 200$$
$$4x_1 + 3x_2 \qquad \leq 100$$
$$2x_1 \qquad + x_3 \leq 50$$
$$x_3 \leq 20$$
$$x_i \geq 0, \, i = 1,2,3$$

Solve by the simplex method.

10. Maximize the following linear programming problem by use of the simplex method.

$$z = 4x_1 + 2x_2 + 3x_3$$

subject to

$$x_1 + 2x_2 + 3x_3 \leq 10$$
$$x_1 + x_2 \qquad \leq 5$$
$$x_1 \qquad\qquad \leq 1$$
$$x_1 \geq 0,\ x_2 \geq 0,\ x_3 \geq 0$$

BIBLIOGRAPHY

The references for this chapter can be found at the end of Chapter 13.

Linear programming II

In the previous chapter linear programming was introduced by solving maximization problems both graphically and by the simplex procedure. The only type of constraints considered were those of a less than or equal to ($\leq$) nature.

This chapter will consider minimization problems and a variety of constraints. Certain special situations that arise in solving linear programming problems will be discussed and the dual linear programming problem will be discussed and solved by the simplex procedure. However, special cases of linear programming problems such as the transportation model, the assignment model, parametric programming, and integer programming are not covered in this introductory text.

The reader will recall from Chapter 12 that an inequality of the less than or equal ($\leq$) type was converted to an equality by the addition of a positive-valued slack variable to the left side of the inequality. Since various types of linear inequalities are encountered in practice, a further discussion of constraints and inequalities is warranted. A review of certain inequality properties therefore follows. **Constraints and Inequalities**

1. An inequality in one direction ($\geq$ or $\leq$) may be changed to an inequality in the opposite direction ($\leq$ or $\geq$) by multiplying through by the quantity -1. For example, the linear constraint

$$a_1 x_1 + a_2 x_2 \geq b$$

is equivalent to

$$-a_1 x_1 - a_2 x_2 \leq -b$$

Also for linear programming purposes, a greater than or equal inequality may be converted to an equality by the subtraction of a slack variable. That is, if

$$a_1 x_1 + a_2 x_2 \geq b, \text{ then}$$
$$a_1 x_1 + a_2 x_2 - S = b$$

The events of a nonpositive resource quantity $-b$ and a negative coefficient -1 for the slack variable present complications in the simplex procedure for solving linear programming problems. A negative-valued b is not allowed and the -1 coefficient for the slack variable S can present problems in easily determining an initial basic feasible solution (the first tableau) in the simplex procedure. The resolution to this latter complication is to add an artificial variable, A, to the equality as

$$a_1 x_1 + a_2 x_2 - S + A = b$$

261

The use of artificial variables arises in greater than or equal ($\geq$) constraints; these may also be added to equality constraints if the obtaining of an initial basic feasible solution is thereby made easier. A more detailed discussion of artificial variables is presented in a later section of the chapter.

2. An equation can be replaced by two inequalities in opposite directions. For example,

$$a_1 x_1 + a_2 x_2 = b$$

is equivalent to the two simultaneous constraints

$$a_1 x_1 + a_2 x_2 \leq b \text{ and } a_1 x_1 + a_2 x_2 \geq b$$

3. An inequality constraint with its left side in the absolute value form can be replaced by two inequalities. That is, for $b \geq 0$,

$$|a_1 x_1 + a_2 x_2| \leq b$$

is equivalent to

$$a_1 x_1 + a_2 x_2 \geq -b \text{ and } a_1 x_1 + a_2 x_2 \leq b. \text{ Or, if}$$

$$|a_1 x_1 + a_2 x_2| \geq b, \text{ then}$$

$$a_1 x_1 + a_2 x_2 \geq b \text{ and } a_1 x_1 + a_2 x_2 \leq -b \text{ are equivalent expressions.}$$

4. A variable which is unconstrained in sign (that is the variable may be zero, positive, or negative) may be represented by the difference between two nonnegative variables. For example, if x_3 is unconstrained in sign, it can be replaced by $(x_3^+ - x_3^-)$ where x_3^+ and x_3^- are both nonnegative. However, in most business applications of linear programming, a variable unconstrained in sign is rarely encountered.

An Example

Suppose the following set of constraints is applicable to some linear programming problem:

$$2x_1 + 2x_2 + 6x_3 \leq 80$$

$$0.5x_1 + 4.5x_2 - 3.5x_3 \geq 25$$

$$2x_1 + x_2 = 15$$

$$|5x_2 + 8x_3| \leq 90$$

where $x_1 \geq 0$, $x_2 \geq 0$, and x_3 is unconstrained in sign.

If it is desired to restate the inequalities such that each is of the less than or equal ($\leq$) form, then we have

$$2x_1 + 2x_2 + 6(x_3^+ - x_3^-) \le 80$$

$$-0.5x_1 - 4.5x_2 + 3.5(x_3^+ - x_3^-) \le -25$$

$$2x_1 + x_2 \le 15$$

$$-2x_1 - x_2 \le -15$$

$$5x_2 + 8(x_3^+ - x_3^-) \le 90$$

$$-5x_2 - 8(x_3^+ - x_3^-) \le 90$$

where $x_1 \ge 0$, $x_2 \ge 0$, $x_3^+ \ge 0$, and $x_3^- \ge 0$

Further modifications to the above inequality constraint set are necessary before entering the first tableau of the simplex procedure. The modifications will be covered later under the discussion of artificial variables.

It will be helpful to slightly modify the simplex table from Chapter 12 for the purposes of development in this chapter. The procedural steps for the solution of a maximization problem will be exactly the same as before, however. The terminology of the simplex table will be modified slightly as follows: **A Modified Simplex Table**

Cost Row	$= C_j$ row (the coefficient associated with the jth variable)
Solution Cost Column	$= C_j$ column (the coefficient associated with the jth variable in solution)
Solution Column	$=$ Solution Variables Column
Reduced Cost Row	$= C_j - Z_j$ row
Solution Cost X Variable Column	$= Z_j$ row (the sum of the products of C_j column values times the jth variable column)

The reader will note that the reduced cost calculation from Chapter 12 has been changed in notation only. That is,

reduced cost = cost − solution cost × variable column

$$= C_j - Z_j$$

With these notational changes, references to the simplex table values can be more conveniently made. The modified simplex table appears in Table 13.1 with the addition of a Z_j row above the $C_j - Z_j$. The addition of the Z_j row merely serves to minimize the chance for arithmetical error in manually working through the simplex procedure.

A problem from Chapter 12 is now recalled, namely,

Maximize

$$P = \$1.5x_1 + \$1.0x_2$$

TABLE 13.1   A Modified Simplex Table

	C_j									b	Ratio
		VARIABLES									
Solution Variables											
Z_j											
$C_j - Z_j$											

Objective Function Value

subject to

$$2x_1 + x_2 \leq 10$$
$$-x_1 + x_2 \leq 6$$
$$x_1 \leq 4.5$$
$$x_2 \leq 4$$
$$x_1 \geq 0, x_2 \geq 0.$$

The initial solution for this problem is given in Table 13.2.

The Z_j total for a given variable column is the sum of the products obtained when the row numbers in the C_j column are multiplied by the corresponding row number for a particular jth variable column. For example, Z_1 (for the x_1 column) = C_j numbers $\times$ x_1 numbers = $0\,(2) + 0\,(1) + 0\,(1) + 0\,(0) = 0$. In matrix algebra terminology, this is the inner product of two vectors. Namely, the vector $x_1 = (2, 1, 1, 0)$ times the vector C_j

$$= \begin{pmatrix} 0 \\ 0 \\ 0 \\ 0 \end{pmatrix}$$ equals the scalar product $Z_1 = 0$. Similarly, a Z value is calculated

	C_j	1.5	1.0	0	0	0	0			
		VARIABLES								
Solution Variables		x_1	x_2	S_1	S_2	S_3	S_4		b	Ratio
S_1	0	2	1	1	0	0	0		10	$\frac{10}{2} = 5$
S_2	0	1	1	0	1	0	0		6	$\frac{6}{1} = 6$
S_3	0	(1)	0	0	0	1	0		4.5	$\frac{4.5}{1} = 4.5$
S_4	0	0	1	0	0	0	1		4	$\frac{4}{0} = \infty$
	Z_j	0	0	0	0	0	0		0	
	$C_j - Z_j$	1.5	1.0	0	0	0	0			

Leaving Variable (← S_3 row)

↑ Entering Variable

for the b column as $Z_0 = (10, 6, 4.5, 4) \cdot \begin{pmatrix} 0 \\ 0 \\ 0 \\ 0 \end{pmatrix} = 0\,(10) + 0\,(6) + 0$

(4.5) + 0 (4) = 0, which is the value of the objective function with the present solution. The Z value for a particular column other than Z_0 represents the amount of profit which is given up by replacing some of the present solution mix with *one* unit of the variable heading the column. In Table 13.2 this amount is zero for all variables. The $C_j - Z_j$ number indicates the net profit (contribution) which would be added, if $C_j - Z_j$ is positive, by one unit of the variable, X_j or S_j; or the amount of profit lost if $C_j - Z_j$ is negative.

From Table 13.2, the $C_1 - Z_1$ value of 1.5 indicates the variable x_1 should add the most profit per unit and the smallest positive ratio of 4.5 indicates that S_3 should leave the solution. This smallest positive ratio indicates the maximum number of units of the new variable which may be brought into solution without causing some other variable to be negative. In this case, 4.5 units of x_1 is the maximum permitted without causing S_3 to be negative. This can be seen from the constraint $x_1 \le 4.5$, or $x_1 + S_3 = 4.5$;

thus S_3 would have to be negative in order to satisfy the equality if x_1 was greater than 4.5 units and a negative-valued variable cannot be in solution.

It is also noted that the coefficients in the simplex table under a given variable column can be considered *substitution coefficients*. For example, in Table 13.2, the vector of elements $\begin{pmatrix} 2 \\ 1 \\ 1 \\ 0 \end{pmatrix}$ is under the variable column x_1. For every unit of x_1 brought into solution, two units of S_1, one unit of S_2, one unit of S_3, and zero units of S_4 must be removed from the solution to avoid violating the constraints. Recall that the constraint set of this problem, after adding slack variables, is

$$
\begin{aligned}
2x_1 + x_2 + S_1 && = 10 && (1) \\
x_1 + x_2 && + S_2 && = 6 && (2) \\
x_1 && + S_3 && = 4.5 && (3) \\
x_2 && + S_4 = 4 && (4)
\end{aligned}
$$

with the initial solution of $x_1 = 0$, $x_2 = 0$, $S_1 = 10$, $S_2 = 6$, $S_3 = 4.5$, and $S_4 = 4$. If 4.5 units of x_1 enter the solution, then 9 units of S_1 must be removed, 4.5 units of S_2 must be removed, 4.5 units (all) of S_3 must be removed, and $S_4 = 4$ remains in order not to violate the constraints. The new solution will be $x_1 = 4.5$, $x_2 = 0$, $S_1 = 1$, $S_2 = 1.5$, $S_3 = 0$, and $S_4 = 4$. The constraints are not violated as seen below (with the variable values substituted in):

$$
\begin{aligned}
2(4.5) + 0 + 1 && = 10 && (1) \\
(4.5) + 0 && + (1.5) && = 6 && (2) \\
(4.5) && + 0 && = 4.5 && (3) \\
0 && + (4) = && 4 && (4)
\end{aligned}
$$

This new solution is seen in the first iteration of the simplex procedure which appears in Table 13.3. The substitution coefficients also provide the rationale for interpreting a Z value, say Z_1, as the *opportunity cost* of introducing a unit of x_1. The profit coefficients for S_1, S_2, S_3, and S_4 (variables which are affected by bringing in x_1) are zero per unit in each case for this particular iteration. The opportunity cost of introducing one unit of x_1 is

$$Z_1 = 2 \text{ (for } S_1) \cdot 0 + 1 \text{ (for } S_2) \cdot 0 + $$
$$1 \text{ (for } S_3) \cdot 0 + 0 \text{ (for } S_4) \cdot 0 = 0$$

In other words, it will cost zero dollars in the objective function to introduce one unit of x_1 into solution. But since x_1 has a profit of $1.5 per unit, the net profit from one unit of x_1 is $C_1 - Z_1 = \$1.5 - 0 = \$1.5$.

It has been the purpose of this section to introduce new notations for

TABLE 13.3 Second Solution to $P = \$1.5x_1 + \$1.0x_2$

Solution Variables	C_j	1.5	1.0	0	0	0	0			
		VARIABLES								
		x_1	x_2	S_1	S_2	S_3	S_4		b	Ratio
S_1	0	0	1	1	0	−2	0		1	1
S_2	0	0	(1)	0	1	−1	0		$\frac{3}{2}$	$\frac{3/2}{1} = 3/2$ ← Leaving Variable
x_1	1.5	1	0	0	0	1	0		4.5	$\frac{4.5}{0} = \infty$
S_4	0	0	1	0	0	0	1		4	$\frac{4}{1} = 4$
Z_j		1.5	0	0	0	1.5	0		$\frac{27}{4}$	
$C_j - Z_j$		0	1	0	0	−1.5	0			
			↑ Entering Variable							

the simplex procedure and to explain the usage thereof. As a consequence, further insight into the mechanics of the simplex procedure has hopefully been provided.

A Minimization Problem

Let us suppose that an objective function in terms of costs, rather than profits, has been formulated to be

Minimize

$$C = \$1.0x_1 - \$3.0x_2 - \$2.0x_3$$

subject to

$$\begin{aligned} 3x_1 - x_2 + 2x_3 &\le 7 \\ -2x_1 + 4x_2 &\le 12 \\ -4x_1 + 3x_2 + 8x_3 &\le 10 \\ x_1 \ge 0,\ x_2 \ge 0,\ x_3 &\ge 0 \end{aligned}$$

This problem can be solved by either of two approaches using the simplex procedure. The first method is to maximize the negative of the cost function, that is, maximize $P = -x_1 + 3x_2 + 2x_3$ by the same procedural steps as previously discussed in Chapter 12. (The constraints remain as above.) Or we can solve as a minimization problem by using a different rule on the $C_j - Z_j$ value for selecting the variable to enter a new solution. All other solution steps are the same. In the maximization problem, the largest positive $C_j - Z_j$ value indicated the new variable to bring into the solution. The optimal solution was found when all the $C_j - Z_j$ values were negative-valued or zero. In the minimization problem, the *most negative* $C_j - Z_j$ value will indicate the new variable to bring into the solution which will lower the objective function cost value the most. The optimal solution will be found when all the $C_j - Z_j$ values are positive-valued or zero. All other simplex procedural steps are the same for the minimization problem as for the maximization problem. In order to illustrate, the above problem is modified to enter the first simplex solution as

Minimize

$$C = \$1.0x_1 - \$3.0x_2 - \$2.0x_3 + \$(0)S_1 + \$(0)S_2 + \$(0)S_3$$

subject to

$$3x_1 - x_2 + 2x_3 + S_1 \qquad\qquad = 7$$
$$-2x_1 + 4x_2 \qquad\qquad + S_2 \qquad = 12$$
$$-4x_1 + 3x_2 + 8x_3 \qquad\qquad + S_3 = 10$$
$$x_1 \geq 0, x_2 \geq 0, x_3 \geq 0, S_1 \geq 0, S_2 \geq 0, S_3 \geq 0.$$

This first solution appears in the simplex table as Table 13.4.

The most negative $C_j - Z_j$ value in Table 13.4 is (-3) under the x_2 column. Thus, x_2 is selected as the entering variable and replaces S_2 which has the smallest positive ratio in the ratio column. We therefore divide the S_2 row in the first solution (Table 13.4) by the pivot element ④ to obtain the x_2 row in the next solution. That is,

	x_1	x_2	x_3	S_1	S_2	S_3	b
row S_2 = (-2	4	0	0	1	0	12)

becomes

	x_1	x_2	x_3	S_1	S_2	S_3	b
row x_2 = ($-1/2$	1	0	0	1/4	0	3)

The reader will recall that we perform elementary operations on the new row x_2 to obtain the new rows for the remaining basis variables S_1 and S_3. We first note that the new column values for x_2 should be

	C_j	1	-3	-2	0	0	0			
		VARIABLES								
Solution Variables		x_1	x_2	x_3	S_1	S_2	S_3		b	Ratio
S_1	0	3	-1	-2	1	0	0		7	$\frac{7}{-1} = -7$
S_2	0	-2	④	0	0	1	0		12	$\frac{12}{4} = 3$
S_3	0	-4	3	8	0	0	1		10	$\frac{10}{3} = 3\frac{1}{3}$
Z_j		0	0	0	0	0	0		0	
$C_j - Z_j$		1	-3	-2	0	0	0			

Leaving Variable ← (S_2 row)

↑ Entering Variable

$$
\begin{matrix}
 & x_2 \\
S_1 \cdots \cdots & \begin{pmatrix} 0 \\ 1 \\ 0 \end{pmatrix} \\
x_2 \cdots \cdots & \\
S_3 \cdots \cdots &
\end{matrix}.
$$

For the S_1 row this zero element is accomplished by adding the new row x_2 to the old S_1 row. That is, add

new $x_2 = (-1/2 \quad 1 \quad 0 \quad 0 \quad 1/4 \quad 0 \quad 3)$ elementally to
old $S_1 = (3 \qquad -1 \quad 2 \quad 1 \quad 0 \qquad 0 \quad 7)$ to get
new $S_1 = (5/2 \quad 0 \quad 2 \quad 1 \quad 1/4 \quad 0 \quad 10)$.

For the S_3 row, multiply elements of the new x_2 row by (-3) and add to the old S_3 row. That is,

new $x_2 \cdot (-3) = (3/2 \quad -3 \quad 0 \quad 0 \quad -3/4 \quad 0 \quad -9)$ added to
old $S_3 \qquad = (-4 \qquad 3 \quad 8 \quad 0 \quad 0 \qquad 1 \quad 10)$ yields
new $S_3 \qquad = (-5/2 \quad 0 \quad 8 \quad 0 \quad -3/4 \quad 1 \quad 1)$.

269

The first iteration (second solution) of the simplex procedure is thus completed and appears in Table 13.5.

The most negative $C_j - Z_j$ value in Table 13.5 is (-2) under the x_3 column. The variable x_3 is therefore selected as the entering variable to replace S_3 which has the smallest positive ratio of $1/8$ in the ratio column. Since the pivot element is ⑧,

$$
\begin{array}{ccccccc}
 & x_1 & x_2 & x_3 & S_1 & S_2 & S_3 & b \\
\text{row } S_3 = (& -5/2 & 0 & 8 & 0 & -3/4 & 1 & 1)
\end{array}
$$

becomes

$$
\text{row } x_3 = (-5/16 \quad 0 \quad 1 \quad 0 \quad -3/32 \quad 1/8 \quad 1/8)
$$

of the next solution. The new column values for x_3 should be

$$
\begin{array}{c}
x_3 \\
S_1 \cdots \cdots \begin{pmatrix} 0 \\ 0 \\ 1 \end{pmatrix}.
\\
x_2 \cdots \cdots \\
x_3 \cdots \cdots
\end{array}
$$

TABLE 13.5 Second Solution to Minimization Problem

Solution Variables		C_j	1	-3	-2	0	0	0		b	Ratio
			\multicolumn{6}{c}{VARIABLES}			
			x_1	x_2	x_3	S_1	S_2	S_3			
S_1	0		$\frac{5}{2}$	0	2	1	$\frac{1}{4}$	0		10	$\frac{10}{2} = 5$
x_2	-3		$\frac{-1}{2}$	1	0	0	$\frac{1}{4}$	0		3	$\frac{3}{0} = \infty$
S_3	0		$\frac{-5}{2}$	0	⑧	0	$\frac{-3}{4}$	1		1	$\frac{1}{8}$ ← Leaving Variable
		Z_j	$\frac{3}{2}$	-3	0	0	$\frac{-3}{4}$	0		-9	
		$C_j - Z_j$	$\frac{-1}{2}$	0	-2	0	$\frac{3}{4}$	0			

Entering Variable

For the S_1 row, this is achieved by

$$
\begin{aligned}
\text{new } x_3 \cdot (-2) &= (5/8 \quad 0 \quad -2 \quad 0 \quad 3/16 \quad -1/4 \quad -1/4) \quad \text{added to} \\
\text{old } S_1 &= (5/2 \quad 0 \quad 2 \quad 1 \quad 1/4 \quad 0 \quad 10) \quad \text{to get} \\
\text{new } S_1 &= (25/8 \quad 0 \quad 0 \quad 1 \quad 7/16 \quad -1/4 \quad 39/4).
\end{aligned}
$$

For the new x_2 row, we need only to enter the old x_2 row because an element of zero already exists under the x_3 column. The second iteration (third solution) now appears as Table 13.6.

The most negative $C_j - Z_j$ value in Table 13.6 is $(-9/8)$ under the x_1 column. The variable x_1 is selected as the entering variable to replace S_1 which has the smallest positive ratio of $78/25$. The pivot element of $(25/8)$ is converted to the element 1 by multiplying row S_1 by $8/25$. That is,

$$
\begin{array}{ccccccc}
x_1 & x_2 & x_3 & S_1 & S_2 & S_3 & b
\end{array}
$$

$$
\text{old } S_1 \cdot (8/25) = (1 \quad 0 \quad 0 \quad 8/25 \quad 7/50 \quad -2/25 \quad 78/25) = \text{new } x_1
$$

The elementary operations on the row x_1 to complete the new solution are

$$
\begin{aligned}
\text{new } x_1 \cdot (1/2) &= (1/2 \quad 0 \quad 0 \quad 8/50 \quad 7/100 \quad -2/50 \quad 78/50) \quad \text{added to} \\
\text{old } x_2 &= (-1/2 \quad 1 \quad 0 \quad 0 \quad 1/4 \quad 0 \quad 3) \quad \text{yields}
\end{aligned}
$$

Third Solution to Minimization Problem **TABLE 13.6**

Solution Variables		C_j	1	-3	-2	0	0	0		b	Ratio
			\multicolumn{7}{c}{VARIABLES}			
			x_1	x_2	x_3	S_1	S_2	S_3			
S_1	0		$\frac{25}{8}$	0	0	1	$\frac{7}{16}$	$\frac{-1}{4}$		$\frac{39}{4}$	$\frac{78}{25}$
x_2	-3		$\frac{-1}{2}$	1	0	0	$\frac{1}{4}$	0		3	-6
x_3	-2		$\frac{-5}{16}$	0	1	0	$\frac{-3}{32}$	$\frac{1}{8}$		$\frac{1}{8}$	$\frac{-2}{5}$
		Z_j	$\frac{17}{8}$	-2	-3	0	$\frac{-9}{16}$	$\frac{-1}{4}$		$\frac{-37}{4}$	
		$C_j - Z_j$	$\frac{-9}{8}$	0	0	0	$\frac{9}{16}$	$\frac{1}{4}$			

Entering Variable

Leaving Variable

new x_2 $\quad = (0 \qquad 1 \quad 0 \quad 8/50 \quad 32/100 \quad -1/25 \quad 114/25)$, and

new $x_1 \cdot (5/16) = (5/16 \quad 0 \quad 0 \quad 8/80 \quad 7/160 \quad -1/40 \quad 78/80) \qquad$ added to

old $x_3 \qquad\quad = (-5/16 \; 0 \quad 1 \quad 0 \qquad -3/32 \qquad 1/8 \qquad 1/8) \qquad$ yields

new $x_3 \qquad\quad = (0 \qquad 0 \quad 1 \quad 1/10 \quad -1/20 \qquad 1/10 \qquad 88/80)$.

The third iteration is then given in Table 13.7.

The $C_j - Z_j$ values of Table 13.7 are all zero or positive which indicates that an optimal solution has been reached. The final solution is $x_1 = 78/25$, $x_2 = 114/25$, $x_3 = 88/80$, $S_1 = 0$, $S_2 = 0$, $S_3 = 0$, and $C = \$-511/4$. Substituting these values of x_j into the original objective function $C = x_1 - 3x_2 - 2x_3$ will yield $C = \$-511/4$, and the x_j values substituted into the constraints will show they are satisfied as equalities. For example, checking the first constraint $3x_1 - x_2 + 2x_3 \leq 7$, we have

$$3(78/25) - 114/25 + 2(88/80) = 7$$

The next section considers a problem having equality constraints and greater than or equal ($\geq$) constraints.

Artificial Variables

Let us assume the following linear programming problem.

TABLE 13.7 Final Solution to Minimization Problem

	C_j	1	-3	-2	0	0	0			
		\multicolumn{6}{c}{VARIABLES}			
Solution Variables		x_1	x_2	x_3	S_1	S_2	S_3		b	Ratio
x_1	1	1	0	0	$\dfrac{8}{25}$	$\dfrac{7}{50}$	$\dfrac{-2}{25}$		$\dfrac{78}{25}$	
x_2	-3	0	1	0	$\dfrac{4}{25}$	$\dfrac{32}{100}$	$\dfrac{-1}{25}$		$\dfrac{114}{25}$	
x_3	-2	0	0	1	$\dfrac{1}{10}$	$\dfrac{-1}{20}$	$\dfrac{1}{10}$		$\dfrac{88}{80}$	
	Z_j	1	-3	-2	$\dfrac{-20}{50}$	$\dfrac{-72}{100}$	$\dfrac{-24}{50}$		$\dfrac{-511}{4}$	
	$C_j - Z_j$	0	0	0	$\dfrac{20}{50}$	$\dfrac{72}{100}$	$\dfrac{24}{50}$			

Maximize

$$P = \$1.0x + \$3.0x_2 - \$5.0x_3$$

subject to

$$
\begin{aligned}
x_1 + x_2 + x_3 &= 7 \\
2x_1 - 5x_2 + x_3 &\geq 10
\end{aligned}
$$
(1)
(2)

$$x_1 \geq 0, x_2 \geq 0, x_3 \geq 0.$$

If constraint (2) is rewritten as an equality, we have

$$2x_1 - 5x_2 + x_3 - S = 10$$
(2)

Using matrix notation to rewrite the constraints yields

$$\binom{1}{2} x_1 + \binom{1}{-5} x_2 + \binom{1}{1} x_3 + \binom{0}{-1} S = \binom{7}{10}$$

The vector coefficients of the variables are of course the elements under the columns of associated variables in the simplex table. In the case of two constraints, the simplex procedure requires two columns in the table

of the form $\binom{1}{0}, \binom{0}{1}$ for every iteration. This can be achieved by modifying the constraint equations to be

$$
\begin{aligned}
x_1 + x_2 + x_3 + A_1 \quad &= 7 \\
2x_1 - 5x_2 + x_3 - S_1 + A_2 \quad &= 10
\end{aligned}
$$
(1)
(2)

or

$$\binom{1}{2} x_1 + \binom{1}{-5} x_2 + \binom{1}{1} x_3 + \binom{1}{0} A_1 + \binom{0}{-1} S_1 + \binom{0}{1} A_2 = \binom{7}{10},$$

where $x_1 \geq 0, x_2 \geq 0, x_3 \geq 0, A_1 \geq 0, A_2 \geq 0, S_1 \geq 0$.

The objective function is then to

Maximize

$$P = x_1 + 3x_2 - 5x_3 + (0)S_1 - MA_1 - MA_2$$

The two variables A_1 and A_2 are termed *artificial variables* and the coefficient M is an arbitrarily large number. For each artificial variable added to the problem, the quantity MA is subtracted from the profit function (or added to a cost function) to assure that the artificial variables do not appear in the final linear programming solution. The use of artificial variables is recommended for each equality ($=$) and greater than or equal to ($\geq$) constraint in the constraint set. Again, the reason for doing so is to obtain an initial basic feasible solution. In a mechanistic sense, this means one obtains basic vectors comprised of the elements zero and one—an identity matrix of size n, where n is the number of constraints in the problem.

A full explanation of artificial variables would require an understanding of matrix algebra beyond the scope of this text. Suffice it to say, then, that the artificial variables are indeed fictitious and have no physical meaning. They are introduced to facilitate the ease of solving a linear programming problem by the simplex procedure. The assignment of the coefficient M (an actual large number relative to other problem coefficients in digital computer programs) insures that the artificial variables are first removed from a solution and do not appear in the final solution. Indeed, if a given problem does not have a feasible solution, at least one artificial variable will appear in the final solution. Once artificial variables are removed from the simplex tableau and become nonbasic variables, the solution procedure prevents their re-entering, and the variables can be removed from the tableau to reduce the computational burden. The initial solution to this particular problem appears in Table 13.8.

TABLE 13.8   First Solution—Artificial Variables Problem

Solution Variables		C_j	1	3	-5	0	$-M$	$-M$		b	Ratio
			VARIABLES								
			x_1	x_2	x_3	S_1	A_1	A_2			
A_1	$-M$		1	1	1	0	1	0		7	$\frac{7}{1} = 7$
A_2	$-M$		(2)	-5	1	-1	0	1		10	$\frac{10}{2} = 5$ ← Leaving Variable
		z_j	$-3M$	$4M$	$-2M$	M	$-M$	$-M$		$-17M$	
		$c_j - z_j$	$1+3M$	$3-4M$	$-5+2M$	$-M$	0	0			

↑
Entering
Variable

The largest positive $C_j - Z_j$ value (maximization) in Table 13.8 is (1 + 3M) under the x_1 variable column and is therefore the entering variable which replaces variable A_2. The variable A_2 will not re-enter the solution and can now be dropped from the procedure. Table 13.9 gives the second solution.

Second Solution—Artificial Variables Problem **TABLE 13.9**

	C_j	1	3	-5	0	-M				
Solution Variables				VARIABLES						
		x_1	x_2	x_3	S_1	A_1	A_2		b	Ratio
A_1	-M	0	$\frac{7}{2}$	$\frac{1}{2}$	$\frac{1}{2}$	1			2	$\frac{4}{7}$ ← Leaving Variable
x_1	1	1	$\frac{-5}{2}$	$\frac{1}{2}$	$\frac{-1}{2}$	0			5	-2
Z_j	1		$\frac{-5-7M}{2}$	$\frac{1-M}{2}$	$\frac{-1-M}{2}$	-M			$5 - 2M$	
$C_j - Z_j$	0		$\frac{1+7M}{2}$	$\frac{-11+M}{2}$	$\frac{1+M}{2}$	0				

↑ Entering Variable

The largest positive $C_j - Z_j$ value in Table 13.9 is $(1/2 + 7/2M)$ under the x_2 variable column and x_2 replaces the variable A_1 which has the minimum positive ratio. The third solution is thus given in Table 13.10.

Since all $C_j - Z_j$ are negative or zero in Table 13.10, the optimal solution has been reached with solution values of $x_2 = 4/7$, $x_1 = 45/7$, $x_3 = 0$, $S_1 = 0$, $A_1 = 0$, $A_2 = 0$, and $P = \$57/7$. That is,

$$P = \$1(45/7) + \$3(4/7) - \$5(0) = \$57/7$$

and the constraints are satisfied from

$$(45/7) + (4/7) + 0 = 7 \tag{1}$$
$$2(45/7) - 5(4/7) + 0 = 10 \tag{2}$$

The solution to a minimization problem involving artificial variables would follow the same procedural steps as for any minimization problem as presented in the previous section of this chapter.

TABLE 13.10 Final Solution—Artificial Variables Problem

C_j		1	3	-5	0					
Solution Variables		VARIABLES							b	Ratio
		x_1	x_2	x_3	S_1	A_1	A_2			
x_2	3	0	1	$\frac{1}{7}$	$\frac{1}{7}$				$\frac{4}{7}$	
x_1	1	1	0	$\frac{6}{7}$	$\frac{-1}{7}$				$\frac{45}{7}$	
Z_j		1	3	$\frac{9}{7}$	$\frac{2}{7}$				$\frac{57}{7}$	
$C_j - Z_j$		0	0	$\frac{-44}{7}$	$\frac{-2}{7}$					

SPECIAL SITUATIONS IN LINEAR PROGRAMMING

This section introduces some special situations which may arise in solving linear programming problems. The examples chosen for illustrative purposes are two-variable problems so that both a graphical and a simplex procedure interpretation can be made. The special cases to be covered are:

1. multiple optimal solutions
2. unbounded solutions
3. nonexisting feasible solutions
4. degeneracy

Multiple Optimal Solutions

Let us assume the linear programming problem
Maximize

$$P = x_1 + 2x_2$$

subject to

$$x_1 + 2x_2 \leq 24 \tag{1}$$
$$3/2x_1 + x_2 \leq 18 \tag{2}$$
$$x_1 \leq 10 \tag{3}$$
$$x_2 \leq 11 \tag{4}$$
$$x_1 \geq 0, x_2 \geq 0$$

276

Note the similarity between the objective function and constraint (1). If constraint (1) is graphically plotted as an equation for $x_1 + 2x_2 = 24$, a graphical plot of the objective function for values of $0 \le P \le 24$ will be a series of parallel lines moving toward the constraint equation. For $P = 24$, the objective function line will be identical to the constraint equation $x_1 + 2x_2 = 24$. Thus, when the objective function is the same as a constraint when written as an equation, *multiple optimal solutions* may result. It can be seen from Figure 13.1 that this is true.

Multiple Optimal Solutions **FIGURE 13.1**

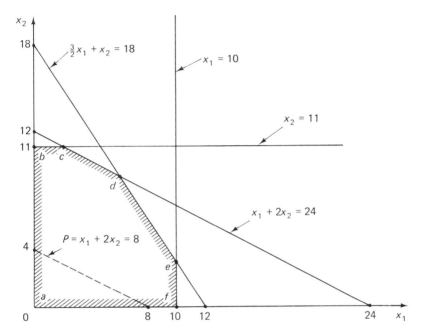

The feasible solution space for this problem is the area of the polygon *abcdef* in Figure 13.1. As the profit function P increases to the optimal value of 24, the iso-profit line P overlays the line segment *cd*. Thus, any combination of x_1, x_2 yielding a point on this line segment *cd* is an optimal solution. At point *c*, $x_1 = 2$ and $x_2 = 11$ yields $P = 24$. At point *d*, $x_1 = 6$ and $x_2 = 9$ yields $P = 24$.

The simplex procedure presented in Chapter 12 will of course locate these two extreme point (*c* and *d*) solutions. The second iteration (third tableau) of the simplex procedure for this problem yields Table 13.11.

The solution shown in Table 13.11 has $x_1 = 2$, $S_2 = 4$, $S_3 = 8$, and $x_2 = 11$ for a profit value of $P = 24$. An inspection of the $C_j - Z_j$ row indicates an optimal solution has been reached (all values are zero or negative). However, a variable *which is not presently in the solution*, namely S_4, has a zero $C_j - Z_j$ value. This says that S_4 could be brought into the solution without changing the profit value of $P = 24$. Then S_4 replaces S_2 in the solution and the next simplex iteration yields Table 13.12.

TABLE 13.11   Final Solution—Multiple Optima

Solution Variables	C_j	1	2	0	0	0	0		b	Ratio
		x_1	x_2	S_1	S_2	S_3	S_4			
x_1	1	1	0	1	0	0	-2		2	-1
S_2	0	0	0	$\frac{-3}{2}$	1	0	(2)		4	2
S_3	0	0	0	-1	0	1	2		8	4
x_2	2	0	1	0	0	0	1		11	11
Z_j		1	2	1	0	0	0		24	
$C_j - Z_j$		0	0	-1	0	0	0			

(VARIABLES header spans x_1 through S_4)

Leaving Variable → (S_2 row)

Alternate Entering Variable ↑ (S_4 column)

The solution shown in Table 13.12 has $x_1 = 6$, $S_4 = 2$, $S_3 = 4$ and $x_2 = 9$ for a profit value of $P = 24$. An inspection of the $C_j - Z_j$ row indicates that of the variables not presently in the solution only S_2 can enter the solution. If S_2 were entered, we would of course have the solution given by Table 13.11. Both optimal solutions for points c and d of Figure 13.1 have therefore been found by the simplex procedure.

Unbounded Solutions

An *unbounded optimal solution* refers to the fact that an objective function may increase (profit maximization) indefinitely or decrease (cost minimization) indefinitely when all the constraints are satisfied. An example follows:

Maximize

$$P = 4x_1 + 2x_2$$

subject to

	C_j	1	2	0	0	0	0			
		\multicolumn{7}{c}{VARIABLES}			
Solution Variables		x_1	x_2	S_1	S_2	S_3	S_4		b	Ratio
x_1	1	1	0	$\frac{-1}{2}$	0	0	0		6	
S_4	0	0	0	$\frac{-3}{4}$	$\frac{1}{2}$	0	1		2	
S_3	0	0	0	$\frac{1}{2}$	0	1	0		4	
x_2	2	0	1	$\frac{3}{4}$	0	0	0		9	
Z_j		1	2	1	0	0	0		24	
$C_j - Z_j$		0	0	-1	0	0	0			

$$2x_1 - 2x_2 \leq 10$$
$$2x_1 - x_2 \leq 40$$
$$x_1 \geq 0,\ x_2 \geq 0$$

It is noted from the constraints above that x_2 can increase without bound and the constraints will remain satisfied. Simultaneously, the objective function P would be increasing without bound. A graphical solution to this problem is given in Figure 13.2.

The initial solution of this problem by the simplex procedure is given in Table 13.13.

From the $C_j - Z_j$ row of Table 13.13, the variable x_1 should be selected as the entering variable and S_1 the departing variable. The $C_j - Z_j$ value for x_2 is positive also, indicating it would be profitable to enter solution. However, all the substitution coefficients in the x_2 column are negative or zero, indicating that an unlimited amount of x_2 could be brought into solution, feasibility maintained, and the objective function increased without bound. If the regular simplex procedure is followed for this problem, x_1 replaces S_1 and x_2 replaces S_2. With this third solution, there would be an indication (positive $C_j - Z_j$ value) that S_1 should again enter solution but both ratio values would be negative, thereby terminating the procedure.

FIGURE 13.2 An Unbounded Optimal Solution

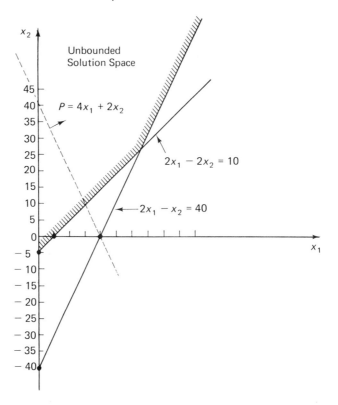

TABLE 13.13 Initial Solution of Unbounded Optimal Solution

	C_j	4	2	0	0		
		VARIABLES					
Solution Variables		x_1	x_2	S_1	S_2	b	Ratio
S_1	0	(2)	-2	1	0	10	$\frac{10}{2} = 5$ ← Leaving Variable
S_2	0	2	-1	0	1	40	$\frac{40}{2} = 20$
	Z_j	0	0	0	0		
	$C_j - Z_j$	4	2	0	0		

↑ Entering Variable

The following problem is an example of an unbounded solution space
with bounded optimal solution.

Maximize

$$P = 3x_1 - x_2$$

subject to

$$2x_1 - x_2 \leq 2$$
$$x_1 \qquad \leq 3$$
$$x_1 \geq 0, x_2 \geq 0$$

A graphical solution to this problem is given by Figure 13.3 and the simplex solution is given in Table 13.14.

The $C_j - Z_j$ values of the third solution in Table 13.14 are all negative or zero, and hence an optimal solution has been found. The solution is $x_1 = 3$, $x_2 = 4$, $S_1 = 0$, and $S_2 = 0$, with $P = 3(3) - 4 = 5$.

An Unbounded Solution Space—Bounded Optimal Solution **FIGURE 13.3**

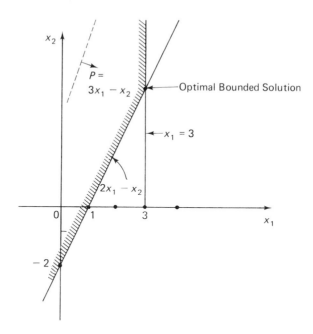

If *all* constraints cannot be met, there is a *nonexisting feasible solution* **Nonexisting** to a linear programming problem. A simple example would be if two of **Feasible** the constraints were, say, $x_1 \geq 9$ and $x_1 \leq 8$. Clearly, both constraints cannot **Solutions** be satisfied and the solution space is termed empty. For a two-variable

TABLE 13.14 Simplex Solution for Unbounded Solution Space; Bounded Optimal Solution

Solution Variables	c_j	3	-1	0	0		
		VARIABLES					
		x_1	x_2	S_1	S_2	b	Ratio
S_1	0	(2)	-1	1	0	2	$\frac{2}{2}=1$ ← Leaving Variable
S_2	0	1	0	0	1	3	$\frac{3}{1}=3$
Z_j		0	0	0	0	0	
$C_j - Z_j$		3 ↑	-1	0	0		
x_1	3	1	$\frac{-1}{2}$	$\frac{1}{2}$	0	1	$\frac{1}{-1/2}=-2$
S_2	0	0	$\left(\frac{1}{2}\right)$	$\frac{-1}{2}$	1	2	$\frac{2}{1/2}=4$ ← Leaving Variable
Z_j		3	$\frac{-3}{2}$	$\frac{3}{2}$	0	3	
$C_j - Z_j$		0	$\frac{1}{2}$ ↑	$\frac{-3}{2}$	0		
x_1	3	1	0	0	1	3	
x_2	-1	0	1	-1	2	4	
Z_j		3	-1	1	1	5	
$C_j - Z_j$		0	0	-1	-1		

problem, a graphical plot readily reveals an empty solution space. However, the simplex procedure may find a solution to the problem in that the optimality condition of the simplex method can be satisfied, but this is not a true optimal solution since the constraints would not all be met. The condition of an empty solution space can be detected in the simplex procedure by the appearance of a positive-valued artificial variable in the optimal solution.

In a problem having an empty solution space, constraints of both the ($\leq$) and ($\geq$) type would be involved. The simplex procedure in this case requires the use of artificial variables to obtain an initial solution. Thus,

an artificial variable could remain in the solution until the optimality conditions
of the simplex procedure are met. The problem therefore would not have
a feasible solution.

Degeneracy

The number of nonzero variables in a given basic feasible solution
by the simplex procedure is equal to the number of constraint equations
(except for the $x_j \geq 0$ restrictions) if the solution is nondegenerate. The
term *degeneracy* in linear programming problems refers to the case where
a given solution contains a smaller number of nonzero variables than the
number of constraints. Alternatively, degeneracy occurs if one or more
of the variables in solution have zero values.

Degeneracy may be temporary during the simplex procedure. That is,
a given solution may be degenerate, but on applying the regular simplex
procedural steps, subsequent iterations are nondegenerate and the optimal
solution is readily found. Further, the optimal solution can be degenerate
by our definition; that is, it can have one or more solution variables with
a zero value. Neither of these two situations constitute any real difficulty
in that the optimal solution is readily found in straightforward fashion by
the simplex procedure. On the other hand, a degenerate solution can lead
to *cycling* or *looping*, which means that from the point of encountering
a degenerate solution, subsequent iterations can lead back to the same
degenerate solution and the optimal solution is never found unless special
procedures are invoked. The severity of this difficulty is lessened by the
claim of several authors that cycling rarely, if ever, occurs in practical
problems. Instances of cycling have arisen through problems theoretically
generated to illustrate the condition.

The existence of redundant constraints in a problem is the condition
which is conducive to degeneracy. For example, if two constraints are (1)
$2x_1 + 3x_2 \leq 9$ and (2) $4x_1 + 6x_2 \leq 18$, it is noted that constraint (2) is a
multiple of constraint (1). Graphically the plot of these inequalities as equalities
would give the same line. Thus, one of the constraints is redundant. Another
example of redundant constraints would be (3) $x_1 + 2x_2 \leq 4$ and (4) $x_1 + 4x_2$
≤ 8. These two are not parallel constraints but a graphical plot of the two
equalities would reveal linear lines intersecting at the point $x_1 = 0$, $x_2 = 0$,
the constraint $x_1 + 2x_2 \leq 4$ as binding, and the constraint $x_1 + 4x_2 \leq 8$ as
redundant. Hence, one prevention of degeneracy is to eliminate redundant
constraints from a linear programming problem before initiating the simplex
procedure. The fallacy of this statement is that redundancy may not readily
be seen in constraints involving several variables.

Further insight into the problem and resolution of degeneracy is best
seen from the following example. Suppose the linear programming problem
is:

Maximize

$$P = 3x_1 + 5x_2$$

subject to

$$x_1 \leq 4$$
$$x_2 \leq 6$$
$$3x_1 + 2x_2 \leq 12$$
$$x_1 \geq 0, x_2 \geq 0$$

The initial solution for this problem is:
Maximize

$$P = 3x_1 + 5x_2 + (0)S_1 + (0)S_2 + (0)S_3$$

subject to

$$x_1 + S_1 = 4$$
$$x_2 + S_2 = 6$$
$$3x_1 + 2x_2 + S_3 = 12$$
$$x_1 \geq 0, x_2 \geq 0$$

and the simplex solution procedure is given in Table 13.15.

In Table 13.15, note the ratio column for the first solution. There is a tie for rows S_2 and S_3 with the minimum positive ratio being 6. This is an indication that the next solution will be degenerate. Procedures exist for breaking the ratio tie but an arbitrary choice between the tied rows may be made. In this case, variable S_2 was arbitrarily chosen to enter the solution for the first iteration. If cycling should occur with such an arbitrary choice (it does not in the instance of choosing S_2), one can return to the solution where the ratio tie was encountered and make the alternate choice.

By choosing S_2 as the leaving variable from the initial solution in Table 13.15, S_3 has a zero solution value in the second solution. In effect, the entering variable x_2 has replaced the two variables S_2 and S_3. Thus, solution two is degenerate. Optimality conditions are not satisfied with solution two. The variable x_1 is selected as the entering variable, and by interpreting a ratio of zero as the minimum positive ratio, S_3 is determined to be the departing variable. Optimality conditions are satisfied with the third solution and a degenerate basic feasible solution is therefore optimal. The final solution is $S_1 = 4$, $S_2 = 0$, $S_3 = 0$, $x_2 = 6$, and $x_1 = 0$ with $P = 3(0) + 5(6) = 30$. A graphical solution to this problem is given in Figure 13.4.

THE DUAL PROBLEM

If a maximization linear programming problem is defined as the "primal" problem, then there is an associated minimization problem known as the "dual" problem. A minimization problem could be defined as the primal, and then an associated maximization problem would be the dual. If an

Solution Variables	C_j	3	5	0	0	0		b	Ratio	
		x_1	x_2	S_1	S_2	S_3				
S_1	0	1	0	1	0	0		4	$\frac{4}{0} = \infty$	
S_2	0	0	①	0	1	0		6	$\frac{6}{1} = 6$	Tie for Leaving Variable
S_3	0	3	2	0	0	1		12	$\frac{12}{2} = 6$	
	Z_j	0	0	0	0	0		0		
	$C_j - Z_j$	3	5	0	0	0				
S_1	0	1	0	1	0	0		4	$\frac{4}{1} = 4$	
x_2	5	0	1	0	1	0		6	$\frac{6}{0} = \infty$	
S_3	0	③	0	0	-2	1		0	$\frac{0}{3} = 0$	Leaving Variable
	Z_j	0	5	0	5	0		30		
	$C_j - Z_j$	3	0	0	-5	0				
S_1	0	0	0	1	$\frac{2}{3}$	$-\frac{1}{3}$		4		
x_2	5	0	1	0	1	0		6		
x_1	3	1	0	0	$\frac{-2}{3}$	$\frac{1}{3}$		0		
	Z_j	3	5	0	3	1		30		
	$C_j - Z_j$	0	0	0	-3	-1				

FIGURE 13.4   Optimal Degenerate Solution

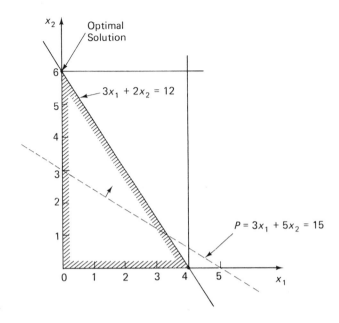

optimal feasible solution exists for the primal problem, then solving the dual problem will yield the same optimal feasible solution. However, there are two primary reasons for considering the dual problem: (1) if the primal problem has a small number of decision variables but a large number of constraints, solving the dual may be computationally more efficient, and (2) the dual formulation can provide insight into the effect of relaxing constraints which are binding. We will show the relationship between the primal problem and the dual problem by means of an example.

An Example   Recall the problem of Chapter 12 which was
Maximize

$$P = \$1.5x_1 + \$1.0x_2$$

subject to

$$
\begin{aligned}
2x_1 + x_2 &\le 10 && (1)\\
x_1 + x_2 &\le 6 && (2)\\
x_1 &\le 4.5 && (3)\\
x_2 &\le 4 && (4)\\
x_1 \ge 0, x_2 &\ge 0
\end{aligned}
$$

Let us designate this maximization problem as the "primal" problem and assume the above formulation represents the following production situation: the decision variable x_1 represents the number of units of Product A to be produced per hour, where the net profit associated with each unit is $1.5. The decision variable x_2 represents the number of units of Product B to be produced each hour, where the net profit per unit is $1.0. A unit of Product A requires 2.0 hours in the machining department, 1.0 hour in the welding department, 1.0 hour in the assembly department, and zero hours in the cleaning department. A unit of Product B requires 1.0 hour in the machining department, 1.0 hour in the welding department, zero hours in the assembly department, and 1.0 hour in the cleaning department. The total number of hours available for the production of these two products in the machining, welding, assembly, and cleaning departments are 10, 6, 4.5, and 4, respectively.

The solution to this primal problem is given below from Chapter 12:

x_1 = 4 units
x_2 = 2 units
S_3 = 0.5 (slack associated with constraint 3)
S_4 = 2 (slack associated with constraint 4)
P = $1.5 (4) + $1 (2) = $8

If y represents the general dual decision variable, then the dual formulation of this same problem is
Minimize

$$C = 10y_1 + 6y_2 + 4.5y_3 + 4y_4$$

subject to

$$2y_1 + 1y_2 + 1y_3 + 0y_4 \geq 1.5$$
$$1y_1 + 1y_2 + 0y_3 + 1y_4 \geq 1.0$$
$$y_1, y_2, y_3, y_4 \geq 0.$$

The following characteristics of the dual problem will serve to explain the above formulation:

1. If the primal is a maximization problem (profit per hour in this example), then the dual is a minimization problem (cost per hour in this example).
2. The number of decision variables in the dual objective function is equal to the number of constraints (excluding the restrictions of $x_j \geq 0$) in the primal problem.
3. The coefficients of the decision variables in the dual objective function are the resource bounds (the right-hand constants) of the primal constraints. In this problem, the first dual variable y_1 has the coefficient of 10 from the first constraint of the primal problem, y_2 has the coefficient of 6 from the second constraint, and so forth. Further, in this dual problem, the coefficients represent the hours available in each processing department and the dual decision variables are the cost per hour of using these resources.
4. The number of constraint equations for the dual problem is equal to the number of original decision variables of the primal (excluding slack and artificial variables). The coefficients for the dual problem constraints are the transpose of the coefficients for the primal problem constraints. That is, if the matrix A of primal coefficients for this problem is

$$A = \begin{pmatrix} 2 & 1 \\ 1 & 1 \\ 1 & 0 \\ 0 & 1 \end{pmatrix}$$

then, the matrix of coefficients for the dual problem is the transpose of A or

$$A^T = \begin{pmatrix} 2 & 1 & 1 & 0 \\ 1 & 1 & 0 & 1 \end{pmatrix}$$

The transpose of a matrix means to interchange rows and columns. In this problem, the first column of A becomes the first row of A^T and the second column of A becomes the second row of A^T.

The constants (or resource bounds) for the dual constraints are obtained from the profit function (the objective function) of the primal. Note that the coefficients for the first column of matrix A are associated with the variable x_1. The profit coefficient for x_1 in the primal problem is \$1.50. The coefficients for the second column of matrix A are associated with the variable x_2. The profit coefficient for x_2 in the primal problem is \$1.00. The constants, or resource bounds, for the dual constraints (1) and (2) are therefore 1.50 and 1.00, respectively.

5. For the maximization primal problem, if the constraints of the primal are ($\leq$), then the constraints of the dual are ($\geq$).

Combining items (4) and (5) above, the dual constraints are written as

$$2.0y_1 + 1.0y_2 + 1.0y_3 + 0y_4 \geq 1.50 \tag{1}$$
$$1.0y_1 + 1.0y_2 + 0y_3 + 1.0y_4 \geq 1.00 \tag{2}$$
$$y_1, y_2, y_3, y_4 \geq 0$$

Before solving the dual problem by the simplex procedure, it is of interest to consider the economic interpretation of the dual formulation.

Economic Interpretation of the Dual

The dual decision variables are opportunity costs. For example, y_1 is interpreted as the dollar cost of using an hour in the machining department. Then recall that the maximum number of hours available in the machining department was 10. The term $10y_1$ in the cost objective function of the dual thereby reflects this reasoning. A similar reasoning for the other three production departments yields the objective function terms of $6y_2$, $4.5y_3$, and $4y_4$. Minimizing $C = 10y_1 + 6y_2 + 4.5y_3 + 4y_4$ will therefore determine minimum values for using an hour of production time in the respective departments for the given products (A and B) in question. One can think of the cost function as the cost of maintaining 10 hours, 6 hours, 4.5 hours, and 4 hours of capacity in the respective departments. The products are then defined by the dual constraints.

We interpret the first dual constraint, $2.0y_1 + 1.0y_2 + 1.0y_3 + 0y_4 \geq 1.50$, as follows: Product A, which is associated with decision variable x_1 in the primal, requires 2.0 hours in the machining department, 1.0 hour of welding, 1.0 hour of assembly, and zero hours of cleaning at the respective *y* dollar per hour usage values. Recall now that a unit of Product A contributed $1.50 per unit of profit in the primal problem. The question we now pose is whether the expenditure of production costs for a unit of Product A equals or exceeds the $1.50 a finished unit is worth. If the production costs equal $1.50, then the product can profitably be made. If production costs exceed $1.50, the resources of the departments should be committed to some other purpose.

A similar argument applies to the second dual constraint.

Solving the Dual

We now proceed to solve the dual problem by first modifying for the initial simplex solution as

Minimize

$$C = 10y_1 + 6y_2 + 4.5y_3 + 4y_4 + (0)S_1 + 0(S_2) + MA_1 + MA_2$$

subject to

$$2.0y_1 + 1.0y_2 + 1.0y_3 + 0y_4 - S_1 + A_1 = 1.5$$
$$1.0y_1 + 1.0y_2 + 0y_3 + 1.0y_4 - S_2 + A_2 = 1.0,$$
where all variables are ≥ 0.

The solution to this problem by the regular simplex procedure is given in either Table 13.16 or Table 13.17.

It is noted that the coefficient for y_3 and y_4 in the constraint equations are of the form $\begin{pmatrix} 1 & 0 \\ 0 & 1 \end{pmatrix}$ which constitute an initial solution to this problem. Thus, the addition of the artificial variables A_1 and A_2 to obtain an initial solution is unnecessary. However, it is of interest to show that the same optimal solution is reached with or without the artificial variables. Table 13.16 gives the simplex solution with the artificial variables in the problem and Table 13.17 gives the solution without the artificial variables.

The optimal solution to the dual problem is $y_1 = 1/2$, $y_2 = 1/2$, $y_3 = 0$, $y_4 = 0$, $S_1 = 0$, and $S_2 = 0$ with $C = 10(1/2) + 6(1/2) = \$8$. The value of the dual objective function (minimization) is $C = \$8$, which is the same value for the primal objective function (maximization) of $P = \$8$.

Economic Interpretation of the Dual Solution

We can interpret the dual solution $y_1 = 1/2$, $y_2 = 1/2$, $y_3 = 0$, and $y_4 = 0$ economically as follows: the dual variable $y_1 = 1/2$ means that an hour of machining time has a value of $0.50 (perhaps unrealistically low, but our problem was chosen to illustrate the solution procedure rather than to represent factual coefficients). If extra time could be added to the machining department, perhaps through overtime or a second shift, it is implied that such time has a value of $0.50 per hour. Also suggested is that, if additional machine time could be subcontracted at a rate lower than $0.50 per hour, then it would be profitable to do so. A similar argument applies to the value of welding time, $y_2 = \$0.50$. The value of assembly time (y_3) and cleaning time (y_4) is zero, implying that there is no potential value in adding

TABLE 13.16 Solution to the Dual Problem with Artificial Variables

Solution Variables		C_j → 10	6	4.5	4	0	0	M	M			
		y_1	y_2	y_3	y_4	S_1	S_2	A_1	A_2	b	Ratio	Leaving Variable
A_1	M	②	1	1	0	-1	0	1	0	$\frac{3}{2}$	$\frac{1.5}{2}=\frac{3}{4}$	←
A_2	M	1	1	0	1	0	-1	0	1	1	$\frac{1}{1}=1$	
	Z_j	$3M$	$2M$	M	M	$-M$	$-M$	M	M	$\frac{5}{2}M$		
	C_j-Z_j	$\begin{matrix}10\\-3M\end{matrix}$	$\begin{matrix}6\\-2M\end{matrix}$	$\begin{matrix}4.5\\-M\end{matrix}$	$\begin{matrix}4\\-M\end{matrix}$	M	M	0	0			
y_1	10	1	$\frac{1}{2}$	$\frac{1}{2}$	0	$\frac{-1}{2}$	0		0	$\frac{3}{4}$	$\frac{0.75}{0}=\infty$	
A_2	M	0	$\frac{1}{2}$	$\frac{-1}{2}$	①	$\frac{1}{2}$	-1		1	$\frac{1}{4}$	$\frac{1}{4}$	← Leaving Variable
	Z_j	10	$5+\frac{M}{2}$	$5-\frac{M}{2}$	M	$-5+\frac{M}{2}$	$-M$		M	$\frac{30}{4}+\frac{M}{4}$		
	C_j-Z_j	0	$1-\frac{M}{2}$	$-\frac{1}{2}+\frac{M}{2}$	$4-M$ ↑	$5-\frac{M}{2}$	M		0			
y_1	10	1	$\frac{1}{2}$	$\frac{1}{2}$	0	$\frac{-1}{2}$	0			$\frac{3}{4}$	$\frac{3}{2}$	
y_4	4	0	① $\frac{1}{2}$	$\frac{-1}{2}$	1	$\frac{1}{2}$	-1			$\frac{1}{4}$	$\frac{1}{2}$	← Leaving Variable
	Z_j	10	7	3	4	-3	-4			$\frac{34}{4}$		
	C_j-Z_j	0	-1	1.5 ↑	0	3	4					
y_1	10	1	0	1	-1	-1	1			$\frac{1}{2}$		
y_2	6	0	1	-1	2	1	-2			$\frac{1}{2}$		
	Z_j	10	6	4	2	-4	-2			8		
	C_j-Z_j	0	0	$\frac{1}{2}$	2	4	2					

Solution to the Dual Problem without Artificial Variables   TABLE 13.17

	C_j	10	6	$\frac{9}{2}$	4	0	0			
				VARIABLES						Leaving Variable
Solution Variables		y_1	y_2	y_3	y_4	S_1	S_2	b	Ratio	
y_3	$\frac{9}{2}$	②$2$	1	1	0	-1	0	$\frac{3}{2}$	$\frac{3}{4}$	←
y_4	4	1	1	0	1	0	-1	1	1	
Z_j		13	$\frac{17}{2}$	$\frac{9}{2}$	4	$\frac{-9}{2}$	-4	$\frac{43}{4}$		
$C_j - Z_j$		-3	$\frac{-5}{2}$	0	0	$\frac{9}{2}$	4			
y_1	10	1	$\frac{1}{2}$	$\frac{1}{2}$	0	$\frac{-1}{2}$	0	$\frac{3}{4}$	$\frac{3}{2}$	
y_4	4	0	②$\frac{1}{2}$	$\frac{-1}{2}$	1	$\frac{1}{2}$	-1	$\frac{1}{4}$	$\frac{1}{2}$	Leaving Variable ←
Z_j		10	7	3	4	-3	-4	$\frac{34}{4}$		
$C_j - Z_j$		0	-1	$\frac{3}{2}$	0	3	4			
y_1	10	1	0	1	-1	-1	1	$\frac{1}{2}$		
y_2	6	0	1	-1	2	1	-2	$\frac{1}{2}$		
Z_j		10	6	4	2	-4	-2	8		
$C_j - Z_j$		0	0	$\frac{1}{2}$	2	4	2			

more capacity (available hours) to these two departments. This seems reasonable since the primal constraints, $x_1 \le 4.5$ and $x_2 \le 4$, were not binding with the optimal primal solution of $x_1 = 4$ and $x_2 = 2$.

These cost or value items from the dual solution are often mentioned in the literature as shadow prices. Essentially, the shadow price measures the value of relaxing a constraint by acquiring an additional unit of that factor (machining, welding, etc.) of production.

It is also of interest to note that the two values in the $C_j - Z_j$ row under the S_1 and S_2 columns for the final dual solution (Table 13.16 or Table 13.17) are 4 and 2. These are the solution values for the primal problem

$(x_1 = 4$ and $x_2 = 2)$. By the same token, refer to Figure 12.13 to see the Reduced Cost, or $C_j - Z_j$, row values of $1/2$ and $1/2$ under the S_1 and S_2 columns of the final solution to the primal problem. These values are of course the solution to the dual problem. Dual ordinary variables (y_1, y_2, y_3, y_4) are associated with primal slack variables $(S_1, S_2, S_3, S_4$ of the primal in this case), and conversely, dual slack variables $(S_1, S_2$ in this case) are associated with primal ordinary variables (x_1, x_2). We recall from the primal optimal solution that $S_1 = 0$ and $S_2 = 0$. This means that the constraints, $2x_1 + x_2 \le 10$ and $x_1 + x_2 \le 6$, were binding and the associated dual ordinary variables (y_1, y_2) turned out nonzero $(y_1 = 1/2, y_2 = 1/2$ in this case). However, the primal constraints, $x_1 \le 4.5$ and $x_2 \le 4$, were not binding and the associated dual variables (y_3, y_4) turned out zero. The primary ordinary variables (x_1, x_2) were nonzero in the optimal solution and the associated dual slack variables (S_1, S_2) turned out zero. If a dual slack variable in the optimal solution had turned out nonzero, say S_1, then the corresponding primal ordinary variable, x_1 in this case, would have been zero in the optimal primal solution. In general these relations are true.

Summary

For every primal linear programming problem there is a dual. The solution of both gives the same optimal value of the objective function, and the variables and constraints of each problem are uniquely related. The dual of the dual is the primal. There are two primary reasons for choosing the dual problem to solve: (1) if the primal problem has a large number of constraints relative to the number of decision variables, the dual solution can be obtained more expediently, and (2) the shadow prices of the dual can provide considerable economic insight into the desirability of relaxing certain constraints. Indeed, much more postoptimal analysis can be given to both the primal and dual solutions than has been presented in this text.

QUESTIONS AND PROBLEMS

1. Define and give an example of substitution coefficients.

2. What is meant by the term degeneracy? unbounded optimal solution? multiple optima?

3. Give individual examples of linear programming problems which (1) have no feasible solution, (2) have multiple optimal solutions, and (3) may have a degenerate feasible solution during the simplex procedure.

4. Rewrite the following equation as three linear equations:

$$\begin{pmatrix} 3 \\ -2 \\ 0 \end{pmatrix} x_1 + \begin{pmatrix} 2 \\ 1 \\ 5 \end{pmatrix} x_2 + \begin{pmatrix} 1 \\ 0 \\ 0 \end{pmatrix} S_1 + \begin{pmatrix} 0 \\ 1 \\ 0 \end{pmatrix} S_2 + \begin{pmatrix} 0 \\ 0 \\ 1 \end{pmatrix} S_3 = \begin{pmatrix} 6 \\ 1 \\ 12 \end{pmatrix}$$

5. Does the following problem qualify as a linear programming problem?

Minimize

$$C = x_2/x_1 + 2x_1$$

subject to

$$x_2 = 20$$
$$x_1 + x_2 \leq 27$$
$$x_1 \geq 1$$

6. Solve the following linear programming problems graphically:
   (a) Minimize

$$C = x_1 + x_2$$

subject to

$$x_1 + 2x_2 \geq 9$$
$$4x_1 + x_2 \geq 8$$
$$x_1, x_2 \geq 0$$

   (b) Minimize

$$C = 7x_1 + 9x_2$$

subject to

$$18x_1 + 7x_2 \geq 250$$
$$9x_1 + 2x_2 \geq 60$$
$$3x_1 + 5x_2 \geq 84$$
$$x_1, x_2 \geq 0$$

   (c) Maximize

$$P = 2x_1 + x_2$$

subject to

$$x_1 + x_2 \geq 5$$
$$2x_1 + 3x_2 \leq 20$$
$$4x_1 + 3x_2 \leq 25$$
$$2x_1 - x_2 = 5$$
$$x_1, x_2 \geq 0$$

7. Solve the following linear programming problems graphically:
   (a) Minimize

$$C = 2x_1 + 5x_2$$

subject to

$$2x_1 + x_2 \le 4$$
$$x_1 + 3x_2 \ge 1$$
$$3x_1 + 2x_2 \le 10$$
$$2/3x_1 + x_2 \ge 1$$
$$x_1, x_2 \ge 0$$

(b) Maximize

$$P = 2x_1 + x_2$$

subject to

$$x_1 + x_2 \ge 5$$
$$2x_1 + 3x_2 \le 20$$
$$4x_1 + 3x_2 \le 25$$
$$x_1 \qquad \le 2$$
$$x_2 \le 2$$
$$x_1, x_2 \ge 0$$

(c) Maximize

$$P = 4x_1 + 5x_2$$

subject to

$$2x_1 + 3x_2 \le 10$$
$$4x_1 + 5x_2 \le 17$$
$$x_1 + x_2 \ge 1$$
$$4x_1 + 6x_2 \le 20$$
$$x_1, x_2 \ge 0$$

8. Solve Problem 6(c) by the simplex procedure.
9. Solve Problem 7(c) by the simplex procedure.
10. Solve the following linear programming problem by the simplex procedure:
   Minimize

$$C = -2x_1 - 3x_2$$

subject to

$$x_1 + x_2 \le 4$$
$$6x_1 + 2x_2 \ge 8$$
$$x_1 + 5x_2 \ge 4$$
$$x_1 \le 3$$
$$x_2 \le 3$$
$$x_1, x_2 \ge 0$$

11. Determine an *initial* solution to the following problem by the simplex procedure.

Linear

programming II

$$C = -x_1 - 2x_2 + 3x_3 - 4x_4$$

subject to

$$-x_1 + x_2 + x_3 - 3x_4 = 5$$
$$6x_1 + 7x_2 - 3x_3 - 5x_4 \geq 8$$
$$12x_1 - 9x_2 + 9x_3 + 9x_4 \leq 20, \text{ where}$$
$$x_1, x_2, x_3 \geq 0, \text{ but } x_4 \text{ is unrestricted in sign.}$$

12. Use the simplex procedure to demonstrate that the following problem does not have a feasible solution:
   Maximize

$$P = 2x_1 + 3x_2 + 5x_3$$

subject to

$$3x_1 + 10x_2 + 5x_3 \leq 15$$
$$33x_1 - 10x_2 + 9x_3 \leq 33$$
$$x_1 + 2x_2 + x_3 \geq 4$$
$$x_1, x_2, x_3 \geq 0$$

13. Use the simplex procedure to demonstrate that the following problem has an unbounded optimal solution:
   Maximize

$$P = 4x_1 + x_2 + 3x_3 + 5x_4$$

subject to

$$-4x_1 + 6x_2 + 5x_3 - 4x_4 \leq 20$$
$$3x_1 - 2x_2 + 4x_3 + x_4 \leq 10$$
$$8x_1 - 3x_2 + 3x_3 + 2x_4 \leq 20$$
$$x_1, x_2, x_3, x_4 \geq 0$$

14. Solve the following problem by the simplex procedure:
   Minimize

$$C = 3x_1 + 2x_2$$

subject to

$$2x_1 - x_2 \geq -2$$
$$2x_1 + x_2 \geq 6$$
$$x_1 + 3x_2 \geq 8$$
$$x_1 - x_2 \leq 4$$
$$x_1, x_2 \geq 0$$

15. A manufacturer of bronze castings wishes to determine the mix of raw materials to include in the melting furnace for each batch of castings. Raw materials are available in three types of ingots. Type 1 costs $0.60 per pound and contains 90 percent copper and 10 percent tin. Type 2 costs $0.55 per pound and contains 80 percent copper, 10 percent tin, and 10 percent lead. Type 3 costs $0.45 per pound and contains 75 percent copper, 5 percent tin, 15 percent lead, and 5 percent zinc. The bronze castings must contain a minimum of 78 percent copper, a minimum of 6.7 percent tin, and a maximum of 10 percent lead. There are no restrictions on the zinc content.

   (a) Ignoring any furnace losses or gains of the chemical elements in the melting process, formulate this problem as a linear programming problem if the objective is to minimize the cost per pound of producing bronze castings. (Let x_1, x_2, and x_3 be the pounds of type 1, 2, and 3 ingots, respectively.)

   (b) Determine an *initial* solution of the problem by the simplex procedure.

16. Assume the following linear programming problem:
   Minimize

$$C = 5x_1 + 2x_2$$

subject to

$$x_1 + 2x_2 \geq 5$$
$$2x_1 - x_2 \geq 12$$
$$x_1 + 3x_2 \geq 4$$
$$x_1, x_2 \geq 0$$

   (a) Formulate and solve the dual of this problem.
   (b) Determine the primal solution from the optimal dual solution.

17. Assume that two products, A and B, are manufactured on two machines, 1 and 2, such that:
   Product *A* requires 6 hours on machine 1; 1 hour on machine 2, and
   Product *B* requires 4 hours on machine 1; 2 hours on machine 2.
   There are 12 hours and 8 hours of available capacity on machine 1 and machine 2, respectively.
   If each unit of Product *A* yields a net profit of $12 and each unit of Product *B* yields a net profit of $4,

   (a) solve the dual of this problem by the simplex procedure,
   (b) determine the primal solution from the dual optimal solution, and
   (c) interpret the shadow prices for the dual optimal solution.

BIERMAN, HAROLD; BONINI, CHARLES P.; AND HAUSMAN, WARREN H. *Quantitative Analysis for Business Decisions.* Homewood, Ill.: Richard D. Irwin, Inc., 1973.

BIERMAN, HAROLD; FOURAKER, LAWRENCE E.; AND JAEDICKE, ROBERT K. *Quantitative Analysis for Business Decisions.* Homewood, Ill.: Richard D. Irwin, Inc., 1961.

COOPER, LEON, AND STEINBERG, DAVID. *Methods and Applications of Linear Programming.* Philadelphia: W. B. Saunders Company, 1974.

FABRYCKY, W. J.; GHARE, P. M.; AND TORGERSEN, P. E. *Industrial Operations Research.* Englewood Cliffs, N.J.: Prentice-Hall, Inc., 1972.

GASS, SAUL I. *Linear Programming: Methods and Applications.* New York: McGraw-Hill Book Company, Inc., 1964.

HILLIER, FREDERICK S., AND LIEBERMAN, GERALD J. *Introduction to Operations Research.* San Francisco: Holden-Day, Inc., 1967.

LEVIN, RICHARD I., AND KIRKPATRICK, CHARLES A. *Quantitative Approaches to Management.* New York: McGraw-Hill Book Company, Inc., 1971.

LLEWELLYN, ROBERT W. *Linear Programming.* New York: Holt, Rinehart and Winston, Inc., 1966.

TAHA, HAMDY A. *Operations Research: An Introduction.* New York: The Macmillan Company, 1971.

Monte Carlo analysis

Probability distributions have been discussed so far only as a method of projecting the likelihood of future possible outcomes. In this sense, they describe the behavior of a stochastic variable. The distribution represents the results of a number of observations considering only the relative values assumed by the variable; for example, the number of heads and the number of tails in the flipping of a coin, and not the sequence in which those values occurred—head, tail, tail, head, and so forth. In some analyses involving stochastic variables the sequence is important. In Monte Carlo analysis it is necessary to produce a sequence of variates whose successive values are random and follow some distribution which describes the likelihood of the event in question.

Monte Carlo is the name given to the technique of selecting numbers randomly from a probability distribution for use in a particular trial or analysis of a model. Although Monte Carlo methods have been known for some time, the application of the term "Monte Carlo" and popularization of the use of the method in scientific studies are attributed to the great mathematician John Von Neumann who used it to study neutron diffusion problems.

Various techniques have been invented for producing "random" sequences of numbers. The simplest examples for producing numbers from a discrete probability distribution are found where the choice is among N different numbers which may each occur with equal probability. A roulette wheel that has that exact number of sections will provide the sequence. If $N = 6$, a six-sided die could be used. Because of these devices for generating random sequences, the name "Monte Carlo" with its connection to gambling has become the general term used to describe just about any computational method using random numbers. The current usage of the term generally refers to the selection of values at random from probability distributions. In this chapter we will investigate Monte Carlo analysis methods in a wide variety of situations. We will investigate its components and how they are assembled to be useful in analyzing many previously discussed models.

THE MONTE CARLO METHOD

The Monte Carlo method of analysis generally requires the production of a sequence of random numbers which are drawn from a distribution that is in general not uniform. Methods for directly generating random numbers with a particular distribution are also not usually available. Methods do, however, exist for generating random numbers with a uniform distribution. Almost all methods for generating nonuniform distribution are therefore based on the principle of transforming a uniformly distributed sequence of random numbers into the prescribed sequence necessary for the analysis.

Uniformly Distributed Random Numbers

In order to get a better appreciation for the use of Monte Carlo methods, and in particular, the use of uniformly distributed random numbers, let us consider one of the oldest examples of the use of a Monte Carlo analysis. In this analysis, Monte Carlo methods are employed to estimate the area of an irregular figure within a unit square. Consider Figure 14.1—a rectangle with an irregularly shaded area contained within. The rectangle is assumed to be a unit square and we wish to estimate the area of the irregular figure within the unit square.

The sides of the unit square are each of length one (Hint: any point along that length can be located by a number between 0 and 1). Assume that two such numbers are available and that the first locates a point on

FIGURE 14.1 Unit Square

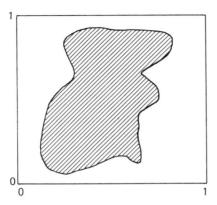

the bottom of the square, the second locates a point on the left-hand side of the square. Then any point within the square can be located as being vertically above the point on the bottom and horizontally to the right of the point on the left side. Obviously, there is an infinite number of decimal fractions between 0 and 1 and we can locate infinite numbers of points along the bottom and along the left-hand side. This provides an infinity of points within the unit square which means we can find as many different ones as we wish.

The Monte Carlo procedure begins with the selection of a large number of random points within the unit square. This is accomplished by continuously choosing two random numbers between 0 and 1 and then using these to identify an exact point within the unit square. The point within the unit square is then tested either by formula or by inspection to see whether or not it lies within the shaded part, and the result of this investigation is recorded. After a predetermined number of points have been evaluated, we can compute the proportion of points falling inside and outside the shaded part and use this proportion as an estimate of the area of the shaded part.

We could fulfill the requirement to produce a sequence of uniform random numbers by drawing chips from a hat. Assume that there are 100 chips of identical size in the hat with numbers 00, 01, 02, . . ., 99 marked on them. We could shake up the chips, draw one and note its number, replace it, reshake the hat, and draw another. By dividing by 100, we could use the first one to locate the point on the bottom of the square and the second to locate the point on the side of the square. Then using these two points, we could locate the point inside the unit square and test to see whether that is within or outside the shaded area. The procedure would continue by repeating the same sequence of steps and drawing digits from the hat until we had located the predetermined number of points in the unit square from which the area is to be estimated.

It should be quite obvious that the accuracy of our estimate is highly dependent on the number of trials we take. The accuracy is furthermore affected by the number of significant digits we choose to maintain on our chips. If instead of the numbers 00 through 99 on the chips, we have the numbers 000 through 999 for the location of our points on the unit square, then a much finer grid can be described and a more precise estimate of the area of the shaded figure could be obtained. We could even put five or six significant digits on the chips and create the number of chips required for experimentation. However, the hat we would need to use to contain them would grow extremely large and the procedure would become impractical.

Let us continue our discussion by assuming that we have selected a great number of pairs of points for the investigation of this area. As we test thousands upon thousands of random points, we would expect that the proportion falling within the shaded part of the figure to approach very closely the area of that shaded portion of the unit square. If the square had an original area other than one, for example, four square feet, we would merely multiply the proportion by four square feet to obtain the desired estimate of the shaded area.

In the previous discussion, the source of our random numbers came from the chips which we placed in our hat. The numbers on the chips ranged from 00 to 99 and these chips were used as the source of uniformly distributed random numbers. By a uniform distribution, we mean that the probability of a single variable X falling in any interval within a certain range of values is proportional to the ratio of the interval size to the range. That is, every point in the range is equally likely to be chosen. Suppose the possible range of the values is from A to B (B greater than A), then the probability that X will fall in an interval ΔX is $\Delta X/(B - A)$. Drawn as a graph, the probability density function is a straight line of height $1/(B - A)$ between the points A and B. One example of a uniform distribution was presented in Figure 5.4 (Chapter 5) in which the probability of the outcome of the toss of a die is illustrated.

However, there is no loss in generality in assuming that the range of a uniform distribution is only from 0 to 1 because any other sequence of uniformly distributed numbers over a different range can be easily transformed to the range 0 to 1.

In dealing with numerical calculations, a certain finite number of digits is collected to represent the desired accuracy and precision. Strictly speaking, it is not possible to represent a continuous variable since any finite number of digits only allows a finite possible number of values. Given enough digits, however, the possible values can be assumed to be sufficiently large to treat the variable as being continuous. It will be assumed that the generated random numbers are generally represented by a sufficient number of digits to make that assumption true. Caution must be employed, however, when the random number is modified subsequent to its generation, because if that number is multiplied by a factor that is greater than one, there is an increase in a phenomena referred to as "granularity" which can cause a loss of accuracy.

Sources of uniform random numbers can be found many places. With the advent of the digital computer, techniques were developed for the production of these random numbers for use in various experiments on the computer. Additionally, several physical processes have been set up which also produce a continuous stream of uniformly distributed random numbers. For purposes of our textbook, however, tables of uniformly distributed random numbers are included in Tables 2 and 3 in the Appendix. These tables may be used to produce random numbers by reading either horizontally or vertically a continuous stream of numbers as necessary.

Suppose that it is decided to generate a sequence of uniformly distributed random numbers between 0 and 1 to an accuracy of 1 part in ten thousand; that is, the numbers are to have four decimal digits. The first column on the left in Table 3 can be read row-by-row. Using this method, we find the first five random numbers are 0.3805, 0.7805, 0.8572, 0.2465, 0.8026. If these numbers with more than four digits were needed, columns could be combined. It is not necessary to start with the first column. Actually, for proper use, particularly when a calculation is being repeated, the starting points should be chosen at random. This could be done by choosing a random number to decide on a page, column, or row at which to start.

**Using the
Cumulative
Distribution**

Now that we have created a source of uniformly distributed random numbers on the interval 0 to 1, we must create the method to transform them into a source of random numbers from another prescribed (but nonuniform) distribution.

This transformation process involves the use of the cumulative distribution function as well as the uniform random number source. By expressing the desired probability distribution in terms of its cumulative distribution function, we are able to construct a representation of the particular event which is most useful for the Monte Carlo analysis. Consider Figure 14.2 which illustrates a typical discrete cumulative distribution function to be used as a source of producing random numbers.

FIGURE 14.2 A Typical Discrete Cumulative Probability Distribution

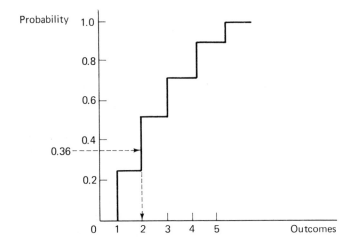

The Monte Carlo method employs the generation of a uniformly distributed random number on the unit interval. This number is then used to locate the point on the abscissa of the cumulative distribution function for the probability distribution in question. By reading over from that entry point on the ordinate to the intersection we can then determine the particular outcome in question. What we are effectively doing is selecting random numbers on the interval 0 to 1 and, depending on where they fall on the unit interval, determining the particular outcome in question. For example, assume a random number was drawn as 0.36. This number would produce an outcome of 2. By drawing a large number of uniformly distributed random numbers and using them with the cumulative distribution function in the same fashion, we can then transform a uniform distribution to numbers distributed as though they had been produced by a process described by any cumulative probability distribution function. In the later sections of this chapter, several examples will be cited which more fully illustrate this concept.

GENERATING NUMBERS FROM OTHER DISTRIBUTIONS

The probability distributions discussed in Chapter 5 may be either discrete or continuous depending on the nature of the events they are used to predict. The Monte Carlo method addresses itself to the production of a sequence of these random variables from a given probability distribution whether it is continuous or discrete. The specific value of that random variable is determined from the method described in the previous section. In this section we will continue our investigation of the Monte Carlo method for generating numbers from both discrete and continuous distributions.

Discrete Distributions

We will demonstrate how our uniform random numbers are used to generate a sequence of numbers from a discrete distribution. When the discrete distribution in question is uniform, the requirement is simply to pick one of N alternatives with equal probability given to each. This process is comparatively simple and involves multiplication of the random number on the unit interval by the total number of alternatives available.

Generally, the requirement is for a discrete distribution which is not uniform so that a different probability is associated with each output. Suppose for example, it is necessary to generate a random variable representing the number of offensive plays a football team executes in one given possession of the football. The probability function is assumed to be a discrete distribution as shown in Table 14.1.

Let us now assume that we have a source for producing uniform random numbers on the unit interval. Let the specific value of one of these numbers be called r. What we wish to do is to compare the value of r with the values of the cumulative distribution function at the various points y_i, a procedure which involves comparing the value of r generated with successive values of y_i. If the value of r falls in an interval $y_i < r \le y_{i+1}$ $(i = 1, 2,$

TABLE 14.1   Number of Offensive Football Plays Per Possession

i	Number of Plays x_i	Probability $P(x_i)$	Cumulative Probability y_i
1	0	.01	.01
2	1	.02	.03
3	2	.05	.08
4	3	.15	.23
5	4	.35	.58
6	5	.20	.78
7	6	.15	.93
8	7	.05	.98
9	8	.01	.99
10	9	.01	1.00

..., 10), the corresponding value of x_i is taken as the expected number of plays for this particular possession. Using the five random numbers which we generated in the previous section, the following sequence of the number of football plays which would have been generated are shown in Table 14.2. In this case the cumulative probability formulation makes it much easier for us to locate and assess the value of the random number produced.

TABLE 14.2   A Sequence

Random Number r	Number of Offensive Plays x
.3805	4
.7805	6
.8572	6
.2465	4
.8026	6

Continuous Distributions

The procedure for generating continuous random variables is basically the same as that for discrete random variables. However, it is usually more convenient to utilize a graph of the cumulative distribution function for continuous random variables than to tabulate the various intervals, because an accurate generation of the random variable would require an extremely large number of intervals.

As a simple illustration of the procedure to generate a continuous random variable, consider the cumulative distribution function shown in Figure 14.3. As in the case of the discrete distribution, we first generate a random number between 0.0 and 1.0 and set the cumulative probability for that distribution equal to this number. We then locate this value in Figure 14.3 on the ordinate of the graph and move horizontally across the graph until the cumulative distribution function is intersected. At that point we drop down to the X-axis and record the value of X as the value of the random variable generated. Examples of random variables generated in this fashion are given in Table

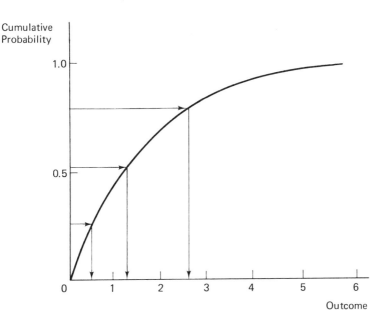

14.3 and Figure 14.3. Remember that in this example and in all examples of a continuous random variable using the cumulative distribution function, that function is nondecreasing and the probabilities lie between 0 and 1. Given a sequence of random numbers that are uniformly distributed over the range 0 to 1, each number of the sequence is considered to be a value of the cumulative distribution function and the corresponding value of the outcome x is determined. The sequence of the numbers x are randomly distributed and have the probability distribution of the original function. In other words, the inverse of the cumulative distribution function is evaluated with the sequence of the uniformly distributed random numbers.

Example Random Variables **TABLE 14.3**

Random Number	x
0.823	2.71
0.557	1.32
0.279	0.50

Problem 1. Suppose we wish to generate binominally distributed random variables with parameters $p = 0.5$ and $n = 5$. In this case the probability of occurrence P is given as: **Some Examples**

$$P(X) = \frac{5!}{X!^{(5-X)!}} (0.5)^5 (0.5)^{5-X}$$

The probabilities associated with this distribution are shown in Table 14.4. The graph of the cumulative distribution is shown in Figure 14.4.

If the method which we employed to generate this random variable is reliable, then out of 100,000 random variables produced we would expect to obtain 3,125 zeroes, 15,625 ones, 31,250 twos, and so on based on the figures in Table 14.4. However, this can be accomplished

TABLE 14.4   Binomial Distribution

X	P(X)	Cumulative Distribution
0	0.03125	0.03125
1	0.15625	0.18750
2	0.31250	0.50000
3	0.31250	0.81250
4	0.15625	0.96875
5	0.03125	1.00000

FIGURE 14.4   Cumulative Distribution of Binomial

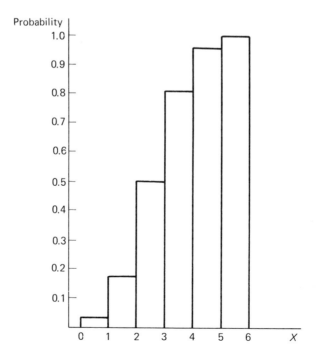

R.N.	x	R.N.	x	R.N.	x	R.N.	x
45523	2	03091	0	82922	4	32757	2
08926	1	84957	4	75342	3	83345	4
95183	4	65728	3	37519	2	03666	1
47551	—	05075	1	88272	4	88388	4
61368	3	18623	1	71864	3	53033	3
57343	3	58320	3	28006	2	26085	2
49719	2	06282	1	18807	2	21998	2
28160	2	15650	1	88182	4	78583	3
82611	4	68008	3	16194	1	42855	2
72711	3	92823	4	02482	0	75321	3
33092	2	45946	2	29198	2	67692	3
16697	1	07138	1	71937	3	70427	3
82384	4	47073	2	34688	2	97423	5
29832	2	28788	2	45523	2	83584	4
15087	1	35283	2	91532	4	28386	2
14903	1	97728	5	47786	2	65902	3
93531	4	12544	1	76861	3	99496	5
33408	2	76900	3	63804	3	87400	4
20825	2	29991	2	61825	3	09749	1
77044	3	21359	2	30469	2	13202	1
76783	3	32517	2	93783	4	61730	5
63409	3	17897	1	63959	3	97316	5
88204	4	97372	5	20661	2	63256	3
10868	1	09166	1	40110	2	96448	4
36252	2	49883	2	76718	3	50457	3
18623	1	92020	4	13689	1	99668	5
30282	2	11265	1	59539	3	02614	0
29351	2	60337	3	72269	3	55698	3
50206	3	88118	4	88833	4	59446	3
82868	4	80142	3	74044	3	66944	3
38515	2	89637	4	02440	0	01486	0
28493	2	24125	2	36954	2	29553	2
29621	2	75289	3	19253	2	47617	2
27012	2	53549	3	46174	2	06833	1
59970	3	24741	2	18288	1	31398	2
14578	1	22065	2	27415	2	72734	3
78644	3	51026	3	31014	2	17332	1
23752	2	14364	1	91924	4	48673	2
85546	4	19611	2	85632	4	74304	3
90960	4	72291	3	73877	3	05303	1
55690	3	37691	2	00508	0	92448	4
71828	3	88265	4	53933	3	15706	1
33894	2	53461	3	68094	3	80296	3
38494	2	40099	2	06119	1	21063	2
56118	3	57016	3	88940	4	99095	5
68063	3	21550	2	94029	4	01548	0
93787	4	74798	3	87827	4	95321	4
72131	3	41250	2	97347	5	30541	2
86749	4	80532	3	88923	4	88789	4
87469	4	03372	1	21759	2	80047	3

by generating five digit random numbers and placing a decimal before each digit. If these random numbers are uniformly distributed, the probability that such a number will fall between 0.00000 and 0.03125 is 0.03125, and the probability that it will fall between 0.03126 and 0.18750 is 0.15625. The same holds true for the rest of each of the remaining intervals. Thus, if the random number generated lies between 0.50001 and 0.81250, the value of the variable generated is 3. An example of this process repeated 200 times is illustrated in Table 14.5. The results of this experiment are shown in Table 14.6 and they indicate a reasonable correspondence to the expected probabilities. It should be noted that as the number of repetitions of the experiment is increased, the difference between the estimated and theoretical probabilities would decrease.

TABLE 14.6   Results of Generation

X	Frequency	Estimated Probability	Theoretical Probability
0	7	0.035	0.03125
1	29	0.145	0.15625
2	61	0.305	0.31250
3	58	0.290	0.31250
4	37	0.185	0.15625
5	8	0.040	0.03125
	200	1.000	1.00000

Problem 2.   An airline has fifteen flights leaving a given airport per day, each with one pilot. The airline has a policy of keeping three reserve pilots on call to replace pilots scheduled for flights who become sick. The probability distribution for the daily number of sick pilots is shown in Table 14.7. Use Monte Carlo methods to estimate the utilization of reserve pilots and also the probability that at least one flight will be cancelled because no pilots are available. Base your estimates on a thirty-day study. Figure 14.5 illustrates the cumulative distribution of the probabilities shown in Table 14.7.

TABLE 14.7   Distribution of Pilots' Sick Call

Number Sick	Probability	Cumulative Probability
0	0.20	0.20
1	0.20	0.40
2	0.25	0.65
3	0.15	0.80
4	0.10	0.90
5	0.10	1.00

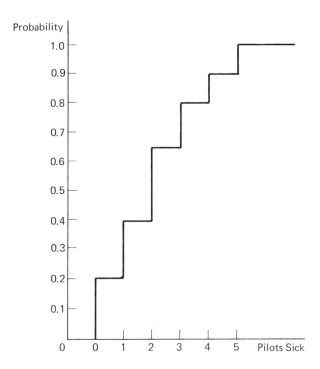

Table 14.8 provides a thirty-day analysis of the situation, including the resultant number of sick pilots, the total number of idle pilots, and the resultants of whether or not the flight was cancelled because of an insufficient number of pilots. You will note that on eight separate days during that thirty-day evaluation there was an insufficient number of pilots to handle the demand. As a result the flights on those days were cancelled; that is, a flight will be cancelled 26 percent of the time. An investigation of the distribution indicates that over a long period three or fewer pilots will be sick 80 percent of the time; therefore, theoretically we would not expect a flight to be cancelled over 20 percent of the time. As the number of investigations increases, we would expect the results of the evaluation to align themselves more closely with the actual probability function, an aspect which was discussed in the previous problem.

If we were to assess the total cost of losing a flight versus the cost per idle pilot, we would begin to develop the optimal strategy for staffing. This cost balancing approach for model building is a fundamental concept in management science and the Monte Carlo analysis facilitates this reasoning to its fullest extent.

TABLE 14.8 Analysis of Pilot Calls

Day	R.N.	No. of Sick Pilots	Idle Pilots	Flight Cancelled?
1	.858	4	—	YES
2	.683	3	0	
3	.059	0	3	
4	.190	0	3	
5	.155	0	3	
6	.314	1	2	
7	.964	5	—	YES
8	.789	3	0	
9	.157	0	3	
10	.783	3	0	
11	.715	3	0	
12	.996	5	—	YES
13	.243	1	2	
14	.861	4	—	YES
15	.289	1	2	
16	.895	4	—	YES
17	.378	1	2	
18	.158	0	3	
19	.247	1	2	
20	.848	4	—	YES
21	.336	1	2	
22	.863	4	—	YES
23	.299	1	2	
24	.636	2	1	
25	.141	0	0	
26	.387	1	2	
27	.532	2	1	
28	.739	3	0	
29	.997	5·	—	YES
30	.321	1	2	

MODEL ANALYSIS

In the previous sections we have introduced the Monte Carlo method and its requirement for producing sequences of numbers from various probability distributions, a technique which is useful in a variety of quantitative study areas. If you were required to study the operation of a certain production process for the purpose of increasing the output of that process, where would you begin? If you were given the assignment of determining the optimal number of spare parts to stock for a given item, how would you approach this problem? If you were asked to determine the number of rooms to construct in a hospital, what would you do? These problems are all very similar in that they involve the determination of some probabilities and consequences associated with different events. They are also similar in that each has a specific objective to be accomplished.

There exists a body of mathematical techniques which are grouped rather loosely under the heading of *Operations Research* and which provide the means whereby questions such as the preceding ones may be answered; many of these techniques have been discussed in this text. Monte Carlo methods can provide data for the mathematical techniques and may be used to analyze situations too complex for mathematical analysis. In this section we will discuss the implications of the Monte Carlo analysis to model building and develop rationale for building simulation models of more advanced systems.

Basic Concepts

In preceding chapters we have characterized specific situations in which mathematical models could be developed to analyze the implications of certain decisions. For instance in Chapter 10, we define the conditions under which a minimum cost operating policy could be determined by specifying the order quantity and reorder point for an inventory situation. Generally speaking, a model is a representation of a system and a system is nothing more than a collection of entities which act and interact toward the accomplishment of some logical end. Obviously, the definition of a system depends on the experiment being conducted. In some cases this may be an inventory system. Other times it might be a quality control system or perhaps a system which defines the activity of a network of traffic lights.

As we pointed out very early in the text, a model is a representation of a system. Through the text we have discussed the employment of certain mathematical and statistical models which capture the pertinent interactions and relations of the entities of the system under investigation. As these models become more complex, we are often able to include interactions which exist in the real world, but which are difficult to express adequately in the mathematical sense. In these cases we often resort to simulation techniques, where *simulation* refers to the activity of performing experiments on a model of a given system. It should be noted that simulation methodology is highly dependent on Monte Carlo procedures. However, simulation can be extended to more complicated studies through the use of a high speed digital computer, which has become a necessity in order to study very complex systems.

The importance of quantitative analysis in the evaluation of complex systems has been well-established for many years. Wide application of the tools of operations research in all phases of analysis serves only to emphasize the importance of the quantitative approach to systems analysis. In most cases the performance of a given system is evaluated through the use of a quantitative model which is a mathematical representation of the system under study. We have spent several chapters developing specific examples of these quantitative models. Often, the model involves an equation or equations which vary in degree of complexity with the complexity of the system being represented by the model.

Generally, in attempting to develop a mathematical model for a specific system, we find that one of three cases arises.

1. The system is amenable to both description and analysis by a pure mathematical model. An example of this is the basic inventory system discussed in Chapter 10.

2. The system is amenable to description by a mathematical model. However, correct analysis of that model is beyond the level of mathematical sophistication of the analyst. An example of this particular problem can be presented by expanding to the concepts of probabilistic lead times as developed in the chapter on inventory systems. In these cases, mathematical models can be developed which represent the total system. However, to analyze these models adequately, one needs to resort to means other than pure mathematical analysis. Remember also that the analyst's level of mathematical sophistication must be considered.

3. The system is so complex that description of the system by mathematical model is totally beyond the capabilities of the analyst.

Cases 2 and 3 lend themselves to simulation techniques because an analyst can prepare a quantitative model of the system even if he possesses a relatively limited background in mathematics.

It is not within the scope of this text to discuss the details of simulation methodology. However, the basics of simulation model building presented in this chapter are such that the reader should have been able to develop an appreciation for the factors involved in employing the simulation technique. Although simulation does generally require the use of a high speed digital computer for most complex analysis, it still stands with Monte Carlo methods as a viable technique for the analysis of various systems.

The basic advantages of simulation and Monte Carlo analysis are:

1. The model of a system once constructed may be employed as often as desired to analyze various situations.

2. Simulation and Monte Carlo methods are handy for analyzing proposed systems in which information is sketchy at best.

3. Usually, data for further analyses can be obtained from the simulation model much more cheaply than it can from a real world system.

4. Simulation models are often easier to apply than pure analytic methods and therefore can be employed by a greater variety of individuals.

There are also several disadvantages in employing Monte Carlo or simulation techniques:

1. The simulation models are often very costly to construct and validate.

2. If computers are employed to run the simulation model, this can be very expensive also.

3. Perhaps the largest single disadvantage of simulation is that people employ it when it is not the best method of analysis. It is obvious that simulation methods give only approximate solutions. Many assumptions underlying simulation techniques once violated render the techniques nearly inoperable and certainly leave them on shaky theoretical ground.

It is not within the scope of this text to discuss the guidelines to be employed to determine when simulation can best be used. It is doubtful that such a set of rules exist, for each analysis is unique in some fashion.

However, it is hoped that the text can provide the basis through which rational decisions can be made.

If possible, it is generally better to formulate mathematical models and to solve them analytically for solution accuracy. As we mentioned earlier, this is not always possible and in such cases, simulation and Monte Carlo analysis provides an alternative method for the solution. It is quite obvious that with either approach the results depend on the validity of the model and utility of input information to the model. A poorly constructed model of the system can do much more harm than good, because a poorly conceived model can lead to false conclusions about the system. The objectives must dictate how "rich" and of what character the model should be.

It should be helpful to characterize the general simulation process of analysis where we build a model of the system which captures its highlights. What are the basic features of a given system? These features have been discussed in various ways in the preceding chapters and are characterized in Figure 14.6 which illustrates a system represented as a black box with three essential characteristics. The *measures of effectiveness* are those quantities which are accepted as the goals of the system; the *decision variables* are those variables of the system under control of the decision maker; and the *uncontrollable variables* are those over which the decision maker has no control whatsoever. The purpose of any systems analysis is to optimize the measures of effectiveness by describing a policy for the decision variables in light of the uncontrollable variables. For example, most inventory systems take as their measure of effectiveness the total system cost. Optimizing the measure of effectiveness means minimizing that cost. The objective, then, is to obtain a set of values for the reorder point and order quantity which minimize that cost in light of demand and other costs which are uncontrollable variables. In order to develop this model, we may need to make some simplifying assumptions to be able to optimize the measure of effectiveness, but when these assumptions are violated the model may become at best a poor representation of the system. It is extremely important in any model analysis to identify each of these characteristics before proceeding: this is the first step in any model building process.

Simulation Methodology

Pertinent Characteristics of a System **FIGURE 14.6**

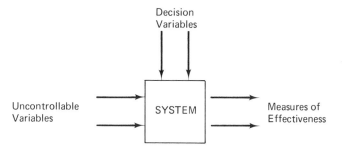

We have stated previously that the simulation or Monte Carlo method is the act of performing experiments on a model of a system. In order to make this a rational technique of analysis in the determination of effective policies, three different objectives must be considered:

1. Objective of the system being studied—This objective generally is to utilize resources allocated to it in such fashion as to optimize some quantity which is recognized in this goal of this system. In the past we have called this the measure of effectiveness.

2. Objective of the simulation model—The objective of the simulation model (assuming that it adequately represents the system) is to efficiently generate output information for further analysis. This output information reflects those parameters which must be known in order to apply the model.

3. Objective of the model analyst—The analyst must allocate resources of the simulation project budget such that the expected benefits from the analysis are maximized.

There already exists a hierarchy among these objectives: the objective of the system under study must necessarily take precedence over all others. Accomplishment of this objective is paramount to the organization and must be kept uppermost in all people's minds. The second most important objective is that of the analyst, and the objective of the model comes last—it is subservient to the objective of the analyst which is subservient to the objective of the system. All this says is that the system does not exist solely for analysis.

These objectives are ever present in each model analysis. They may either be explicit or implicit, but they must be considered in order to derive maximum benefits from the project. It is desirable to qualify these objectives whenever possible. This is always very difficult and often impossible, but it is helpful to attempt to quantify as much as one can. As in so many of the techniques, the attempt alone is often sufficient to provide great insight into the system being studied.

In the determination of rational policies through the use of model building and simulation, you must recognize that simulation of a given system is not an end in itself. The model is but a vehicle from which data for further analyses can be collected, and in this manner the simulation model becomes a pure representation of the real system providing information which may be analyzed in order to draw conclusions about the system under study.

The use of the simulation or Monte Carlo model provides a means for collecting information about the performance of a complex system based on conditions established by the analyst. Using this methodology, we can create systems for study without affecting real life situations, and for this reason alone, Monte Carlo and simulation analysis has become a viable and reliable tool for analysis of complex systems.

An Example *Problem 3.* Using Monte Carlo techniques, estimate the average number of lost sales per week for the inventory system of a part for the Doright Supply System. The system operates such that whenever inventory level falls to or below five units, an order is placed. The size of each order is equal to $20 - X$ where X is the inventory level when the order was placed. If a demand occurs during a period when the inventory level is zero, the sale is lost. Daily demand is binomially distributed with $p = .5$ and $n = 5$. The order lead time (that time in days between placing and receiving the order) is also binomially distributed with $p = 0.5$ and $n = 5$.

Analyze the system for a period of thirty days assuming that the inventory level on the first day is twenty units. For simplicity also assume that all demands occur at noon and all orders are placed at the same time. It will be further assumed that all orders are received after the demand occurred on a given day.

Table 14.9 summarizes the activities of this analysis carried on for a period of thirty working days or six working weeks. The total number of lost sales for this period was 8 or 1.33 per week. Note that this

Estimation of Lost Sales of 30 Days Operation   **TABLE 14.9**

Day	R. N. Demand	Demand	R. N. Lead Time	Lead Time	Sales	Lost Sales	Inventory Level	Receipts
0							20	
1	703	3			3		17	
2	962	4			4		13	
3	072	1			1		12	
4	431	2			2		10	
5	027	0			0		10	
6	845	4			4		6	
7	323	2	331	2	2		4	
8	356	2			2		2	
9	720	3			2	1	16	16
10	881	4			4		12	
11	084	1			1		11	
12	455	2			2		9	
13	841	4	644	3	4		5	
14	515	3			3		2	
15	769	3			2	1	0	
16	149	1			0	1	15	15
17	047	1			1		14	
18	596	3			3		11	
19	994	5			5		6	
20	687	3	942	4	3		3	
21	840	4			3	1	0	
22	164	1			0	1	0	
23	173	1			0	1	0	
24	334	2			0	2	17	17
25	041	1			1		16	
26	409	2			2		14	
27	637	3			3		11	
28	927	4			4		7	
29	965	4	743	3	4		3	
30	284	2			2		1	

analysis treated an inventory model which we were not prepared to treat in the inventory chapter due to the random nature of the demand and lead time patterns. If cost modeling were involved, the appropriate cost figures could be introduced to arrive at system costs.

PROBLEMS

1. Crumpler Manufacturing, Inc., stocks purchased units of item A, a component used in subsequent assembly. It is known that:

    a. Each unit of item A costs $500.

    b. The cost of holding item A in inventory is 20 percent of its price per year.

    c. The cost of processing an order for any number of units is $15 per order processed.

    d. An annual demand of 365 units is expected.

    e. All items of A demanded but not available are back ordered and are filled immediately when a new shipment arrives.

Two uncertainties stand out:

    1. Crumpler is uncertain about the day-to-day demand rate.

    2. Crumpler is uncertain about the lead time.

However, Crumpler has the records of last year's operation and believes this year's will be nearly equivalent. Specifically, the records show that the demand rate and lead time last year were as shown in the tables below.

Demand

Units Demanded Per Day	Frequency of Demand
0	40% of the days
1	30% of the days
2	25% of the days
3	5% of the days

Lead Time

Lead Time (Days)	Frequency of Lead Time
1	25%
2	50%
3	25%

In order to minimize total inventory cost: (1) how many units of item A should Crumpler order at a time, and (2) at what point as the stock level drops should an order be placed?

2. Each day a man leaves his home, A, and goes to work at G. As indicated in the diagram below, the routes he may take are

      1-3-7,   1-4-8,   2-5-8,   2-6-9

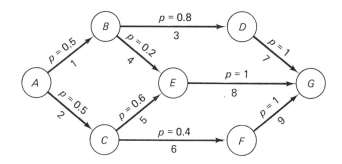

The value, p, for each route is the probability that he takes that route. That is, if he arrives at point C, the probability that he takes route 5 is 0.6 and the probability he takes 6 is 0.4. The distribution of the time spent on each route is normal with parameters given below:

Route 1—time = 20 minutes
Route 2—time = 15 minutes
Route 3—time = 5 minutes
Route 4—time = 7 minutes
Route 5—time = 6 minutes
Route 6—time = 10 minutes
Route 7—time = 4 minutes
Route 8—time = 5 minutes
Route 9—time = 3 minutes

Examine by Monte Carlo methods this man's routes for thirty working days. On the average how long will he likely take to reach work?

3. A particle moves on the following circle. The particle starts at zero. At any point on the circle, the particle will take one step which may be to either adjacent point on the circle. The probability that the particle moves clockwise or counterclockwise at any point is 0.5. By simulation determine the probability distribution of the number of steps until the particle returns

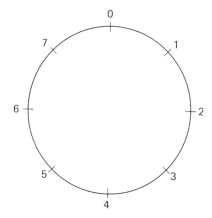

to 0 and the expected number of steps until the particle returns to zero.

4. A professor grades homework sets (always with six problems) on the following basis: A coin is flipped and if it lands a "head" then no grading is performed that day. If a "tail" lands then a die is rolled to see which of the six problems will be graded. By Monte Carlo methods investigate and discuss the following student strategies:

   a. Work all problems on every other day.
   b. Flip a coin to determine whether or not to work all problems.
   c. Work 1/2 of assigned problems each day.

Base your comparisons on 100 days of class.

5. A computer center operates twenty-four hours per day requiring three computer operators per eight-hour shift. Each operator is paid at a rate of $4 per hour. If an operator cannot work his shift, either he must be replaced or the machine he operates must be shut down for that shift at a cost of $100 per hour. To provide insurance against the possibility of loss of machine time, it has been proposed that several of the operators be put "on call" during those shifts on which they are not working. The proposal calls for paying operators "on call" at a rate of $0.50 per hour for remaining available. Each operator is paid time and a half for all work over eight hours per day. The probability that an operator can work his shift is 0.95. The probability that an operator "on call" can be reached when needed is 0.90. By simulation, determine the number of "on call" operators to minimize the total cost of keeping the computers running. Assume that an operator "on call" is paid $0.50 per hour whether he is called or not.

6. A greeting card company has observed the demand pattern for their cards during the previous year. They expect, however, that the demand for cards may increase in the future but are unsure what the amount of change may be. In order to help in the planning for purchases of newer and higher volume equipment, they are more concerned with the expected rate of increase per year than with the absolute change in demand. Given the following information, provide the information the company seeks.

Change in Demand (units/month)	Frequency
−2	.05
−1	.05
0	.05
1	.10
2	.15
3	.30
4	.20
5	.10

7. Cars arrive at a police road block periodically throughout the day. Cars are chosen at random with probability of 0.6 for an intensive search. The time required to search a car is also a random variable. Given the following frequency distributions for arrival rate and search time, determine the expected number of cars searched per hour and the expected amount of time per hour spent conducting the search of cars.

| Arrival Rate | | Search Time | |
# of Cars/Hr.	Frequency	Time/Car Searched	Frequency
0	.05	5 min	.20
1	.10	10 min	.45
2	.25	15 min	.20
3	.40	20 min	.10
4	.10	25 min	.05
5	.05		
6	.05		

8. Weigger Industries manufactures a component part in lots of 10,000 units which are subsequently shipped to another plant. The lot fraction defective (percent defective units in a lot) has been observed to be 0.05, 0.10, or 0.15 with probability 0.60, .30, and .10, respectively. The quality control inspectors make every effort to keep defective lots from being shipped out of Weigger Industries. The probability that an inspector catches a lot having fraction defective 0.05 is 0.60; having fraction defective 0.10 is 0.80; and having fraction defective 0.15 is 0.95. If a defective lot passes by the inspectors a cost of $5.00 per defective unit is incurred by Weigger Industries. If a defective lot is identified by the inspectors, each defective unit in the lot is repaired at a cost of $1 per unit. Determine the expected number of defective units shipped from the plant and the total expected cost of defective units shipped and repaired per lot produced.

9. A local fire department wishes to determine the expected dollar losses due to fire damage. The probability that a fire will occur during any given hour of the day is 0.10. The department has been able to categorize the fires into three classes. The probability that a fire is a class A fire is .50; class B is .30; and class C is .20. The expected dollar loss from a class A, B, or C fire is $1000, $3000, and $5000, respectively. Determine the expected dollar loss from fire damage.

BIBLIOGRAPHY

EMSHOFF, JAMES R., AND SISSON, ROGER L. *Computer Simulation Models.* New York: The Macmillan Company, 1970.

GORDON, GEOFFRY. *System Simulation.* Englewood Cliffs, N.J.: Prentice-Hall, Inc., 1969.

MCMILLAN, CLAUDE, AND GONZALEZ, RICHARD F. *Systems Analysis: A Computer Approach to Decision Models.* Homewood, Ill.: Richard D. Irwin, Inc., 1968.

MEIER, ROBERT C.; NEWELL, WILLIAM T.; AND PAZER, HAROLD L. *Simulation in Business and Economics.* Englewood Cliffs, N. J.: Prentice-Hall, Inc., 1969.

MIZE, JOE H., AND COX, J. GRADY. *Essentials of Simulation.* Englewood Cliffs, N.J.: Prentice-Hall, Inc., 1968.

NAYLOR, THOMAS; BALINTFY, JOSEPH L.; BURDICK, DONALD S.; AND CHU, KONG. *Computer Simulation Techniques.* New York: John Wiley & Sons, Inc., 1966.

SCHMIDT, J. W., AND TAYLOR, R. E. *Simulation and Analysis of Industrial Systems.* Homewood, Ill.: Richard D. Irwin, 1970.

Waiting line analysis

The mathematical study of waiting lines has been termed queueing theory. The formation of waiting lines is, of course, a very common occurrence and arises whenever a current demand for some service exceeds the current capacity to provide that service. Personal, every day examples of waiting lines include waiting in line to purchase tickets to an entertainment event, waiting at barber shops, grocery store check-out stations, toll booths on highway turnpikes, and bank teller windows. Ships waiting to unload at docks, aircraft waiting to land, raw materials waiting for processing, purchase orders waiting to be filled, and finished goods inventory waiting for distribution to customers are but a few of an almost infinite number of business and industrial examples of units waiting in line for service.

A multiple-channel waiting line system is illustrated schematically in Figure 15.1. For convenience, we will hereafter refer to the units arriving for service, units waiting for service, or units being served simply as *customers*. The entity which provides service to the customers will be referred to as the *service facility*. The manner in which customers are chosen from the waiting line for service is termed the *queue discipline*. Examples of a queue discipline include selecting customers from a line on a "first-come, first-served" basis, a "last-come, first-served" basis, at random, or according to one of several priority rules. An example of a priority rule is at any given selection time, always select the customer in line which requires the shortest processing time. As the descriptive queueing models are presented later in the chapter, these dimensions will become more clear.

A Multiple-Channel Waiting Line System **FIGURE 15.1**

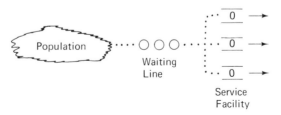

THE QUEUEING SYSTEM

Certain characteristics of waiting lines, such as the expected length of the line over a given time interval or the expected time a customer spends waiting for service and being served, are directly influenced by the capacity of the service mechanism and the queue discipline. A knowledge of the interaction among arriving customers, the queue discipline, and the service mechanism may prove beneficial to a decision maker. Queueing theory can provide a basis for describing this interaction and thereby enable predictions of waiting line behavior. For example, assume that customers arrive for service to receive a hair cut and/or a shave in a barber shop in random fashion at an average rate of twenty customers per hour. The service mechanism—the six barbers—can process an average of twenty-four customers per hour. Although the service rate exceeds the arrival rate, a waiting line may form and extend over one or more intervals of time due to the randomness of arrivals and the varying processing times the customers require. It seems logical that the average time a customer spends waiting in line would be decreased if the service rate were increased by adding a barber and being able to process an average of twenty-eight customers per hour. However, seven barbers are likely to spend a larger proportion of the day idle than six barbers. Queueing theory can serve to quantify such intuition.

Increasing the capacity of any service mechanism will most likely increase the cost of providing that service. However, the cost of waiting in line may then be reduced. The decision maker may wish to effect an economic balance between these opposing costs, that is, the optimization of a total cost expression for the queueing system formulated as a function of the average service rate. In most queueing systems in the business world, the decision maker can control the service mechanism and queue discipline but generally not the arrival rate and pattern of arrivals. Queueing theory itself does not directly answer the economic optimization question but can provide necessary descriptive information for the development of an economic evaluation.

The literature on queueing theory is extensive and the applications of the theory, numerous and diverse. As the individual elements of a queueing system are subsequently discussed, it will be apparent that the various combinations of customer arrival patterns, queue disciplines, number of servers, and service patterns comprise an almost limitless set of possible queueing systems. For our purposes, simplification is warranted and indeed necessary, because an in-depth understanding of queueing theory requires a considerable background in advanced mathematics and probability theory. It is also appropriate to state that mathematical closed-form models have not yet been developed for many queueing systems, and in these situations, Monte Carlo simulation methods may be better employed to gain insight. Thus, mathematical analysis and Monte Carlo simulation are the two basic approaches used to describe queueing systems.

In order to further motivate our discussion of waiting line analysis, an example is now offered. Let us assume that we are concerned with a production situation where the operation of interest is a final manual inspection. Units arrive singly at the inspection station by conveyor belt from several final assembly stations which are not part of a machine-paced assembly line; that is, they arrive randomly rather than periodically. The final inspection task consists of visual examination, taking certain measurements, and making minor repairs if required. Customers are selected from the line on a first-come, first-served basis, and after inspection, the serviced customers are either sent to a packaging station or rejected.

At the beginning of a workday, an analyst takes a sample observation of the inspection task for 100 minutes and compiles the data as shown in Table 15.1.

Unit Number	Arrival Time	Operation Begins	Operation Completed
1	0	0	4
2	10	10	16
3	14	16	22
4	15	22	30
5	18	30	34
6	19	34	45
7	23	45	47
8	31	47	52
9	39	52	62
10	43	62	70
11	61	70	82
12	63	82	86
13	77	86	97
14	92	—	—

Note from Table 15.1 that for simplification of analysis one unit is immediately available for inspection at the beginning of the study and this first unit requires four minutes to inspect. There could have been zero, two, three, four, or n units waiting for service when the study began. This "initial condition" of the queueing system would affect our description of the waiting line, of course, but we will return to this point later in a brief discussion of the transient versus the steady-state condition of a queueing system. Returning to Table 15.1, the second customer arrives at time $t = 10$, can be processed immediately and requires a six-minute service time. The third customer arrives at time $t = 14$, must wait two minutes until service can begin, then requires six minutes to be serviced, and so forth, until the arrival of the fourteenth customer completes the study period. The fourteenth customer arrives at $t = 92$ while the thirteenth customer is being served. After completing the thirteenth customer at $t = 97$, the inspector did not begin the inspection task on the fourteenth customer during the remaining three minutes of the 100 minute study period. From the data of Table 15.1, some arithmetic will reveal other items of interest about the inspection station waiting line. From Table 15.2, the average time between arrivals for thirteen customers is calculated to be 7.154 minutes, while the average service time for a customer is 7.000 minutes. The inverse of the 7.154 minutes/customer interarrival time is 0.140 customers/minute or 8.40 customers/hour. This figure is interpreted as the average, or mean, arrival rate. Similarly, the inverse of the 7.000 minutes/customer average service time yields 8.58 customers/hour as the mean service rate. Thus, on the average, the inspector should be able to keep ahead of the arriving customers. That this is not the case can be seen from Figure 15.2 which has been developed from the data in Table 15.1.

TABLE 15.2   Unit Interarrival and Service Times—Inspection Task

Unit Number	Time Between Arrivals, Minutes	Operation Time Minutes
1	—	4
2	10	6
3	4	6
4	1	8
5	3	4
6	1	11
7	4	2
8	8	5
9	8	10
10	5	8
11	18	12
12	2	4
13	14	11
14	15	—

FIGURE 15.2   Number in the System as a Function of Time

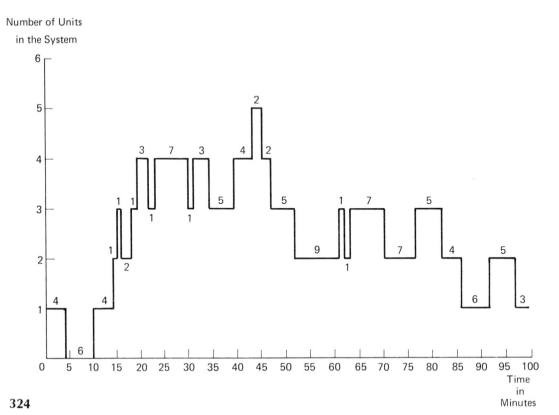

In Figure 15.2, the number of customers in the system consists of those in the waiting line plus one customer being served. The number in the system reaches a maximum of five during the forty-three to forty-five-minute time interval of the 100-minute study. The random nature of the arrivals result in random fluctuations of the number in the system. The numbers above the bar graph in Figure 15.2 have no particular significance except as an aid to the compilation of Table 15.3. In Table 15.3 the proportion of time that the system contained various numbers of customers is shown. The mean number of customers in the system for the study period is calculated from Table 15.3 data to be $(0 \times .06) + (1 \times 0.17) + (2 \times 0.29) + (3 \times 0.27) + (4 \times 0.19) + (5 \times 0.02) = 2.42$ customers.

Proportion of Time in the System—Inspection Task   **TABLE 15.3**

Number of Units in System	Proportion of Time
0	.06
1	.17
2	.29
3	.27
4	.19
5	.02

We also note from Table 15.3 that the proportion of time when there were zero customers in the system was 0.06. This is the proportion of time when the service mechanism, that is, the inspector, was idle. The data in Table 15.1 can be manipulated to yield the information of Table 15.4. The time each customer spends waiting in line before being served is calculated as the difference in the customer's arrival time and the time his service begins. Using the information in Table 15.4 for the first thirteen customers, the mean waiting time is $143/13 = 11$ minutes.

The example of the final inspection task serves to illustrate the basic elements of a single-server queueing system. Namely, customers arrive as inputs into the system, wait in line for service and are selected from the line by a particular policy, are processed by a service mechanism, and then depart from the system. An analysis of the waiting line can yield data of possible benefit to managerial decision making. Our analysis of the final inspection task is summarized below, and such results are typical of those provided by queueing theory:

Mean arrival rate	= 8.40 units/hour
Mean service rate	= 8.58 units/hour
Mean number in the system	= 2.42 units
Mean waiting time in line/unit	= 11.00 minutes
Proportion of idle time for the service facility	= 0.06

TABLE 15.4   Time Spent Waiting in the System—Inspection Task

Unit Number	Waiting Time (Arrival Time— Operation Begin Time)
1	0
2	0
3	2
4	7
5	12
6	15
7	22
8	16
9	13
10	19
11	9
12	19
13	9
14	8

ELEMENTS OF A QUEUEING SYSTEM

We will now proceed with a more detailed discussion of queueing system elements and present mathematical results for particular systems. As a preface to further discussion, it should be stated that queueing systems may be categorized as either deterministic or probabilistic in nature. If each customer arrives at known and constant interarrival times and the service times for each customer are likewise known and constant, then the system is deterministic. The substantial majority of the queueing literature is based on the premise that one or more of the elements of the system (interarrival or service time) can be characterized only in probabilistic terms. Experience suggests that probabilistic systems are also the more commonplace in the business world. For these reasons, only the probabilistic view will be considered in this chapter.

Input Population   The input population refers to the source of customers for the queueing system. All the people in a city or any region may be considered the potential population of customers for a bank, hospital, grocery store, or other queueing situation. Such a large population may be considered infinite; however, the concept of an infinite population of customers is theoretical. The assumption of an infinite population is often made for mathematical convenience in the solution of certain queueing models with the judgment that resulting errors (between the assumed model and the real situation) are negligible. On the other hand, there are many industrial and business situations where the assumption of an infinite population would be unrealistic and lead to gross errors in results. For example, twenty looms in a textile manufacturing firm which are candidates for service by a maintenance crew cannot be considered an infinitely large population but rather, a finite

population. Removing one customer from a small, finite population for service has a more noticeable effect on the number of service calls expected from the remaining population than if one customer is removed from an infinite population.

In addition to whether the population is finite or infinite, the pattern by which the customers leave the population for service is an important variable in the analysis. Customers could leave the population at fixed, regular intervals of time such as parts leaving a numerically-controlled machine tool to arrive at a final, manual inspection station. Conversely, automobiles may arrive at a highway toll booth randomly within a given time interval. With random arrivals, the number of customers arriving per unit time follow a statistical pattern and thus may be described by a probability function. In practice either of two statistical measures, the number arriving per unit time or the time between arrivals, is used to hypothesize the probability function which describes the arrival pattern. Although random arrivals may follow any statistical pattern, many queueing models have been developed under the assumption that the Poisson probability function adequately describes the number of customers arriving per unit time period. The validity of this assumption has been supported by many real world queueing studies and the term, *Poisson input*, is often used to mean this assumption is being made.

The mean rate of arrivals can be another variable characterizing the input population. With a fixed mean, or average, rate of arrivals per unit time, the number of arrivals per unit time can be random as previously mentioned. However, the mean rate of arrivals itself could vary over time or indeed, be set by the decision maker. This would be true in a production situation where units arrive at production stage two from production stage one and the production rate at stage one can be set by the decision maker. Such control over the arrival population is usually not the case in actual random arrival queueing situations and the mean rate of arrivals, once determined by data collection, is usually assumed constant over time and not under the control of the decision maker.

Another characteristic of the input population is whether customers arrive for service singly or in bulk. Bulk arrivals are typical of many material handling situations—parts delivered to a machining station in tote boxes by fork lift truck or ships discharging cargo at an unloading dock. Most elementary queueing models consider single arrivals.

The input population may be heterogeneous in nature; that is, they may have different priorities once they arrive at the service facility. Patients arriving at a hospital and rush orders in a manufacturing firm are but two examples of a heterogeneous input population. For modeling purposes, this characteristic is normally considered under the selection policy or queue discipline.

Another interesting characteristic of the input population occurs when there are limits on time and space at the service facility. Customers may elect not to enter a barber shop or a service station if the waiting line is too long, a condition termed *balking,* and then they may either return to the input population for service at a later time or leave the input population altogether. A somewhat special case of balking can occur in a material handling situation where units arrive at production stage two from production stage one by a conveyor which has a fixed number of storage locations. When the storage locations are full, units cannot leave production stage one and blocking of that stage occurs. We are also familiar with the common experience of customers entering a waiting line, but then leaving the line if the wait is too long.

Service Mechanism

Many of the characteristics of the input population may be used to describe the characteristics of the service mechanism. Bulk arrivals may be serviced singly or as a group. Service may require a fixed interval of time for each customer (for example, an automatic machine) or the service time may be a random variable having any probability distribution.

A service mechanism characteristic of considerable importance is the number of service channels. In a broad context, the service mechanism may consist of one or more service facilities and each service facility may contain one or more channels or servers. Elementary multichannel queueing models consider a single service facility but with two or more parallel service channels. A channel is simply a server and the term "parallel" implies that each server in the service facility provides the same type of service to the customer. Everyday examples of multichannel queueing are check-out stations in a grocery store, teller windows in a bank, and gasoline pumps at a service station. The grocery store, bank, or service station is the service facility with more than one server providing essentially the same type of service.

The service mechanism is considered the design element in the queueing system. That is, the number of servers to provide and the service rate for each server are often under the control of the decision maker and the level of service to provide is, therefore, primarily an economic consideration. It should be noted that a single server need not be a single individual or single machine. A repair crew, an installation crew, or an unloading crew may function as a single server since the members of the crew simultaneously work to service one customer.

Service mechanisms which process each customer through multiple, single server stages in series are considered in queueing networks. For example, the machining of steel bar stock may consist of cut-off, turning, drilling, grinding, and packaging operations each performed by different single servers in series. The total processing system from raw material to packaging comprises a queueing network.

Returning to the elementary multichannel queueing system, a fundamental assumption is that arriving customers enter one parent waiting line. Customers then depart the line one at a time to enter the next empty service station. This assumption of one parent waiting line is for mathematical simplicity and may or may not accurately represent some real world multiple channel systems. We note, for example, that multiple check-out stations in a grocery store may each have waiting lines longer than the one customer being served.

However, one can reason that only one customer at a time is serviced by each facility and that the numerous lines can be considered one parent waiting line for the store and the standard multichannel model used to approximate the actual situation. An alternate view is to consider each check-out station as an independent, single channel queueing system.

The example of grocery store check-out stations seems at first reasonably straightforward to analyze, but actually, other input population or service channel characteristics that occur in the practical situation complicate the matter. Customers may switch lines or "jockey" to enter the fastest moving line; they may "balk" or refuse to enter long lines and leave the store. Cash register attendants may have different mean service rates and indeed may individually have service rates that vary as a function of the waiting line length, thus increasing the service rate as the line increases. Queueing models which incorporate such modifications into either the single-server or multichannel model are far more complex.

Queue Discipline

At the outset it should be noted that it is not necessary for there actually to be a physical waiting line in front of a physical structure in order to constitute a queue of customers. A fork-lift truck which is dispatched to perform materials handling service for various production departments in fixed locations is a queueing system and a counterexample to the physical waiting line in front of a physical structure. Production departments demanding the services of the fork-lift truck are the customers in "queue" and the mobile truck is the server.

Queue discipline refers to the order by which customers are selected from the waiting line for service. Although the type of service demanded by the arriving customers can dictate the queue discipline, this element may also be a matter of management policy.

A common queue discipline is one in which all customers are served in order of their arrival—first-come, first-served. This discipline usually simplifies the mathematical analysis in deriving queueing results and is the policy implicitly assumed by queueing models unless otherwise stated.

Customers may be selected from the waiting line for service at random. In the instance of the example above, the fork-lift truck may service the requesting production departments in no particular order or at random. On the other hand, it may be more important to always serve Department A first if that department is in the line. Such priority disciplines are quite common and exist whenever arriving units must be classified and served in order of importance. The priority can be either preemptive or nonpreemptive. A preemptive priority exists when an arriving unit not only goes to the head of the waiting line but causes the removal of a unit already in process from the service unit. An emergency production order which preempts a regular production order while in process is such an example. A nonpreemptive priority exists when an arriving unit may move to the head of the line but does not remove the unit already being served until service is completed on that unit. Other queue disciplines are possible, but these are basic and the ones most commonly encountered.

Because an almost limitless number of queueing models can be developed through combinations of the input population, service mechanism, and queue discipline characteristics, a shorthand method of classifying queueing systems is usually employed in the following format:

$$(a|b|c) : (d|e|f)$$

where

- a represents the arrival distribution, that is, the number of arrivals per increment of time,
- b represents the departure (or service time) distribution, that is, the time interval between departures (or units being serviced),
- c represents the number of parallel service channels in the system,
- d represents the service discipline,
- e represents the maximum number allowed in the system (in service plus waiting line), and
- f represents the input population size.

The following codes are conventionally used to replace the symbols in the above format; for symbols a and b,

- M—Poisson arrival or exponential departure distributions (or equivalently, exponential interarrival times or Poisson units-serviced distributions)[1]
- D—deterministic interarrival or service times, for example, a constant service time
- G—general distribution of departures (or service time)

For symbol d,

- $FCFS$—first-come, first-served
- $LCFS$—last-come, first-served
- $SIRO$—service in random order
- GD—general service discipline

The symbol c is replaced by any positive integer representing the number of parallel servers. The symbols e and f represent finite (usually denoted by N) or infinite (∞) numbers in the queueing system and input population, respectively.

The above material does not cover all the queueing system characteristics, but it will suffice for the elementary queueing models presented in this chapter. For example, the shorthand notation $(M|M|1) : (FCFS|\infty|\infty)$ describes the first model we will discuss. Namely, the arrivals are Poisson distributed, service times are exponentially distributed, a single server is

---

[1]An abbreviated treatment of these two distributions will be provided in this chapter. It can be demonstrated that if the number of arrivals per unit time is Poisson distributed, the interarrival times are exponentially distributed. Also, if the service times are exponentially distributed, the number of customers departing the system per unit time is Poisson distributed.

involved, the queue discipline is first-come, first-served, an infinite number of customers can enter the queueing system, and the input population is assumed infinite in size.

PREREQUISITE NOTATION AND PROBABILITY DISTRIBUTIONS

The mathematical description of a probabilistic queueing system consists of a set of "state equations" which express the probability that exactly n customers are in the queueing system (waiting line plus in-service) at a given time t, for all values of n. The number of customers in the system at time t is the state of the system. In this introductory presentation, only the results for selected elementary queueing systems will be presented. Further, only particular results for these models will be presented, namely, *steady-state results*. Such mathematical results assume the queueing system is in a steady-state condition or rather, the probability of n customers in the system does not depend on the time the queueing system is observed or the number of customers in the system when observed. The state probabilities become constants and independent of time. Recall the earlier final inspection task illustration; only one customer was in the system when the inspector began the workday and the study of the task was over a 100-minute period. Two results from the study were an 11.0 minute average waiting time per unit and an average 2.42 units in the system at any time during the study period. Both of these results would have been significantly increased if more than one customer had been in the system when service began. Thus, the state of the system (number of units in the system) can be greatly affected by the initial state and the time elapsed since starting the system. When this is true the system is said to be in a *transient* condition. Thus, in the solution of state equations for a particular queueing system, both a "transient" solution and a "steady-state" solution may be of interest. Steady-state solutions are usually more easily obtained, and thus steady-state conditions are commonly assumed and the majority of published results are based on this assumption.

The steady-state assumption is that, after sufficient time has elapsed, the state of the system becomes essentially independent of the initial state of the system and of the elapsed time the system has been operating. Only extensive data collection can support the validity of the assumption for a given operating queueing system.

The following additional notation will be needed, and this *terminology* **Terminology**
and notation assumes steady-state conditions in all instances:

Line length = the number of customers in the queueing system
Queue length = the number of customers waiting for service
= line length minus the number of units being served[2]
Waiting time = the elapsed time between the arrival of a customer and the time service actually begins

[2] Even in the case of serving one customer at a time, the expected number of customers in the service facility is usually less than 1.0 if the service facility has a nonzero probability of being idle a portion of the time.

c = the number of servers (parallel service channels) in the service facility

λ = the mean arrival rate, customers per unit time

$1/\lambda$ = the expected time between arrivals

μ = the mean service rate, customers per unit time, for a busy server

$1/\mu$ = the expected service time per customer

ρ = $\lambda/c\mu$ = the utilization factor for the service facility, that is, the expected fraction of time the servers are busy[3]

p_n = the probability that exactly n customers are in the queueing system at any given time t

L = the expected line length

L_q = the expected queue length

W = the expected waiting time in the system (includes service time)

W_q = the expected waiting time in the queue (excludes service time)

The Poisson Distribution

The Poisson and exponential probability distributions have not been developed previously. Knowledge of these probability functions is not critical to an understanding of the results to be presented but the usage of these two functions is so common in queueing theory that a basic introduction is in order.

The Poisson distribution is applicable when the opportunity for the occurrence of an event is large but when an actual occurrence is rather unlikely. For example, every male (and some female) member of the community may be a candidate for a haircut during a specific five-minute interval of a specified day of the month. The probability of any one individual electing to have his hair cut at that time is unlikely. Then, the probability of exactly x occurrences of an event in a time interval of length t is

$$P(x) = \frac{(\lambda t)^x \, e^{-\lambda t}}{x!}, \, x = 0, 1, 2, \ldots$$

with e an irrational number and an approximate value 2.7183. For the Poisson distribution, the mean value of x, designated μ_x, is λ and the variance of x, designated σ_x^2, is λ also for $t = a$ designated *unit* time interval such as one hour, five minutes, three weeks, or whatever measure is designated unity for time.

Example. For a Poisson distribution of arrivals every five minutes to our barber shop having $\lambda = \mu_x = 2.0$, the following probability values can be calculated:

$$P(0) = \frac{2^0 e^{-2}}{0!} = \frac{1}{e^2} \qquad = 0.135$$

$$P(1) = \frac{2^1 e^{-2}}{1!} = \frac{2}{e^2} \qquad = 0.271$$

[3] In most all queueing results, it is necessary that ρ have a value < 1.0 or else steady-state conditions can theoretically never occur and the waiting line will grow without bound.

$$P(2) = \frac{2^2 e^{-2}}{2!} = \frac{4}{2e^2} = 0.271$$

$$P(3) = \frac{2^3 e^{-2}}{3!} = \frac{8}{(3 \cdot 2 \cdot 1)\, e^2} = 0.180$$

$$P(4) \qquad\qquad = 0.090$$

$$P(5) \qquad\qquad = 0.036$$

$$P(6) \qquad\qquad = 0.012$$

$$P(7) \qquad\qquad = 0.004$$

$$P(8) \qquad\qquad = \underline{0.001}$$

$$\qquad\qquad\qquad\quad 1.000$$

In effect, the probability of zero arrivals during a five-minute interval is $P(0) = 0.135$; the probability of one arrival is $P(1) = 0.271$, and so forth.

This continuous probability distribution is given by:

The Exponential Distribution

$$f(x) = \mu e^{-\mu x}, \; o \le x \le \infty$$

The mean and variance of the distribution are given by $1/\mu$ and $1/\mu^2$ respectively.

The exponential is a continuous distribution and the probability that x will be less than some value a, Prob $(x < a)$, or greater than some value b, Prob $(x > b)$ can be obtained through use of the cumulative function. For example, if it is desired to find $P(x < a)$, the cumulative function is evaluated (integration of the probability function $f(x)$) at $x = a$, or

$$P(x < a) = F_x(a) = \int_{x=o}^{x=a} f(x)\, dx$$

$$= \int_{x=o}^{x=a} \mu e^{-\mu x}\, dx$$

$$= 1 - e^{-a\mu}$$

The cumulative probability function has the property that

$$F_x(\infty) = \int_{x=o}^{x=\infty} f(x)\, dx = 1.0$$

when integrated over the total range of values for the variable x, which is $x \ge o$ in the exponential case. This property and the result $P(x < a)$ above permits the probability statement, $P(x > a)$, to be obtained readily as

$$P(x > a) = 1 - P(x < a)$$
$$= 1 - [1 - e^{-a\mu}]$$
$$= e^{-a\mu}$$

If we desire the probability that the random variable x will have a value between two positive constants, a and b, where $b > a$, then

$$P(a < x < b) = 1 - P(x < a) - P(x > b)$$

As a numerical example of these probability statements, assume an exponentially distributed variable x has an expected (mean) value of $1/\mu = 2.0$. It is desired to find $P(x < 4)$, $P(x > 6)$, and $P(4 < x < 6)$. Thus,

$$\mu = 0.5 \text{ and } P(x < 4) = 1 - e^{-4(.5)} = 1 - \frac{1}{e^2} = 0.865, \ P(x > 6) = e^{-6(.5)}$$

$$= \frac{1}{e^3} = 0.050, \text{ and } P(4 < x < 6) = 1 - 0.865 - 0.050 = 0.085.$$

For queueing systems that have random service times t which are exponentially distributed with mean $1/\mu$, the probability function for service time is given by

$$f(t) = \mu e^{-\mu t}, \quad \text{for} \quad t \geq o$$

The mean service time per customer is $1/\mu$ and the mean service rate for the busy server is μ.

QUEUEING MODELS

The first model to be presented—the $(M|M|1) : (FCFS|\infty|\infty)$—is a classic in the sense that it is inevitably used as an introduction to waiting line theory and appears quite commonly in applications. The mathematical logic necessary to describe this and subsequent models requires an understanding of basic probability theory and the solution of differential-difference equations. We will forego such development and merely present the steady-state results.

Single-Server, Poisson Input, Exponential Service Times, Infinite Queue Model— $(M|M|1)$: $(FCFS|\infty|\infty)$

From our previous discussion, the model assumes a single server, the queueing system has unlimited capacity, and the input population is infinite in size. One steady state result of interest is

$$p_o = \left(1 - \frac{\lambda}{\mu}\right)$$

This is the probability of zero customers in the system at any time or alternatively, the proportion of time the server is expected to be idle. We note that if $(\lambda/\mu) > 1$, then p_o will have a negative value which violates the laws of probability. The interpretation in such a case is that the queue will grow without bound and there is no steady-state solution to the original state equations. Hence, a restriction on the expression for p_o and the other results to follow is that $(\lambda/\mu) < 1$ or $\lambda < \mu$.

The probability of n customers in the system is given by

$$p_n = p_o(\lambda/\mu)^n = (1 - \lambda/\mu)(\lambda/\mu)^n$$

Other steady-state results for this queueing model are

Expected line length $= L = \dfrac{\lambda}{\mu - \lambda}$

Expected queue length $= L_q = \dfrac{\lambda^2}{\mu(\mu - \lambda)}$

Expected time in the system/unit $= W = \dfrac{1}{\mu - \lambda}$

Expected waiting time/unit $= W_q = W - \dfrac{1}{\mu}$

$$= \dfrac{\lambda}{\mu(\mu - \lambda)}$$

It is noted that the expected waiting time in the queue, W_q, is the expected time spent in the system, W, minus the expected service time for one unit, $1/\mu$. A little reflection on the results above will reveal that $L = \lambda W$ and $L_q = \lambda W_q$. These relationships are true under essentially general conditions and permit the determination of all the fundamental quantities L, W, L_q, and W_q, once any one of these is determined analytically. It is also interesting to note from the steady-state results above that, for a constant λ, if the mean service rate is increased, all the fundamental quantities are reduced which supports one's intuition about the behavior of the queueing system.

An Example

Units of Product A arrive at a final inspection station from several assembly stations such that the arriving customers follow a Poisson probability function. The mean arrival rate to the inspection station is 20 units per hour. The inspector can process an average of 25 units per hour and data analysis reveals that inspection times are approximately exponentially distributed—some units are quickly inspected with no repair required and other units require considerable time to inspect and repair. An infinite population of Product A is assumed, there are no limits of space or time at the inspection station, and arriving units are inspected on a *FCFS* basis. Determine

(1) the probability that 10 units will be at the inspection station at any time the system is observed,

(2) the expected proportion of time the inspector will be idle,

(3) the fundamental quantities L, W, L_q, and W_q for the queueing system,

(4) the probability that a unit of Product A will require less than 6 minutes to inspect, and

(5) the effect on W_q if the inspector increases his mean service rate to 30 units per hour.

Solution.

(1) The probability of 10 units in the system is

$$P_n = \left(1 - \frac{\lambda}{\mu}\right)\left(\frac{\lambda}{\mu}\right)^{10}$$

$$P_{10} = (1 - 20/25)(20/25)^{10}$$

$$= (.2)(.8)^{10} = (.2)(.1074)$$

$$= 0.02148$$

(2) The proportion of idle time is equal to the probability of zero in the system and given by

$$P_o = \left(1 - \frac{\lambda}{\mu}\right)\left(\frac{\lambda}{\mu}\right)^{0}$$

$$= (1 - 20/25)(1) = 0.20,$$

or 20 percent of the time.

(3) The quantities L, W, L_q, and W_q are

$$L = \frac{\lambda}{\mu - \lambda} = \frac{20}{25 - 20} = 4.0 \text{ units}$$

$$L_q = \frac{\lambda^2}{\mu(\mu - \lambda)} = \frac{(20)^2}{25(25 - 20)} = 3.2 \text{ units}$$

$$W = \frac{1}{\mu - \lambda} = \frac{1}{25 - 20} = 0.2 \text{ hour per unit}$$

$$W_q = W - \frac{1}{\mu} = 0.2 - \frac{1}{25}$$

$$= 0.2 - 0.04 = 0.16 \text{ hour per unit}$$

The difference between the expected line length L of 4.0 units and the expected queue length L_q of 3.2 units is not 1.0 unit, which is so because the server will not be busy all the time ($p_o = 0.20$) but a 0.80 proportion of the time. The expected busy time for the server is λ/μ, or 0.80 in this case. This can also be seen from the fact that

$$L_q = L - \frac{\lambda}{\mu}$$

$$= \frac{\lambda}{\mu - \lambda} - \frac{\lambda}{\mu} = \frac{\lambda\mu - \lambda\mu + \lambda^2}{\mu(\mu - \lambda)}$$

$$= \frac{\lambda^2}{\mu(\mu - \lambda)}$$

(4) Service times are exponentially distributed. The mean service rate μ equals 25/hour. The exponential distribution is then

$$f(t) = \mu e^{-\mu t}$$
$$= 25 e^{-25t}$$

The probability that service time is less than six minutes or 0.1 hour is $P(t < 0.1)$ or

$$P(t < 0.1) = F_t(.1) = 1 - e^{-25(.1)}$$
$$= 1 - e^{-2.5}$$
$$= 1 - .082$$
$$= 0.918$$

(5) If $\mu = 30$ units/hour, then

$$W_q = \frac{\lambda}{\mu(\mu - \lambda)} = \frac{20}{30(30 - 20)} = \frac{20}{300}$$
$$= .0667 \text{ hours}$$

a reduction of $[(0.1600 - 0.0667)/0.1600] \times 100 = 58.31\%$ in expected waiting time in the queue.

It is reasonable to assume that the Poisson distribution adequately describes arrivals if the input source, at a fixed mean rate, generates customers at random. However, many real world service time distributions are other than exponential. Machines, for example, often process units at essentially a constant time per unit. If minor deviations from the constant time commonly occur, then either the uniform or the normal probability distributions would be more realistic as service time distributions than either the exponential distribution or a deterministic (constant) time. The type of interarrival or service time distribution that is applicable for a given queueing situation can be resolved by data collection and statistical curve fitting. However, knowledge of the process, particularly of the server, may permit a logical estimate of the probability distribution without the expense of data collection,

Single-Server, Poisson Input, Arbitrary Service Times, Infinite Queue Model—$(M|G|1)$: $(GD|\infty|\infty)$

other than to determine the mean and variance estimates by data analysis. The hypothesized distribution is then assumed the true distribution and the associated model analytical results used with the understanding that a small error may result. But these queueing model results which can be used for any service time distribution arc particularly useful.

This model is usually described as a non-Poisson queue in that Poisson departures do not occur if the service time distribution is other than exponential. In general, non-Poisson queues cover those systems where other than Poisson arrivals and/or Poisson departures occur. The particular model of this section deals with Poisson arrivals but non-Poisson departures from the system. The result for L is called the Pollaczek-Khintchine formula and the remaining quantities L_q, W, W_q can then be determined.

The notation, $(GD|\infty|\infty)$, means that the model is applicable for a general queue discipline. More precisely, the results hold for the FCFS, LCFS, and SIRO queue disciplines but not other priority disciplines.

Assuming Poisson arrivals with mean arrival rate λ, that the service times for the respective customers are independent with some common probability distribution whose mean $1/\mu$ and variance σ^2 are known, and that $\lambda < \mu$, the steady state results are given below. (It is convenient to use $\rho = \lambda/\mu$ in the subsequent formulations.)

$$p_o = 1 - \rho$$
$$L_q = \frac{\lambda^2 \sigma^2 + \rho^2}{\lambda(1 - \rho)}$$
$$L = L_q + \rho$$
$$W_q = \frac{L_q}{\lambda}$$
$$W = W_q + \frac{1}{\mu}$$

It should be noted from the above results that, for given values of λ and μ, if the variance σ^2 of the service time distribution can be reduced, then all the values L_q, L, W_q, and W are reduced. This fact is perhaps intuitive, but it points out that the consistency of the server, as well as the server's average speed, has a bearing on the performance of the service facility. A reduction in variability has a general beneficial effect on the behavior of the lines and is therefore a goal management may wish to work toward.

An Example   Units of product A arrive at a numerically-controlled milling machine for a final machining operation, after Product A has been cast and manually cleaned. Except for short-time cycles of loading and unloading for Product A, the machining operation is essentially a constant time for each customer. Data collection and analysis reveals that an average of ten units per hour arrive at the milling machine. An average of twelve units per hour can be processed by the milling machine. Determine:

(1) the proportion of time the milling machine is idle,

(2) the fundamental quantities L_q, L, W_q, and W, and

(3) the effect on L_q if the mean service rate was increased by 25% by increasing the machine's cutting speed.

Solution.

(1) The proportion of idle time is:

$$p_o = 1 - \rho = 1 - \frac{\lambda}{\mu} = 1 - \frac{10}{12} = 0.1667$$

(2) Since a constant service time implies the variance of service time is equal to zero, we have:

$$L_q = \frac{\lambda^2 \sigma^2 + \rho^2}{\lambda(1 - \rho)} = \frac{(10)^2(0) + \left(\frac{10}{12}\right)^2}{2\left(1 - \frac{10}{12}\right)}$$

$$= \frac{(.8333)^2}{2(.1667)} = 2.083 \text{ customers}$$

$$L = L_q + \frac{\lambda}{\mu} = 2.083 + \frac{10}{12}$$

$$= 2.916 \text{ customers}$$

$$W_q = L_q/\lambda = 2.083/10$$

$$= 0.2083 \text{ hours}$$

$$W = W_q + \frac{1}{\mu} = 0.2083 + \frac{1}{12}$$

$$= 0.2916 \text{ hours}$$

(3) An increase of 25 percent in the mean service rate would yield a new $\mu' = (1 + .25)\mu = 1.25(12) = 15$. Then,

$$L'_q = \frac{(10)^2(0) + \left(\frac{10}{15}\right)^2}{2\left(1 - \frac{10}{15}\right)}$$

$$= \frac{(.667)^2}{2(.333)} = 0.667 \text{ customers}$$

A 25 percent increase in μ results in a $[(2.083 - 0.667)/2.083] \times 100 = 68\%$ decrease in expected queue length.

When the service time distribution is exponential with $\sigma^2 = 1/\mu^2$, the above results for L, L_q, W, W_q will reduce to those for the $(M|M|1)$: (FCFS $|\infty|\infty$) model previously.

Multiple-Servers, Poisson Input, Exponential Service Times, Infinite Queue Model— $(M|M|C)$: $(GD|\infty|\infty)$

We can now return to the first model presented except that the service facility is characterized by c parallel servers and the results derived are applicable for a general queue discipline rather than limited to *FCFS*. The model is important primarily because c, the number of servers, is a design element which usually can be controlled by the decision-maker. Again, note that multiple servers are considered parallel servers in that each server provides essentially the same type of service to the customers one at a time rather than in bulk. Also, the stringent assumption that each server has independent service time distributions with the same mean $1/\mu$ service time must be made. Finally, the steady-state results below assume $(\lambda/c\mu) < 1$. Then,

$$p_o = 1 \bigg/ \left[\sum_{n=o}^{n=c-1} \frac{(\lambda/\mu)^n}{n!} + \frac{(\lambda/\mu)^c}{c!(1 - \lambda/c\mu)} \right]$$

$$p_n = \begin{cases} \dfrac{\left(\dfrac{\lambda}{\mu}\right)^n}{n!} p_o, & \text{if } o \le n \le c \\[20pt] \dfrac{\left(\dfrac{\lambda}{\mu}\right)^n}{c!\,c^{n-c}} p_o, & \text{if } n \ge c \end{cases}$$

$$L_q = \frac{p_o \left(\dfrac{\lambda}{\mu}\right)^c \left(\dfrac{\lambda}{c\mu}\right)}{c!(1 - \lambda/c\mu)^2}$$

$$L = L_q + \lambda/\mu$$

$$W_q = L_q/\lambda$$

$$W = W_q + \frac{1}{\mu}$$

The quantity p_o is again the proportion of idle time but for the system (all servers) rather than a given server. If one customer were in the system, one server would be busy and $c - 1$ servers would be idle. If two customers were in the system, two servers would be busy and $c - 2$ servers would be idle, and so forth, until $n \ge c$ and then all servers would be busy. We see then that the expected system service rate, μ_n, is given by:

$$\mu_n = \begin{cases} n\mu, & \text{if} \quad o \le n \le c \\ c\mu, & \text{if} \quad n \ge c \end{cases}$$

If a *FCFS* queue discipline is assumed, probability distributions for waiting time is presented in the following way:

Let t = the variable, the elapsed time a random arrival has to wait in the queue before service begins.

Then the probability that the elapsed time will be greater than some value a is given by:

$$p(t > a) = e^{-c\mu a(1 - \lambda/cu)} \cdot p(t > o)$$

where

$$p(t > o) = \frac{p_o \left(\dfrac{\lambda}{\mu}\right)^c}{c!(1 - \lambda/c\mu)}$$

Let T = the random variable, the elapsed time a random arrival has to wait from arrival until completion of service.

Then, the probability that the elapsed time will be greater than some value a is given by:

$$p(T > a) = e^{-\mu a}\left[1 + \frac{p_o \left(\dfrac{\lambda}{\mu}\right)^c}{c!(1 - \lambda/cu)} \left(\frac{1 - e^{-\mu a(c-1-\lambda/\mu)}}{c - 1 - \lambda/\mu} \right) \right]$$

The quantities, p_o, L_q, $P(t > a)$, $P(T > a)$ are particularly tedious to calculate.

An Example

Let us again assume the final inspection station for Product A, which arrives from several manual assembly stations. Inspection involves visual inspection, some measuring, and minor repairs such that an exponential service time distribution seems a reasonable approximation. It has been estimated that the mean arrival rate of units to the service facility is twenty-five units per hour. The mean service rate for a single inspector is estimated to be ten units per hour. An infinite input population, an infinite queue length, and *FCFS* queue discipline is assumed. Management is interested in estimating the system characteristics L, L_q, W, W_q if three inspection stations are provided, each of which has approximately the same service rate. Management realizes that more than two inspectors are required but expect that with three inspectors, at least one will be idle a considerable portion of the time. They feel some insight into this idleness can be gained by determining the probability of less than three customers in the system. Finally, management wishes an estimate of the probability that the elapsed time a customer must wait in the queue before service begins will exceed 0.10 hours.

Solution. It is convenient to first solve for p_o from:

$$p_o = 1 \Big/ \left[\sum_{n=o}^{n=c-1} \frac{(\lambda/\mu)^n}{n!} + \frac{\left(\dfrac{\lambda}{\mu}\right)^c}{c!(1-\lambda/c\mu)} \right]$$

$$= 1 \Big/ \left[\sum_{n=o}^{n=3-1} \frac{\left(\dfrac{25}{10}\right)^n}{n!} + \frac{\left(\dfrac{25}{10}\right)^3}{3!(1 - 25/3(10))} \right]$$

$$= 1 \Big/ \left[\frac{\left(\dfrac{25}{10}\right)^0}{0!} + \frac{\left(\dfrac{25}{10}\right)^1}{1!} + \frac{\left(\dfrac{25}{10}\right)^2}{2!} + \frac{15.625}{3\cdot2\cdot1(1 - .833)} \right]$$

$$= 1/[1 + 2.5 + 3.125 + 15.594] = 1/22.22$$

$$= 0.0450$$

Then, the system characteristics are:

$$L_q = \frac{p_o \left(\dfrac{\lambda}{\mu}\right)^c \left(\dfrac{\lambda}{c\mu}\right)}{c!(1-\lambda/cu)^2}$$

$$= \frac{0.045 \left(\dfrac{25}{10}\right)^3 \left(\dfrac{25}{30}\right)}{3!(1 - 25/30)^2} = \frac{0.5857}{6(.0279)}$$

$$= 3.50 \text{ customers}$$

$$L = L_q + \frac{\lambda}{\mu} = 3.50 + 25/10$$

$$= 6.00 \text{ customers}$$

$$W_q = L_q/\lambda = 3.50/25 = 0.14 \text{ hours}$$

$$W = W_q + \frac{1}{\mu} = 0.14 + 1/10$$

$$= 0.24 \text{ hours}$$

Less than three customers are in the system when there are 0, 1, or 2 customers in the system. From basic laws of probability,

$$P(\text{less than 3 customers}) = P(0 \text{ customers}) + P(1 \text{ customer})$$
$$+ P(2 \text{ customers}), \quad \text{or}$$

$$P(<3) = p_o + p_1 + p_2.$$

We know that $p_o = 0.045$ from above. Since $n = 1$ and $n = 2$ are both less than $c = 3$, then

$$p_1 = \frac{\left(\dfrac{\lambda}{\mu}\right)^n}{n!} p_o = \frac{\left(\dfrac{25}{10}\right)^1}{1!} (.045)$$

$$= 0.1125$$

$$p_2 = \frac{\left(\dfrac{\lambda}{\mu}\right)^n}{n!} p_o = \frac{\left(\dfrac{25}{10}\right)^2}{2!} (.045)$$

$$= 0.1406. \quad \text{Thus,}$$

$$P(< 3) = 0.0450 + 0.1125 + 0.1406$$

$$= 0.2981$$

Finally, the probability of elapsed time from arriving until service begins for a unit exceeding 0.10 hours is determined as:

$$P(t > 0) = \frac{p_o \left(\dfrac{\lambda}{\mu}\right)^c}{c(1 - \lambda/cu)} = \frac{(0.045) \left(\dfrac{25}{10}\right)^3}{3!(1 - 25/30)}$$

$$= 0.70$$

$$P(T > 0.1) = e^{-c\mu t(1 - \lambda/cu)} \cdot P(t > o)$$

$$= e^{-3(10)(0.1)(1 - 25/30)} \cdot 0.70$$

$$= e^{-0.5} (0.70) = 0.425$$

This model is similar to the first model presented in the chapter except the system can accommodate only a finite number of customers, N, at a given time. This situation may arise due to a limited storage space in front of the server, such as a conveyor between two production stages, or when customers refuse to enter a system because the queue reaches a size of $N - 1$ customers, such as waiting lines in barber shops, in banks, and so forth.

The steady-state results for the mathematical model holds for FCFS, LCFS, and SIRO queue disciplines rather than only for FCFS. The input population is still assumed infinite and whether or not the customer who cannot or chooses not to enter the queue returns to the input population has no effect on the analysis.

Single-Server, Poisson Input, Exponential Service Times, Finite Queue Model— $(M|M|1)$: $(GD|N|\infty)$

The model results do not depend on the constraint of $(\lambda/\mu) < 1$ as have the previous models. In this model it is necessary to introduce an effective arrival rate, $\tilde{\lambda}$. Our conventional arrival rate λ is the average rate at which customers arrive at the system. Since not all arrivals enter the system, $\tilde{\lambda}$ is the average, or expected, rate at which customers *enter* the system. Customers do not enter the system when N units are already in the system. The probability of N customers in the system, or alternatively that a customer does not enter the system, is given by p_N. Thus, $(1 - p_N)$ is the probability that a customer enters the system, and it can be interpreted as the proportion of λ which enters the system. Hence,

$$\tilde{\lambda} = \lambda(1 - p_N)$$

In the results below, ρ is used for convenience and the expression for L involves $\rho = \lambda/\mu$ rather than $\rho = \tilde{\lambda}/\mu$. The expression for L is then modified by the use of $\tilde{\lambda}$ to obtain expressions for L_q, W, and W_q. The steady-state results are:

$$p_n = \left(\frac{1 - \rho}{1 - \rho^{N+1}}\right)\rho^n \quad \text{for} \quad n = 0, 1, 2, \ldots, N$$

It is noted that if $\rho > 1$, the quantity p_n will still be positive for all values of n. However, let us add the constraint of $\rho < 1$ such that, as N gets large or approaches infinity, the quantity ρ^{N+1} will approach zero. The quantity p_n then approaches $\rho^n(1 - \rho)$, which is the same result for p_n we found in our first model of this chapter, namely, the nontruncated queue model $(M|M|1) : (FCFS|\infty|\infty)$. This is merely saying that if a line is truncated at a large value of N, we can assume an infinite queue length is permitted with little loss in accuracy.

$$L = \frac{\rho[1 - (N + 1)\rho^N + N\rho^{N+1}]}{(1 - \rho)(1 - \rho^{N+1})}$$

$$L_q = L - \tilde{\lambda}/\mu$$

$$W_q = L_q/\tilde{\lambda}$$

$$W = W_q + 1/\mu$$

An alternate expression for L_q is given as: $L_q = L - (1 - p_o)$. The reader may wish to show that $(1 - p_o) = \tilde{\lambda}/\mu$ as an exercise and reason why $L_q = L - (1 - p_o)$.

An Example   The final inspection station example with modifications is again used to illustrate this model. Units of Product A are finally assembled at a single assembly station and then transported by conveyor to the inspection station. Units are assumed to arrive in Poisson fashion at the inspection station with a mean arrival rate λ equal to twenty per hour. Inspection times are approximated by an exponential distribution with mean $1/\mu = 0.04$ hours per unit. The connecting conveyor only has storage space for four units, which excludes one unit which can be in-service at the inspection station. That is, the queueing system can only accommodate five units and the assembly station will be "blocked" when five units are in the system.

Determine (1) the probability that a customer will arrive and be able to enter the "system" and (2) the operating characteristics L, L_q, W, and W_q for the system.

Solution. It is convenient to first calculate:

$$\mu = 1/.04 = 25 \text{ customers/hour}$$

$$\rho = \lambda/\mu = 20/25 = 0.8$$

$$
\begin{aligned}
p_N = p_5 &= \left(\frac{1 - \rho}{1 - \rho^{5+1}} \right) \rho^5 \\
&= \left(\frac{1 - 0.8}{1 - (0.8)^6} \right) (0.8)^5 \\
&= \left(\frac{0.2}{1 - .2621} \right) (.3277) \\
&= 0.0655/0.7379 = 0.0888
\end{aligned}
$$

The probability of more than five customers in the system is zero and thus, the probability that a customer can enter the system is the probability that less than five customers are in the system or:

$$P(n < N) = P(n < 5) = 1 - p_5 = 0.9112$$

The expected number of customers in the system is:

$$
\begin{aligned}
L &= \frac{\rho \left[1 - (N + 1) \rho^N + N\rho^{N+1} \right]}{(1 - \rho)(1 - \rho^{N+1})} \\
&= \frac{0.8 \left[1 - (6)(0.8)^5 + (5)(0.8)^6 \right]}{(0.20)[1 - (0.8)^6]} \\
&= \frac{0.8 \left[1 - (6)(0.3277) + 5(0.2621) \right]}{(0.20)(1 - 0.2621)} \\
&= 0.2754/0.1476 = 1.866 \text{ customers}
\end{aligned}
$$

Then,

$$\tilde{\lambda} = \lambda(1 - p_N) = 20(1 - 0.0888)$$

$$= 18.224$$

$$L_q = L - \tilde{\lambda}/\mu = 1.866 - 18.224/25$$

$$= 1.866 - 0.729 = 1.137 \text{ customers}$$

$$W_q = L_q/\tilde{\lambda} = 1.137/18.224$$

$$= 0.0624 \text{ hours}$$

$$W = W_q + 1/\mu = 0.0624 + 0.04$$

$$= 0.1024 \text{ hours}$$

QUESTIONS AND PROBLEMS

1. Contrast a deterministic queueing system with a probabilistic queueing system.

2. From your own experience, briefly describe five queueing systems. Of these, describe one system where it is reasonable to assume service times are exponentially distributed.

3. In your own words, suggest four queueing situations where a priority queue discipline seems appropriate. For each situation, what priority rule would you establish?

4. From the chapter's discussion on the elements of a queueing system, conceive of and describe eight different types of queueing situations or models. For example, $(M|M|1) : (FCFS|\infty|\infty)$ is a description of one such system; three others are presented in the chapter.

5. What is (are) the difference(s) between a transient and a steady-state condition of a queueing system?

6. What is a queueing network? How does this differ from a multichannel queueing model?

7. Create graphic models for each of the four queueing models presented in the chapter.

8. What is meant by the term balking in a queueing sense? a truncated queue? a preemptive priority queue discipline?

9. Advance arguments, your own or the text's, as to why waiting line problems should be solved.

10. Assume the results for the $(M|G|1) : (GD|\infty|\infty)$ queueing model. By using $\sigma^2 = 1/\mu^2$, show that these results will reduce to the L, L_q, W, and W_q formulations for the $(M|M|1) : (FCFS|\infty|\infty)$ model.

11. If $\sigma^2 = 0$ for the $(M|G|1) : (GD|\infty|\infty)$ queueing model, derive expressions for L, L_q, W, and W_q in terms of λ and μ.

12. What is your interpretation of an $(M|G|C) : (GD|\infty|\infty)$ queueing model?

13. Assume a $(M|G|1) : (GD|N|N)$ model. However, the single server is a crew of three persons who unload trucks that arrive at an unloading dock. The crew presently uses one fork-lift truck and two hand carts in

the unloading process. As a manager, what things might be done to increase the mean service rate μ? (Results for the $(M|G|1) : (GD|N|N)$ model are not required to answer the question.)

14. The jobs to be performed on a particular machine arrive according to a Poisson input process with a mean rate of one per hour. Suppose that the machine breaks down and will require two hours to be repaired. What is the probability that the number of new jobs that will arrive during this time is (a) zero, (b) two, (c) five or more?

15. Assume a $(M|M|1) : (FCFS|\infty|\infty)$ queueing model. If units arrive for servicing at the average rate of 8 per hour and the mean service time is five minutes per unit, determine the:
   (a) mean number in the system
   (b) mean number in the waiting line
   (c) mean time in the system
   (d) mean waiting time in the system
   (e) probability of 6 units in the system
   (f) probability that the service facility is busy
   (g) probability of 2 arrivals in a 30 minute interval

16. Jobs arrive for processing by turret lathe A in accordance with the $(M|M|1) : (GD|N|\infty)$ queueing model. The mean rate of arrival, over a long study period, is sixteen jobs per week based on a forty-hour week. The average processing time for a job is two hours.
   (a) Assuming that jobs are routed to another turret lathe if three jobs are in the "turret lathe A system," calculate the operating characteristics L, L_q, W, and W_q for the "A" system.
   (b) What is the probability that an arriving job will be routed to another turret lathe? What is the probability that the job enters the "A" system?
   (c) If the mean service rate for turret lathe A were increased by 50 percent, what effect would this have on the expected number of jobs in the "A" system?
   (d) If the mean service rate for turret lathe A remains the same but λ increases to twenty-two jobs per week, what effect does this have on the probability that an arriving job will be routed to another turret lathe if $N = 3$ as before?

17. Plans are being made for opening a small car wash operation, and the decision must be made as to how much space to provide for waiting cars. It is estimated that customers would arrive according to a Poisson input with a mean rate of one every five minutes, unless the waiting area is full, in which case the customer would take his car elsewhere. The time that can be attributed to washing one car has an exponential distribution with a mean of four minutes. Compare the expected fraction of potential customers that would be lost because of inadequate waiting space if (a) zero, (b) two, or (c) four spaces (not including the car being washed) were to be provided. Hint: Compute the proportion of time busy for $N = 5$ from $1 - p_o$ of the appropriate model. Then, compute the expected number of customers served from $(1 - p_o) \cdot (\mu$, units/hr.$)$. Similar calculations for $N = 3$ and $N = 1$ permit a relative comparison.

18. A business office has a pool of three secretaries who do essentially the same type of work. Although somewhat unrealistic, it is assumed that there are no job priorities involved and the $(M|M|C) : (GD|\infty|\infty)$ model

is an appropriate representation of the actual situation. If each secretary processes jobs at an average rate of five per hour and the mean rate of arrivals is twelve jobs per hour, determine (1) the quantities L_q, L, W_q, and W for the secretarial pool, and (2) what is the probability that an arrival must wait longer than 12 minutes before service begins?

19. Consider a small local plant that manufactures garments for women. There are 200 machines maintained by two men, and each man is capable of repairing any machine. A maintenance record over the past year reveals that machine breakdowns (of all types) occur at an average rate of twenty per day (an eight-hour working day). A one-week time study of both men reveals that the average repair job by either man requires thirty minutes. Further, the men complain that they cannot keep up with the work. Determine:

(a) the probability that both men will be idle at any given time,

(b) the expected time in hours that any machine will wait for servicing, and

(c) the expected number of machines in the maintenance "system" at any time.

Note: For the purposes of this problem, assume that only the results of the following models are available to you:

(1) $(M|M|1):(FCFS|\infty|\infty)$

(2) $(M|M|1):(GD|N|\infty)$

(3) $(M|M|C):(GD|\infty|\infty)$

State any assumptions you may make in selecting the model to use in answering (a), (b), and (c) above.

BIBLIOGRAPHY

CONWAY, RICHARD W.; MAXWELL, WILLIAM L.; AND MILLER, LOUIS W. *Theory of Scheduling*. Reading, Mass.: Addison-Wesley Publishing Company, 1967.

COX, D. R., AND SMITH, WALTER L. *Queues*. London: Methuen and Company, 1961.

CULLINANE, THOMAS P. "A Transient Analysis of Two Link Fixed Conveyor Systems," unpublished Ph.D. dissertation, Virginia Polytechnic Institute and State University, January 1972.

FABRYCKY, W. J.; GHARE, P. M.; AND TORGERSEN, P. E. *Industrial Operations Research*. Englewood Cliffs, N.J.: Prentice-Hall, Inc., 1972.

GRIFFIN, WALTER C. *Introduction to Operations Engineering*. Homewood, Ill.: Richard D. Irwin, Inc., 1971.

HILLIER, F. S., AND LIEBERMAN, G. J. *Introduction to Operations Research*. San Francisco: Holden-Day, Inc., 1967.

MORRIS, WILLIAM T. *Analysis of Materials Handling Systems*. Homewood, Ill.: Richard D. Irwin, Inc., 1962.

TAHA, HAMDY A. *Operations Research: An Introduction*. New York: The Macmillan Company, 1971.

WHITE, J. A.; SCHMIDT, J. W.; AND BENNETT, G. K. *Analysis of Queueing Systems*. New York: Academic Press, 1975.

Appendices

APPENDIX A

TABLE 1   Cumulative Binomial Probabilities

n = 2

X	p = 01	02	03	04	05	06	07	08	09	10
1	0199	0396	0591	0784	0975	1164	1351	1536	1719	1900
2	0001	0004	0009	0016	0025	0036	0049	0064	0081	0100

X	p = 12	14	16	18	20	24	28	32	40	50
1	2256	2604	2944	3276	3600	4224	4816	5376	6400	7500
2	0144	0196	0256	0324	0400	0576	0784	1024	1600	2500

n = 3

X	p = 01	02	03	04	05	06	07	08	09	10
1	0297	0588	0873	1153	1426	1694	1956	2213	2464	2710
2	0003	0012	0026	0047	0072	0104	0140	0182	0228	0280
3	0000	0000	0000	0001	0001	0002	0003	0005	0007	0010

X	p = 12	14	16	18	20	24	28	32	40	50
1	3185	3639	4073	4486	4880	5610	6268	6856	7840	8750
2	0397	0533	0686	0855	1040	1452	1913	2417	3520	5000
3	0017	0027	0041	0058	0080	0138	0220	0328	0640	1250

n = 4

X	P=01	02	03	04	05	06	07	08	09	10
1	0394	0776	1147	1507	1855	2193	2519	2836	3143	3439
2	0006	0023	0052	0091	0140	0199	0267	0344	0430	0523
3	0000	0000	0001	0002	0005	0008	0013	0019	0028	0037
4	0000	0000	0000	0000	0000	0000	0000	0000	0001	0001

X	P=12	14	16	18	20	24	28	32	40	50
1	4003	4530	5021	5479	5904	6664	7313	7862	8704	9375
2	0732	0968	1228	1509	1808	2450	3132	3837	5248	6875
3	0063	0098	0144	0202	0272	0453	0694	0996	1792	3125
4	0002	0004	0007	0010	0016	0033	0061	0105	0256	0625

n = 5

X	P=01	02	03	04	05	06	07	08	09	10
1	0490	0961	1413	1846	2262	2661	3043	3409	3760	4095
2	0010	0038	0085	0148	0226	0319	0425	0544	0674	0815
3	0000	0001	0003	0006	0012	0020	0031	0045	0063	0086
4	0000	0000	0000	0000	0000	0001	0001	0002	0003	0005
5	0000	0000	0000	0000	0000	0000	0000	0000	0000	0000

X	P=12	14	16	18	20	24	28	32	40	50
1	4723	5296	5818	6293	6723	7464	8065	8546	9222	9687
2	1125	1467	1835	2224	2627	3461	4303	5125	6630	8125
3	0143	0220	0318	0437	0579	0933	1376	1905	3174	5000
4	0009	0017	0029	0045	0067	0134	0238	0390	0870	1875
5	0000	0001	0001	0002	0003	0008	0017	0034	0102	0313

n = 6

X	.01	.02	.03	.04	.05	.06	.07	.08	.09	.10
1	0585	1142	1670	2172	2649	3101	3530	3936	4321	4686
2	0015	0057	0125	0216	0328	0459	0608	0773	0952	1143
3	0000	0002	0005	0012	0022	0038	0058	0085	0118	0159
4		0000	0000	0000	0001	0002	0003	0005	0008	0013
5					0000	0000	0000	0000	0000	0001
6										0000

X	.12	.14	.16	.18	.20	.24	.28	.32	.40	.50
1	5356	5954	6487	6960	7379	8073	8607	9011	9533	9844
2	1556	2003	2472	2956	3446	4422	5356	6220	7667	8906
3	0261	0395	0560	0759	0989	1539	2196	2936	4557	6562
4	0025	0045	0075	0116	0170	0326	0557	0875	1792	3437
5	0001	0003	0005	0010	0016	0038	0079	0148	0410	1094
6	0000	0000	0000	0000	0001	0002	0005	0011	0041	0156

n = 7

x \ P	01	02	03	04	05	06	07	08	09	10
1	0679	1319	1920	2486	3017	3515	3983	4422	4832	5217
2	0020	0379	0171	0294	0444	0618	0813	1026	1255	1497
3	0000	0003	0009	0020	0038	0063	0097	0146	0193	0257
4		0000	0000	0001	0002	0004	0007	0012	0018	0027
5				0000	0000	0000	0000	0001	0001	0002
6								0000	0000	0000

x \ P	12	14	16	18	20	24	28	32	40	50
1	5913	6521	7049	7507	7903	8535	8997	9328	9720	9922
2	2012	2556	3115	3677	4233	5298	6266	7113	8414	9375
3	0416	0620	0866	1154	1480	2231	3081	3987	5801	7734
4	0054	0094	0153	0231	0333	0617	1016	1534	2898	5000
5	0004	0009	0017	0029	0047	0107	0213	0380	0963	2266
6	0000	0000	0001	0002	0004	0011	0026	0055	0188	0625
7			0000	0000	0000	0000	0001	0003	0016	0078

353

n = 8

P	01	02	03	04	05	06	07	08	09	10
x										
1	0773	1492	2163	2786	3366	3904	4404	4868	5297	5695
2	0027	0103	0223	0381	0572	0792	1035	1298	1577	1869
3	0001	0004	0013	0031	0058	0096	0147	0211	0289	0381
4	0000	0000	0001	0002	0004	0007	0013	0022	0034	0050
5			0000	0000	0000	0000	0001	0001	0003	0004
6							0000	0000	0000	0000

P	12	14	16	18	20	24	28	32	40	50
x										
1	6404	7008	7521	7956	8322	8887	9278	9543	9832	9961
2	2480	3111	3744	4366	4967	6075	7031	7822	8936	9648
3	0608	0891	1226	1608	2031	2967	3973	4987	6846	8555
4	0097	0168	0267	0397	0563	1004	1594	2319	4059	6367
5	0010	0021	0038	0065	0104	0230	0438	0750	1737	3633
6	0001	0002	0003	0007	0012	0034	0078	0159	0498	1445
7	0000	0000	0000	0000	0001	0003	0008	0020	0085	0352
8	0000				0000	0000	0000	0001	0007	0039

n = 9

x	01	02	03	04	05	06	07	08	09	10
1	0865	1663	2398	3075	3698	4270	4796	5278	5721	6126
2	0034	0131	0282	0478	0712	0978	1271	1583	1912	2252
3	0001	0006	0020	0045	0084	0138	0209	0298	0405	0530
4	0000	0000	0001	0003	0006	0013	0023	0037	0057	0083
5			0000	0000	0000	0001	0002	0003	0005	0009
6						0000	0000	0000	0000	0001
7										0000

x	12	14	16	18	20	24	28	32	40	50
1	6835	7427	7918	8324	8658	9154	9480	9689	9899	9980
2	2951	3657	4348	5012	5638	6750	7660	8372	9295	9805
3	0833	1202	1629	2105	2618	3713	4829	5894	7682	9102
4	0158	0269	0420	0615	0856	1475	2260	3173	5174	7461
5	0021	0041	0075	0125	0196	0416	0762	1252	2666	5000
6	0002	0004	0009	0017	0031	0081	0179	0348	0994	2539
7	0000	0000	0001	0002	0003	0010	0028	0064	0250	0898
8			0000	0000	0000	0001	0003	0007	0033	0195
9						0000	0000	0000	0003	0020

n = 10

x	01	02	03	04	05	06	07	08	09	10
1	0956	1829	2626	3352	4013	4614	5160	5656	6106	6513
2	0043	0162	0345	0582	0861	1176	1517	1879	2254	2639
3	0001	0009	0028	0062	0115	0188	0283	0401	0540	0702
4	0000	0000	0001	0004	0010	0020	0036	0058	0088	0128
5			0000	0000	0001	0002	0003	0006	0010	0016
6					0000	0000	0000	0000	0001	0001
7									0000	0000

x	12	14	16	18	20	24	28	32	40	50
1	7215	7787	8251	8626	8926	9357	9626	9789	9940	9990
2	3417	4184	4920	5608	6242	7327	8170	8794	9536	9893
3	1087	1545	2064	2628	3222	4442	5622	6687	8327	9453
4	0239	0400	0614	0883	1209	2012	2979	4044	6177	8281
5	0037	0073	0130	0213	0328	0670	1181	1867	3669	6230
6	0004	0010	0020	0037	0064	0161	0342	0637	1662	3770
7	0000	0001	0002	0004	0009	0027	0070	0155	0548	1719
8		0000	0000	0000	0001	0003	0010	0025	0123	0547
9					0000	0000	0001	0003	0017	0107
10							0000	0000	0001	0010

n = 15

x	01	02	03	04	05	06	07	08	09	10
1	1399	2614	3667	4579	5367	6047	6633	7137	7570	7941
2	0096	0353	0730	1191	1710	2262	2832	3403	3965	4510
3	0004	0030	0094	0203	0362	0571	0829	1130	1469	1841
4	0000	0002	0008	0024	0055	0104	0175	0273	0399	0556
5		0000	0001	0002	0006	0014	0028	0050	0082	0127
6			0000	0000	0001	0001	0003	0007	0013	0022
7					0000	0000	0000	0001	0002	0003
8								0000	0000	0000

x	12	14	16	18	20	24	28	32	40	50
1	8530	8959	9269	9490	9648	9837	9928	9969	9995	10000
2	5524	6417	7179	7813	8329	9065	9505	9752	9948	9995
3	2654	3520	4392	5234	6020	7358	8355	9038	9729	9963
4	0959	1476	2092	2782	3518	5022	6416	7580	9095	9824
5	0265	0478	0778	1167	1642	2810	4154	5523	7827	9408
6	0057	0121	0227	0387	0611	1272	2220	3393	5968	8491
7	0010	0024	0052	0102	0181	0463	0965	1722	3902	6964
8	0001	0004	0010	0021	0042	0135	0338	0711	2131	5000
9	0000	0000	0001	0003	0008	0031	0094	0236	0950	3036
10	0000	0000	0000	0000	0001	0006	0021	0062	0338	1509
11	0000	0000	0000	0000	0000	0001	0003	0012	0093	0592
12	0000	0000	0000	0000	0000	0000	0000	0002	0019	0176
13	0000	0000	0000	0000	0000	0000	0000	0000	0003	0037
14	0000	0000	0000	0000	0000	0000	0000	0000	0000	0005
15	0000	0000	0000	0000	0000	0000	0000	0000	0000	0000

n = 20

X	01	02	03	04	05	06	07	08	09	10
1	1821	3324	4562	5580	6415	7099	7658	8113	8484	8784
2	0169	0599	1198	1897	2642	3395	4131	4831	5484	6083
3	0010	0071	0210	0439	0755	1150	1610	2121	2666	3231
4	0000	0006	0027	0074	0159	0290	0471	0706	0993	1330
5		0000	0003	0010	0026	0056	0107	0183	0290	0432
6			0000	0001	0003	0009	0019	0038	0068	0113
7				0000	0000	0001	0003	0006	0013	0024
8						0000	0000	0001	0002	0004
9								0000	0000	0001
10										0000

X	12	14	16	18	20	24	28	32	40	50
1	9224	9510	9694	9811	9885	9959	9986	9996	10000	10000
2	7109	7916	8529	8982	9308	9698	9877	9953	9995	9998
3	4369	5450	6420	7252	7939	8915	9474	9765	9964	9987
4	2127	3041	4010	4974	5886	7431	8534	9235	9840	9941
5	0827	1375	2059	2849	3704	5439	6981	8173	9490	9793
6	0260	0507	0870	1356	1958	3427	5048	6574	8744	9423
7	0067	0153	0304	0537	0867	1838	3169	4693	7500	8684
8	0014	0038	0088	0177	0321	0835	1707	2922	5841	7483
9	0002	0008	0021	0049	0100	0320	0784	1568	4044	5881
10	0000	0001	0004	0011	0026	0103	0305	0719	2447	4119
11		0000	0001	0002	0006	0028	0100	0279	1275	2517
12			0000	0000	0001	0006	0027	0091	0565	1316
13					0000	0001	0006	0025	0210	0577
14						0000	0001	0006	0065	0207
15							0000	0001	0016	0059
16								0000	0003	0013
17									0000	0002
18										0000
19										

n = 50

X	P=01	02	03	04	05	06	07	08	09	10
1	3950	6358	7819	8701	9231	9547	9734	9845	9910	9948
2	0894	2642	4447	5995	7206	8100	8735	9173	9468	9662
3	0138	0784	1892	3233	4595	5838	6892	7740	8395	8883
4	0016	0178	0628	1391	2396	3527	4673	5747	6697	7497
5	0001	0032	0168	0490	1036	1794	2710	3710	4723	5688
6	0000	0005	0037	0144	0378	0776	1350	2081	2928	3839
7	0000	0001	0007	0036	0118	0289	0583	1019	1596	2298
8	0000	0000	0001	0008	0032	0094	0220	0438	0768	1221
9	0000	0000	0000	0001	0008	0027	0073	0167	0328	0579
10	0000	0000	0000	0000	0002	0007	0022	0056	0125	0245
11	0000	0000	0000	0000	0000	0002	0006	0017	0043	0094
12	0000	0000	0000	0000	0000	0000	0001	0005	0013	0032
13	0000	0000	0000	0000	0000	0000	0000	0001	0004	0010
14	0000	0000	0000	0000	0000	0000	0000	0000	0001	0003
15	0000	0000	0000	0000	0000	0000	0000	0000	0000	0001
16	0000	0000	0000	0000	0000	0000	0000	0000	0000	0000

X	P=12	14	16	18	20	24	28	32	40	50
1	9983	9995	9998	10000	10000	10000				
2	9869	9951	9983	9994	9998	10000				
3	9487	9779	9910	9965	9987	9998	10000			
4	8655	9330	9688	9863	9943	9992	9999	10000		
5	7320	8472	9192	9601	9815	9967	9995	9999		
6	5647	7186	8323	9071	9520	9893	9981	9997		
7	3935	5616	7081	8199	8966	9720	9941	9990	10000	
8	2467	4010	5594	6996	8096	9377	9842	9969	9999	

9	10000	9998	9914	9635	8794	6927	5576	4071	2605	1392
10	9998	9992	9794	9260	7934	5563	4122	2718	1537	0708
11	9995	9978	9563	8663	6822	4164	2813	1661	0824	0325
12	9987	9943	9168	7817	5544	2893	1768	0929	0402	0135
13	9967	9867	8564	6749	4233	1861	1022	0475	0179	0051
14	9923	9720	7732	5534	3023	1106	0544	0223	0073	0018
15	9836	9460	6698	4286	2013	0607	0266	0096	0027	0006
16	9675	9045	5530	3121	1247	0308	0120	0038	0009	0002
17	9405	8439	4328	2130	0718	0144	0050	0014	0003	0000
18	8987	7631	3197	1359	0384	0063	0019	0005	0001	
19	8389	6644	2220	0809	0191	0025	0007	0001	0000	
20	7601	5535	1447	0449	0088	0009	0002	0000		
21	6641	4390	0882	0232	0038	0003	0001			
22	5561	3299	0503	0112	0015	0001	0000			
23	4439	2340	0267	0050	0006	0000				
24	3359	1562	0133	0021	0002					
25	2399	0978	0061	0008	0001					
26	1611	0573	0026	0003	0000					
27	1013	0314	0011	0001						
28	0595	0160	0004	0000						
29	0325	0076	0001							
30	0164	0034	0000							
31	0077	0014								
32	0033	0005								
33	0013	0002								
34	0005	0001								
35	0002									
36	0000									
37										
38										
39										

Z	0.09	0.08	0.07	0.06	0.05	0.04	0.03	0.02	0.01	0.00
−3.5	0.00017	0.00017	0.00018	0.00019	0.00019	0.00020	0.00021	0.00022	0.00022	0.00023
−3.4	0.00024	0.00025	0.00026	0.00027	0.00028	0.00029	0.00030	0.00031	0.00033	0.00034
−3.3	0.00035	0.00036	0.00038	0.00039	0.00040	0.00042	0.00043	0.00045	0.00047	0.00048
−3.2	0.00050	0.00052	0.00054	0.00056	0.00058	0.00060	0.00062	0.00064	0.00066	0.00069
−3.1	0.00071	0.00074	0.00076	0.00079	0.00082	0.00085	0.00087	0.00090	0.00094	0.00097
−3.0	0.00100	0.00104	0.00107	0.00111	0.00114	0.00118	0.00122	0.00126	0.00131	0.00135
−2.9	0.0014	0.0014	0.0015	0.0015	0.0016	0.0016	0.0017	0.0017	0.0018	0.0019
−2.8	0.0019	0.0020	0.0021	0.0021	0.0022	0.0023	0.0023	0.0024	0.0025	0.0026
−2.7	0.0026	0.0027	0.0028	0.0029	0.0030	0.0031	0.0032	0.0033	0.0034	0.0035
−2.6	0.0036	0.0037	0.0038	0.0039	0.0040	0.0041	0.0043	0.0044	0.0045	0.0047
−2.5	0.0048	0.0049	0.0051	0.0052	0.0054	0.0055	0.0057	0.0059	0.0060	0.0062
−2.4	0.0064	0.0066	0.0068	0.0069	0.0071	0.0073	0.0075	0.0078	0.0080	0.0082
−2.3	0.0084	0.0087	0.0089	0.0091	0.0094	0.0096	0.0099	0.0102	0.0104	0.0107
−2.2	0.0110	0.0113	0.0116	0.0119	0.0122	0.0125	0.0129	0.0132	0.0136	0.0139
−2.1	0.0143	0.0146	0.0150	0.0154	0.0158	0.0162	0.0166	0.0170	0.0174	0.0179
−2.0	0.0183	0.0188	0.0192	0.0197	0.0202	0.0207	0.0212	0.0217	0.0222	0.0228
−1.9	0.0233	0.0239	0.0244	0.0250	0.0256	0.0262	0.0268	0.0274	0.0281	0.0287
−1.8	0.0294	0.0301	0.0307	0.0314	0.0322	0.0329	0.0336	0.0344	0.0351	0.0359
−1.7	0.0367	0.0375	0.0384	0.0392	0.0401	0.0409	0.0418	0.0427	0.0436	0.0446
−1.6	0.0455	0.0465	0.0475	0.0485	0.0495	0.0505	0.0516	0.0526	0.0537	0.0548
−1.5	0.0559	0.0571	0.0582	0.0594	0.0606	0.0618	0.0630	0.0643	0.0655	0.0668
−1.4	0.0681	0.0694	0.0708	0.0721	0.0735	0.0749	0.0764	0.0778	0.0793	0.0808
−1.3	0.0823	0.0838	0.0853	0.0869	0.0885	0.0901	0.0918	0.0934	0.0951	0.0968
−1.2	0.0985	0.1003	0.1020	0.1038	0.1057	0.1075	0.1093	0.1112	0.1131	0.1151
−1.1	0.1170	0.1190	0.1210	0.1230	0.1251	0.1271	0.1292	0.1314	0.1335	0.1357
−1.0	0.1379	0.1401	0.1423	0.1446	0.1469	0.1492	0.1515	0.1539	0.1562	0.1587
−0.9	0.1611	0.1635	0.1660	0.1685	0.1711	0.1736	0.1762	0.1788	0.1814	0.1841
−0.8	0.1867	0.1894	0.1922	0.1949	0.1977	0.2005	0.2033	0.2061	0.2090	0.2119
−0.7	0.2148	0.2177	0.2207	0.2236	0.2266	0.2297	0.2327	0.2358	0.2389	0.2420
−0.6	0.2451	0.2483	0.2514	0.2546	0.2578	0.2611	0.2643	0.2676	0.2709	0.2743
−0.5	0.2776	0.2810	0.2843	0.2877	0.2912	0.2946	0.2981	0.3015	0.3050	0.3085
−0.4	0.3121	0.3156	0.3192	0.3228	0.3264	0.3300	0.3336	0.3372	0.3409	0.3446
−0.3	0.3483	0.3520	0.3557	0.3594	0.3632	0.3669	0.3707	0.3745	0.3783	0.3821
−0.2	0.3859	0.3897	0.3936	0.3974	0.4013	0.4052	0.4090	0.4129	0.4168	0.4207
−0.1	0.4247	0.4286	0.4325	0.4364	0.4404	0.4443	0.4483	0.4522	0.4562	0.4602
−0.0	0.4641	0.4681	0.4721	0.4761	0.4801	0.4840	0.4880	0.4920	0.4960	0.5000

TABLE 2   Cumulative Normal Probabilities   **(continued)**

Z	0.00	0.01	0.02	0.03	0.04	0.05	0.06	0.07	0.08	0.09
+0.0	0.5000	0.5040	0.5080	0.5120	0.5160	0.5199	0.5239	0.5279	0.5319	0.5359
+0.1	0.5398	0.5438	0.5478	0.5517	0.5557	0.5596	0.5636	0.5675	0.5714	0.5753
+0.2	0.5793	0.5832	0.5871	0.5910	0.5948	0.5987	0.6026	0.6064	0.6103	0.6141
+0.3	0.6179	0.6217	0.6255	0.6293	0.6331	0.6368	0.6406	0.6443	0.6480	0.6517
+0.4	0.6554	0.6591	0.6628	0.6664	0.6700	0.6736	0.6772	0.6808	0.6844	0.6879
+0.5	0.6915	0.6950	0.6985	0.7019	0.7054	0.7088	0.7123	0.7157	0.7190	0.7224
+0.6	0.7257	0.7291	0.7324	0.7357	0.7389	0.7422	0.7454	0.7486	0.7517	0.7549
+0.7	0.7580	0.7611	0.7642	0.7673	0.7704	0.7734	0.7764	0.7794	0.7823	0.7852
+0.8	0.7881	0.7910	0.7939	0.7967	0.7995	0.8023	0.8051	0.8079	0.8106	0.8133
+0.9	0.8159	0.8186	0.8212	0.8238	0.8264	0.8289	0.8315	0.8340	0.8365	0.8389
+1.0	0.8413	0.8438	0.8461	0.8485	0.8508	0.8531	0.8554	0.8577	0.8599	0.8621
+1.1	0.8643	0.8665	0.8686	0.8708	0.8729	0.8749	0.8770	0.8790	0.8810	0.8830
+1.2	0.8849	0.8869	0.8888	0.8907	0.8925	0.8944	0.8962	0.8980	0.8997	0.9015
+1.3	0.9032	0.9049	0.9066	0.9082	0.9099	0.9115	0.9131	0.9147	0.9162	0.9177
+1.4	0.9192	0.9207	0.9222	0.9236	0.9251	0.9265	0.9279	0.9292	0.9306	0.9319
+1.5	0.9332	0.9345	0.9357	0.9370	0.9382	0.9394	0.9406	0.9418	0.9429	0.9441
+1.6	0.9452	0.9463	0.9474	0.9484	0.9495	0.9505	0.9515	0.9525	0.9535	0.9545
+1.7	0.9554	0.9564	0.9573	0.9582	0.9591	0.9599	0.9608	0.9616	0.9625	0.9633
+1.8	0.9641	0.9649	0.9656	0.9664	0.9671	0.9678	0.9686	0.9693	0.9699	0.9706
+1.9	0.9713	0.9719	0.9726	0.9732	0.9738	0.9744	0.9750	0.9756	0.9761	0.9767
+2.0	0.9773	0.9778	0.9783	0.9788	0.9793	0.9798	0.9803	0.9808	0.9812	0.9817
+2.1	0.9821	0.9826	0.9830	0.9834	0.9838	0.9842	0.9846	0.9850	0.9854	0.9857
+2.2	0.9861	0.9864	0.9868	0.9871	0.9875	0.9878	0.9881	0.9884	0.9887	0.9890
+2.3	0.9893	0.9896	0.9898	0.9901	0.9904	0.9906	0.9909	0.9911	0.9913	0.9916
+2.4	0.9918	0.9920	0.9922	0.9925	0.9927	0.9929	0.9931	0.9932	0.9934	0.9936
+2.5	0.9938	0.9940	0.9941	0.9943	0.9945	0.9946	0.9948	0.9949	0.9951	0.9952
+2.6	0.9953	0.9955	0.9956	0.9957	0.9959	0.9960	0.9961	0.9962	0.9963	0.9964
+2.7	0.9965	0.9966	0.9967	0.9968	0.9969	0.9970	0.9971	0.9972	0.9973	0.9974
+2.8	0.9974	0.9975	0.9976	0.9977	0.9977	0.9978	0.9979	0.9979	0.9980	0.9981
+2.9	0.9981	0.9982	0.9983	0.9983	0.9984	0.9984	0.9985	0.9985	0.9986	0.9986
+3.0	0.99865	0.99869	0.99874	0.99878	0.99882	0.99886	0.99889	0.99893	0.99896	0.99900
+3.1	0.99903	0.99906	0.99910	0.99913	0.99915	0.99918	0.99921	0.99924	0.99926	0.99929
+3.2	0.99931	0.99934	0.99936	0.99938	0.99940	0.99942	0.99944	0.99946	0.99948	0.99950
+3.3	0.99952	0.99953	0.99955	0.99957	0.99958	0.99960	0.99961	0.99962	0.99964	0.99965
+3.4	0.99966	0.99967	0.99969	0.99970	0.99971	0.99972	0.99973	0.99974	0.99975	0.99976
+3.5	0.99977	0.99978	0.99978	0.99979	0.99980	0.99981	0.99981	0.99982	0.99983	0.99983

38	28	27	9	11	81	85
78	95	72	70	73	10	96
85	49	23	96	70	56	5
24	94	42	7	63	14	19
80	10	39	43	5	43	15
96	41	80	2	95	48	31
51	29	7	84	35	52	96
5	63	34	32	86	25	78
42	46	91	35	86	99	15
1	69	99	71	39	88	78
69	12	50	88	75	60	83
57	89	18	8	79	2	99
72	39	83	45	17	97	24
68	92	35	84	86	60	86
73	68	44	51	11	5	28
25	89	14	76	31	94	89
83	92	8	14	12	41	37
49	53	81	4	95	28	15
35	69	96	59	85	76	86
37	41	12	99	87	31	99
12	83	86	68	33	81	88
4	25	11	43	59	59	24
13	55	16	0	47	85	84
37	58	18	84	36	59	33
64	83	23	86	4	55	86
22	57	42	39	54	70	29
46	7	31	16	16	52	63
10	87	33	17	98	32	14
89	10	54	33	14	84	77
8	54	49	4	80	43	38
43	15	96	40	76	90	53
8	70	50	63	30	7	73
75	85	34	43	45	84	99
37	26	21	92	63	50	32
36	32	64	92	72	98	39
50	53	62	96	14	17	76
99	7	49	28	26	2	78
48	80	47	59	33	65	90
53	9	68	31	69	35	84
90	82	77	20	28	83	45
20	11	87	21	40	51	40
82	27	18	66	35	11	47
83	73	84	50	36	66	72
38	74	3	52	81	20	89
52	5	61	20	70	38	97
37	45	34	98	84	20	61
88	73	42	99	10	69	24
20	0	19	13	5	10	16
3	75	19	34	31	75	68
32	81	97	53	39	57	89
25	44	36	25	20	91	66
76	64	98	12	84	95	14
29	48	25	15	64	47	0
74	43	94	72	88	74	52

46	4	8	15	12	34	95
63	26	82	60	17	58	98
62	86	56	59	47	46	54
5	46	32	70	32	61	81
31	57	58	30	57	72	20
70	37	90	0	94	58	3
92	21	93	70	78	36	8
26	79	39	18	52	49	28
25	95	46	18	89	72	29
19	53	46	99	77	67	9
47	96	57	72	17	51	57
77	50	3	62	49	28	31
27	84	59	97	48	14	46
48	77	28	71	71	89	91
40	20	55	52	14	13	48
68	75	33	24	46	55	20
17	23	82	86	79	94	51
63	11	99	95	78	14	81
55	2	8	34	25	45	42
42	72	49	46	35	96	53
58	63	59	82	58	7	16
34	58	35	88	10	70	25
17	77	7	51	42	86	40
65	25	64	56	64	74	71
53	79	96	63	8	82	14
48	60	23	95	66	36	24
18	89	72	28	22	75	50
21	75	64	2	36	96	46
14	65	66	9	58	68	81
74	13	14	60	38	83	53
69	33	73	40	78	9	49
9	9	67	24	34	91	37
99	63	83	27	17	56	77
55	38	31	41	61	98	35
26	35	77	46	77	53	17
24	94	45	23	29	62	10
98	99	10	69	24	23	19
5	59	10	25	65	58	63
56	63	76	85	25	84	78
8	46	2	1	81	77	33
2	12	55	21	29	84	40
87	56	55	23	37	16	61
17	55	69	19	92	79	46
63	61	93	9	11	88	23
48	76	27	70	80	45	48
82	61	21	79	80	64	63
3	47	55	8	46	5	10
16	4	72	98	34	24	33
81	90	4	18	67	40	30
19	41	77	89	38	25	7
10	99	1	11	53	19	30
11	93	58	9	36	33	67
5	23	91	36	94	39	84
53	57	63	61	2	56	21

14	94	41	97	5	60	11
27	57	99	81	92	25	17
80	22	9	52	31	19	28
98	34	18	4	56	1	99
83	5	83	50	45	20	15
10	22	38	24	0	83	97
36	37	98	52	25	79	48
76	27	72	87	77	74	48
26	18	72	65	44	78	68
1	93	46	42	31	9	73
56	83	89	86	12	94	57
91	32	74	54	53	29	95
9	93	75	13	2	92	29
40	83	31	43	74	55	67
1	2	97	66	14	91	20
99	12	73	31	26	80	40
20	57	64	66	20	29	87
59	71	94	19	66	22	38
29	30	19	39	64	31	11
81	89	2	9	34	26	46
38	13	31	68	24	26	43
21	37	30	45	95	59	2
77	46	74	34	34	94	55
80	86	88	57	46	61	55
74	50	34	49	86	69	39
15	32	60	68	63	62	5
74	91	79	57	26	46	40
19	54	53	25	73	11	5
32	49	99	52	24	70	1
80	66	73	43	98	1	22
26	53	84	24	84	81	32
61	75	97	5	53	73	55
77	60	70	76	21	42	56
60	53	76	81	99	60	68
68	98	70	37	92	19	83
20	74	62	7	82	21	89
44	60	59	14	45	49	84
59	95	39	76	4	43	17
14	28	35	58	31	58	69
92	30	49	21	88	30	93
81	46	49	77	20	26	73
2	54	8	58	73	12	16
88	76	65	3	30	53	48
11	31	83	15	38	89	93
54	85	27	94	15	45	31
76	82	99	58	57	14	69
86	0	19	14	10	27	75
4	43	22	42	57	60	43
12	86	7	64	19	34	26
49	63	32	26	67	66	91
49	78	21	24	51	85	50
34	46	73	19	55	57	44
48	88	94	66	52	13	10
40	46	15	74	5	61	22

82	90	98	74	66	27	63
32	20	36	27	39	90	91
29	54	64	94	84	59	96
47	14	56	10	58	49	76
9	69	37	95	34	49	89
86	18	29	12	10	52	21
57	56	22	20	24	60	41
5	55	86	20	41	64	14
8	18	31	23	53	14	4
90	3	12	38	24	98	69
27	39	88	72	38	76	8
64	12	95	55	75	55	51
4	66	57	51	92	85	82
27	20	73	62	10	0	6
34	50	92	98	58	65	62
86	54	48	4	87	88	43
59	66	65	94	75	2	35
92	36	84	80	21	6	43
1	22	21	24	50	87	69
27	40	93	92	18	75	88
52	17	35	51	94	99	53
21	47	93	26	24	3	4
89	1	98	81	97	54	51
19	49	21	88	31	96	91
85	88	61	72	82	44	21
29	87	61	75	99	23	43
48	97	45	95	63	24	71
9	13	96	63	8	79	1
93	46	35	92	35	78	58
39	12	19	4	49	57	98
73	59	92	23	5	24	98
71	42	11	85	10	0	2
16	70	79	38	19	72	56
89	22	34	0	91	47	59
29	45	5	20	79	91	30
60	88	80	88	8	53	44
88	32	96	88	56	47	71
5	86	70	45	38	18	62
8	92	79	40	29	14	22
2	12	51	3	50	76	2
28	44	11	69	18	82	29
31	20	42	69	38	2	65
75	59	77	31	92	69	88
2	23	16	87	77	76	57
61	47	37	91	17	80	19
95	98	33	11	72	29	22
73	36	62	44	5	32	44
74	47	11	41	49	19	73
67	44	65	88	44	70	24
10	45	79	67	91	39	16
44	15	92	16	68	60	50
56	84	2	51	86	57	69
94	44	10	68	13	63	59
86	79	99	79	83	85	67

33	90	40	30	16	25	7
16	29	33	36	12	48	74
16	23	95	58	90	15	81
50	68	57	28	56	81	76
31	97	2	34	82	88	87
31	2	30	58	75	19	42
78	88	18	19	46	6	18
54	57	52	0	27	59	10
27	66	50	9	98	4	45
28	66	42	54	43	68	22
19	10	87	35	23	19	7
66	36	16	74	97	14	8
25	72	3	72	99	44	78
64	82	16	51	65	26	74
2	47	64	54	47	0	70
23	2	6	11	10	66	98
96	88	65	98	1	19	3
51	74	85	40	72	77	7
47	19	90	65	80	91	27
40	91	86	93	79	38	9
16	8	6	59	5	91	4
99	59	64	50	21	72	41
0	27	61	15	45	30	72
62	24	84	86	60	86	73
67	40	37	54	95	78	12
69	10	33	9	50	21	68
22	17	97	31	11	84	0
41	45	97	75	72	57	95
52	54	52	27	92	4	95
27	8	1	28	60	8	4
49	55	92	53	86	36	44
35	13	61	50	47	36	85
89	66	92	60	28	25	1
78	55	33	96	78	4	21
86	27	83	54	78	79	69
2	94	40	92	94	31	38
51	59	91	19	92	76	27
74	1	39	29	15	31	49
10	18	18	45	5	26	5
98	39	48	32	64	87	50
11	13	80	59	33	62	75
88	49	98	47	95	48	25
20	94	82	38	95	21	73
41	92	77	35	13	62	52
53	46	95	52	55	60	62
30	13	9	38	43	13	90
27	46	32	73	48	31	56
50	97	25	79	42	40	63
18	38	65	45	89	22	33
94	69	65	67	17	94	11
17	96	23	73	28	10	4
35	71	6	91	96	49	29
34	39	31	28	88	74	51
41	83	26	3	86	83	19

TABLE 4   Four Digit Uniform Random Numbers

3805	2833	2747	982	1172	8188	8584
7805	9575	7201	7032	7384	1012	9613
8572	4908	2300	9627	7054	5680	598
2465	9402	4224	725	6336	1488	1903
8026	1027	3927	4314	538	4399	1546
9686	4198	8009	272	9550	4848	3137
5194	2923	792	8446	3546	5260	9646
530	6365	3421	3233	8611	2566	7896
4280	4619	9188	3559	8659	9917	1572
179	6921	9916	7198	3945	8889	7826
6950	1265	5032	8808	7558	6070	8397
5754	8947	1894	836	7967	278	9963
7274	3977	8391	4551	1785	9750	2434
6852	9201	3537	8409	8619	6031	8611
7387	6816	4417	5150	1148	538	2892
2504	8998	1444	7685	3110	9493	8959
8321	9291	852	1489	1267	4198	3781
4902	5378	8146	474	9526	2887	1585
3530	6910	9693	5965	8548	7606	8699
3740	4145	1208	9940	8767	3137	9916
1263	8337	8649	6857	3304	8106	8898
431	2507	1159	4392	5912	5948	2473
1305	5575	1697	8	4775	8577	8484
3704	5868	1871	8407	3606	5970	3362
6441	8387	2347	8603	489	5506	8632
2238	5734	4265	3976	5470	7038	2995
4626	794	3133	1646	1676	5242	6365
1004	8738	3396	1729	9808	3282	1417
8960	1008	5402	3338	1408	8405	7753
875	5470	4940	410	8001	4314	3871
4397	1538	9656	4091	7638	9011	5323
832	7085	5024	6372	3019	761	7392
7506	8505	3476	4302	4529	8455	9971
3724	2605	2112	9227	6351	5062	3211
3699	3298	6494	9279	7221	9816	3905
5080	5333	6276	9655	1446	1780	7662
9952	751	4933	2840	2640	274	7884
4832	8032	4708	5955	3358	6545	9050
5392	901	6875	3141	6966	3529	8476
9091	8260	7737	2080	2848	8365	4551
2019	1155	8758	2152	4087	5147	4099
8267	2707	1844	6693	3563	1141	4776
8385	7327	8492	5009	3621	6643	7265
3803	7428	344	5211	8162	2073	8981
5227	531	6138	2049	7053	3875	9769
3738	4509	3405	9849	8446	2034	6191
8838	7303	4274	9918	1040	6970	2461
2031	37	1946	1339	518	1052	1644
399	7594	1971	3481	3140	7511	6806
3234	8146	9771	5309	3914	5700	8971
2525	4404	3697	2546	2005	9108	6603
7646	6448	9875	1213	8406	9514	1430
2956	4860	2553	1579	6492	4741	15
7417	4364	9425	7274	8818	7437	5260

4628	424	894	1544	1219	3415	9521
6387	2628	8284	6046	1717	5889	9878
6264	8675	5674	5964	4722	4650	5400
549	4692	3208	7016	3223	6194	8157
3196	5763	5813	3008	5722	7262	2072
7070	3773	9007	84	9442	5895	389
9274	2143	9393	7070	7876	3630	890
2667	7995	3961	1809	5205	4949	2846
2532	9578	4674	1841	8977	7284	2915
1930	5341	4672	9966	7746	6778	953
4711	9690	5740	7228	1706	5183	5739
7786	5064	311	6285	4908	2882	3114
2746	8447	5965	9760	4877	1416	4601
4864	7770	2843	7130	7193	8981	9149
4060	2020	5577	5279	1478	1359	4849
6859	7513	3346	2455	4615	5592	2010
1733	2307	8241	8683	7929	9426	5190
6304	1109	9917	9519	7858	1480	8153
5598	213	892	3436	2586	4589	4261
4260	7212	4928	4657	3588	9615	5393
5822	6396	5972	8267	5856	731	1679
3489	5825	3542	8827	1080	7039	2513
1722	7710	761	5176	4206	8655	4071
6528	2526	6401	5672	6423	7489	7125
5350	7972	9681	6333	869	8215	1468
4874	6028	2301	9553	6605	3649	2445
1825	8943	7229	2886	2255	7553	5017
2125	7594	6436	266	3669	9612	4652
1402	6542	6634	929	5864	6818	8131
7426	1374	1411	6095	3871	8372	5386
6972	3353	7370	4036	7887	995	4988
968	915	6773	2404	3464	9151	3722
9976	6352	8327	2790	1792	5642	7725
5568	3883	3181	4135	6181	9868	3571
2615	3550	7760	4605	7792	5306	1703
2465	9463	4591	2377	2940	6244	1004
9824	9906	1014	6929	2448	2323	1904
512	5934	1000	2587	6522	5844	6369
5614	6360	7629	8534	2543	8451	7815
827	4621	284	115	8133	7755	3334
207	1234	5539	2132	2933	8412	4073
8723	5681	5575	2324	3765	1671	6140
1797	5517	6933	1939	9237	7970	4687
6388	6143	9366	911	1170	8816	2362
4824	7689	2714	7077	8038	4531	4845
8290	6135	2197	7966	8019	6422	6353
321	4747	5594	838	4680	534	1084
1696	424	7273	9821	3469	2427	3336
8172	9005	485	1860	6796	4035	3040
1924	4180	7763	8955	3864	2584	723
1082	9985	169	1150	5376	1905	3045
1119	9313	5800	983	3699	3344	6777
560	2367	9159	3651	9468	3950	8485
5352	5748	6321	6186	228	5695	2112

1416	9489	4184	9702	560	6035	1171
2711	5722	9936	8115	9259	2521	1793
8066	2252	919	5243	3184	1919	2854
9853	3425	1875	423	5659	147	9946
8352	594	8392	5009	4522	2048	1589
1099	2288	3836	2426	29	8342	9788
3646	3783	9882	5244	2518	7913	4817
7680	2722	7213	8775	7732	7415	4899
2657	1855	7209	6562	4489	7873	6833
136	9318	4678	4205	3125	904	7304
5681	8350	8968	8657	1231	9467	5722
9129	3275	7489	5459	5348	2954	9587
935	9330	7560	1390	295	9260	2902
4069	8300	3171	4328	7425	5599	6762
184	243	9799	6605	1435	9166	2082
9992	1210	7335	3116	2677	8023	4037
2015	5757	6408	6628	2099	2938	8735
5968	7194	9447	1941	6618	2234	3840
2937	3057	1909	3936	6432	3167	1110
8154	8936	223	917	3488	2676	4663
3890	1368	3196	6862	2404	2667	4363
2175	3779	3096	4561	9502	5960	240
7795	4608	7493	3485	3471	9464	5544
8084	8603	8859	5726	4619	6181	5515
7455	5094	3471	4977	8621	6929	3981
1521	3297	6087	6850	6316	6240	596
7413	9112	7953	5709	2679	4690	4028
1957	5491	5328	2549	7341	1101	533
3285	4915	9920	5284	2428	7007	186
8053	6636	7339	4313	9822	113	2277
2648	5388	8495	2479	8412	8165	3278
6177	7560	9764	540	5362	7307	5580
7719	6092	7080	7650	2177	4207	5649
6027	5320	7674	8164	9914	6009	6827
6878	9820	7022	3748	9285	1979	8308
2035	7433	6283	794	8217	2156	8982
4481	6052	5979	1402	4598	4972	8445
5925	9540	3913	7617	486	4362	1792
1495	2837	3568	5871	3110	5823	6945
9258	3041	4928	2193	8806	3098	9333
8108	4651	4933	7742	2052	2631	7318
225	5482	864	5850	7319	1262	1697
8822	7657	6537	309	3022	5348	4888
1199	3197	8387	1550	3817	8946	9321
5413	8583	2781	9434	1577	4550	3108
7696	8204	9953	5886	5731	1414	6905
8699	47	1983	1477	1013	2782	7577
422	4336	2221	4296	5790	6072	4319
1259	8685	778	6498	1982	3407	2603
4957	6308	3238	2647	6744	6637	9121
4991	7852	2192	2479	5147	8569	5091
3417	4686	7357	1965	5577	5780	4482
4868	8873	9423	6675	5241	1373	1067
4045	4663	1568	7439	519	6160	2286

8268	9037	9804	7489	6695	2770	6358
3220	2098	3601	2724	3935	9090	9124
2933	5473	6445	9406	8430	5926	9683
4761	1416	5639	1093	5802	4971	7609
912	6991	3740	9517	3438	4974	8905
8660	1809	2915	1209	1014	5205	2104
5772	5696	2224	2080	2463	6057	4173
519	5558	8678	2040	4136	6453	1494
884	1854	3168	2319	5394	1491	405
9003	372	1207	3892	2487	9892	6970
2788	3995	8875	7291	3873	7615	835
6467	1289	9526	5555	7596	5579	5107
428	6605	5774	5197	9220	8542	8270
2740	2008	7389	6262	1066	38	635
3465	5074	9256	9867	5892	6548	6260
8626	5415	4860	421	8780	8892	4327
5934	6663	6568	9441	7533	224	3547
9258	3630	8452	8038	2162	628	4303
168	2278	2153	2409	5077	8775	6961
2786	4064	9307	9265	1820	7538	8846
5230	1763	3504	5157	9401	9994	5352
2160	4791	9301	2692	2437	393	422
8988	128	9876	8103	9733	5463	5183
1930	4927	2194	8818	3160	9600	9158
8544	8838	6130	7239	8261	4410	2109
2964	8799	6116	7507	9991	2386	4393
4880	9744	4540	9540	6382	2427	7126
908	1311	9692	6346	847	7968	183
9386	4671	3545	9235	3502	7891	5830
3955	1261	1965	439	4945	5718	9804
7358	5914	9255	2305	531	2438	9848
7145	4234	1102	8501	1087	12	287
1607	7061	7900	3846	1977	7249	5694
8923	2293	3444	26	9161	4729	5923
2975	4547	501	2083	7983	9156	3084
6095	8814	8029	8848	823	5309	4442
8874	3259	9693	8820	5685	4723	7174
537	8652	7076	4591	3857	1821	6208
857	9271	7912	4027	2952	1468	2240
228	1208	5197	307	5068	7649	277
2818	4413	1119	6989	1867	8294	2960
3115	2045	4233	6992	3859	220	6585
7532	5922	7740	3146	9212	6953	8808
271	2350	1654	8775	7765	7608	5764
6110	4783	3706	9191	1788	8003	1928
9535	9854	3310	1172	7242	2904	2241
7306	3666	6242	4457	561	3251	4456
7472	4729	1122	4167	4901	1902	7303
6700	4469	6510	8836	4429	7045	2406
1032	4537	7931	6750	9119	3958	1676
4436	1525	9230	1647	6815	6061	5029
5623	8474	231	5121	8649	5798	6944
9485	4409	1091	6863	1356	6366	5989
8643	7949	9911	7918	8309	8595	6785

3349	9033	4052	3013	1609	2536	738
1603	2972	3398	3642	1265	4814	7495
1641	2388	9556	5835	9010	1541	8150
5030	6834	5731	2873	5661	8107	7687
3161	9782	241	3401	8239	8818	8758
3188	298	3097	5897	7509	1977	4280
7890	8815	1878	1929	4670	654	1892
5462	5742	5289	60	2752	5977	1089
2737	6621	5086	931	9807	461	4504
2869	6682	4265	5451	4321	6862	2280
1922	1014	8781	3562	2335	1955	710
6668	3612	1659	7446	9740	1427	899
2554	7227	376	7216	9908	4499	7824
6449	8274	1605	5163	6527	2693	7415
253	4781	6407	5407	4781	19	7087
2345	287	615	1105	1095	6621	9866
9605	8835	6564	9865	114	1900	374
5137	7461	8526	4005	7297	7733	725
4748	1961	9035	6559	8037	9188	2791
4051	9190	8675	9344	7984	3806	978
1608	847	602	5987	509	9163	400
9930	5973	6470	5061	2128	7223	4179
65	2783	6104	1579	4538	3010	7222
6238	2426	8410	8621	6034	8615	7383
6755	4083	3704	5475	9514	7807	1208
6987	1045	3391	935	5089	2114	6884
2279	1714	9770	3186	1190	8462	56
4178	4562	9763	7518	7244	5794	9567
5255	5429	5275	2791	9269	494	9540
2789	868	110	2845	6077	854	434
4916	5585	9268	5340	8622	3671	4428
3528	1315	6142	5010	4782	3600	8556
8937	6616	9262	6027	2800	2556	135
7802	5590	3322	9625	7849	465	2142
8666	2720	8323	5459	7840	7914	6919
283	9429	4023	9273	9431	3126	3879
5135	5900	9180	1978	9241	7646	2705
7410	114	3990	2913	1564	3167	4920
1021	1839	1849	4536	576	2630	591
9880	3957	4819	3298	6413	8794	5046
1132	1374	8058	5980	3352	6292	7583
8866	4945	9876	4745	9585	4804	2552
2075	9479	8201	3892	9536	2190	7315
4178	9229	7769	3547	1365	6264	5294
5388	4675	9557	5266	5580	6087	6297
3001	1330	968	3838	4309	1313	9096
2756	4672	3227	7314	4838	3198	5645
5090	9732	2584	7910	4203	4030	6350
1830	3830	6509	4584	8921	2267	3311
9457	6944	6547	6778	1749	9489	1188
1723	9644	2357	7346	2860	1039	491
3599	7168	619	9199	9618	4920	2951
3426	3995	3132	2836	8827	7440	5190
4183	8381	2637	397	8647	8301	1982

APPENDIX B

Calculation of
Probabilities
for the Quality
Inspection
Example
Problem of
Chapter 9

For the example problem mentioned above, we recall that two states of nature were involved, namely, let

S_1 = a lot comes from a process producing 8% defective units, and
S_2 = a lot comes from a process producing 3% defective units.

Then,

$P(S_1) = 0.50$ = the *a priori* probability of S_1, and

$P(S_2) = 0.50$ = the *a priori* probability of S_2.

If a sample of size two is taken per the example problem, one of the following outcomes could result:

x_1 = zero defective units
x_2 = one defective units
x_3 = two defective units

From Chapter 5, the probability of exactly x defective units out of a sample of size n can be calculated using the binominal distribution, as follows:

$$P(x) = \frac{n!}{x!(n-x)!}(p)^x(1-p)^{n-x}$$

where x is the number of defectives in question and p is the percent defective of the population (lot).

Applying this to our example problem, we would have: for future S_1 (8 percent defective),

$P(x_1|S_1) = P(x = 0 \text{ defectives, given future } S_1)$

$= P(x = 0) = \frac{2!}{0!(2-0!)}(0.8)^0(.92)^2 = .8464$

$P(x_2|S_1) = P(x = 1) = \frac{2!}{1!1!}(.08)^1(.92)^1 = 1472$

$P(x_3|S_1) = P(x = 2) = \frac{2!}{2!0!}(.08)^2(.92)^0 = .0064$

for future S_2 (3 percent defective),

$P(x_1|S_2) = P(x = 0) = \frac{2!}{0!2!}(.03)^0(.97)^2 = .9409$

$$P(x_2|S_2) = P(x=1) = \frac{2!}{1!1!}(.03)^1(.97)^1 = .0582$$

$$P(x_3|S_2) = P(x=2) = \frac{2!}{2!0!}(.03)^2(.97)^0 = .0009$$

As a point of information, the $P(x|S)$ statements are termed *likelihood statements*.

Given the above results, the probabilities of obtaining 0, 1, or 2 defectives from a sample of size two can then be calculated. Since the outcomes x_1, x_2, or x_3 could occur if the sample of two were taken from either an 8 percent defective lot (future S_1) or a 3 percent defective lot (future S_2), we employ the additive law of probability to calculate the probabilities of the outcomes as

$$P(x_1) = P(x_1|S_1)P(S_1) + P(x_1|S_2)P(S_2)$$
$$= .8464(.5) + .9409(.5) = .89365$$
$$P(x_2) = P(x_2|S_1)P(S_1) + P(x_2|S_2)P(S_2)$$
$$= .1472(.5) + .0582(.5) = .10270$$
$$P(x_3) = P(x_3|S_1)P(S_1) + P(x_3|S_2)P(S_2)$$
$$= .0064(.5) + .0009(.5) = .00365$$

We note that because the outcome of the sample must be either 0, 1, or 2 defectives, these three probabilities sum to 1.0.

Finally, in order to calculate the conditional probabilities about the futures S_1 and S_2, given the outcomes x_1, x_2, and x_3, let us recall a basic form of Bayes Theorem to be:

$$P(A|B) = \frac{P(B|A)P(A)}{P(B)}$$

We now adapt this to our example problem and calculate:

If x_1 is observed,

$$P(S_1|x_1) = \frac{P(x_1|S_1)P(S_1)}{P(x_1)}$$
$$= \frac{(.8464)(.5)}{.89365} = .473$$

Because there are only two futures S_1 and S_2,

$$P(S_2|x_1) = 1 - .473 = .527$$

If x_2 is observed,

$$P(S_1|x_2) = \frac{P(x_2|S_1)\,P(S_1)}{P(x_2)}$$

$$= \frac{(.1472)(.5)}{(.10270)} = .717$$

$$P(S_2|x_2) = 1 - .717 = .283$$

If x_3 is observed,

$$P(S_1|x_3) = \frac{P(x_3|S_1)\,P(S_1)}{P(x_3)}$$

$$= \frac{(.0064)(.5)}{.00365} = .877$$

$$P(S_2|x_3) = 1 - .877 = .123$$

Index